LIFE AND LETTERS OF LAFCADIO HEARN

VOLUME II

THE LIFE AND LETTERS
OF
LAFCADIO HEARN

BY

ELIZABETH BISLAND

WITH ILLUSTRATIONS

IN TWO VOLUMES
VOL. II

BOSTON AND NEW YORK
HOUGHTON MIFFLIN COMPANY
The Riverside Press Cambridge

ILLUSTRATIONS

Lafcadio Hearn in Japanese Costume (photogravure)
                               Frontispiece

The City of Matsue, seen from Castle Hill 40
  1. The Prefecture Office. The Middle School, in which Mr.
     Hearn was a teacher, is hidden from view by the Prefecture
     Office Building.
  2. The Normal School. Mr. Hearn also taught here.
  3. Here on the beach of Lake Shinyi Mr. Hearn lived for some time.

The Shintō Temple of Kizuki described in "Glimpses
  of Unfamiliar Japan" 104
    Lafcadio Hearn was the first foreigner who was allowed to enter
    the inner part of this temple.

A Group of Graduates of the Middle School 162
  1. Mr. Hearn.
  2. Mr. Nishida.
  3. The old teacher of Chinese Classics.

Lafcadio Hearn's Favourite Dwelling-House 192
    This house, an old Samurai's residence, is situated in front of a
    castle. The river before the house is an outer moat of the
    castle.

Mr. Hearn's Garden in Tōkyō 282

Writing-Room in Mr. Hearn's Tōkyō House 344
  His three sons on the verandah. In this house he died.

Facsimile of Mr. Hearn's Later Handwriting 410

Kazuo and Iwao, Lafcadio Hearn's Older Children,
  exercising at Jū-Jutsu 476

Lafcadio Hearn's Grave 516

LETTERS OF LAFCADIO HEARN

TO ELIZABETH BISLAND

1890.

DEAR ELIZABETH, — . . . I feel indescribably towards Japan. Of course Nature here is not the Nature of the tropics, which is so splendid and savage and omnipotently beautiful that I feel at this very moment of writing the same pain in my heart I felt when leaving Martinique. This is a domesticated Nature, which loves man, and makes itself beautiful for him in a quiet grey-and-blue way like the Japanese women, and the trees seem to know what people say about them, — seem to have little human souls. What I love in Japan is the Japanese, — the poor simple humanity of the country. It is divine. There is nothing in this world approaching the naïve natural charm of them. No book ever written has reflected it. And I love their gods, their customs, their dress, their bird-like quavering songs, their houses, their superstitions, their faults. And I believe that their art is as far in advance of our art as old Greek art was superior to that of the earliest European art-gropings — I think there is more art in a print by Hokusai or those who came after him than in a $10,000 painting — no, a $100,000 painting. *We* are the barbarians! I do not merely *think* these things: I am as sure of them as of death. I only wish I could be reincarnated in some little Japanese baby, so that I could see and feel the world as beautifully as a Japanese brain does.

And, of course, I am studying Buddhism with heart and soul. A young student from one of the temples is my companion. If I stay in Japan, we shall live together. —Will write again if all goes well.

My best love to you always.

LAFCADIO HEARN.

TO ELIZABETH BISLAND

1890.

DEAR MISS BISLAND, —Do you think well enough of me to try to get me employment at a regular salary, somewhere in the United States. I have permanently broken off with the Harpers: I am starved out. My average earnings for the last three years have been scarcely $500 a year. Here in Japan prices are higher than in New York, — unless one can become a Japanese employee. I was promised a situation; but it is now delayed until September.

I shall get along somehow. But I am so very tired of being hard-pushed, and ignored, and starved, — and obliged to undergo moral humiliations which are much worse than hunger or cold, — that I have ceased to be ashamed to ask you to say a good word for me where you can, to some newspaper, or some publishing firm, able to give me steady employ, later on.   LAFCADIO HEARN.

TO ELIZABETH BISLAND

1890.

MY DEAR SISTER ELIZABETH, — . . . Now, as for myself, — I am going to become country schoolmaster in Japan, — probably for several long years. The language is unspeakably difficult to learn; — I believe it can only be learned by ear. Teaching will help me to learn it; and before learning it, to write anything enduring upon Japan would be absurdly impossible. Literary work will not support one here, where living costs quite as much as in New York. What I wish to do, I want to do for its own sake; and so intend to settle, if possible, in this country, among a people who seem to me the most lovable in the world.

I have been living in temples and old Buddhist cemeteries, making pilgrimages and sounding enormous bells and worshipping astounding Buddhas. Still, I do not as yet know anything whatever about Japan. I have nothing else worth telling you to write just now, and no address to give, — as I do not know where I am going or what I shall be doing next month.

Later on, I shall write again.

Best wishes and affection from   L. H.

TO BASIL HALL CHAMBERLAIN

KIZUKI, July, 1890.

DEAR PROFESSOR CHAMBERLAIN, — I am writing to you from the little beach of Inasa, mentioned in the "Kojiki," — the etymology of which name, as given by Hirata, I think you say is incorrect, or at least fantastic. But I think you may not know that Inasa beach is in some respects the nicest bathing-place imaginable — certainly by far the best I have ever visited in Japan. The hotels face a beach without a pebble in its sand, and when the water is not rough, it is clear as a diamond; when roughened by a west wind, however, the water sometimes becomes dirty with seaweed, drift and such refuse. This is the great bathing resort of Izumo. But it is much more quiet and pleasant than other Japanese bathing resorts I have seen — such as Ōiso. After the bath, moreover, one can have a hot salt water bath or a cold fresh-water douche. And there is plenty of deep water for swimming. Right opposite our window is the "thousand draught rock" which the son of Ohokuni, etc., lifted on the tips of his fingers.

Kaka is famous for its sea cave, and legend of Jizō. I think I wrote you of this beautiful legend of the child ghosts and the fountain of milk. But it is really too pretty to publish in a matter-of-fact record.

The term "arrows of prayer" which I use, might deceive the reader. The arrows put into the rice-fields to scare away crows are very different in appearance and purpose. I hope to send you some of the former from Mionoseki.

I will stay here some weeks — the sea-bathing is too good to lose. Will write again soon.

Most truly ever,
LAFCADIO HEARN.

TO BASIL HALL CHAMBERLAIN

KIZUKI, July, 1890.

DEAR PROFESSOR CHAMBERLAIN, — We are still at Kizuki — enjoying exquisite weather and delicious sea-bathing. Last evening I dined with the Kokuzō; and I never ate so much dinner or drank so much sake anywhere in Japan. It was a royal feast. I also saw some things that would interest you. A series of letters of Motoori's, — also two MSS. of flute-music made by him, and the brushes with which his commentaries were written. One of the Senke family, who was his pupil, received these as bequests, and they are preserved in the family.

The conversation turned upon you; and I was asked many questions about you, which I answered as best as I could. From the extreme interest shown, I am sure that Kizuki would be turned inside out to please you if you come down here.

I asked about the deity of Mionoseki; and the learned priest Sasa and others state positively that deity is not Hiruko. The legend concerning him would prove the same fact. The deity detested the cock, and no hens or chickens or eggs or feathers are allowed to exist in Mionoseki. No vessel would take an egg to Mionoseki. It is wrong even to eat eggs the day before going to Mionoseki. A passenger to Mionoseki was once detected smoking a pipe which had the figure of a cock upon it, and that pipe was immediately thrown into the sea. The dislike of the god for the cock is attributed to some adventure of his youthful days, — when the cock had been instructed to wake him up, or call him at a certain hour. The cock did not perform his duty, and Koto-shiro-nushi-no-Kami, had his hand bitten by a crocodile in hurrying to get back home.

There is a temple of Ebisu in Nishinomiya near Ōsaka, where the deity is believed to be identical with Hiruko, but this is not the case at Mionoseki.

Regarding the Deity of Marriage, I must correct an error in my last. The learned priest Sasa states (quoting many ancient poems and authors to prove the fact) that the ancient Deity of Marriage was the Deity of Kizuki. But at Yaegaki Jinja, where there is a tree with two trunks, or two trees with trunks grown into one, and other curious symbolic things, the popular worship of the Deities Susa-no-o and Inada-Hime gradually centred and finally wrested away the rights and privileges of the Kizuki deity in favour of the gods of Yaegaki.

I have had some fine *shōryō-bune* made. And I can send you one if you would like. There is a special kind of *shōryō-bune* made here. Mine, though of straw, is an elaborate model of a junk and could sail for miles. Would you like to send one to Dr. Tylor? Anthropologically, these little boats in which to send the souls home have a rare interest.

LAFCADIO HEARN.

TO BASIL HALL CHAMBERLAIN

MATSUE, September, 1890.

DEAR PROFESSOR, — I have just returned from my first really great Japanese experience, — a trip to Kizuki. The two trips were beautiful. From Shōbara the route lies through a superb plain of rice fields, with mountain ranges closing the horizon to left and right.

Reaching Kizuki at night, I sent a letter of introduction from Mr. Nishida of the Chūgakkō to Senke Takamori, — the princely person whose family for 82 generations have been in charge of the great temple. I paid a visit to the grounds the same evening, and was amazed by the great scale and dignity of the buildings, and the nobility of the approaches to them, under succession of colossal *torii*.

Next morning a messenger came from Mr. Senke, announcing that I would be received at the temple. My attendant had, however, to put on *hakamas* and perform other personal corrections of dress before entering the august presence.

We were then received with a courtesy and kindness impossible to praise sufficiently or to qualify too gratefully. After performing the requisite ablution of hands, we were received into the inner shrine of the chief deity—(my baggage not yet having arrived, I have not your "Kojiki" by me to correct misspelling, but I think the name is Ōnamuji-no-Mikoto). I was told that I was the first European ever allowed to enter the shrine, though seven or eight other foreigners had visited the grounds.

There are some 19 shrines not consecrated to any particular deities, — in which the Kami are supposed to assemble during the Kami-ari-zuki, — after a preliminary visit to a much smaller temple erected on the seashore,— where, it is said, the sovereignty of Izumo was first divinely guaranteed by the great deity.

We were received by the Gūji (Senke) in ceremonial costumes. His robes were white, those of the attendant priests purple with gold figuring — very beautiful. I acknowledge that I felt considerable awe in the presence of these superb Japanese, who realized for me all that I had imagined about the daimyōs, and grandees of the past. He who used to be called the Iki-gami — said to descend from Susa-no-o-no-Mikoto — is a fine portly man, with a full beard. The ceremonial was imposing, and the sense of the immense antiquity and dignity of the cult, and of the generations of its officiants, might have impressed even a more unbelieving mind than my own.

The temple is really very noble, with its huge pillars, and the solidity of its vast beamwork. Since the prehistoric era it has been rebuilt 28 times. It is said to be the oldest of all Shintō places of worship, and holier than Ise. There are many curiosities and valuable historical documents. The chief shrine faces west, — unlike others.

We were shown the primitive method of lighting the sacred fire — a simple board in holes of which a rapidly revolving stick kindles the spark. Also we saw the hierophantic dance, and heard the strange old song sung — An-un — to the accompaniment of sticks tapped on curiously shaped wooden boxes, or drums.

Subsequently we were invited to the house of Mr. Senke, where other curious things were shown to us.

I have had a rare and delightful experience, and I hope to write of it for one of the English reviews later on.

My attendant — unwarrantably, perhaps — mentioned me as a friend of yours; and the statement provoked a murmur of pleasure. Your name is held, I can assure you, in very great reverence at Kizuki; and I feel assured, should you go there, that you would be received as if you were the chief of the Kami. And I am also sure you would like these really fine and noble men.

I have written enough to tire you perhaps, but I believe the subject may, at least, suggest questions of value from you, if not otherwise interesting. Kizuki is certainly the chief place of interest in Izumo; and I have all details and documents. They will take me some months to digest, but I shall do something pretty.

The jinrikisha ride is a little tiring. Kizuki is very, very pretty. From 200,000 to 250,000 pilgrims go there yearly. All day the sound of the clapping of hands is unbroken, like the sound of a cataract. At least it was when I was there.

Best regards to you.

LAFCADIO HEARN.

TO BASIL HALL CHAMBERLAIN

MATSUE, September, 1890.

DEAR PROFESSOR, — On second thought I have set to work to obtain the information you wish as fully as possible from trustworthy Japanese, — as I fear it could only be gathered by my own exertions alone, too late to be serviceable. I shall send as soon as possible, and if there be time I will supplement the notes with some observations of my own.

I think I shall be very happy in Matsue, and every one assures me it is not so cold as in Tōkyō in winter, although there is more snow.

On the way here I stopped at a very primitive village where there are volcanic springs, and nearly every house has a "natural bathtub" always hot and fresh. And the good old man in whose house I stopped said he only once before in all his life saw a European, — but he did not know whether the European was a man or a woman. The European had very long hair, of a curious colour, and wore a long dress reaching its feet, and its manners were gentle and kind. I found out afterwards it was a Norwegian missionary-girl, having the courage to travel alone.

LAFCADIO HEARN.

TO BASIL HALL CHAMBERLAIN

MATSUE, October, 1890.

DEAR PROFESSOR CHAMBERLAIN, — I received your last kind letter just after having posted a note to you. As for what information I could send, I am surprised and delighted to find that it was of some use. I never expected to be so kindly thanked for it, — deeming it too scanty.

I do not think I shall have any difficulty in getting a model made of the fire-drill, which at Kizuki is a thick board of dense white wood, all the holes being drilled near one edge, in an almost parallel line. Perhaps it may take some little time to arrange the matter; but if there be no hurry, I am almost certain I can get the model made. I am a member of the society now for the preservation of the Kizuki buildings, and am sure my request will be kindly considered.

There are coloured prints here enough: *Samurai-no-ehon* they call the old picture-books here. But they do not relate to Izumo. I hope to procure some soon which will do.

I am more and more impressed with the ascendency of Shintō here. Everybody is a Shintōist; and every house seems to have both its *kamidana* and its *butsudan*. One street is almost entirely composed of Buddhist temples — the Teramachi; but all the worshippers also attend the Shintō services on certain days. The charms suspended over doors, etc., are Shintō. Most of the *mamori* on the *kamidana* of a house are sure to be Shintō. The Gods (1) Ebisu and (2) Daikoku, here respectively identified with (1) Koto-shiro-nushi-no Kami and (2) Oho-kuni-nushi-no-Kami, are monopolized by Shintō. Its signs and mysteries are everywhere: the atmosphere is full of magic.

I suppose some people would think this sort of worship shocking, but I must say I could not laugh at it: the childish naïveté of the prayers and the offerings — the idea of a *kami* in the tree, able to heal — seemed to me rather touching than absurd, and delightfully natural. One feels what pastoral

life in the antique world must have been, on studying
the artless notions of these good country-folk, whom
no one could live among without loving, — unless he
were strangely brutal or bigoted.

I had to make a speech before the educational
association of Izumo the other day, and in citing the
labours of Darwin, Lubbock, Huxley, and others, I
quoted also Tylor's delightful little book on Anthropology. My speech was on the Value of the Imagination as a Factor in Education. The Governor ordered
it to be translated and printed; — so that I am being
for the moment perhaps much more highly considered
than I ought to be.

I have become so accustomed to Japanese food
and habits, that it would now be painful to me to
change them. The only extras, besides sake, which
I take, are plenty of fried and raw eggs. So far I am
in better health than I hoped to be in Japan.

I am very sorry you are not quite well. Here the
weather is what they call "mad weather" — rain
alternating with sun, and chilly winds.

With best regards,
Faithfully yours,
LAFCADIO HEARN.

TO BASIL HALL CHAMBERLAIN

NOVEMBER, 1890.

DEAR PROFESSOR CHAMBERLAIN, — You will remember having invited humble me to make a few
criticisms if I could, about "Things Japanese." I
am now going to pray you with all my heart and soul

to change that article about Japanese Music in the
next edition of the book.   I am, and have been for
months unspeakably charmed with Japanese music,
— I think it is as dainty and playfully sweet and
pretty as the Japanese girls who sing it and play it;
and I feel sure there is a very fine subtle art-feeling
in it.   I am sorry to say, however, that while making
this plea, I must in honesty confess that I am not an
appreciant of Wagner, and that I have always been
much impressed and charmed by primitive music.
African music, and Spanish-American melodies I am
quite infatuated about, and neither of these would be
considered as related to the higher musical sense.
But I feel sure if you were in Izumo, I could make
you hear some music, both instrumental and vocal,
which you would acknowledge to be more than
"pretty."

I think I will be able to get a model of the fire-
drill made in a while.   I have arranged for a week
at Kizuki during the coming vacation.

The importance of Shintō here as compared with
Buddhism impresses me more and more every day.
Most of the *kakemono* in the *tokonomas* are Shintō
rather than Buddhist.   The story of the Sun-goddess
is a favourite theme with local artists.   Here also the
gods of Good-Fortune have become after a fashion
adopted by Shintō.

I expect to send you some *mamori* shortly from two
places — Ichibata and Sakusa.   The Shintō shrine
at Sakusa would probably interest you.   Lovers in
doubt go there to pray to the *kami* who set the
single in family, and who have decided in advance

the coupling of all human creatures. In this shrine are the spirits of Susa-no-o-no-Mikoto and his wife enshrined,—his first wife whom he met accompanied by her father before he went to kill the Serpent. The ghost of the father-in-law, "Foot-stroking Elder," is supposed to reside in the same place, — also that of the mother-in-law. Almost every spot in hill or valley here has a shrine marking an act or footstep of Susa-no-o. Every place where the Serpent (Orochi) could possibly have been, still holds a legend of it.

I am no longer in a hotel, but have a very beautiful house, fronting on the lake, and from my window I could see with a telescope almost to Kizuki over a beautiful stretch of blue water. And every peak I see has some divine story attached to it, and several are named after the primæval gods.

I am perfectly treated here, and would be very, very happy if I had only a little more time to work. It is now a busy season. The examinations have come upon me; and I interrupted this letter twice before sending it, in order to get some examination papers done. I have twelve large classes to examine and give marks to on Dictation, Reading, Composition, and Conversation. But now the trouble is over, and I shall have plenty of time to write again.

Hoping you will excuse silence, I am always

Sincerely yours,

LAFCADIO HEARN.

I enclose a few *mamori* of Kishibojin, — the Sanscrit Harite, — to whom wives pray for children.

I suppose you know more about her worship than I do. But in the Northern temples of her the votive offerings of children dresses are large dresses. Here the dresses are only models of dresses — doll size. The pregnant woman picks one out of a thousand, keeping her eyes shut. When she looks, if she has picked out a girl's dress, she is sure the child in her womb is a boy!—and vice versa. When the child is born she makes another dress and brings it to the temple. I am very fond of Kishibojin, and I think her worship beautiful.

Verily I have become quite as much of an idolater as any of these.

L. H.

TO BASIL HALL CHAMBERLAIN

Matsue, 1890.

Dear Professor Chamberlain, — I returned last Sunday from Ichibata, but was too tired and busy to write at once. I have already sent you some *mamori* from the famed temple of Yakushi Nyorai.

The little steamer — the very smallest I ever saw — which carries pilgrims and others from Matsue to Kozakai — makes the trip to the latter village in about two hours. Then the task of climbing the mountain is not over-easy. The scenery, however, both on the lake and at Ichibata is grand, and the peaks of the ranges have all their legends. There are nearly 600 steps of stone to climb before the temple, — situated on a windy summit whence the view extends for many luminous miles. The temple is new, — the ancient one having been destroyed by fire. There is a large hotel where guests are entertained upon a strictly Buddhist diet — no fish, no eggs; but a little cheap sake is tolerated. No girls, — only young men as servants and waiters. The priests made some demonstrations at my appearance in their courts; but a few words from the pilgrims with me settled me in their good opinions, and they became kind, and showed me their *kakemonos* of the Great Physician. All afflicted with eye-troubles journey here and pray, — repeating always the same prayer according to long established usage — "On koro-koro Sendai," etc. Little water vessels are sold bearing the *mon* of the temple, and these are filled from the temple spring, and the sick bathe their eyes therewith. The trip was altogether a very charming one for me, and not the less interesting because I had to get back to Matsue in a sampan.

I am becoming a good pilgrim.

I do not think I am the first European to visit Ichibata, however: there were some German naval officers here, according to tradition, eight or ten years ago.

With best regards, always yours,

LAFCADIO HEARN.

TO SENTARŌ NISHIDA

MATSUE, 1890.

DEAR MR. NISHIDA, — . . . Last evening, the servant of Governor Koteda came to the house with a curious-looking box, which contained a present from Miss Koteda, — an uguisu: the bird which sings "*Hokkekyō*," and ought, therefore, for its piety, according to the *sutra* of the good law, to be endowed with six hundred good qualities of Eye, six hundred good qualities of Hearing, twelve hundred good qualities of Smelling power, and twelve hundred supernatural excellences of the tongue, or of Speech.   I am almost ready to believe the last compensation has been given it, — for its voice is superlatively sweet. — But what to say or do in the way of thanking the giver I don't know: this is really too kind.

So yesterday, despite the hideous weather, was a fortunate day: it brought to my house the sacred bird and your delightful postal news; — and for all things my grateful thanks and best wishes.

Most faithfully,

LAFCADIO HEARN.

TO YRJÖ HIRN

Tōkyō, December, 1890.

DEAR PROFESSOR, — I have just finished the reading of your "Origins of Art." . . . Some years ago I remember that I wanted very much to produce an ideal essay upon the "ghostliness" of fine art, — the element of *thrill* common to all forms of it: painting, sculpture, music, or architecture.   The notion is not original, I suppose, — but it came to me with such an intensity that I imagined a general truth behind it.   This was the possible fact that no existing æsthetic sentiment had a primarily æsthetic origin,

and that all such sentiment must simply represent
emotional accumulation, — organic memory or inherited tendency. But I could not develop my notion
judiciously. Your fine book shows me how such
things should have been done, and it expresses con-
victions and ideas which I lacked the scientific
training to utter consistently.

I found a particular satisfaction in your critique of
the Darwinian hypothesis as to sexual æsthetic sensibility in animals and birds. Though I am an "extreme" evolutionist, this hypothesis always seemed
to me essentially wrong, — essentially opposed to the
facts of psychical evolution. You have more than
convinced me of what I suspected. Also I think that,
even while occasionally diverging from Spencer's
views, you have reënforced his main positions, and
shed fresh light upon various shadowy regions of the
new psychology. I liked very much your treatment
of the difficult topic of pleasure-pain: indeed, I like
the whole book more than I feel able to tell you.

My own slight knowledge of these matters is
based chiefly upon a study of Spencer. Although I
have played "æsthetically" with metaphysical ideas
in my books, I believe that I have a fair knowledge
of the whole system of Synthetic Philosophy, and
that I may call myself a disciple of its author. Therefore, — or rather by reason of this private study
only, — can I presume even to discuss your work as
an admirer. You place the study of æsthetics upon
a purely natural and common-sense basis, even while
considering its multiple aspects; and I am persuaded
that this must be the system of the future. Psycho-

physics and psycho-dynamics have of late years been applied to æsthetic problems with the naked result of leaving the main question exactly where it was before, or of landing the student in a *cul-de-sac;* and I imagine that much intellectual labour has been wasted in such paths merely through cowardice of conventions. It is a delight to meet with a book like this, in which science quietly ignores cant, and opens a new clearing through the blinding maze of mediæval cobwebs. Again, I must say that a more lucid, strong, and pleasing style I have not found in any modern work on æsthetics.

I want, however, to make a small protest about the second paragraph on page 233. Perhaps in the second edition you might think it worth your while to modify the statement as to the "gross" character of Japanese dancing. I should question the fairness of classing together—except as to probable emotional origins — Asiatic and African dances (i. e. *negro* dances). But I shall speak of the Japanese dances only. To make any general statement about anything Japanese is always risky; for customs here (differing in every province and every period) exhibit a most bewildering variety. It is not correct to say that the dancing is performed by "outcast women" mostly; for there are many respectable forms of dancing. The *maiko* is not perhaps a very respectable person; — but the *miko*, or Shintō priestesses (daughters of priests), certainly are worthy of all respect. Well, there are the temple-dances, before the old gods, — the dances of children at the temples upon holidays, — the dances of the peasants, etc.,

etc. None of these could be called gross,—however amorous their origin. Men dance as well as women: all children dance; and in some conservative provinces dancing is a part of female education. To come back to the *maiko* or *geisha*, however, let me assure you that although some of their dances may be passionally mimetic, even the passionate acting could not be termed "gross" with justice: on the contrary it is a very delicate bit of refined acting, — acting of eyes and lips and hands, — which requires a sharp eye to follow. There are in Japan, as everywhere else, dances that would not bear severe moral criticism; but the fine forms of Oriental dancing are really dramatic performances, — silent monologues of a most artistic kind. — Perhaps you will be interested in a book which an acquaintance of mine, Mr. Osman Edwards, is bringing out through Mr. Heinemann of London, "The Theatre in Japan." The fact of the old lyric drama seems to me to call for a modification of the statement on page 233. Of course I am not questioning the suggestion of origins.

Excuse these hasty and insufficient expressions of appreciation. Now to the question of a former letter received from you, on the subject of a selection of papers translated from various books of mine, by Mrs. Hirn.

You have my full consent to publish such a translation. . . . I should certainly accept no pay either from translator or publisher; and a single copy of such translation, when published, would be favour enough. . . .

On the subject of a photograph and biographical

notice, however, will you not excuse me for saying that I do not think the circumstances justify such an introduction to a strange public? . . .

With renewed thanks for your most precious book, believe me, dear Professor, very sincerely yours,

LAFCADIO HEARN.

TO BASIL HALL CHAMBERLAIN

MATSUE, January, 1891.

DEAR PROFESSOR CHAMBERLAIN, — I am sorry not to have heard from you, — fearing you may have been ill. The weather here has become something very disagreeable — I was going to say infernal; but I think this word better describes the weather of the North Atlantic Coast. The changes of temperature here are less extreme, the cold is milder, but the temperature may change three times in twenty-four hours, — which seems to me extraordinary. There is almost perpetual rain and gloom, and I would almost dislike Izumo were it not that one lovely day in a month is enough to make me forgive and forget all the bad weather. The "Izumo Fuji"—Dai sen (which is not, however, in Izumo at all) — was beautifully visible the day before yesterday, and the landscape was unspeakably beautiful.

I am now arranging, as best I can, to get the fire-drill model made in Kizuki. My friends have been ill and my best friend, Mr. Nishida, is still so ill that he cannot travel with me. But I think the drill can be made very soon now. I have a passport for all Izumo; but the weather is diabolical; and though my chest is very strong, I feel that it is a severe strain to keep well even at home. So I shall not travel much before the summer.

I send you some clean new "fire-insurance mamori." I found out only two weeks ago where they are sold, — at the great Inari temple in the grounds of Matsue Castle, where there are enormous stone foxes, and perhaps two thousand small foxes sitting all round the court with their tails perpendicularly elevated. The most extraordinary thing of the kind I ever saw. They showed me at the temple a *kakemono* of a ghostly fox, with a phosphoric jewel in its tail, — said to have been painted ages ago. I think I shall buy it from them. It is not beautiful, but quite curious.

I wish you a very, very happy new year and many of them.   Faithfully,

LAFCADIO HEARN.

TO BASIL HALL CHAMBERLAIN

MATSUE, January, 1891.

DEAR PROFESSOR CHAMBERLAIN, — Your kindness in sending me a postal card while suffering so much yourself from sickness, is something that touches me very much. I hope to thank you better later on.

I myself am very sick. I boasted too soon about my immunity from cold. I have been severely touched where I thought myself strongest — in my lungs — and have passed some weeks in bed. My first serious discouragement came with this check to

my enthusiasm; I fear a few more winters of this kind
will put me underground. But this has been a very
exceptional winter, they say. The first snowstorm
piled five feet of snow about my house, which faces
the lake, looking to Kizuki. All the mountains are
white, and the country is smothered with snow, and
the wind is very severe. I never saw a heavier snow-
fall in the United States or Canada. The thermometer does not go so low as you might suppose, not
more than about 12 above zero; but the houses are
cold as cattle barns, and the *hibachi* and the *kotatsu*
are mere shadows of heat, — ghosts, illusions. But
I have the blues now; perhaps to-morrow everything
will be cheerful again. The authorities are astonishingly kind to me. If they were not, I do not know
what I should do.

I trust you are now strong again. I send you
a few *mamori* from the famous shrine of Sakusa
(county I-yu) where Yaegaki-san are worshipped,
the "Deities who couple and set the single in families." It is said that these, so soon as a boy or
girl is born, decide the future love and marriage of
the child, — betrothing all to all from the moment
of birth. Three Shintō deities are the presiding
gods: Susa-no-o-no-Mikoto, his wife Inada-Hime-
no-Mikoto, and their son Sakusa-no-Mikoto, from
whom, I suppose, the place takes its name. The
mother of Inada-Hime and Taka o gami-no-Mikoto,
and Ama-terasu-Omi-Kami, are also there enshrined.

Here, amid stone foxes and stone lions, a priest
sells love-charms. Some of these consist of the
leaves of *Camellia Japonica*.

There is a tree in the temple court (or rather two trees, which have grown into one); this is considered both symbolical and magical. There is also a pond in which newts live. The flesh of these newts, reduced to ashes, is considered an efficacious aphrodisiac. It is also the custom for lovers to throw offerings wrapped in bits of white paper into the pond, and watch. If the newts at once run to it, the omen is good; if they neglect it, it is bad.

In the Middle Ages this temple used to be in the village of Ushio, on the boundary of the counties of O hara and Ni ta, but was removed to its present site many hundred years ago. There are curious traditions and poems, mostly of an erotic character, regarding this shrine.

Trusting you will soon be quite well, believe me always sincerely yours,

LAFCADIO HEARN.

TO BASIL HALL CHAMBERLAIN

MATSUE, April, 1891.

DEAR PROFESSOR CHAMBERLAIN, — I am delighted to hear the fire-drill is at last in your hands.

About Shintō . . . Of course, as far as its philosophy is concerned (which I am very fond of, in spite of my devotion to Herbert Spencer), and romance of religious sentiment, and legends, and art, — my Izumo experiences have not at all changed my love of Buddhism. If it were possible for me to adopt a faith, I should adopt it. But Shintō seems to me like an occult force, — vast, extraordinary, —

which has not been seriously taken into account as a force. I think it is the hopeless, irrefragable obstacle to the Christianization of Japan (for which reason I am wicked enough to love it). It is not all a belief, nor all a religion; it is a thing formless as a magnetism and indefinable as an ancestral impulse. It is part of the Soul of the Race. It means all the loyalty of the nation to its sovereigns, the devotion of retainers to princes, the respect to sacred things, the conservation of principles, the whole of what an Englishman would call sense of duty; but that this sense seems to be hereditary and inborn. I think a baby is Shintō from the time its eyes can see. Here, too, the symbolism of Shintō is among the very first things the child sees (I suppose it is the same in Tōkyō). The toys are to a great extent Shintō toys; and the excursions of a young mother with a baby on her back are always to Shintō temples. How much of Confucianism may have entered into and blended with what is a striking characteristic of Japanese boys in their attitude toward teachers and superiors, I do not know; but I think that what is now most pleasing in these boys is the outer reflection of the spirit of Shintō within them, — the hereditary spirit of it.

The Shinshū sect is the only one, as far as I can learn, whose members in Izumo are not also Shintōists; but the sect is very weak here. Even the Nichirenites are Shintōists. The two religions are so perfectly blended here that the lines of demarcation are sometimes impossible to find.

Well, I think we Occidentals have yet to learn the

worship of ancestors; and evolution is going to teach it to us. When we become conscious that we owe whatever is wise or good or strong or beautiful in each one of us, not to one particular inner individuality, but to the struggles and sufferings and experiences of the whole unknown chain of human lives behind us, reaching back into mystery unthinkable, — the worship of ancestors seems an extremely righteous thing. What is it, philosophically, but a tribute of gratitude to the past, — dead relatively only, — alive really within us, and about us.

With best regards, in momentary haste,

LAFCADIO HEARN.

TO BASIL HALL CHAMBERLAIN

MATSUE, May, 1891.

DEAR PROFESSOR CHAMBERLAIN, — I have just returned from a pilgrimage to the famous Kwannon temple of Kiyomizu — about 18 miles from Matsue — where it is said that the sacred fire has never been extinguished for a thousand years, to find your postal card. I do not wait to receive the delightful gift in order to thank you for it; as I hope to have the pleasure of writing you a letter on my impression of it after reading it. You could have imagined nothing to send me more welcome. Mr. Lowell has, I think, no warmer admirer in the world than myself, though I do not agree with his theory in the "Soul of the Far East," and think he has ignored the most essential and astonishing quality of the race: its genius of eclecticism. The future holds many problems we cannot presume to guess, in regard to the fate of races. But there is not wanting foundation for the belief that the Orient may yet dominate the Occident and absorb it utterly. China seems to many a far greater question than Russia.

About your kind question regarding books. I think I shall be able to get all the books on Japan — in English — that I need; and your "Things Japanese" is a mine of good advice on what to buy. But if I need counsel which I cannot find in your book, then I will write and ask.

I venture to say that I think you have underrated the importance of my suggestion about the Sacred Snake, — of which I have not been able to find the scientific name. If they have such a snake at Ise then I am wrong. But, if not, I think the little snake would be worth having. It does not — like the fire-drill of Kizuki—possess special interest for the anthropologist; but it certainly should have interest for the folk-lorist, as a chapter in one of the most ancient and widely spread (if not universal) religious practices, — the worship of the Serpent. If you ever want an enshrined snake, let me know. It is dried and put into a little *miya* for the *kamidana*.

Speaking of folk-lore, I have been interesting myself in the fox-superstition in Izumo. Here, and in Iwami, the superstition has local peculiarities. It is so powerful as to affect the value of real estate to the amount of hundreds of thousands of yen, and keen men have become rich by speculating upon the strength of it. If you want any facts about it, please tell me.

The scenery at Kiyomizu is superb. But there is
no clear water except the view of Nanji-umi from the
pagoda and the hills. The *mamori*, I regret to say,
are uninteresting. There is, however, a curious Inari
shrine. Beside it is a sort of huge trough filled with
little foxes of all shapes, designs, and material. If
you want anything, you pray, and put a fox in your
pocket, and take it home. As soon as the prayer is
granted you must take the fox back again and put it
just where it was before. I should like to have taken
one home; but my servants hate foxes and Inari and
tofu and *azuki-meshi* and *abura-gi* and everything
related to foxes. So I left it alone.

You will not be sorry to hear that I am to have the
same publishers as Mr. Lowell, — at least according
to present indications. I am not vain enough to
think I can ever write anything so beautiful as his
"Chosön" or "Soul of the Far East," and will
certainly make a poor showing beside his precise,
fine, perfectly worded work. But I am not going to
try to do anything in his line. My work will deal
wholly with exceptional things (chiefly popular) in
an untilled field of another kind.

I gave 72 boys, as subject for composition the
other day, the question: "What would you most like
in this world?" Nine of the compositions contained
in substance this answer: "To die for our Sacred
Emperor." That is Shintō. Is n't it grand and
beautiful? and do you wonder that I love it after
that?

Most grateful regards from yours most sincerely,
LAFCADIO HEARN.

TO BASIL HALL CHAMBERLAIN

Matsue, 1891.

Dear Professor Chamberlain, — I went to Kōbe by rail, and thence by jinrikisha across Japan over mountains and through valleys of rice-fields — a journey of four days; but the most delightful in some respects of all my travelling experiences. The scenery had this peculiar effect, that it repeated for me many of my tropical impressions — received in a country of similar volcanic configuration, — besides reviving for me all sorts of early memories of travel in Wales and England which I had forgotten. Nothing could be more beautiful than this mingling of the sensations of the tropics with those of Northern summers. And the people! My expectations were much more than realized: it is among the country-people Japanese character should be studied, and I could not give my opinion of them now without using what you would call enthusiastic language. I felt quite sorry to reach this larger city, where the people are so much less simple, charming, and kindly, — although I have every reason to be pleased with them. And in a mountain village I saw a dance unlike anything I ever saw before — some dance immemorially old, and full of weird grace. I watched it until midnight, and wish I could see it again. Nothing yet seen in Japan delighted me so much as this Bon-odori — in no wise resembling the same performance in the north. I found Buddhism gradually weaken toward the interior, while Shintō emblems surrounded the fields, and things suggesting the phallic worship of antiquity were being adored in remote groves.   LAFCADIO HEARN.

TO BASIL HALL CHAMBERLAIN

MATSUE, June, 1891.

DEAR MR. CHAMBERLAIN, — I am horribly ashamed to confess my weakness; but the truth must be told! After having lived for ten months exclusively upon Japanese fare, I was obliged to return (for a couple of days only! ! ! !) to the flesh-pots of Egypt. Having become sick, I could not recuperate upon Japanese eating — even when reënforced with eggs. I devoured enormous quantities of beef, fowl, and sausage, and fried solid stuffs, and absorbed terrific quantities of beer, — having had the good luck to find one foreign cook in Matsue. I am very much ashamed! But the fault is neither mine nor that of the Japanese: it is the fault of my ancestors, — the ferocious, wolfish hereditary instincts and tendencies of boreal mankind. The sins of the father, etc.

Do you know anything about Chōzuba-no-Kami? There are images of him. He has no eyes — only ears. He passes much of his time in sleep. He is angry if any one enters the *koka* without previously hemming, — so as to give him notice. He makes everybody sick if the place in which he dwells is not regularly cleaned. He goes to Kizuki and to Sada with the other gods once a year; and after a month's absence returns. When he returns, he passes his hand over each member of the family as they go to the Chōzuba, — to make sure the family is the same. But one must not be afraid of the invisible hand. I think this kami is an extremely decent, respectable person, with excellent views on the subjects of morality and hygiene. I could not refuse him a lamp nor — for obvious reasons — the worship of incense.

I have not been able to travel yet far enough to find anything novel, but hope soon to do so. Meanwhile I am planning to make, if possible, not only a tour of Izumo, but also a very brief visit to Tōkyō in company with Mr. Nishida. Perhaps — I may be able to see both you and Mr. Lowell for a tiny little while — you will always have a moment to spare.

I am always haunted by a particularly sarcastic translation Mr. Lowell, in one of his books, made of the name of a gate, — "The Gate of Everlasting Ceremony." (Only an American could have dared to make such a translation.) I have been through the Gate and into the Court of Everlasting Ceremony; but the gate is a marvellous swarming of carven dragons and water, and the court is full of peace and sweetness. Most truly,

LAFCADIO HEARN.

TO BASIL HALL CHAMBERLAIN

MATSUE, 1891.

DEAR PROFESSOR CHAMBERLAIN, — Your welcome letter has just reached me, on the eve of a trip to Kizuki, and — unless extraordinary circumstances prevent—Oki islands. My guest has departed. He

was so petted and made much of here, that I could
not help regretting you also would not come. I
think I could make you comfortable here, — even in
regard to diet, — at any time when you could make
the trip; and, as far as the people go, they would
embarrass you with kindness. Your name here is
— well, more than you would wish it to be.

Your last delightful letter I did not fully answer in
my last, being hurried. What you said about the
influence of health or sickness on the spiritual life of
a man went straight to my heart. I have found, as
you have done, that the possessor of pure horse-health
never seems to have an idea of the "half-lights."
It is impossible to see the psychical undercurrents
of human existence without that self-separation
from the purely physical part of being, which
severe sickness gives — like a revelation. One in
good health, who has never been obliged to separate
his immaterial self from his material self, always
will imagine that he understands much which, even
recorded in words, cannot be understood at all without sharp experience. We are all living two lives, —
but the revelation of the first seems only to come by
accident. There is an essay worth reading, entitled
"Sickness is Health," — dealing with the physical
results of sickness only; but there is a much larger
psychological truth in the title than the author of it,
whose name I forget, ever dreamed of. All the
history of asceticism and self-suppression as a religion, appears to me founded upon a vague, blun-
dering, intuitive recognition of the terrible and glorious fact, that we can reach the highest life only

through that self-separation which the experiences of illness, that is, the knowledge of physical weakness, brings; perfect health always involves the domination of the spiritual by the physical — at least in the present state of human evolution.

Perhaps it will interest you to know the effect of Japanese life upon your little friend after the experiences of a year and a half. At first, the sense of existence here is like that of escaping from an almost unbearable atmospheric pressure into a rarefied, highly oxygenated medium. That feeling continues: in Japan the law of life is not as with us, — that each one strives to expand his own individuality at the expense of his neighbour's. But on the other hand, how much one loses! Never a fine inspiration, a deep emotion, a profound joy or a profound pain — never a thrill, or, as the French say so much better than we, a *frisson*. So literary work is dry, bony, hard, dead work. I have confined myself strictly to the most emotional phases of Japanese life, — popular religion and popular imagination, and yet I can find nothing like what I would get at once in any Latin country, a strong emotional thrill. Whether it is that the difference in our ancestral history renders what we call soul-sympathy almost impossible, or whether it is that the Japanese are psychically smaller than we, I cannot venture to decide — I hope the former. But the experience of all thinking persons with whom I have had a chance to speak seems to be the same.

But how sweet the Japanese woman is ! — all the possibilities of the race for goodness seem to be con-

centrated in her. It shakes one's faith in some
Occidental doctrines. If this be the result of suppression and oppression, — then these are not
altogether bad. On the other hand, how diamond-
hard the character of the American woman becomes
under the idolatry of which she is the subject. In
the eternal order of things which is the highest being, — the childish, confiding, sweet Japanese girl,—
or the superb, calculating, penetrating Occidental
Circe of our more artificial society, with her enormous power for evil, and her limited capacity for
good? Viscount Torio's idea haunts me more and
more; — I think there are very formidable truths
in his observations about Western sociology. And
the question comes: "In order to comprehend the
highest good, is it necessary that we must first learn
the largest power of evil?" For the one may be the
Shadow of the other.

I am very much disappointed with Rein. I got
much more information about my own particular
line of study from your "Things Japanese" than
from Rein. Rein himself confesses, after seven or
eight years' labour, that he has only been able to make
"a patchwork"! What, then, can a man like myself hope to do, — without scientific knowledge, and
without any hope of even acquiring the language of
the country so as to read even a newspaper? Really
it seems to me almost an impertinence on my part to
try to write anything about Japan at all, and the
only fact which gives me courage is that there exists
no book especially devoted to the subject I hope
to consider.

The deity of Mionoseki is called always by the
people Ebisu, or Koto-shiro-nushi-no-Kami; — in
the guide the deity is said to be Hiruko, who, I believe, has been identified by Shintō commentators
with Hiruko, as I find in the article on the Seven
Gods of Good Fortune, in the Asiatic Transactions.
But I am not sure what to say about Hiruko being
the deity of Mio Jinja, as a general statement. My
friends say that only a Shintō priest can decide, and
I am going to see one.

Most truly,

LAFCADIO HEARN.

TO BASIL HALL CHAMBERLAIN

MATSUE, August, 1891.

DEAR PROFESSOR CHAMBERLAIN, — I have just
received and read your most interesting letter on my
return from Kizuki, — where I should have liked to
remain longer, but I must go to see the Bon-odori at
Shimo-ichi, where it is danced differently from anywhere else, so far as I can learn, and in a thrillingly
ghostly manner, — so that one thinks he is looking at
a Dance of Souls.

Before leaving I had a copy of Murray's Guide
sent to the Kokuzō, who was more than pleased to
see the picture of the great temple reproduced and to
hear what was said about it. Before I went away, he
gave me another singular entertainment, such as he
alone could do — for he is King of Kizuki. (By the
way, the old reverence for the Kokuzō is not dead.
Folks do not believe now that whoever he looks at

immediately becomes unable to move; but as I and
my companion followed him to the great shrine, the
pilgrims fell down and worshipped him as he passed.)

This was the entertainment he gave me: —
Having invited me to the temple grounds, where
seats were prepared, and a supper got ready for us,
Mr. Senke gave some order, and the immense court
immediately filled with people, — thousands. Then
at a signal began a round dance, such as I had never
seen before, — the Hōnen-odori, as anciently performed in Kizuki. It was so fascinating that I
watched it until two o'clock in the morning. At least
three hundred dancers were in the ring; — and the
leader, standing on a mochi-mortar turned upside
down, with an umbrella over his head, formed the
axis of the great round, and turned slowly within it
upon his pedestal. He had a superb voice. The
Kokuzō also got the beautiful *miko* dances photographed to please me, and presented me with many
curious MSS., some of which I hope to show you later
on. They were written expressly for me.

Now as to the shōryō-bune. Just as the Bon-odori
differs in every part of Japan, and just as everything
at Kizuki is totally different from everything at Ise,
even to the Miko-kagura, so is the custom of sending
away the Ships of the Souls different here. In many
parts the ships are launched at two or three o'clock in
the morning of the day after the Bon; or if ships are
not launched, then floating lanterns are sent out by
way of guiding the dead home. But in Kizuki the
shōryō-bune are launched only by day and for those
who have been drowned at sea, and the shapes of

the ships vary according to the kind of ship in which the lost man or woman perished. And they are launched every year for ten years after the death: — and when the soul returns yearly to visit the home, the ship is made ready, and a little stick of incense is lighted before launching it to take the beloved ghost back again, and a little stock of provisions is placed in it upon *kawarake* (principally *dango*). And the *kaimyō* of the dead is written upon the sail. And these boats are launched, — not at night, as elsewhere, but in the daytime.

I have had the shōryō-bune boxed and addressed to you, and a priest wrote for me the kaimyō upon the sail and the date of death, according to the usual custom. But you will not get the thing before three weeks, as I am forwarding it by express, and you know how slow the process is!

As for my letters, use anything you wish, and, if you desire, my name. The only matter is this: that I am so small a personage as an author that I am much in doubt whether the use of my name attached to any opinion would give the opinion more weight than if expressed impersonally. Unless it should, it might not be good for the book. I leave the decision entirely to you.

I have been reading Mr. Lowell's book over again; for it is one thing to read it in Philadelphia, and quite another thing to read it after having spent a year and a half in Japan. And the power and the charm impress me more than ever. But I am so much horrified by its conclusions — at least a few of them — that I try very hard to find a flaw therein.

I think the idea that the degree of the development of individuality in a people necessarily marks its place in the great march of mind is not true necessarily. At least it may be argued about. For as the tendency of the age is toward class specialization and interdependent subdivision of all branches of knowledge and all practical application of that knowledge, the development of the individuality of every integer of a community would seem to me to unfit the unit to form a close part of any specialized class. In brief, I doubt, or rather I wish to doubt, that the development of individuality is a lofty or desirable tendency. Much of what is called personality and individuality is intensely repellent, and makes the principal misery of Occidental life. It means much that is connected with pure aggressive selfishness: and its extraordinary development in a country like America or England seems a confirmation of Viscount Torio's theory that Western civilization has the defect of cultivating the individual at the expense only of the mass, and giving unbounded opportunities to human selfishness, unrestrained by religious sentiment, law, or emotional feeling.

What you say about your experience with Japanese poetry is indeed very telling and very painful to one who loves Japan. Depth, I have long suspected, does not exist in the Japanese soul-stream. It flows much like the rivers of the country, — over beds three quarters dry, — very clear and charmingly beshadowed; — but made temporarily profound only by some passional storm. But it seems to me that some tendencies in Japanese prose give hope of

THE CITY OF MATSUE

some beautiful things. There was a story some time ago in the *Asahi Shimbun* about a *shirabyōshi* that brought tears to my eyes, as slowly and painfully translated by a friend. There was tenderness and poetry and pathos in it worthy of Le Fanu (I thought of the exquisite story of Le Fanu, "A Bird of Passage," simply as a superb bit of tender pathos) or Bret Harte — though, of course, I don't know what the style is. But the Japanese poem, as I judge from your work and the "Anthologie Japonaise," seems to me exactly the Japanese coloured print in words, — nothing much more. Still, how the sensation of that which has been is flashed into heart and memory by the delicious print or the simple little verse.

I go to-morrow or the next day to Shimo-ichi. If you get the shōryō-bune, let me know. Any of your servants can, I think, fix the little masts and pennons in place. A small incense vessel and *kawarake* with *dango*, or models of *dango*, might be added by Dr. Tylor to the exhibit; but I suppose these are not essential.

With sincerest regards, ever truly,

LAFCADIO HEARN.

TO BASIL HALL CHAMBERLAIN

MATSUE, August, 1891.

DEAR MR. CHAMBERLAIN, — Before leaving, I must trouble you with another note or two.

For "Things Japanese," I would like to make a suggestion about the article "Theatre." The reference to O-Kuni seems to me extremely severe; for her story is very beautiful and touching. She was a *miko* in the Great Temple of Kizuki, and fell in love with a *ronin* named Nagoya Sanza, and she fled away with her lover to Kyōto. On the way, another *ronin*, who fell in love with her extraordinary beauty, was killed by Sanza. Always the face of the dead man haunted the girl.

At Kyōto she supported her lover by dancing the Miko-kagura in the dry bed of the river Kamogawa. Then they went to Tōkyō (Yedo) and began to act. Sanza himself became a famous and successful actor. The two lived together until Sanza died.

Then she came back to Kizuki. She was learned, and a great poet in the style called *renga*. After Sanza's death she supported herself, or at least occupied herself, in teaching this poetic art. But she shaved off her hair and became a nun, and built the little Buddhist temple in Kizuki called Rengaji, in which she lived, and taught her art. And the reason she built the temple was that she might pray for the soul of the *ronin* whom the sight of her beauty had ruined. The temple stood until thirty years ago. Nothing is now left of it but a broken statue of Jizō. Her family still live in Kizuki, and until the restoration the chief of the family was always entitled to a share of the profits of the Kizuki theatre, because his ancestress, the beautiful *miko*, had founded the art.

So I would like to suggest that poor O-Kuni have a kind word said for her. And I am sure we would both think very highly of her if she were alive.

There is a little Japanese book about her history; but I do not know the title. With best regards,

LAFCADIO.

TO PAGE M. BAKER

MATSUE, August, 1891.

DEAR PAGE, — I answer your dear letter at once, as you wished me to do. It reached me to-day, on my return from Kizuki, the Holy City of Japan, — where I have become something of a favourite with the high pontiff of the most ancient and sacred shrine of the land, — which no other European was ever permitted to enter before me. And I am travelling now, — stopping at home only on my way to other curious and unknown places. For this part of Japan is so little known that I was the first to furnish Murray's Guidebook editors with some information thereabout. . . .

But I had unknown friends here who knew me through my "Chinese Ghosts" — so they applied to the Government for me, and I got an educational position under contract. The contract was renewed last March for a year — the extreme term allowed by law. My salary is only $100 per month; but that is equal here to more than double the sum in America. So that I am able to keep up nearly the nicest house in town, — outside of a few very rich men, — to have several servants, to give dinners, and to dress my little wife tolerably nicely. Moreover, life in Japan is something so placid and kindly and gentle — that it is just like one of those dreams in which everybody is good-natured about everything. The missionaries have no reason to like me, — for one had to be discharged to secure me; and I teach the boys to respect their own beautiful faith and the gods of their fathers, and not to listen to proselytism. However, the missionaries leave me alone. We have a tiff about Spencer in the *Japan Mail* sometimes; but as a rule I am completely isolated from all Europeans. It is only at long intervals one ever gets so far, — with the exception of an austere female stationed here in the vague hope of making a convert.

Of course I will send you a photograph of my little wife. I must tell you I am married only in the Japanese manner as yet, — because of the territorial law. Only by becoming a Japanese citizen, which I think I shall do, will it be possible to settle the matter satisfactorily. By the present law, the moment a foreigner marries a native according to English law, she becomes an English citizen, and her children English subjects, if she have any. Therefore she becomes subject to territorial laws regarding foreigners, — obliged to live within treaty limits, and virtually separated from her own people. So it would be her ruin to marry her according to English form, until I become a Japanese in law; — for should I die, she would have serious reason to regret her loss of citizenship.

As for going abroad — I mean back to you all — I don't know what to say. Just now, of course, I could not if I would; for I am under legal contract. Then my plans for a book on Japan are but a quarter finished. Then, my little woman would be very

unhappy, I fear, away from her people and her gods;
— for this country is so strange that it is impossible
for any who have never lived here for a long time
to understand the enormous difference between the
thought and feeling of the Japanese and our own.
But, later on, perhaps I *must* go back for a time to
see about getting out a book. Then I will probably
appeal to you for a year's employ or something. The
Orient is more fascinating than you may suppose:
here, remember, the people *really* eat lotuses: they
form a common article of diet. But no human being
can tell exactly what the future has in store for
him. So I cannot for the life of me say now what
I shall do. . . .

We are many years behind you here. In Matsue
there is a little newspaper of which I must send you a
copy as a curiosity. Every week or two there is an
article in it about me. For "the foreigner's" every
act is a subject for comment. There is no such
thing in Japan as privacy. There are no secrets.
Every earthly thing a man does is known to everybody, and life is extravagantly, astoundingly frank.
The moral effect is, in my opinion, extremely good,
— though the missionaries, who lie hard about this
country, say the reverse. Think of nothing but a
paper screen dividing all your life from the lives
about you, — a paper screen to poke a hole through,
which is not considered outrageous, unless the screen
be decorated with celebrated paintings. That is
common life here. As for me, I have a secluded
house, with three gardens round it. But, according
to popular custom, I must never shut the door, or

lock myself up except at night. One must not be nervous here, or impatient: it is impossible to remain either in such an atmosphere, or to be ill-natured, or to hide anything. And just think of it! — I having to give lectures and make speeches through an interpreter, which lectures and speeches are duly printed in a Japanese magazine! To speak before a Japanese audience, however, is delightful. One look at all the placid smiling faces reassures the most shrinking soul at once.

Well, at all events, I shall write you often, and send you something queer betimes. I must now get ready to take the little steamer by which I start.

With best regards to all, and to you best love, I remain, LAFCADIO HEARN.

This is my legal seal.

TO BASIL HALL CHAMBERLAIN

YABASE, August, 1891.

DEAR PROFESSOR CHAMBERLAIN, — I have discovered Yabase. No European seems to have ever been here before. On arriving at Shimo-ichi to see the Bon-odori, I found I had come three days too soon, and the little town is very hot and uncomfortable.

Well, Yabase is an extremely quiet, pretty little town, with a much better hotel than I have seen for quite a while, — and a superb beach. Strange to say, there are no boats and nobody ever thinks of going into the sea, except children. So whenever I go to swim, the entire population crowd the beach to look on. Happily I am a very good swimmer, — could swim for twenty-four hours without fatigue. Thus the people have a *mezurashii mono* to behold. Another queer thing about Yabase is that it is the only place I have seen in Japan where there is no shrine of Inari. It is a strictly Buddhist town, and Nichiren prevails. There is a *yashiro* on a neighbouring mountain, however. There is no Bon-odori here, one must go to the next town to see it, which I will do to-night. There has been much rough weather —tremendous seas breaking along the coast. At Kizuki I thought the hotel was going to be carried away; and all the approaches to it, bridges, etc., were dashed to pieces. Here, the sea is opposed by a loftier coast, but it becomes something one cannot laugh at on a windy day.

I must tell you an incident of the revival of pure Shintō. At Kizuki, until very recently, two of the hotels were kept by families belonging to some Buddhist sect, as well as to the Kizuki sect of Shintō, and so in their establishments, as in nearly every Izumo household, there was a *butsudan* as well as a *kamidana*. But some pilgrims who came to Kizuki, full of fiery Shintō zeal, were wroth to see a *butsudan* in the inns of the Sacred City, and girded up their loins, and sought out an hotel where no Buddha was, and went there, — and sent out word to their fellow pilgrims. The result has been that all the hotels in Kizuki have suppressed Buddhism, or at least its externals: they have become pure Shintō. This incident is rather anomalous, but it is a confirmation of what I said before, regarding the predominance of Shintō.

From Mionoseki, I hope to send you some *o fuda* of interest. The prospects of getting to Oki are growing small, however, — for the time being.

P. S. Alas! I have not discovered Yabase! Some detestable missionary was here before me — for one hour only, it is true, but he was here! — And to-day, being a day of high surf, there came down to the beach with planks, divers boys, who swam far out and came in, as the Americans say, "a-kite-ing," on the crests of waves — swimming unspeakably well, after the fashion of the Polynesian islanders. So that I feel small! I offered to teach them what I know in exchange for instruction as to how to come "a-kite-ing" on the top of a wave.

As for the little Japanese pipe: —

I cannot think that its form and dimensions simply evidence the Japanese fondness for "small things." The ancient Samurai pipes, of which I have seen many fine specimens, were very much larger than the modern *kiseru*. The pipe seems to me rather the natural evolution of a utensil in its relation to the domestic life of Japan. The little pipe is admirably adapted to the multifarious interruptions of Japanese occupations. Long-sustained effort, protracted and unbroken study, are things foreign to Japanese existence. The Western pipe is good between the teeth of a man trained to remain on duty without remission of mental labour or relaxation of muscle for five or six hours at a stretch. But the Japanese idea of labour is blessed and full of interruptions as his year is full of *matsuri*. Thus, the little pipe, with its three conventional whiffs, exactly suits his wants. Its artistic evolution is also a matter worthy of study. Some of the best metal-work has been done upon it. From the pipe of 3 sen to the pipe of 30 yen, there is as great a range of artistic design and finish as in the realm of *kakemono*. Pipes of silver are the fashion. Without engraving, the silver must be very heavy. If the two metal parts be elaborately engraved and inlaid, the metal may be made as light as possible. A really fine pipe becomes an heirloom.

The introduction of European costume among the class of officials and teachers necessarily produced a change in the smoking paraphernalia which formed a part of the native Japanese outfit. The *tabako-ire* was reshaped, so as to accommodate itself to a breast or side pocket, and the little pipe shortened so as to be enclosed without the tobacco pouch, much as a pencil is enclosed in a pocket-book. Many beautifully designed things thus came into existence. A nice small pipe of silver may now be had to order for about 3 yen, — (designed). The *netsuke* has, of course, no place in this form of the *tabako-ire*. I have collected over a hundred different forms of the new pipe. This has no bamboo: the whole thing is one solid piece of metal. The best are inlaid or engraved: — the bowl and mouthpiece (at least) being usually of silver, worked into steel or brass.

Pipes with long stems are preferable for house use. They do not burn the tongue so quickly as the short pipe. However, the tobacco itself has much to do

with this matter. Those jōros, geishas, and others,
who smoke the greater part of the time, use a special tobacco which does not blister the tongue or
lips.

With the pipe for an evolutionary centre, a whole
intricate and complex world of smoking-furniture
has come into existence, — of which the richest specimens are perhaps those lacquered *tabako-bon* for
the use of aristocratic ladies, with plated or solid
silver *hibachi* and *haifuki*. The winter *hibachi* for
smoking purposes has, of course, many forms; —
some of the daintiest being those invented for use
in theatres, to be carried in the hand. The smoker,
who finds a handsome bronze *hibachi* placed before
him on a winter's day, is not supposed to empty his
pipe into it by knocking the metal head of the pipe
upon the rim: if genteel, he will always insert the
leather flap of his tobacco pouch between the pipehead and the *hibachi* — so as to prevent the tapping
of the pipehead from causing a dent in the bronze.
At present the most genteel *tabako-bon* for summer
use has a small cup of bronze, instead of the usual
cup of porcelain. The smoker empties his pipe, not
into the *hibachi* of bronze or porcelain, but into the
bamboo *haifuki* which is an indispensable part of
the summer *tabako-bon*.

The foreigner who uses the Japanese pipe com-
mences his experience with that apparently simple
article by burning small round holes in everything
near him — the *tatami*, the *zabuton*, and especially
his own *yukata* or *kimono*. The small pellet of
ignited tobacco contained in the *kiseru* becomes,

after a few whiffs, a fiery pill, loose, and ready to leap from the pipe at a breath. Wherever it falls, it pierces holes like a red-hot shot. But the Japanese expert smoker rarely burns anything. He draws from his pipe at the very most three whiffs and at once empties it into the *haifuki*. To smoke a Japanese pipe to the bottom, moreover, results in clogging up the pipe. The art of cleaning it out afterwards is quite elaborate. A common plan is to heat the pipehead in the charcoal of the *hibachi*, and then blow out the refuse. But this method corrodes and spoils a fine pipe. The cleaning of the fine pipe must be done with a twist of tough fine paper passed up the stem and pulled out through the head.

Besides smoking-furniture, a special code of politeness has been evolved around the Japanese pipe.

The pipe, I regret to say, is in vulgar circles used as a domestic rod. The wife or child who is very naughty may receive a severe blow with the *kiseru*, or even many. However, it is not so bad as the instruments of punishment in vogue elsewhere.

I am not sure if I have been able to say anything worth your while to read about the pipe, but I think the Japanese pipe is really worth more consideration than is usually given it.

NOTE. Women's pipes have a special, delicate form — and are made very small and dainty — also their *tabako-ire*.

TO BASIL HALL CHAMBERLAIN

DEAR PROFESSOR CHAMBERLAIN, — If you are not frightfully busy, which I suppose nobody is at this time of the year, perhaps some of my adventures will interest you.

I found that the Bon-odori is different, not only in every village, but even in every commune. So I was very anxious to see all the varieties of this curious dance that I could. I heard that at Ōtsuka, near Yabase, there was a very remarkable kind of dance danced; and I went, in Japanese costume, with a dozen citizens of Yabase, to see it. It turned out to be not worth seeing at all: the people had no more knowledge of dancing — or rather, much less, than Sioux or Comanches.

Ōtsuka is a stony, large, primitive-looking village, — full of rude energy and, I am sorry to say, of bad manners, — a terrible thing to say about any Japanese town. But I have been in about 50 Japanese villages, where I loved all the people, and always made a few of them love me, and Ōtsuka is the first exception I found to the general rule about the relation between foreigners and *hyakushō-no-jin*. At Ōtsuka the people left their dance to pelt the foreigner with little pellets of sand and mud, — crying out: "Bikki ! — bikki !" What that means I do not know. So both I and the whole of the Yabase people turned back. The pelting was not very savage — it was just like the work of naughty children: a foreign mob would have thrown stones,

which these folk were very careful not to do — in
spite of the fact that there were no police. I passed
through this village twice since, and found the
attitude of its people peculiarly rough — bordering
upon hostility. Compared with the roughness of
— say a Barbadoes mob — it was a very gentle
thing, but it gave me the first decidedly unpleasant sense of being an alien that I have ever had in
Japan.

I have just returned from Togo-ike, — a place
described in your Guide.

Frankly, I detest Togo-ike. But it is extremely
popular with travelling Japanese — especially the
shōbai. Imagine a valley of rice-fields, ringed in by
low jagged wooded hills, with a lakelet in the middle
of it about a mile and a quarter long (at most) by
half a mile broad, and hotels built out into the water.
The coldest place I have yet been in Japan. The
hotels are supplied with hot water from the volcanic
springs through bamboo pipes, but the baths do not
compare with those of the much humbler Izumo
resort — Tama-tsukuri. The cold air to me was
penetrating, sickly, but this may be idiosyncrasy.
To one who has lived in the tropics the chill of rice-
fields means fever and death; and some of my old
tropical fears came up. Then the hotel has only
mishido, no *karakami*, — so that one is never alone.
One hour of Yabase is worth a season at Togo-ike —
free of expense — to one who loves quiet and simple
ways. So I shall spend a couple more days there
before going to Mionoseki.

I have given up Oki, until winter. The health

and strength I get from seawater bathing have made me delay too long. But I will get to Oki later.

Ever yours,

LAFCADIO HEARN.

TO SENTARŌ NISHIDA

YABASE, August, 1891. .

DEAR MR. NISHIDA, — I have had a pleasant time in different little drowsy sea-villages, — sleeping, eating, drinking sake, and bathing. Yabase is about the most pleasant place I ever stopped at here.

But, alas ! — *I saw no Bon-odori* at all at Shimo-ichi. I seemed to have gone too soon; — at Yabase, there is no Bon-odori; and at Ōtsuka, where I next travelled, on foot, to see the Bon-odori, I had an adventure of a peculiar kind.

Ōtsuka seems to be a rough sort of place. Its folk are big hustling noisy countrymen; and when they are full of sake inclined to be mischievous. They stopped dancing to see the foreigner. The foreigner took refuge from the pressure of the crowd in a house, where he sat upon the floor, and smoked. The crowd came into the house and round the house, and uttered curious observations and threw sand and water at the foreigner. Therefore the people of Yabase, who had accompanied the foreigner to Ōtsuka, arose and made vigorous protests; and we all returned to Yabase together. At Yabase, the police and some of the principal people more than made up to me for the rudeness of the Ōtsuka folk,—

they apologized for the Ōtsuka folk until I was really ashamed of being so kindly looked after; and I was entertained very generously; and the police told me that anything in the world I wished their advice or help about, only to send them word. (The hostility of the Ōtsuka folk was really a very childish sort of thing, not worth making a fuss about; — a Western crowd would have thrown stones or rotten eggs. Indeed I am not sure whether the crowd was really hostile at all. I rather think that they wanted to see the foreigner move, — so they tried to make him stir about, — like a *kedamono* in a cage.)

To-morrow I return to Matsue, by way of Miono-seki; — I really regret leaving Yabase: the people are the kindest, most honest, straightforward folk imaginable. And I have made several friends; — at the temple of Nichiren here, I got some beautiful *o fuda*.

LAFCADIO HEARN.

TO BASIL HALL CHAMBERLAIN

MATSUE, August, 1891.

DEAR PROFESSOR CHAMBERLAIN, — Having reached a spot where I can write upon something better than a matted floor, I find three most pleasant letters from you. The whole of the questions in them I cannot answer to-night, but will do so presently, when I obtain the full information.

However, as to cats' tails I can answer at once. Izumo cats — (and I was under the impression until recently that all Japanese cats were alike) — are

generally born with long tails. But there is a belief
that any cat whose tail is not cut off in kittenhood,
will become an *obake* or a *nekomata*, and there are
weird stories about cats with long tails dancing at
night, with towels tied round their heads. There are
stories about petted cats eating their mistress and
then assuming the form, features, and voice of the
victim. Of course you know the Buddhist tradition
that no cat can enter paradise. The cat and the
snake alone wept not for the death of Buddha. Cats
are unpopular in Izumo, but in Hōki I saw that they
seemed to exist under more favourable conditions.
The real reason for the unpopularity of the cat is its
powers of mischief in a Japanese house; — it tears
the *tatami*, the *karakami*, the *shōji*, scratches the
woodwork, and insists upon carrying its food into
the best room to eat it upon the floor. I am a great
lover of cats, having "raised," as the Americans say,
more than fifty; — but I could not gratify my desire
to have a cat here. The creature proved too mischievous, and wanted always to eat my uguisu.

The oscillation of one's thoughts concerning the
Japanese — the swaying you describe — is and has
for some time been mine also.

There are times when they seem so small! And
then again, although they never seem large, there is
a vastness behind them, — a past of indefinite complexity and marvel, — an amazing power of absorbing and assimilating, — which forces one to suspect
some power in the race so different from our own
that one cannot understand that power. And as you

say, whatever doubts or vexations one has in Japan, it is only necessary to ask one's self: — "Well, who are the best people to live with?" For it is a question whether the intellectual pleasures of social life abroad are not more than dearly bought at the cost of social pettinesses which do not seem to exist in Japan at all.

Would you be horrified to learn that I have become passionately fond of *daikon*, — not the fresh but the strong ancient pickled *daikon?* But then the European Stilton cheese, or Limburger, is surely quite as queer. I have become what they call here a *jōgo*, — and find that a love of sake creates a total change in all one's eating habits and tastes. All the sweet things the *geko* likes, I cannot bear when taking sake. By the way, what a huge world of etiquette, art, taste, custom, has been developed by sake. An article upon sake, — its social rules, — its vessels, — its physiological effects, — in short the whole romance and charm of a Japanese banquet, ought to be written by somebody. I hope to write one some day, but I am still learning.

As to Dr. Tylor and the anthropological institute. If he should want any paper that I could furnish, I would be glad and consider myself honoured to please him. As for your question about the *o fuda*, why, I should think it no small pleasure to be mentioned merely as one of your workers and friends. Though the little I have been able to send does not seem to me to deserve your kindest words, it is making me very happy to have been able to please you at all.

Whatever I can write or send, make always any use of you please.

About "seeing Japan from a distance," — I envy you your coming chance. I could not finish my book on the West Indies until I saw the magical island again through regret, as through a summer haze, — and under circumstances which left me perfectly free to think, which the soporific air of the tropics makes difficult. (Still the book is not what it ought to be, for I was refused all reasonable help, and wrote most of it upon a half-empty stomach, or with my blood full of fever.) But to think of Japan in an English atmosphere will be a delicious experience for you after so long an absence. I should not be surprised should the experience result in the creation of something which would please your own feelings as an author better than any other work you have made. Of course it is at the time one is best pleased that one does one's real best in the artistic line.

By the way, since you like those Shintō prints, — and I might get you others, — what about a possible edition of your "Kojiki" illustrated by Japanese conceptions of this kind, colours and all? Such work can be so cheaply done in Japan! And an index! How often I wished for an index. I have made an imperfect one of my own. It is believed here that Hahaki is the ancient name of the modern Hōki. I was told this when I wanted to go to the legendary burial-place of Izanami.

As usual, I find I have been too presumptuous in writing offhand about cats' tails. On enquiring, I learn that there are often, born of the same mother, Izumo kittens with short tails, and kittens with long tails. This would show that two distinct species of cats exist here. The long-tailed kittens are always deprived when possible of the larger part of their caudal appendage. The short tails are spared. If an old cat be seen with a short tail, people say, — "this cat is old, but she has a short tail: therefore she is a good cat." (For the *obake* cat gets two tails when old, and every wicked cat has a long tail.) I am told that at the recent *bon*, in Matsue, cats of the evil sort were seen to dance upon the roofs of the houses.

What you tell me about those Shintō rituals and their suspicious origin seems to me quite certainly true. So the *kara-shishi* and the *mon* and the dragon-carvings and the *tōrōs*, — all stare me in the face as pillage of Buddhism. But the funeral rite which I saw and took part in, on the anniversary of the death of Prince Sanjō, struck me as immemorially primitive. The weird simplicity of it — the banquet to the ghost, the covering of the faces with white paper, the moaning song, the barbarian music, all seemed to me traditions and echoes of the very childhood of the race. I shall try to discover the genesis of the book you speak of as dubious in character. The Shintō christening ceremony is strictly observed here, and there are curious facts about the funeral ceremonies — totally at variance with and hostile to Buddhism.

By the way, when I visited a *tera* in Mionoseki after having bought *o fuda* at the Miojinja, I was told I must not carry the *o fuda* into the court of the *tera*. The Kami would be displeased.

For the moment, good-bye.

Ever faithfully,

LAFCADIO HEARN.

TO ELLWOOD HENDRICK

MATSUE, 1891.

DEAR HENDRICK, — . . . My household relations have turned out to be extremely happy, and to bind me very fast here at the very time that I was beginning to feel like going away. It does not now seem possible for me ever to go away. To take the little woman to another country would be to make her extremely unhappy; for no kindness or comfort could compensate for the loss of her own social atmosphere — in which all thoughts and feelings are so totally different from our own.

I find literary work extremely difficult here. The mental air about one has a totally disintegrating effect upon Western habits of thinking; — no strong emotion, no thrills or inspirations ever come to me, so I am still in doubt how to work. Whether I shall ever be able to make a really good book on Japan is still a question; but if I do, it will require years of steady dry work, without one real flash in it. The least fact in this Oriental life is so different from ours, and so complex in its relationship to other facts, that to explain it requires enormous time and patience.

I was made a little homesick by your letter about

New Orleans, mentioning so many familiar names. It brought back many pleasant memories.

Ah! you are in a dangerous world now. You will meet some charming, unsophisticated Southern girl, so much nicer than most Northern girls, that the South may fascinate you too much.

My correspondents have all dropped off except you. Sometimes a letter wanders to me — six months old — announcing my nomination as vice-president of some small literary society; but the outer world is slowly and surely passing away. At the same time the harder side of Japanese character is beginning to appear — in spots. The women are certainly the sweetest beings I have ever seen, as a general rule: all the good things of the race have been put into them. They are just loving, joyous, simple-hearted children with infinite surprises of pretty ways. About the men, — one never gets very close to them. One's best friends have a certain far-offness about them, even when breaking their necks to please you. There is no such thing as clapping a man on the back and saying, "Hello! old boy!" There is no such thing as clapping a fellow on the knee, or chucking a fellow under the ribs. All such familiarities are terribly vulgar in Japan. So each one has to tickle his own soul and clap it on the back, and say "Hello" to it. And the soul, being Western, says: "Do you expect me always to stay in this extraordinary country? I want to go home, or get back to the West Indies, at least. Hurry up and save some money." As it is, I have two hundred dollars saved up, even after dressing my little wife like a queen.

And now I am about to journey to outrageous places, among very strange gods. Good-bye for a while.   Ever most affectionately,

LAFCADIO HEARN.

TO ELLWOOD HENDRICK

MATSUE, October, 1891.

DEAR DEVILISHLY DELIGHTFUL OLD FELLOW, — I have been dancing an Indian war-dance of exultation in my Japanese robes, to the unspeakable astonishment of my placid household. After which I passed two hours in a discourse in what my Japanese friends ironically term "The Hearnian Dialect." Subject of exultation and discourse, — the marriage of Miss Elizabeth Bisland. If she only knew how often I have written her name upon the blackboard for the eyes of the students of the Normal School to look upon when they asked me to tell them about English names! And they pronounce it after me with a pretty Japanese accent and lisp: "*Aileesabbet Beeslan!*" Well, well, well!—you most d——nably jolly fellow!!

. . . Civilization is full of deadly perils in small things, — isn't it? and horrors in large things — railroad collisions, steamboat explosions, elevator accidents, — all nightmares of machinery. How funny the quiet of this Oriental life. The other day a man brought a skin to the house to sell, — a foreign skin. Very beautiful the animal must have been, and the price was cheap. But the idea of murder the thing conveyed was horrible to me, and I was

glad to find my folks of the same mind. "No, no! —
we don't like to see it," they said. And the man
departed, and in his heart pain was lord.

Oh! as for vacation, I always get two months,
or nearly two months, — the greater part of July
and all of August. This time I have been travelling
alone with my little wife, who translates my "Hearnian dialect" into Japanese, — eating little dishes of
seaweed, and swimming across all the bays I could
find on the Izumo coast. They take me to be a good
swimmer out here; but I am a little afraid to face
really rough water at a distance from shore. — About
getting to you, I don't really see my way clear to do
it for another year or two — must wait till I feel very
strong with the Japanese. Just now friend Chamberlain is trying to get me south, to teach Latin and
English, at $200 per month, in a beautiful climate.
I would like it — but the Latin — "*hic sunt leones!*"
I am awfully rusty. Should I be offered the place
and dare to take it, you would find me at Kumamoto,
in Kyūshū, — much more accessible than Matsue.
I think I have a better chance of seeing you here
than you of seeing me. But what a dear glorious
chap you are to offer me the ways and means; — I 'll
never forget it, old boy — never!

Pretty to talk of "my pen of fire." I 've lost it.
Well, the fact is, it is no use here. There is n't any
fire here. It is all soft, dreamy, quiet, pale, faint,
gentle, hazy, vapoury, visionary, — a land where
lotus is a common article of diet, — and where there
is scarcely any real summer. Even the seasons are
feeble ghostly things. Don't please imagine there

are any tropics here. Ah! the tropics — they still pull at my heart-strings. Goodness! my real field was there — in the Latin countries, in the West Indies and Spanish-America; and my dream was to haunt the old crumbling Portuguese and Spanish cities, and steam up the Amazon and Orinoco, and get romances nobody else could find. And I could have done it, and made books that would sell for twenty years yet. Perhaps, however, it 's all for the best: I might have been killed in that Martinique hurricane. And then, I think I may see the tropics on this side of the world yet, — the Philippines, the Straits Settlements, — perhaps Reunion or Madagascar. (When I get rich!)

Besides, I *must* finish my work on Japan, and that will take a couple of years more. It is the hardest country to learn — except China — in the world. I am the only man who ever attempted to learn the people seriously; and I think I shall succeed. But there is work ahead — phew! I have sent away about 1500 pp. MSS., and I have scarcely touched the subject — merely broken ground.

. . . Fact is, there is only one way to really marry a Japanese legally, — to be adopted into a Japanese family after marrying the daughter, and so become a Japanese citizen. Otherwise the wife loses her citizenship — a terrible calamity to a good girl. She would have to live in the open ports, unless I could always live in the interior. And the children — the children would have no rights or prospects in Japan. I don't see any way out of it except to abandon my English citizenship, and change my name to *Koi-*

zumi, — my wife's name. I am still hesitating a little — because of the Japanese. *Would* they try to take advantage, and cut down my salary? I am thinking, and waiting. But meantime, I am morally, and according to public opinion, fast married.

By the way, she would very much like to see E. B. If E. has a yacht, make her "sail the seas over" and come to this place; and she will be much pleased and humbly served and somewhat amused.

Well, so long, with best heart-wishes and thanks,

LAFCADIO HEARN.

I have accepted a new position, in Southern Japan. Oh! read Zola's "L'Argent"—you will appreciate it. There are delicious *financial* characters in it. For goodness' sake, don't read a translation.

TO SENTARŌ NISHIDA

KUMAMOTO, 1891.

DEAR FRIEND NISHIDA, — Your very welcome letter came to-day. I was beginning to be anxious about you, as my cook, who arrived here only yesterday, said that it was extremely cold in Matsue; and I was afraid the bitter weather might have given you cold. I am very glad you are taking care of yourself. . . .

I am now a little more reconciled to Kumamoto; but it is the most uninteresting city I was ever in, in Japan. The famous shrines of Katō Kiyomasa (the Katō-sha and the Hommyōji) are worth visiting; they are at Akitagun, a little outside the town. The

city is packed with soldiers. Things are dear and
ugly here — except silks. This is quite a place for
pretty silks, and they are cheaper than in Matsue:
but there is nothing pretty in the shape of lacquer-
ware, porcelain, or bronze. There is no art, and
there are no *kakemonos,* and no curio-shops.

The weather here is queer — something like that
of the Pacific slope, a few hundred miles north of
San Francisco. The nights and the mornings are
cold; and at sunrise, you see the ground covered with
white frost, and mists all over the hills. But by noon
it gets warm, and in the afternoon even hot; then
after sundown it turns cold again.

Mr. Kano was too modest when he told me there
were other teachers who spoke English better than
he. There are not. He speaks and writes better
English than any Japanese I know. However, there
is a Mr. Sakuma here, from Kyōto, who has a very
uncommon knowledge of *literary* English: he has
read a great deal, has a good library, and has made
a special study of Old English and Middle English.
He teaches literature (English) and grammar, etc.
Mr. Ōzawa (*I think*) is the second English teacher:
I like him the best personally. He has that fine consideration for others which you have, — and which
is not a common quality of men anywhere. He
speaks French. The Head-master, Mr. Sakurai,
a young and very silent man, also speaks French.
Nearly all the teachers speak English, — except the
delightful old teacher of Chinese, who has a great
beard and a head like Socrates. I liked him at
once, — just as I liked Mr. Katayama at first sight.

I wonder if there is anything in the learning of Chinese which makes men amiable. Perhaps it is the constant need of patience and the æsthetic sentiment also involved by such studies, that changes or modifies character so agreeably. I don't know much, however, about the teachers yet. I say good-morning and good-evening, and sit in my corner, and smoke my pipe. So far they all seem very gentle and courteous. I think I shall be able to get along pleasantly with them; but I don't think I shall become as friendly with any of them as I was with you. Indeed there is nobody like you here — no chats in the ten minutes, — no curious information, — no projects and discoveries. I often look at your pretty little tea-tray, with the *semi* and the dragonflies upon it, —and wish I could hear your voice at the door. . . .

LAFCADIO HEARN.

I have become very strong, and weigh about 20 lbs. more than I did last summer. But I can't tell just why. Perhaps because I am eating three full meals a day instead of two. My house is not quite so large as the one I had in Matsue. We are five here now — myself and wife, the cook, the *kurumaya*, and O-Yone. It was very funny about O-Yone when she first came. Nobody could understand her Izumo dialect (she is from Imaichi); but both she and the *kurumaya* can now get along. The hotels here are outrageously expensive: at least some of them. I cannot recommend the Shirakuin for cheapness. I paid, including tea-money, 24 yen for 6½ days. No more of that!

About the boys? Yes, Ōtani writes to me, and Azukizawa, — and I got a charming letter from Tanabe, late of the 5th Class.

I was surprised to hear of the decision of the Council. But I cannot help thinking this is much better than that the boys should be taught by a missionary; 99 out of 100 will not teach conscientiously and painstakingly. And a clever Japanese teacher can do so much. I have now no one to prepare some of my classes for the English lesson; and I know what it means. The main use of a foreign teacher is to teach accent and conversational habits. But I suspect that within another generation few foreign teachers will be employed for English — except in higher schools and for special purposes. There will be thousands of Japanese teachers, speaking English perfectly well. I hope you will be the new Director. Please kindly remember me to Mr. Sato, Mr. Katayama, Mr. Nakamura (I wish I could hear him laugh now), and all friends.

P. S. Setsu insists that I shall tell you that the *kurumaya* of this town are *oni*, and that one must be careful in hiring them; — so that if you should come down here when the weather is better, you must be as careful as in Tōkyō, — where they are also *oni*. Also that rent is high: my house is eleven yen. But with any Izumo cook, living is just as cheap as in Matsue; and there is much good bread and meat and sake and food of all kinds.

I am sorry about that Tamatsukuri affair; for I wrote, as you will see, words of *extreme* praise, —

never suspecting such possibilities. Why, the first duty of gentlemen is to face death like soldiers, — not like sailors on a sinking ship, who stave in the casks — sometimes. However, don't such things make you wish for the chance to do the same duty better? They do me. That is one good effect of a human weakness: it makes others wish to be strong and to do strong things.

TO MASANOBU ŌTANI

KUMAMOTO, November, 1891.

MY DEAR ŌTANI, — I have just received your most kind letter, for which my sincerest thanks. But I don't want to correct it, and send it back to you: I would rather keep it always, as a pleasant remembrance.

It has been very cold in Kumamoto — a sharp frost came last night, with an icy wind. Everybody says such cold is extraordinary here; but I am not quite sure if this is really true, because they have told me everywhere I have been during the last twenty years: "Really we never saw such weather before."

Kumamoto is not nearly so pretty a city as Matsue, although it is as neat as Tenjin-machi. There are some very beautiful houses and hotels, but the common houses are not so fine as those of Matsue. Most of the old Shizoku houses were burned during the Satsuma war, so that there are no streets like Kita-bori-machi, and it is very hard to find a nice house. I have been fortunate enough to find one nearly as nice as the one I had in Matsue, but the garden is not nearly so pretty; and the rent is eleven

dollars — nearly three times more than what I paid
in Matsue. There is, of course, no lake here, and no
beautiful scenery like that of Shinji-ko; but on clear
days we can see the smoke rising from the great
volcano of Aso-san.

As for the Dai Go Kōtō-Chūgakkō, the magnificence of it greatly surprised me. The buildings are
enormous, — of brick for the most part; and they
reminded me at first sight of the Imperial University
of Tōkyō. Most of the students live in the school.
There is a handsome military uniform; but all the
boys do not wear it, — some wear Japanese clothes,
and the rules about dress (except during drilling-time,
etc.) are not very strict. There is no bell. The
classes are called and dismissed by the sound of a
bugle. There are ten minutes between class-hours
for rest; but the buildings are so long, that it takes
ten minutes to walk through them to the teacher's
room, which is in a separate building. Two of the
teachers speak French, and six or seven English:
there are 28 teachers. The students are very
nice, — and we became good friends at once. There
are three classes, corresponding with the three
higher classes of the Jinjō Chūgakkō, — and two
higher classes. I do not now teach on Saturdays.
There are no stoves — only *hibachi*. The library is
small, and the English books are not good; but this
year they are going to get better books, and to
enlarge the library. There is a building in which
jū-jutsu is taught by Mr. Kano; and separate buildings for sleeping, eating, and bathing. The bath-
room is a surprise. Thirty or forty students can

bathe at the same time; and four hundred can eat
at once in the great dining-hall. There is a separate
building also for the teaching of chemistry, natural
history, etc.; and there is a small museum.

You have been kind enough to offer to find out
for me something about Shintō. Well, if you have
time, I will ask you to find out for me as much as you
can about the *miya* of the household, — the household shrine and *kamidana* in Izumo. I would like
to know what way the *kamidana* should face —
north, south, east, or west.

Also, what is the origin of the curious
shape of the little stoppers of the *omiki-
dokkuri?*

Also, whether the ancestors are ever
worshipped before the *kamidana* in the
same way as they are worshipped before the
butsudan.

Are the names of the dead ever written upon something to be placed in the *miya*, in the same way, or
nearly the same way, as the *kaimyō* is written upon
the *ihai* or Buddhist mortuary tablet.

In the Shintō worship of *family* ancestors (if
there is any such worship, which I doubt), what
prayers are said?

Are any particular *family*-prayers said by Buddh-
ists when praying before the *kaimyō*, or do the
common people utter only the ordinary prayer of
their sect — such as *"Namu Amida Butsu,"* or,
"Namu Myōhō Rengekyō?"

But do not give yourself too much trouble
about these things, and take your own time; — in a

month, or two months, or even three months will be
quite time enough. And if you have no time, do not
trouble yourself about it at all; and write to me that
you cannot, or would rather not, — then I will ask
some one who is less busy.

I shall be hoping really to see you in Kumamoto
next year. You would like the school very much.
Perhaps you would not like the city as well as Matsue; but the school is not in the city exactly; it is a
little outside of it, and you would live in the school,
probably, — or very near it. The students make
excursions to Nagasaki and other places, by railroad
and steamer.

Now about your letter. It was very nice. You
made a few mistakes in using "*will*," — and in
saying "if I would have promote my school." It
ought to have been "if I should go to a higher
school."

"This will be a bad letter" ought to have been
"I fear this *is*. . . etc." But you and I and everybody learn best by making mistakes.

With best remembrance from your old teacher,
believe me   Ever truly yours,

LAFCADIO HEARN.

TO SENTARŌ NISHIDA

KUMAMOTO, December, 1891.

DEAR FRIEND NISHIDA, — Your letter has just
reached me. I am more sorry than I can express to
hear of the death of Yokogi. Nature seems strangely
cruel in making such a life, and destroying it before

the time of ripeness. And the good hearts and the fine brains pass to dust, while the coarse and the cunning survive all dangers. . . .

The name of the delightful old Samurai who teaches Chinese here, I think you know, — Akizuki. He was at Aizu, and made a great soldier's name; and he is just as gentle and quiet as Mr. Katayama, — and still more paternally charming in his manner. He is sixty-three years old. . . .

I have made no friends among the teachers yet. I attended my first Japanese dinner with them the night before last; and, because *you* were not there, I think I made some queer mistakes about the dishes — when to use chopsticks, etc. There were no *geishas :* the former director had forbidden their employment at teachers' dinners; and I don't think that Mr. Kano is going to revoke the order. The reason for it was not prudery; but the opposition paper used to take advantage of the presence of *geishas* at the teachers' banquets to print nasty things against the school. So it was determined not to give the paper a chance to say anything more. . . .

I have been very cautious in writing you about the climate, because I wanted to be very sure that, in case you should come here, it would be for the best. So far the climate is like this: every morning and night cold, with white frost; afternoons so warm that one can go out without an overcoat. Very little rain. No snow yet; but I am told that it will come.

As for me, I have become stronger than I have been for years. All my clothes, even my Japanese *kimono*, have become too small!! But I cannot say whether this be the climate or the diet or what. Setsu says it is because I have a good wife; — but she might be prejudiced, you know! My lungs are sound as a bell; I never cough at all. This is all that I can tell you at present.

No: O-Yone came with us. She took O-Yoshi's place, when O-Yoshi went back to live with her mother. I am sorry to say I had to send the *kuru-maya* away. He abandoned his wife in Matsue, and she went to the house of the Inagaki, crying and telling a very pitiful story. When I heard this, I told the man he must go back. But on the same days later, I found he had been doing very wrong things, — trying to make trouble among the other servants, and playing tricks upon us by making secret arrangements with the shopkeepers. I had bought him clothes, and given him altogether 14 yen and 50 sen, besides his board and lodging — including 5 yen to go back with. But he had squandered his little money and how he managed afterward I don't know. I could not help him any more; for his cunningness and foolishness together made it impossible to keep him a day longer in the house. The cook is from the *Nisho-tei*, — to which you first introduced me. The *kurumaya's* place would have been a nice place for a good man. I shall be very careful about employing another *kurumaya* by the month.

Now about the question you asked me. The words you underlined are from the Jewish Bible. The ideas of VALUE and of WEIGHT were closely connected in the minds of the old Semites, as they are still, to some extent, in our own. Everything was sold by WEIGHT, and according to the WEIGHT was the VALUE. The weighing was done with the SCALES or BALANCE, of which there were several kinds. The balancing was done by suspending a weight at one end of the "balance," or scales, as in Japan, and the article to be sold in the other. If too light, the article was "found wanting" — (i. e.: in weight). So in such English expressions as "to make LIGHT of" (to ridicule, to belittle, to speak contemptuously of) — the idea of WEIGHT thus estimated survives. Now, in the mythology of the Jews God is represented as one who WEIGHS, in a scale or balance, the good that is in a man — (his MORAL WEIGHT or VALUE) — and sends him to hell if he proves too light. Public opinion is now the God with the scales. If I am an author, for example, I (that is, my work) will be WEIGHED in the BALANCE (of public or of literary opinion) and found perhaps WANTING. Poor Ito was weighed many, many times, and found wanting — before being expelled. I am afraid he will be found wanting also by the world into which he must enter.

As for the phrase, "not a hair of their *head*," the singular is often used for the plural in the old English of the Bible, and other books. (To-day, we should use only the plural, — as a general rule.)

Examples from the Bible:

1. "The fire had no power upon their bodies, nor
singular
was the hair of *their* HEAD singed."
— *Daniel, 3d Chap. 27th verse.*

plural singular

2. "But the very hairs of your HEAD are all numbered." — *Luke* 12. 7.

singular

3. "And he bowed the HEART of *all the men of Judah.*" — *II Samuel* 19. 14.

Poets to-day, or writers of poetical prose, may take similar liberties with grammar as that in No. 3.

There are very many quotations in the Bible about the words "weighed in the balance;" the most famous being that in the story of Belshazzar, in the book of Daniel. The first poetical use of the phrase is in the book of Job — supposed, you know, to have been written by an Arab, not a Jew.

Now I hope and pray that you will take good care of yourself, and not allow your Samurai-spirit of self-denial to urge you into taking any risks on bitterly cold days. Many, many happy new years to you and yours.   LAFCADIO HEARN.

TO BASIL HALL CHAMBERLAIN

KUMAMOTO, November, 1891.

DEAR PROFESSOR, — Your welcome postal to hand. One must travel out of Izumo after a long residence to find out how utterly different the place is from other places, — for instance, this country. Matsue is incomparably prettier and better built and in every way more interesting than Kumamoto. What Kumamoto is religiously, I have not yet been able to find out. There are no shops here full of household shrines of *hinoki*-wood for sale, no display of *shimenawa* over doors, no charms in the fields, no *o fuda* pasted upon house-doors, no profusion of Shintō emblems, no certainty of seeing a *kamidana* or a *butsudan* in every house, and a strange scarcity of temples and images. Religiously, the place seems to be uninteresting; and to-day it is infernally cold. Everything is atrociously dear, and the charming simplicity of the Izumo folk does not here exist. My own people — four came with me — feel like fish out of water. My little wife said the other morning, with an amusing wonder in her eyes, that there was a *mezurashii kedamono* in the next yard. We looked out, and the extraordinary animal was a goat. Some geese were also a subject of wonder, and a pig. None of these creatures are to be seen in Izumo.

About Inari. I may enquire again, but I think that the representation of Inari as a man with a beard, riding upon a white fox, in the pictures of Toyokuni, for instance, and in the sacred *kakemono* is tolerably good evidence. Also the relief carving I have seen representing him as a man. Also the general popular idea concerning him, about which there is no mistake. Also the letter of Hideyoshi to Inari Daimyōjin cited in Walter Dening's Readers, under the heading: "Hideyoshi's Letter to Gods."

As to Kwannon, it is true that in Buddhist history she figures both as a man and woman (as also does the daughter of the Serpent-King in the astounding *sutra* of the Lotus of the Good Law), — she is identified with the Sanscrit Avalokitesvara, —

about whose sex there may be some doubt. I have a translation of her Japanese *sutra*, in which she is female, however; — and in China and in Japan she has come to be considered the ideal of all that is sweet in womanliness, and her statues and the representations of her in the numerous pictures of the Buddhist pantheon are of a woman, — maiden. And after all, the people, not the scholars, make the gods, and the gods they make are the best.

I cannot help thinking that the identification of the Japanese Buddhas and Bodhisattvas with those of India is not sufficiently specified by Eitel and others as an identification of origin only. They have become totally transformed here, — they have undergone perfect avatars, and are not now the same. Shaka, Amida, Yakushi, Fudō, Dainichi, etc., may have been in India distinct personalities: in Japan they are but forms of the One, — as indeed are the innumerable Buddhas of the Lotus of the True Law. All are one. And Kshitigarbha is not our Japanese Jizō, — and Kwannon is not Avalokitesvara, and the Ni-ō are not the figures of Indra, and Emma-O is not Yama. "They were and are not." Don't you agree with me that the popular idea of a divinity is an element of weight in such questions of doubt as we are chatting about?

With every wish that you may enjoy your journey in Shikoku, I remain, most truly ever,

LAFCADIO HEARN.

P. S. . . . I have been teaching three days, and find no difference in the boys from those of Izumo,

— they are gentle, polite, manly and eager. But I am
greatly hampered by the books. There are not books
enough, and the reading-books chosen are atrociously
unsuited for the students. Fancy "Silas Marner"
and "John Halifax," with the long double-com-
pound complex semiphilosophical sentences of George
Eliot, as text-books for boys who can scarcely speak
in English ! A missionary's choice ! Ye gods of old
Japan ! I think the Mombushō is economical in
the wrong direction. Too much money cannot be
spent on good reading-books. Less money on buildings and more for books would give better results.
Buildings worth a quarter of a million (as building
costs in America), and "Lovell's Library" and
"George Munro's" piracies bought for text-books.
I could scream ! !

TO MASANOBU ŌTANI

KUMAMOTO, January, 1892.

DEAR ŌTANI, — Your long and most interesting
letter gave me much pleasure, as well as much information. I am very glad to have had my questions
so nicely answered; for I am writing an essay on
Shintō home-worship in Izumo, — all about the
kamidana, etc. I know a good deal about general
forms and rules, but very little about the reverence
paid *in the house* to the family dead (forefathers,
father, mother, dead children, etc.) — in Shintō,
which is very interesting to know. I think much of
the modern customs shows a Chinese origin, though
the spirit of pure Shintō seems to be wholly Japanese.

I think your first explanation of the form of the
omiki dokkuri no kuchi-sashi is the correct one, —
so far as this is concerned. I am not sure, but
the shape is strikingly like that of the mystic
jewel of Buddhist art. There is another form
in brass, which I have, that seems intended to
represent a folded paper; but I am not sure
what it means.

Many thanks for your very valuable notes about
the January customs. You told me quite a number
of things I did not know before, — such as the rules
about the twist of the straw-rope, and the symbolism
of the charcoal and many other articles. But I
would like to know why the pendent straws should
be 3–5–7: is there any mystic signification in those
numbers? I thought the Japanese mystic number
was 8. . . .

Take good care of your health.

Ever very truly yours,

LAFCADIO HEARN.

TO ELLWOOD HENDRICK

KUMAMOTO, January, 1892.

DEAR HENDRICK,— Your jolly letter just came —
Jan. 3rd, — to find me celebrating the new year
after the Japanese fashion. There is not one New
Year's day here, but three. Over the gate, and all the
alcoves of each apartment, the straw rope (*shimenawa*), which is the Shintō emblem of the gods,
is festooned; upon the *kamidana*, or "god-shelf,"
lights are burning before the tablets of those deities

who have pledged themselves in Japanese ideo-
graphs to love and protect this foreigner, — and I
have given to them offerings of rice-cakes and sake.
For the guests are dishes of raw fish, and others
which it would take too long to describe, and hot
sake. My little wife does the honours. Before the
gate are Japanese flags and pine-trees — emblems of
green old age and unflinching purpose.

— Well, here I am in Kyūshū, a thousand miles
and more south of Yokohama, at a salary of 200 yen
a month. All my Izumo servants came with me.
Our house is not nearly so beautiful as that in
Matsue, and the city is devilishly ugly and commonplace, — an enormous, half-Europeanized garrison-
town, full of soldiers. I don't like it; but Lord! I
must try to make money, for nothing is sure in
Japan, and I am now so tied down to the country
that I can't quit it, except for a trip, whether the
Government employs me or not. I have nine lives
depending on my work — wife, wife's mother,
wife's father, wife's adopted mother, wife's father's
father, and then servants, and a Buddhist student.
How would *you* like that? It would n't do in America. But it is nothing here — no appreciable burden.
The *moral* burden, however, is heavy enough. You
can't let a little world grow up around you, to depend
on you, and then break it all up — not if you are
a respectable person. And I indulge in the luxury
of "filial piety"— a virtue of which the good and
evil results are only known to us Orientals.

I translated into Hearnian dialect all you said.
And my wife, whose name is Setsu, or Chi-yo (alter-

native), knows you well by your photograph, and
said such nice things about that photograph that
I dare not tell you. Which is all the more extraordinary because when I showed her some pictures of
"distinguished foreigners" she and the girls all said
that if they should ever meet such people they would
"become Buddhas for fear"— i. e., die of fright.
American and English faces—their deep-set eyes —
terrify unsophisticated Japanese. Children cry with
fear at the sight of a foreigner. So your photo must
reveal exceptional qualities to make such an impression. . . .

Everybody gets drunk here to-day; but a cultivated Japanese is never offensively drunk. To
get *properly*, politely drunk upon sake is the *sum-
mum bonum*. . . . Although a gentleman knows
how to act, however drunk, it is the custom, when
your host makes you drunker than usual (which
delights him), to call at the house next morning, and
thank him for the entertainment — at the same
time apologizing for any *possible* mistakes. Of
course, there are no ladies at men's dinners — only
professional dancing-girls, *maiko* or *geisha*.

Work progresses; but the barrier of language is
a serious one. My project to study Buddhism must
be indefinitely delayed on that account. For the
deeper mysteries of Buddhism cannot be explained
in the Hearnian dialect.

What some people say about Miss Bisland —
ah! I mean Mrs. Wetmore — being only beautiful
when she wants to be is, I think, perfectly true. She
can change into seventeen different women. She

used to make me almost believe the stories about
Circe and Lilith. She laughed to scorn the terrible
scientific test of the photograph — of the science
which reveals new *nebulae* and tells a man in advance
whether he is going to get the small-pox or not. No
two photos of her ever represented the same human
being. In ordinary mortals the sort of thing called
Ego, which is not "I" but "They," is worked up
into a recognizable composite photo. But in her
case, 't is quite otherwise. The different dead that
live in her, live quite separately from each other, in
different rooms, and receive upon different afternoons. And yet — if even Rudyard Kipling were
to write the truth about that person — or rather that
ghostly congregation of persons called Elizabeth
Bisland, — who but a crazy man would believe that
truth? Assuredly Mr. W. ought to think himself
lucky. Ever to get tired of Elizabeth is out of human
possibility. There are too many different Elizabeths,
belonging to different historical epochs, countries,
and conditions. If he should tire of one Elizabeth,
—lo! there will appear another. And there is one
very terrible Elizabeth, whom I had a momentary
glimpse of once, and whom it will not be well for
Mr. W. or anybody else to summon from her retire-
ment. But I am glad for the compound Elizabeth
that she has this Protector in reserve. — Lord!
how irreverently I have been talking! But that is
because you can read under the irreverence. . . .

What can't be insured against is earthquake. I
have become afraid. Do you know that the earthquake the other day in Gifu, Aichi, etc., destroyed

nearly 200,000 houses and nearly 10,000 lives? My house in far-off Matsue rocked and groaned like a steamer in a typhoon. It isn't the quake one's afraid of: it is being held down under a ton of timber and slowly burned alive. That is what happened to most of the dead. Five millions of dollars will scarcely relieve the distress. . . .

Well, here's a thousand happy New Years to you and yours, — all luck, all blessings, all glorious sensations.

Ever from your old disoccidentalized chum,

LAFCADIO HEARN.

TO ELLWOOD HENDRICK

KUMAMOTO, April, 1892.

DEAR HENDRICK, — Just had a long and delightful letter from you, and Mallock's book. I hate the Jesuit; but he has a particular cleverness of his own indeed. I hate him first because he is insincere, as you suggest; then I hate him because he is morbid, with a priestly morbidness — sickly, cynical, unhealthy. I like Kipling's morbidness, which is manly and full of enormous resolve and defiance in the teeth of God and hell and nature, — but the other — no! This book is not free from the usual faults. It is like Paul Bourget boiled into thin soup, and flavoured with a dash of M. de Camors. The Markham girl was certainly Feuillet's imagination; but she is excellently done. Really, I don't know; — I asked myself: "If it was I?" . . . And conscience answered: "If it was *you*, in spite of love and

duty and honour and hellfire staring you in the face
you would have gone after her, — and tried to console yourself by considering the Law of Attraction
of Bodies and Souls in the incomprehensible cosmical order of things, which is older than the gods."
And I was very much inclined to demur; but conscience repeated: "Oh! don't be such a liar and
quibbler; — you know you would! That was the
only part of the book you really liked. Your
ancestors were not religious people: you lack constitutional morality. That's why you are poor,
and unsuccessful, and void of mental balance, and
an exile in Japan. You know you cannot be happy
in an English moral community. You are a fraud —
a vile Latin — a vicious French-hearted scalawag."

And I could not say anything, because what conscience observed was true — to a considerable
extent. "*Vive le monde antique!*" . . .

I have been thinking a heap, because of being
much alone. (The Japanese do not understand
Western thought at all — at least not its emotional
side. Therefore devour time and devour thought
even while they stimulate it.) . . .

Now about these Shadows. Yes, there are forces
about one, — vague, working soundlessly, imper-
ceptibly, softening one as the action of air softens
certain surfaces of rock while hardening others.
The magnetism of another faith about you necessarily polarizes that loose-quivering needle of desire
in a man that seeks source of attraction in spite of
synthetic philosophy. The general belief in an
infinite past and future interpenetrates one some-

how. When you find children who do wrong are always warned, "Ah! your future birth will be unhappy;" when you find two lovers drinking death together, and leaving behind them letters saying, "This is the influence of our last birth, when we broke our promise to become husband and wife;" and last, but not least, when some loving woman murmurs, laughingly: "In the last life thou wert a woman and I a man, and I loved thee much; but thou didst not love me at all,"— you begin to doubt if you do not really believe like everybody else.

About the training of the senses. The idea is admirable, but *alas!* — a very clever Frenchman five years ago, in the *Revue Politique et Littéraire*, almost exhausted it. He represented a man who had cultivated his eye so that he could see the bacteria in the air, and the grain of metals, — also being able to adjust his eyes to distance. He had trained his ear so as to hear all sounds of growth and decomposition. He had trained his nose to smell all substances supposed to have no smell. He made a diagram of the five senses thus: —

The way impressions come to —

YOU ＝＝＝＝ (sight, smell, hearing, taste, touch) ME (sight, smell, hearing, taste, touch)

I translated it for the *T.-D.*

For a little while, good-bye and best happiness.

LAFCADIO HEARN.

TO ELLWOOD HENDRICK

KUMAMOTO, 1892.

DEAR E. H., — . . . Your thoughts about the Shadows of the East are touching. You ought to be able to write something beautiful and quite new if you had time. . . .

You have been seized by the fascination of monstrous cities built up to heaven, and eternally sending their thunder to the smoke-blacked sky, — cities where we live by machinery. I can shudder now only to think of walking down a street between miles of houses two hundred feet high, with a roaring of traffic through them as of a torrent in a cañon. And that fascination means elegance, fashion, social duties. . . . I have been trying to deal with these two problems: "What has been the moral value of Christianity to mankind?" and "Why is Western civilization still in slavery to religious hypocrisy?" The answer to the former seems to be that without the brutal denial of the value of life and pleasure by Christianity, we could never have learned that the highest enjoyments are, after all, intellectual, and that progress can be effected only by self-sacrifice to interest and indifference to physical gratifications. And the latter question, though I have not yet solved it, seems to suggest that the hypocrisy itself may have large hidden value, — may be in process of transmutation into a truth.

Yes, Japanese women are all that your question implies you would wish them to be. They are children, of course. They perceive every possible shade of thought, — vexation, doubt, or pleasure, — as it passes over the face; and they know all you do not tell them. If you are unhappy about anything, then they say: "I will pray to the Kami-sama for my lord," — and they light a little lamp, and clap their hands and pray. And the ancient gods hearken unto them; and the heart of the foreign barbarian is therewith lightened and made luminous with sunshine. And he orders the merchants of curious textures to bring their goods to the house, which they do — piling them up like mountains; and there is such choice that the pleasure of the purchase is dampened by the sense of inability to buy everything in this world. And the merchants, departing, leave behind them dreams in little Japanese brains of beautiful things to be bought next year.

Also Japanese women have curious Souls. The other day in Nagano, a politician told a treacherous lie. Whereupon his wife robed herself all in white as those are robed who are about to journey to the world of ghosts, and purified her lips according to the holy rite, and, taking from the storeroom an ancient family sword, thereupon slew herself. And she left a letter, regretting that she had but one life to give in expiation of the shame and the wrong of that lie. And the people do now worship at her grave, and strew flowers thereupon, and pray for daughters with hearts as brave. . . . But the worms are eating her.

Because you sent me that horrid book, I revenge myself. I send you a much more horrid book. But if you do not enjoy it, I shall commit *hara kiri*, or *seppuku,* which is the polite name. And a woman wrote it — a woman! Christopher Columbus! what a *terrible* woman she must be! . . .

The "tract" you sent is giving much amusement to friends here. Send anything *really* good of that sort you can find: it makes life happier for the exile.

I am not easy about my book, of which I now await the proofs. It lacks colour — it is n't like the West Indian book. But the world here is not forceful: it is all washed in faint blues and greys and greens. There are really gamboge, or saffron-coloured valleys, — and lilac fields; but these exist only in the early summer and the rape-plant season, and ordinarily Japan is chromatically spectral. My next book will probably be on Buddhism in common life.

You write me delightful letters, which, alas ! I can't answer. Well, they are not answerable in themselves. They are thinking. I can only say this about one point: the isolation ought — unless you are physically tired by the day's work — to prove of value. All the best work is done the way ants do things — by tiny but tireless and regular additions. I would n't recommend introspection, — except in commentary. You *must* see interesting life. Of course only in flashes and patches. But preserve in writing the memory of these. In a year you will be astounded to find them self-arranging, kaleidoscopically, into something symmetrical, — and trying to live. Then play God, and breathe into the nostrils, — and be astonished and pleased.

Lovingly ever yours,

LAFCADIO HEARN.

TO PAGE M. BAKER

KUMAMOTO, June, 1892.

DEAR PAGE, — To-day, second of June, your kind
letter came, enclosing a draft for £163; and I write
in haste to catch the mail. . . . And now, ten
thousand thanks, from the bottom of my much-
scarified heart.

I am sorry I did not get the *T.-D.*, as it would have
helped me to get out my book quicker, — my first
book. It ought to be out this Fall; and I think it
will be tolerably large, — a little larger than "Two
Years in the French West Indies;" but it is only
an introductory book.

Really, it is very queer; but you seem to be the
best friend I 've got outside of Japan. You really
do things for a fellow — great big things; and nobody else seems inclined to do much of anything. . . .

I send you to-day a better photo of my little wife,
and some other things; and you will shortly get a
copy of Chamberlain's "Things Japanese" I have
ordered for you. . . . As for making a present to
Setsu (that is her name in Japanese; in Chinese
Chi-yo, or Tchi-yo[1]), I don't think you could send
her anything Western she would understand. And
I would not wish you to take so much trouble. The
best thing you can do to please her is to be good to
me. She has really everything she wants (you know
Japanese women wear no earrings, necklaces, or

---

[1] (Like Tchi-Nim?) — It means "Life-for-a-Thousand-Years," — a name
of good omen.

jewelry as ours do); and what she really wants is only made in Japan; and I am wickedly trying to keep her as innocent of foreign life as possible. So whenever she shows a liking even for foreign textures (many are now thrown on the market) I persuade her that Japanese goods are twice as pretty and durable, and for fear she might not believe me I usually manage to find some Japanese stuff that really is much better than the foreign article on sale. . . .

Oh, about distances. I am in Kyūshū, the southern island, you know, — very far from Tōkyō, and by the route much farther than as the crow flies. What I meant by 2000 miles south of Tōkyō was the Loochoo Islands. You know they belong to Japan, but perhaps I am wrong as to distance. The Loochoo Islands compose what is called *Okinawa Ken* (ken is province). . . . I find I shall not be able to go to Loochoo this summer, however; I must make studies somewhere else for a new book. Of course you will get my book as soon as it comes out.

In that book you will find a good deal about what you ask in relation to my way of living, etc. But as to eating, I have said very little. The fact is I lived for one year exclusively on Japanese food, which Europeans, among others Mr. Chamberlain, consider almost impossible. I must confess, however, that it broke me down. After twelve months I could not eat at all. You know Japanese food is raw fish and fresh fish, rice, bean-curds (they look like custard), seaweed, dried cuttle-fish, — rarely chicken or eggs. In short, of five hundred Japanese dishes, the basis is rice, fish, beans, lotus, various vegetables, including bamboo shoots, and seaweed. Confectionery is eaten between meals only, and sparingly. Tea is never allowed to become strong: it is a pale straw-colour, without sugar or milk, and once used to it, you cannot bear the sight of European tea any more. But I had to return to the flesh-pots of Egypt. I now eat Japanese food only once a day; and morning and evening indulge in beefsteak, bread, and Bass's Ale.

One becomes fond of Japanese sake (rice-wine); but it can only be eaten with Japanese food. A barrel of the best costs about $3.50. It is extremely deceiving. It looks like lemonade; but it is heavy as sherry. Happily it has not the after-effects of sherry. There is no liquor in the world upon which a man becomes so quickly intoxicated, and yet none of which the effects last so short a time. The intoxication is pleasant as the effect of opium or hasheesh. It is a soft, pleasant, luminous exhilaration: everything becomes brighter, happier, lighter; — then you get very sleepy. At Japanese dinners it is the rule to become slightly exhilarated; but not to drink enough to talk thickly, or walk crooked. The ability to drink at banquets requires practice — long practice. With European wines, the rule is, I believe, that hearty eating prevents the drink from taking too much effect. But with Japanese sake it is exactly the opposite. There are banquets of many kinds, and the man who is invited to one at which extensive drinking may be expected is careful to start in upon

an empty, or almost empty, stomach. By not eating
one can drink a good deal. The cups are very small,
and of many curious shapes; but one may be expected
to empty fifty. A quart of sake is a good load; two
quarts require iron nerves to stand. But among
the Japanese there are wonderful drinkers. At a
military officer's banquet a captain offered me a
tumbler holding a good pint of sake, — I almost
fainted at the sight of it; for it was only the first.
But a friend said to me: "Only drink a little, and
pass it back" — which I did. Stronger heads emp-
tied cup after cup like water. "Oh, that is nothing,"
my friend said; "wait till you see an old-fashioned cup." He showed me something like a wash-
basin for size, — a beautiful lacquered bowl, holding,
I should guess, at the very least a quart and a half.
"A valiant warrior was expected," he said, "to
swallow this at one draft, and wait for more." I
should not like to attempt it, unless I were suffering
very badly from chills and fever. When very tired
and cold, one can drink a great deal of sake without
harm.

About my every-day life. Well, it is the simplest
and most silent of lives, — in a simple Japanese
house. I use one chair, only for writing at a high
table on account of my eyes. Most of my life I spend
squatting on the floor. Europeans can seldom get
used to this; but it has become second nature to me.

I always wear Japanese clothes in the house, of
course. We rest, eat, talk, read, and sleep on the
floor. But then, you do not know, perhaps, what a
Japanese floor is. It is like a great soft mattress:

the real floor is covered by heavy mats, fitted to one another like mattresses set edge to edge; and these cannot be lifted up except by a workman: they are really part of the building. Then this floor is spotlessly clean. No dust is ever suffered upon it, — not a speck. Therefore we live barefooted in summer, or wearing only stockings in winter. The bed consists of a series of heavy quilts of pretty colours — like very thick comforts, piled one upon the other on the floor. By day these are rolled up and stowed out of sight. So in a Japanese house you see no furniture, — only in some recess, a graceful vase, and one *kakemono*, or hanging picture painted on silk. That is all — except the smoking-box (*hibachi*) in the middle of the room, surrounded by kneeling-cushions. In the evening the Japanese bath is ready. It is *almost* scalding always — hard to get used to; but the best in the world because you can't take cold after it. It consists of an immense tub, with a little furnace *in* it which heats the water. For amusements we have the Japanese theatres, the street-festivals, visits of friends, Japanese newspapers, occasional pilgrimages to curious places, and — delight of delights in some cities — *shopping*, Japanese shopping.

Bad boys, — and not obliged to give good and great moral examples, — people who are not strictly moral in their virtues like you and me, — sometimes hire *geisha* or dancing girls to amuse them. . . .

At all banquets — except those of teachers here — there are *geisha*. When you sit down (I mean kneel down) to eat, a band of beautiful girls come in to wait upon you, with exquisite voices, and beautiful dresses, etc. These are *geisha*. After a while they dance. If you wish to fall in love with them, you may. . . .

In Matsue I often saw *geisha* dance: they were at all banquets. But at teachers' banquets in Kumamoto they are not allowed. We are strictly moral in Kyūshū. . . .

Lo ! — it 's nearly time to close the mail for the outgoing steamer. So, dear Page, I must conclude for the moment in great haste.

With best regards to Mrs. Baker, best remembrances and gratitude to you, excuse this scrawl, and believe me ever faithfully

Your friend,

LAFCADIO HEARN.

Really, it seems to me as if I had n't thanked you at all. You are simply divine about doing kind things. My little wife sends you this greeting with her own hand, —

萬 歳

It means: "*May you live a thousand years!*"

TO SENTARŌ NISHIDA

KAGAWA, SAKAI, August, 1892.

DEAR NISHIDA, — . . . It made us both very happy to hear you had been persuaded to stop at our little house; for although it is hot and small, still you would feel more homelike there, with Izumo folk, than at the big dreary hotels of Kumamoto. I hope you will be able to stop a little while with us now at Mionoseki.

I like Oki very, very much — much better than Kumamoto. I like country people, fishermen, sailors, primitive manners, simple ways: all these delight me, and they are in Oki. To watch the life and customs of those people is very pleasant, and would be profitable to me in a literary way if I had time to spare. Oki is worth six months' literary study for me. I hope to see it again. The only unpleasant thing is the awful smell of the cuttle-fish. But I will tell you all my impressions when we meet. . . .

With kindest regards from myself and Setsu, — hoping to see you soon, as ever,

LAFCADIO HEARN.

TO SENTARŌ NISHIDA

MIONOSEKI, August, 1892.

DEAR NISHIDA, — We felt quite lonesome after you went away, and especially at supper-time, — when there were only two mats, instead of three, laid upon the *suzumi-dai*, overlooking the bay, and the twinkling of the Golden Dragon.

Next morning the water was rough, and made a great noise; and I said, "That is because Nishida San has sent us some eggs." But in the afternoon the bay again became like a mirror; and I succeeded in teaching Masayoshi to lie on his back in the water. Quite late in the afternoon the little Sakai Maru came in, and brought a magnificent box of eggs, and your letter, and a copy of the *Nippon*.

You are too good; and I felt not less pleased to find myself so kindly remembered than sorry to think of the trouble you took for us. But the eggs were more than welcome. The landlord cooked them in a little quadrangular pan; and each one looked like a Japanese flag, with the Red Sun in the middle. A thousand thanks to you, and to your kindest mother, — and to all your family warmest regards.

By the way, speaking of the Great Deity of Mionoseki, last evening we had a good laugh at the arguments of a clever barber, who came to cut my *kappa*-hair. I noticed he had a soldier's belt instead of an *obi*. I questioned him, through Setsu; and found he had been many years in the army. In the army they gave the soldiers eggs; and he hated eggs at first. But he learned to eat them, and found that they made him stronger. Whenever he ate many eggs, he could blow his bugle much better. Then he became fond of eggs. Still he gets his friends secretly to send him eggs; and the Great Deity of Mionoseki is not angry. He says: "What nonsense ! Suppose the Cock *did* crow at the wrong hour, is not Koto-shiro-nushi no Mikoto a *Kami sama?* — and how are we to believe that a *Kami sama* does not know the right time? And suppose the *wanizame* did bite him, — then it is at the *wanizame* he ought to have been angry, — not at the Cock. I don't believe Koto-shiro-nushi no Kami could be so foolish. Indeed it is very wrong to tell such

a story about him. I like eggs. I pity the people
of Mionoseki, who do not know the rare pleasure of
eating a well-cooked egg" (etc., etc.). "If the
Deity was angry with the Cock, he should have
eaten him." . . .

With many grateful regards,

Ever most truly,

LAFCADIO HEARN.

TO ELLWOOD HENDRICK

November, 1892.

DEAR OLD FELLOW, — . . . What a beastly
nightmare that woman who married the preacher!
High-pressure civilization only produces these
types. — But, Lord! what is to be the end? . . .
The race will still be to the mentally strong as well
as to the physically strong. But the women fit for
fertile maternity, and equally fit to discuss the fourth
dimension of space, are yet rare, — and apt to be
a little terrible. The cost of intellectual race-expan-
sion is more terrible, — is frightful; and then the
expansion cannot *ever* become universal. The
many must profit by the few. To make 1 of the
few, there must be, I suppose, at least 111,111 of
such monstrosities created as that one you wrote
of.

Isn't the hunger for the eternal feminine much
like the other hunger? —to be completely exorcised
in the same way. Marriage seems to me the certain
destruction of all that emotion and suffering, — so
that one afterwards looks back at the old times with

wonder. One cannot dream or desire anything more after love is transmuted into the friendship of marriage. It is like a haven from which you can see the dangerous sea-currents, running like violet bands beyond you out of sight. It seems to me (though I'm a poor judge of such matters) that it does n't make a man any happier to have an intellectual wife — unless he marries for society. The less intellectual, the more lovable: so long as there is neither coarseness nor foolishness. For intellectual converse a man *can't* have really with women: womanhood is antagonistic to it. And emotional truth is quite as plain to the childish mind as to the mind of Herbert Spencer or of Clifford. The child and the god come equally near to the eternal truth. But then marriage in a complex civilization is really a terrible problem: there are so *many* questions involved.

Oh! — *you* talk of being without intellectual companionship! O ye Eight Hundred Myriads of Gods! What would you do if you were me. Lo! the illusion is gone! — Japan in Kyūshū is like Europe; — except I have no friend. The differences in ways of thinking, and the difficulties of language, render it impossible for an *educated* Japanese to find pleasure in the society of a European. Here is an astounding fact. The Japanese child is as close to you as the European child — perhaps closer and sweeter, because infinitely more natural and naturally refined. Cultivate his mind, and the more it is cultivated, the *further you push him* from you. Why? Because there the race-antipodalism shows itself. As the Oriental thinks naturally to the left where we

think to the right, the more you cultivate him the
more strongly will he think in the opposite direction
from you. Finis sweetness, sympathy, friendship.
Now, my scholars in this great Government school
are not boys, but men. They speak to me only in
class. The teachers never speak to me at all. I go to
the college (two miles away) by jinrikisha and return after class, — always alone, no mental company
but books. But at home everything is sweet.

At the college there is always a recess of half
an hour at noon, for dining. I do not dine, but
climb the hill behind the college. There is a grey
old cemetery, where "the rude forefathers of the
hamlet sleep." From between the tombs I can look
down on the Dai Go Kōtō Chūgakkō, with its huge
modern brick buildings and its tumultuous life, as
in a bird's-eye view. I am only there never alone.
For Buddha sits beside me, and also looks down
upon the college through his half-closed eyelids of
stone. There is moss on his nose and his hands, —
moss on his back, of course! And I always say to
him: "O Master, what do you think of all this? —
is it not vanity? There is no faith there, no creed,
no thought of the past life nor of the future life, nor
of Nirvana, — only chemistry and cube-geometry
and trigonometry, — and the most damnable 'English language.'" He never answers me; but he looks
very sad, — smiles just like one who has received an
injury which he cannot return, — and you know that
is the most pathetic of all smiles. And the snakes
twist before my feet as I descend to the sound of the
bell. — There is my only companion for you! but I

like him better than those who look like him waiting
for me in the classroom.   Ever with best regards,

LAFCADIO HEARN.

TO SENTARŌ NISHIDA

KUMAMOTO, January, 1893.

DEAR NISHIDA, — I do not know how to thank
you enough for your last letter; — indeed I must tell
you frankly that I felt ashamed of having put you to
such trouble involuntarily, for I had no idea how
complicated the matter was when I wrote to you for
information about the origin of the belief.   And now
let me beg of you never to take so much trouble
again on my account.   I think I can hear you pro-
testing that it was only a pleasure.   I am sure it was
a pleasure to help me; but I am too much of a literary
man not to know exactly the time-cost of the work,
especially in a language not your own.   So I will
again beg you not to take so much trouble for me
at any future time — as it would cause me pain.

And now let me say something else about other
letters.   You spoke of *mistakes*.   Do you know that
I think your letters are very wonderful?   There are
extremely few mistakes; and there are very seldom
even incorrectnesses in the use of idioms.   This is rare
in Japan.   Very few Japanese, even among those
who have been abroad, can write an informal letter
without mistakes of a serious kind.   You write letters
much as a well-educated German or Frenchman
would — showing only rarely, by some unfamiliar
turn of expression, by the elision of a preposition, or

(but this is very seldom indeed) by a sudden change
of tense, that it is not an Englishman who writes.
And in a few years more, even these little signs will
disappear. It is very wonderful to me to see how
a few Japanese have been able to master English
without ever leaving Japan.

A point of much value to me in your explanation
was the fact that too many souls are held to be as
bad as too few. I had imagined the opposite to be
the case, and had so written. But as I put the
statement into the mouth of a story-teller, it will
read all right enough; and I can correct the erroneous impression by a footnote.

There is rejoicing here over the non-abolition of
the school. Your predictions have been well fulfilled. Several new books I recommended have
been adopted; but there were changes made in my
list, I think for the worse. Kingsley's "Greek
Heroes" (Ginn, Heath & Co.'s school-text edition)
has been adopted for the younger class. I recommended this book for the extreme purity and simplicity of its English, which reads like a song. I
tried to get "Cuore" adopted, but could not succeed:
they said it was "too childish." I tried Macaulay's
"Lays of Ancient Rome;" and that I think they will
get. Then some classic texts — Burke's Essays
(selected) were adopted instead of a volume of
stories I proposed. They adopted also "The Book
of Golden Deeds," a volume of anecdotes of virtue
and courage. As for my own classes, they still give
me no books at all; and I teach entirely by word of
mouth and chalk. Still, considering the short time

given to each class, I believe this is best. The main thing is to teach them to express themselves in English without books to help them. I have noticed that at one period of the course there is always a sudden improvement, as if there had been also a sudden development of intelligence, — between the third and fourth class. It corresponds to a change of capacity I noticed also in the Jinjō Chūgakkō. It might be indicated by lines, thus: —

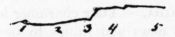

Between 3 and 4 the increase of power is like a leap. But after that (in the higher schools) I don't think there is much progress. Thereafter I fancy that in most cases the highest capacity has been reached, and then the strain comes. The students attempt to do on rice and gruel what foreign students can only do on beef, eggs, puddings, heavy nutritious diet. In the eternal order of things the overstrain comes. The higher education will not give the desired results for at least another generation, — because the physique of the student must be raised to meet it. The higher education requires a physiological change, — an increase of brain capacity in actual development of tissue, an increase of nervous energy, and consequently a higher standard of living. That there have been wonderful exceptions in Japanese scholarship makes no difference: it is a question of general averages. The student of to-day is not sufficiently strong and sufficiently nourished to bear the tremendous strain put upon him at the higher schools and the university. Wherefore he loses some of his best qualities in mere effort. The higher schools don't feed their boys well — not so well by half as the Government feeds the soldiers. At least so I have been assured. . . . Yours faithfully,

LAFCADIO HEARN.

TO SENTARŌ NISHIDA

KUMAMOTO, January, 1893.

DEAR NISHIDA, — Your charming letter has just come, full of news and things to be grateful for. There is some news here too. Mr. Kano is gone! We are all very, very sorry. . . .

Perhaps I might go to Niigata during the summer. Setsu is always, always, always talking about Tōkyō. I suppose I shall have to take her there. And I want to visit Kompira, and Zenkōji in Nagano (?) — where all the Souls of the Dead go, — and one might do all that and see Niigata too. I am very anxious to see the dear kind Governor and his daughter again. That kind of Governor is rare, and I think will soon cease to exist in Japan. He always seemed to me a delightful type of the old days, — like the princes of the *ehon:* the modernized Governor scarcely seems to belong to the same race. And the Japanese of the next generation will not be kind and open-hearted and unselfish, I fear: they will become hard of character like the Western people, — more intellectual and less moral. For old Japan, in unselfishness, was as far in advance of the West as she was materially behind it.

THE SHINTŌ TEMPLE OF KIZUKI

The curling-up of the toe in the statue of Inada-Hime is not according to the canons of Western sculpture (which is still generally governed by the Greek spirit), — because it shows the member in what is considered an ungraceful position. But I thought after looking awhile at it, that it was really natural. Not natural from the standpoint of a modern people whose toes have lost both symmetry and flexibility owing to the wearing of leather shoes; but natural among a people whose feet are well shaped and whose toes remain supple, and to some degree, prehensile. Among tropical races the toes retain extraordinary flexibility; but I don't think any English girl could put her great-toe into the attitude taken by that of Inada-Hime. I imagined that this movement represented in the statue a little nervous feeling, — the involuntary shrinking of a woman from sharp cold steel. But that is only a guess. What it really means I should like to know.

I forgot in another letter to tell you that Herbert Spencer, in one of his recent volumes ("Individual Life") severely criticized some of the Mombushō Readers and other publications as immoral, — because appealing to the desire of revenge and the passion of hatred and bloodshed. . . . One thing is certain, that Readers for Japanese students ought to be edited in Japan, and edited in a particular manner with especial reference to national character and feeling. I prize the Mombushō Readers, because I learn so much from them; but as text-books they are not well written, and they do not appeal to the student's natural love of novelty. It is hopeless to interest boys in stories they know already by heart in their own language. They want what is new and strange and beautiful. — But no thanks will ever be given to the man who tries to do the work well; and his work itself will almost certainly be spoiled by the emendations and interpolations of a committee of men without knowledge or taste, — unless the thing should be done quite independently of officialdom.

I am trying to teach Setsu English by a fast memory-system. I can't tell whether I will succeed or not: if I find it strains her too much I must stop, — for the system is exhausting. In the course of teaching I notice something of what you tell me about Izumo pronunciation. It makes the difficulty much greater. LAFCADIO HEARN.

TO ELLWOOD HENDRICK

KUMAMOTO, February, 1893.

DEAR HENDRICK, — This is not going to be a pleasant letter, — though it may have interest for you. I don't hesitate to tell my friends about shadows as well as lights, and I rather think the latter alone would cease to be interesting. Besides, we are all most interested in what most closely relates to the realities of life; and the realities of life are ugly to no small degree. Dreams are realities — of desire for things out of reach; but the diet of dreams is not substantial enough for the sense of friendship to live upon. So here goes for the lamentations, — or as a Frenchman would say, a *jérémiade.* . . .

I might cite a fourth, a fifth; — but happily there

are lights. I made one delightful friend here, Professor Chamberlain, and I told you about Major McDonald. . . .

I am perfectly conscious that to a thorough man of the world I must be only a contemptible fool. Even to a friend like you who are not spoiled and cannot be spoiled by your *milieu*, I must seem something of a fool. Be that as it may, — here I am. Now what is this fool to do? . . .

Suppose I should seek a place as teacher of English literature. Everybody thinks he can teach English literature, and the public doesn't care particularly: it takes its pabulum largely on trust. On whose trust? Oh! the trust of the trustees, — and the respectable people. Now I am not respectable. I am under the *odium theologicum* of every Christian faith. Small and mean as I am, I am spotted. Don't imagine this is vanity! It doesn't require any greatness to be spotted. It is just like a prostitute trying to become an honest woman, or a convicted thief endeavouring to get employment. There is nothing great about it. If I had any position worth hunting up, the cry would be raised that an atheist, a debauchee, a disreputable ex-reporter was corrupting the morals of the young under pretence of teaching literature. That is position No. 3. As Fiske says, the heretic is not now burned at the stake; but there is an organized policy to starve him by injuring his reputation and lying about him. And even Fiske (because he is poor) dares not take the whole position of Spencer. But I don't want to pretend myself a martyr for

any worthy cause. I am not. I am *not respectable:*
that is the whole matter, — and the pardoning influence of women would never be exerted for me, because
I am physically disagreeable, — and what I could
win by my own merit I could not keep, because I have
no aggressiveness and no cunning. And I am only
now learning all this, — with my hair grey. There
is no chance of becoming independent, as I will never
be allowed to hold a position that pays well. I shall
never be able to do my best in literary matters; for
I shall never have the leisure, the means, or the
opportunities of travel I want. . . .

To all this *jérémiade,* then, you must think for
reply, in the words of Herbert Spencer: "My
dear friend, the first necessity for success in life is
to be a good animal. As an animal you don't work
well at all. Furthermore you are out of harmony
mentally and morally with the life of society: you
represent broken-down tissue. There is some good in
the ghostly part of you, but it would never have been
developed under comfortable circumstances. Hard
knocks and intellectual starvation have brought your
miserable little *animula* into some sort of shape. It
will never have full opportunity to express itself,
doubtless; but perhaps that is better. It might
otherwise make too many mistakes; and it has not
sufficient original force to move the sea of human
mind to any storm of aspiration. Perhaps, in some
future state of —" But here Spencer stops. . . .

I think civilization is a fraud, because I don't
like the hopeless struggle. If I were very rich I
should perhaps think quite differently — or, what

would be still more rational, try not to think at all about it. Religion under an empire preaches the divinity of autocracy; under a monarchy, the divinity of aristocracy. In this industrial epoch it is the servant of the monster business, and is paid to declare that religion is governed by God, and business by religion, — "whoever says the contrary, let him be anathema!" Business has its fixed standard of hypocrisy; everything above or below that is to be denounced by the ministers of the gospel of God and business. Hence the howl about Jay Gould, who, with splendid, brutal frankness, exposed to the entire universe the real laws of business, — without any preaching at all, — and overrode society and law and became supreme. Wherefore I hold that a statue should be erected to him. Here we have been having a newspaper fight. All the missionaries are down on "that anonymous writer" as usual. I wrote an article to prove that Gould was the grandest moral teacher of the century. Even sermons were preached in Tōkyō denouncing the writer of that article. I was accused of declaring that the end justified the means. I had not said so; but I quoted American authorities to show Gould had created and made effective the railroad-transportation system of the West; and then I quoted English financial authorities to prove that that very transportation system alone was now saving the United States from bankruptcy. The facts were unanswerable (at least by the clerics); and they proved that in order to get power to save a whole nation from ruin, — Gould had to ruin a few thousand people. Wherefore I am called "immoral, low, beastly." Nobody *knows* it is I; but some suspect. I am already deemed the "moral plague-spot" of Japan by the dear missionaries. Next week I'll try them with an article on "The Abomination of Civilization." . . .

But I have at home a little world of about eleven people, to whom I am Love and Light and Food. It is a very gentle world. It is only happy when I am happy. If I even look tired, it is silent, and walks on tiptoe. It is a moral force. I dare not fret about anything when I can help it, — for others would fret more. So I try to keep right. My little wife and I have saved nearly 2000 Japanese dollars between us. I think I'll be able to make her independent. When I've done that, I can let the teaching go, and wander about awhile, and write "sketches" at $10 per page.   Ever affectionately,

LAFCADIO HEARN.

TO ELLWOOD HENDRICK

KUMAMOTO, April, 1893.

DEAR HENDRICK, — . . . You never wrote a more wonderful letter than that last letter full of penetrating things. Now one of my shortcomings is a total ignorance of practical worldly wisdom; — for instance, I could not sit down and talk to a man in polite enigmas which both of us would understand, at all. All that world of business is to me a mystery and a marvel incomprehensible. Moreover, it is the revelation of mental powers of a very subtle order, as much beyond me as mathematics, — so

that I cannot but respect the forces manifested, even
if I deplore the directions in which they are sometimes exercised. Your sketch of the two men, and
the interview, and the psychological relations was
perfectly delicious, — and like nearly everything you
write to me, gave me the pleasure of a novel sensation. . . .

Your criticism about ——'s criticism was not
exactly what I thought you might make: — it *is* true
that we like to be thought, and to believe ourselves,
capable of doing vast harm, and credit ourselves
more for our goodness perhaps on account of that
belief. But I don't agree with you in thinking the
remark uncomplimentary. I think it was true, and
in the sense I take it, beautiful. Ask yourself could
you really do anything you knew to be terribly cruel
under any personal provocation, — at least after
the first burst of sudden anger was over? And you
will find you *could not*. Any nature sincerely sympathetic — with a complex nerve-system — cannot
inflict pain without receiving at least as much, if not
more pain than it gives. I believe you could kill a
man, under just provocation; but that is not bad, or
cruel — indeed, it might be a duty. The terrible
men are the men who do everything in cold blood,
icily, with calculation, infinite patience, and infinite
pleasure. But the capacity to be thus dangerous
means also a low development of those qualities
which give sweetness to character and amiability to
life, — and chivalry to a man's soul.

Now here is the very immoral side of Western
civilization. Being wholly aggressive and selfish,

the hard, cold qualities of character are being pro-
digiously developed by it. The emotional qualities,
you might suggest, are also indirectly developed by
the suffering the others inflict; — there is action and
reaction. Yes, that is true. But the terrible men —
the men of the type of that manager — represent
not only a constantly increasing class, but a leading
one — the class whose name is Power. Now Power
multiplies. In wealth and luxury multiplication is
rapid and facile. They are less fertile comparatively
than other classes; but the cost of their individuality
is infinitely greater, and one type can outlive, out-
work, outplan a hundred of the emotional sort, — as
a general rule. The ultimate tendency is to settle all
power in the hands of those without moral scruple.
It may take another few centuries to do this; but
the tendency is obvious, and the danger is steadily
growing. I think the West can never become as
moral as the Orient. But it may become infinitely
more wicked.

This is one way of seeing the matter. Another
I wrote you about in my last letter, — the sexual
question in the West, — something never dreamed
of in the East. What must be the ultimate results
of this Western worship of the Eternal Feminine?
Must not one be, the contempt of old age, and
universal irreverence for things the most naturally
deserving of reverence? Already, in the West, the
Family has almost ceased to exist.

To an Oriental it seems utterly monstrous that
grown-up children should not live with their father,
mother, and grandparents, and support and love

them more than their own children, wives, or hus-
bands. It seems to him sheer wickedness that a man
should not love his mother-in-law, — or that he
should love his own wife even half as well as his own
father or mother. Our whole existence seems to him
disgustingly immoral. He would deem worthy of
death the man who wrote —

> "He stood on his head on the wild seashore,
>   And joy was the cause of the act; —
> For he felt, as he never had felt before,
>   Insanely glad, in fact.
> And why? Because on that selfsame day
>   His mother-in-law had sailed
> To a tropical climate, far away,
>   *Where tigers and snakes prevailed.*"

He first most loves his father, — then his mother, —
then his father-in-law and mother-in-law, — then
his children, — and lastly, his wife. His wife is not
of the family proper, — a stranger, — not of the
blood of the ancestors, — how can he love her like
his own parents!
Now I half suspect the Oriental is right.
To him the people of the West with their novels
and poems about love seem a race of very lascivious
people. If indeed he should think more kindly of
them at all, it would be through pity, — as a race of
sexually starved beings, frantic with nymphomania
and all forms of erotomania, through refusal to obey
the laws of nature. "They talk about their wives! —
they write novels about their lusts! — they do not
support their parents! — they do not obey their
mothers-in-law! Truly they are savages!" Now

they write love-stories in Japan. But who are the women of these love-stories? Dancing-girls. "If one must write stories about the passion of sex, let him at least not write such things about wives and daughters of honest men — let him write about whores! A whore's business is to excite passion. That of a pure woman is to quench it. What horribly immoral people the Western people are!"

— Don Juan is the imagination of the West. No Japanese Don Juan — no Chinese Don Juan — ever existed or could exist. He is a common type at home. But the Orient rejoices also in exemption from one of the most terrible creations of Western life; — no Oriental is haunted by "the Woman thou shalt never know."

What a curse and a delusion is that beautiful spectre! How many lives she makes desolate! How many crimes does she inspire, "the Woman thou shalt never know!"— the impossible ideal, not of love, but of artistic passion, pursued by warm hearts from youth till age, always in vain. As her pursuer grows more old, she becomes ever more young and fair. He waits for her through the years, — waits till his hair is grey. Then, — wifeless, childless, blasé, ennuyé, cynical, misanthropic, — he looks in the glass and finds that he has been cheated out of youth and life. But does he give up the chase? No! — the hair of Lilith — just one — has been twisted round his heart, — an ever-tightening fine spider-line of gold. And he sees her smile just ere he passes into the Eternal darkness.

Then again, our social morals! We never in

the West talk to people of their duties. Do orators make speeches about duties? Do any, except priests, talk about social duties? But what do we talk to the people about? We talk to them about their *rights*, — "by G—d!" Always, incessantly, *ad nauseam*, about their *rights*. Now to talk to people who know nothing of social science, of political economy, of ethical ideas in their relation to eternal truths, — to talk to such people about their *rights*, is like giving a new-born baby a razor to play with. Or putting a loaded revolver in the hands of a mischievous child. Or inviting a crowd of urchins to make a bonfire in the immediate vicinity of ten thousand barrels of gunpowder. And the Oriental knows this. (Wherefore in China it was a law that he who should say or invent anything new should be put to death, — an extreme view of the necessities of the case, but not much more extreme than our own philistinism.)

The Japanese of the new school do not, however, keep to the Chinese wisdom. They show evidence now of a desire to put to death those who say anything older than yesterday. They are becoming infected with the Western moral poison. They are beginning to love their wives more than their fathers and mothers; — it is much cheaper. . . .

By the way, I am in a world of new sensations. My first child will be born, I expect, about September next. The rest of my family have come from Matsue, — father-in-law, father's father also, a nice old man of 84. We are now all together. There is universal joy because of the birth in prospect. And

I am accused of not seeming joyful enough. I am not sorry. But I hope my little one will never have to face life in the West, but may always dwell in a Buddhist atmosphere.

Ever most faithfully,

LAFCADIO HEARN.

TO ELLWOOD HENDRICK

KUMAMOTO, April, 1893.

DEAR HENDRICK, — Your most welcome lines of March 1 came to me during a lonesome spring vacation — to brighten it up. Your wish about a Japanese love-story has been partly answered in the March *Atlantic;* and in the June number, you will have a paper of mine, entitled the " Japanese Smile," which you will find as philosophical as you could wish. — No, I have been working well, but for a book only; and of that book only five or six chapters can be published in a magazine. I am not yet sure if the book will be published in the shape I want, — although the publishers show some signs of yielding.

So much for me. I was too egotistic last time, and will not be so much so again, unless I get a very awful attack of the blues within the next five years. . . .

To return to Japan and Japanese life. What do you think of the following? It happened near Kumamoto. A peasant went to consult an astrologer what to do for his mother's eyes: she had become blind. The astrologer said that she would get her sight back if she could eat a little human liver, —

taken fresh and from a young body. The peasant
went home crying, and told his wife. She said:
"We have only one boy. He is beautiful. You can
get another wife as good, or better than I, very easily,
but might never be able to get another son. Therefore, you must kill me instead of the son, and give
my liver to your mother." They embraced; and
the husband killed her with a sword, and cut out the
liver and began to cook it, when the child awoke
and screamed. Neighbours and police came. In the
police court, the peasant told his tale with childish
frankness and cited stories from the Buddhist scrip-
tures. The judges were moved to tears. They did
not condemn the man to death; — they gave only
nine years in prison. Really the man who ought to
have been killed was the astrologer. And this but
a few miles off from where they are teaching integral
calculus, trigonometry, and Herbert Spencer! yet
Western science and religion could never inspire
that idolatrous self-devotion to a mother which the
old ignorant peasant and his wife had. She thought
it her sacred duty to die for her mother-in-law. . . .

I am going to have the delight of a visit from the
author of "The Soul of the Far East." He is a lucky
man, — wonderful genius, strength, youth, and
plenty of money. He spends six months of each
year in the Orient. Professor Chamberlain, my
other friend, spent a few days with me last week. He
speaks Japanese better than the Japanese; — in
fact, he is *Professor of Japanese in the Imperial
University of Japan.* He mentions me in his books;
and Conder, who writes those beautiful books about

Japanese flower arrangement and Japanese gardens, has just written a book with a kindly reference to me.

Enough to tire you, I fear, already. Well, *au revoir*, till the next mail. Affectionately ever,

LAFCADIO HEARN.

TO SENTARŌ NISHIDA

KUMAMOTO, April, 1893.

MY DEAR NISHIDA, — About the sentence that puzzles you (as it well might puzzle anybody unaccustomed to what we call "rant"), — the phrase simply signifies the Bible. It is based on the idea that Christ is the "*Light* of the World" (Light and Glory being used synonymously); and the origin of this expression again goes back beyond Christianity into ancient Gnostic ideas, — *probably* based on the Iranian belief of Ormuzd, the (Persian or Iranian) God of *Light*, as distinguished from Ahriman, the Spirit of Evil and Darkness. The common Christian people know nothing of this; but from childhood, they are accustomed to hear the word "Bible" coupled with the words "light" and "glory" and "illumination," — and to see pictures representing a Bible surrounded with rays of light beaming from it as from a sun. "The glory of the mechanic's shop," i. e., illuminating the darkness of labour, the suffering and gloom, by light of consolation, etc. — But I must say that all this is what we call "rant" (worse than "cant"); — it is of no earthly use to let the boys read it. I used always to skip it. The article is not even good English: it is fanatical "gush" and humbug. If I were you, I would not bother with it at all, — except for your own amusement, as a study of queer ideas. I don't mean to say *all* writing of this sort is bad; — some of it is very beautiful, although the ideas be false. But that stuff in Sanders's Reader is the sort we call "*cheap rant,*" — such as any uneducated Sunday-school teacher can spout by the mile. . . .

I do not think Setsu can travel again this year. I expect to become a father about September, or perhaps even sooner. So we shall not see Tōkyō in 1893, at all events. And the chances are that I shall not be able to travel very far; — as I shall have to be in constant weekly communication with the mail-steamers for America. The preparation of the printed proofs will be hard work.

I am sorry about Goto. You summed him up, however, very keenly a long time ago. — We have a wonderful drawing-master here, who painted a wonderful oil-portrait of Mr. Akizuki. And that man is only getting $12 a month (counting the deduction of his salary for building warships)! Yet he is really a fine artist.

Besides the letter of introduction I gave you to Mr. Kano, I also wrote him a long letter about you last year. Should you go to Tōkyō, therefore, remind him of that. Or, if you wish, I will write you at once a third letter to take with you. You will like Mr. Kano at sight. He charms even the most reserved foreigners, and still he is perfectly easy and simple in his manners. Faithfully yours,

LAFCADIO HEARN.

TO ELLWOOD HENDRICK

KUMAMOTO, April, 1893.

DEAR HENDRICK, — . . . I hear rarely from
America, and have no definite news from Boston up
to date. They send me a paper — the Sunday
edition, full of poetry about love, woodcuts of beauties of fashion, and all sorts of chatter about women
and new styles of undergarments. To-day, after
three years in the most Eastern East, when I look
at that paper, I can hardly believe my eyes. The
East has opened my eyes. How affected the whole
thing seems ! Yet it never seemed so to me before.
My students say to me, "Dear Teacher, why are
your English novels all filled with nonsense about
love and women? — we do not like such things."
Then I tell them partly why. "You must know,
my dear young gentlemen, that in England and
America, marriage is a most important matter, —
though it is something you never even speak about
in Japan. For in Japan, it is as easy to get married
as it is to eat a bowl of rice. But for educated young
men in the West, it is very difficult and dangerous
to marry. It is necessary to be rich to marry well, —
or to be, at least, what *you* would call rich. And the
struggle for life is very bitter and very terrible — so
bitter and terrible that you cannot possibly imagine
what it means. It is hard to live at all, — made
harder to marry. Therefore the whole object of
life is to succeed *in order to get married*. And the
parents have nothing to do with the matter, as in
Japan; the young man must please the girl, and

must win her away from all other young men who
want to get her. That is why the English and others
write all that stuff about love and beauty and marriage, and why everybody buys those books and
laughs or weeps over them — though to you they are
simply disgusting."

But that was not all the truth. The whole truth
is always suggested to me by the Sunday paper. We
live in the musky atmosphere of desire in the West; —
an erotic perfume emanates from all that artificial
life of ours; — we keep the senses perpetually stimu-
lated with a million ideas of the eternal feminine; and
our very language reflects the strain. The Western civilization is using all its arts, its sciences, its
philosophy in stimulating and exaggerating and ex-
acerbating the thought of sex. An Oriental would
almost faint with astonishment and shame to see
a Western ballet. He would scream at the sight of a
French nude. He would be scandalized by a Greek
statue. He would rightly and instantly estimate all
this as being exactly what it is, — artificial stimulus
of dangerous senses. The whole West is steeped in
it. It now seems, even to me, almost disgusting.

Yet what does it mean? Certainly it pollutes
literature, creates and fosters a hundred vices,
accentuates the misery of those devoted by the law
of life as the victims of lust. It turns art from
Nature to sex. It cultivates one æsthetic faculty at
the expense of all the rest. And yet — perhaps its
working is divine behind all that veil of vulgarity
and lustfulness. It is cultivating also, beyond any
question, a capacity for tenderness the Orient knows

nothing of. Tenderness is not of the Orient *man*. He is without brutality, but he is also without that immense reserve force of deep love and forgiving-power which even the rougher men of the West have. The Oriental is intellectually, rationally capable of all self-sacrifice and loyalty: he does the noblest and grandest things without even the ghost of a tender feeling. His feeblest passion is that of sex, because with him the natural need has never been starved or exasperated. He marries at sixteen or seventeen perhaps, — is a father of two or three children at twenty. All that sort of thing for him belongs to the natural appetites: he would no more talk about his wife or tell you he had a child born, than he would tell you that his organs performed their function regularly at 6.30 A.M. He is ashamed of appearing to have any sexual love at all in public; — and his family live all their lives in the shadow — do not appear to visitors. Well, his nature may lose something by this. It loses certainly in capacities that mean everything for us — tenderness, deep sympathy, a world of sensations not indeed sexual with us, yet surely developed out of sexualism to no small extent, — just as the sense of moral beauty developed out of the sense of physical beauty.

I guess this must bore you, however. More anon of other matters.

Ever faithfully,

LAFCADIO HEARN.

KUMAMOTO, June, 1893.

DEAR HENDRICK, — I am not quite sure that you are right about the Oriental view of things. It is very difficult to understand at first. It is not want of refinement or sensibility to beautiful things. It is rather a tendency to silence and secrecy in regard to the highest emotions. So that a cultivated Japanese never even speaks of his wife and family, or hints of his fondness for them. Of course, our idea is nobler and higher. But it is a question with me whether it cannot be, and has not been, developed to excess. I think we have filled the whole universe with an ideal of woman. Star-swarms and all cosmical glories exist for us only in an infinity of passional pantheism. I suspect that we see Nature especially through the beauty of woman. A splendid tree, a fragrant bud, delicacy of petals, songs of birds, undulations of hills, mobility of waters, sounds of foliage, murmur of breezes and their caress, laughter of streamlets, even the gold light — do not all these things remind us of woman? You might cite the ruggedness of oaks and the grimness of crags as masculine. True, we have visions of Nature as masculine—for rugged and mighty contrasts. But how enormously preponderant is the eternal feminine! Even our language is a language of gender, — in which I think the feminine predominates. But in our thought the masculine at once suggests the feminine, and creates a new idea. All precious things, too, remind us of what is not masculine, because "far and from the uttermost coasts is the price of *her.*"

Now the Oriental sees Nature in no such way. His language has no gender. He does not think of a young girl when he sees a palm, nor of the lines of a beautiful body when he sees the undulations of the hills. Neither does he see Nature as masculine. He sees it as *neuter*. His geographical nomenclature shows this. He sees things as they are. The immediate inference would be that he finds less enjoyment in them. But his art shows that he finds *more*. He sees in Nature much that we can't see at all. He sees beauty in stones, — in common stones, — in clouds, fogs, smoke, curling water, shapes of trees, shapes of insects. In my friend's alcove is a stone. When you can learn that that stone is more beautiful than a beautiful painting, you can begin to understand that there is another way of seeing Nature. In my own garden there are a number of large stones. Their value is seven hundred dollars. No American would give five cents for them — no! he would not dream of taking them as a gift — no! he would consider himself highly insulted by the offer! Then why are they worth seven hundred dollars? Because they are beautiful. You would say: "I can't see it!" You can't see it because you see all Nature through the idea of woman. And it is just faintly possible (I don't say certain) that our way — your way of seeing Nature is all wrong. It is like peeping through an atmosphere which makes everything iridescent and deflects the lines of forms.

Now, why do I suspect that our way of looking at Nature may not be the highest, — besides the plain fact that it is not according to the Eternal order of

things? I suspect it because the evolution of the
ideal has been chiefly physical. It has not been an
ideal of soul. Is the soul of a woman more beautiful
than that of a man — outside of maternal tenderness? You have just had a divine glimpse of two
souls — excuse the personal question (for it is a
highly important one): which seemed to you the
largest and deepest? — in which were the glories
more profound and radiant? And is it not essential
that the woman-beauty of soul must be the lesser;
for its scope must be limited by its eternal duty. We
are in the presence, however, of the undeniable fact
that we rarely get glimpses of the higher possibilities
of the man-soul. Life is too hard and bitter. But in
the twilight of every home one sees the woman-souls
glowing like fireflies. We think only of the lights
we see. The circling darknesses are opaque to us,
— like burnt-out suns.

Reading over the list of things in your notebook I was impressed by several facts. It is well to
set down everything that impresses you. But — I
cannot help thinking that you do not look for the
highest, — that you miss a universe of beautiful
things. The obtrusive, the eccentric, the sharply
bitter, the "Distorted Souls" as you call them,
naturally compel attention first, — just as in real life
the forward, the selfish, the aggressive, force themselves upon us. It is of the highest possible value,
as a means of self-preservation, to understand them.
But I suspect that it is of no value at all to draw
them, to photograph them, to give them artistic
treatment *except in a contrast-study*. They are not

beautiful. They are not good. They are, using
the word in the Miltonic sense, obscene — like owls.
On the other hand the beautiful in life must be
sought, and coaxed, and caressed to make it show its
colours. It does not appear very often spontaneously.
Yet I feel convinced it is all about us. It travels on
railroads too, and lodges at hotels. It fights for life
against ugliness and wickedness and apathy and
selfishness: it is Ormuzd against Ahriman. Now
what is the artist's moral duty? (Of course he may
take any subject he pleases and be great in it.) But
what is his duty in the eternal order of things, to art
and to ethics? Is it not to extract the gold from the
ore, —the rubies and emeralds from the rubble?
I think it is — though many may laugh at me. Thus
newer and higher ideals are created. We advance
only by new ideals. I don't mean to say we should
make statues of pure gold, or a table, like that of
some Caliph, out of a single emerald. But I think
that in modern life we should use the dross and slag
only when their lightness, worthlessness, or rudeness
brings out in higher relief the light of the pure jewel,
the weight of the pure metal, the value of that which
gives the radiance or the gravity. And in the order
of research I would seek the lodes and veins first; —
the rest is always easy to find and handle, though
requiring much scientific skill, of course, to use
artistically.

There *is* a world, I suppose, almost as barren as
the Alkali Plains, where convention has strangled
all feeling, and where the development of selfish
capacities has choked the other growths. But either

below this world or above it there are Americas to discover — full of warmth, light, and beauty — continents chained to each other by snow-peaks, watered by Amazons and Mississippis.

Below, I think, more than above, — for the nearer to Nature, the nearer to truth. And the value, artistically, of our high-pressure civilization seems to me to be that its monstrosities and glooms and tragedies infernal give an opportunity for the grandest contrasts ever made. What I would pray you to do is "to put a lily in the mouth of Hell" — using one of Carlyle's phrases. Then the petals of the lily will change into pure light, like those of the Lotus of Amida Buddha. . . .

Good-bye, with affectionate wishes,

LAFCADIO HEARN.

TO ELLWOOD HENDRICK

KUMAMOTO, July, 1893.

DEAR HENDRICK, — To continue from my last: — It seems to me you might have mistaken my meaning in my half-criticism of the contents of your notebook. I don't wish you should think I find any fault with them *per se*. Indeed you cannot set down too much. Only I think you have been collecting only shadow-and-fire material. You have no sky-blues, — no rose and violet and purple and gold-yellow, — no cadmium, no iridescences. You have that which will give them all value — artistic value. Even if you have only one light for ten darknesses, it will be enough to illume them all.

And now for Ego and Egotisms. In my home
the women are all making baby-clothes, — funny
little Japanese baby-clothes. All the tender Buddhist
divinities, who love little children, have been invoked
except one, — he who cares for them only when
they are dead, and plays little ghostly games with
them in the shadowy world. Letters of congratula-
tion come from all directions, and queer, pretty presents; for the announcement of pregnancy is a subject of great gladness in Japan. And one theme
of rejoicing is that the child will look more like
a Japanese than the children of other foreigners,
because the father is dark. Behind all this, of
course, there is a universe of new sensations, — new
ideas, — revelations of things in Buddhist faith
and in the religion of the more ancient gods, which
are very beautiful and touching. About the world
an atmosphere of delicious, sacred naïveté, — difficult to describe, because resembling nothing in
the Western world. — Some doubts and fears for
me, of course; but they are passing away gradually. I have only some anxiety about *her:* still
she is so strong that I trust the gods will be kind
to us. . . .

This summer I shall not be able to travel far.
First, of course, I can't leave my little woman too
long alone; second, I have proofs to correct; third,
I am economizing. We have now nearly $3500 be-
tween us; and I want to try to provide for her as
soon as I can, — so that once the chances of ill luck
are off my mind, I can make a few long voyages to
other places east of Japan. The Chinese ports are

only a few days distant; and there is Manila, there is the French Orient to see. I hope to be able to do this in a few years more. You will be glad to hear I am very strong, though getting grey, — much stronger than I was at thirty.

Professor Chamberlain and I have a secret project in hand, — a book on Japanese folk-lore. Whether we can carry it out I do not know; but if the dear Professor's health keeps up we shall do something together. . . .

Ever faithfully,
LAFCADIO HEARN.

TO SENTARŌ NISHIDA

KUMAMOTO, August, 1893.

DEAR NISHIDA, — I got your kind letter, — and the money, — and the ballads; for all of which a thousand thanks. I feel you have been very, very kind in all this, even while you were sick: so that my poor thanks signify little of what I really feel towards you. It has given me much pleasure to hear of your being better; but I am disappointed at your being unable to travel, — very much disappointed, as I fear I will not be able to leave Kumamoto again this vacation. . . .

I see that, as regards Kyūshū compared with Tōkyō, you take the moral aspect of the question, while I have possibly been ruled too much by the artistic side. I cannot fully understand the moral side, of course: I can only perceive that the Kyūshū students are allowed to dress as simply as possible, —

are encouraged to be frugal and frank, and rough
in their sports, — and are generally said to be extremely independent and what you call *katai*,
is n't it? But whether they are really any better than
Matsue students, I don't know. Certainly they have
no pleasures to soften their minds. There is nothing
to see, and nowhere to go. And Kyōto is the most
delightful city in the whole of Japan. However, I
suppose it has also temptations for students of a
dangerous sort. . . .

I had no luck with Kumagae Masayoshi, and was
obliged to send the boy back to Oki, after he had
worried and made unhappy everybody in the house.
He was an extraordinarily clever boy, — both at
school, and at everything he undertook, — extremely
skilful with his hands, and almost diabolically intelligent. But he had no affection at all, and seemed
to be naturally very cruel and cunning. He was
strictly honest, and trustworthy, — for all that. But
his character was supremely selfish and malignant.
He made nasty songs about people, and sang them,
and gave us the impression of being a small devil.

I am trying to do some literary work. Your ballad
of Shuntoku-maru proved quite useful to me in the
course of an essay I wrote on the difficulty expe-
rienced by Japanese in understanding a certain class
of English poetry and fiction. It revealed a popular
conception of things, — that ballad, which I took
for an illustration, in showing the total unlikeness of
Western to Oriental society — especially in the
family relation; the absence of flirting and kissing
and woman-worship which we have in the West.

Indeed I think the great difficulty of mutual comprehension between the Japanese and the English
is chiefly due to the predominance of *a feminine idea*
in our language, our art, and our whole conception
of Nature. Therefore the Oriental can see aspects
of Nature to which we remain blind. . . .

LAFCADIO HEARN.

TO OCHIAI

KUMAMOTO, August, 1893.

MY DEAR OCHIAI, — It has given me much
pleasure to hear of your success at the examinations.
I wish you all good fortune for the coming year, and
good health to aid you.

I want also to talk to you about another matter
very much to your interest. Please pay attention to
my words, and think about them. I only wish your
happiness; — therefore remember that what I say
deserves your attention and your thought.

I want to talk to you about Christianity, as a
religion, — not as a *shū*, or sect. I hope you will
understand the distinction I make. A religion is a
moral belief which causes men to live honestly and
to be kind and good to each other. A sect is made
by a *difference* of belief as to what is true religious
teaching. Thus in Buddhism there are many sects
or *shū;* and in Christianity, there are also many
sects or *shū*. But it is not what makes the sects
that has made Buddhism. Neither is it what has
made the Christian sects that has made Christianity.
Truth makes a religion — moral truth; sects are

made by differences of opinion about the meaning of *kyō*, or the meaning of other sacred texts.

So much for this. I want now to tell you, as your friend, that it is *not* Christianity to refuse to bow before the portrait of the Emperor, or before the tombs of the great dead. If anybody tells you that is Christianity, — that person is not a Christian, but a bigot, and an enemy of his country. Whenever we sing the English national anthem, we take off our hats. Whenever we enter into the presence of one of Her Majesty's representatives, we take off our hats. We stand up to drink Her Majesty's health. We are taught that the Queen rules by divine command. It is the same in Germany, in Austria, in Italy, in Spain, — in all except republican countries. So much for that. It is quite right, even for a Christian, to bow before the Emperor's picture; — it is loyal, noble, and good to do it. To refuse to do it is ignorant and vulgar. It is not Christian at all.

Now about the question of tombs and temples. What is the Christian custom? The Christian custom is to pay proper and just respect to the religion which other people believe in. If I go into a Christian church, — although I am not a Christian, — I must take off my hat. If I go into a Mohammedan mosque, I must take off my shoes. Such tokens of respect are purely social, — they are just and right. In Mexico, for example, when a religious procession passes, everybody who is polite takes off his hat. That means, — "Although I am not of your religion, I respect your religion, — your prayers to heaven, and your wish to be good."

Again, when a funeral goes by, we take off our hats. That means, "Although none of *my* friends have died, I sympathize with your sorrow." It is courteous and it is right.

Whatever you believe, my dear Ochiai, you need never refuse to show respect to the tomb of an Emperor, to the memory of an ancestor, or the religion of another people or another country. Christianity teaches no such discourtesy. Only bigots teach it, — and even they teach it for reasons you are not able to understand. I do not want to question your religious belief at all; — that is not my duty. I want only to talk to you about social action in reference to *real* religion. No honest religion ought to cause you any unhappiness, or to cause you to be blamed by others. Religion ought to be of the heart. It is not a question of hats and shoes. Do not refuse to show respect to honest customs and honest reverence for ancestors, by a bow, or a removal of the hat. It will injure your prospects in life to make ill will for yourself by refusing to show respect to the beliefs of your nation and country. Such respect has nothing to do with your faith; — it is a question of social politeness and gentlemanliness. And when you refuse, you will not be judged for your belief, — not at all. You will simply be thought vulgar, — not a true gentleman.

A true gentleman respects *all* religions. That is the real Western idea. Do not deceive yourself.

This from your true friend and teacher,

LAFCADIO HEARN.

TO ELLWOOD HENDRICK

KUMAMOTO, August, 1893.

DEAR HENDRICK, — . . . And now for a letter.
Your last two letters were full of curious things
that call for no answer, but, in connection with fore-
going ones, certainly invite comment. More and
more, reading your lightning-flash glimpses of life,
I think how terribly tragical modern life is becoming.
What is its law? Is it not something like this? —

General: (1) Theoretically, you must be good. (2)
Practically you must be not very good, —
unless you wish to starve or live in the
slime. (3) Reconcile these facts very intel-
ligently, without making any blunders.

Special: (1) If you are not more intelligent than
the average man, you must be both theoretically and practically good, — and resign
yourself to remaining poor and despised all
your blessed life. Don't kick: if you do,
you'll die! (2) In proportion as you are
more intelligent than your fellow man, the
more to your interest to depart from abstract
moral rules; — the more, indeed, you *must*.
It is quite true that vice and crime lead to
ruin. Still, you must perform your part of
both without getting into trouble. If you
don't, you will die. (3) Reconcile intelli-
gently these seeming contradictions.

The contradictions can only be fully recognized

and reconciled through a profound knowledge of
social conditions, not in the abstract only, but in the
most complex operation. This is the theoretical
recognition. But the practical recognition requires
special hereditary gifts, — intuitions, — instincts, —
powers. Mere education in business alone won't do.
That only makes servants. Masters must be *natural*
masters of men. Life is an intellectual battle, but
not a battle to be fought out by mere chess-com-
binations. It is also a battle of characters. The
combinations required for success are of the most
difficult — comprising force, perception, versatility,
resource, — and enough comprehension of morals as
factors in sociology to avoid fatal mistakes. He
who has all this, and strong health, goes to the top.
But he has there to fight for his standing-room.
Besides all other fighting, he has to fight against
himself.

In the Buddhist system, the soul, by self-suppression and struggle against temptation, obtains
Light and effects progress. The Past begins to be
remembered, the Future to be foreseen. But always
in proportion to the progress and the enlightenment,
the temptations increase. For example, one reward
of virtue is beauty and high sexual power (!) The
more indulgence is despised, the greater these gifts.
The Soul reaches heaven. Then is the greatest of
all temptations. Life for thousands of ages, —
supreme beauty and power, — supreme loveliness
of celestial beings offered to feast upon. And here
can be no *sin:* it is only a question of further progress.
Indulgence means retrogression. The wise only pass

to Nirvana. — Now I fancy the battle of life has the same moral.

It is a terrible battle now, though; and is becoming fiercer every year, — and aggravating with a velocity beyond all precedent. (I see there is a falling-off in the birth-rate of the U.S.—which means increased difficulty of living.) And ultimately what must come out of all this? Pain is certainly the only reliable creator, — the only one whose work endures. Extraordinary intelligence and mental dynamical power will be results, of course, — up to a certain time. I do not see much likelihood, however, of *moral* development. Indeed, as Mackintosh long ago said, morals have been at a standstill since the beginning of history: we have made no apparent progress in that. Then comes the question, Are we not developing immorally?

I have begun to think immorality must be, in the eternal order of things, a *moral* force. That is, some kinds of it, — the aggressive kinds: those which the whole world agrees to call immoral. For the physical value and excellence of a life in its relation to other lives is primarily in its capacity to meet all hostile influences by changes correspondingly effected within itself. This is called adaptation to environment. If this be the physical side of the question, what is the moral side? That the perfect character must be able to oppose or to meet all hostile influences by corresponding changes within itself. This necessarily involves a prodigious experience of evil, — a deep, personal, intimate, artistic, loving knowledge of evil. I see a frightful dualism only in prospect. No love or mercy outside of the circle of each active life. As Spencer holds, absolute morality can only begin where the struggle for existence has ceased. This is not new. The appalling prospect is this, — How infinitely worse the world must become before it begins to improve at all ! — And surely education ought to be conducted with a knowledge of these things.

But will the existing state of things continue indefinitely? Surely, it can't! It is too monstrous, and the suffering too infernal! There must be social smashings, earthquakes, chaos-breakings-up, recrystallizations to lighten the burthen. And what will these be?

I cannot send you, because there is no copy here, but I recommend you a book, — Pearson's "National Character," a study. He takes the ground that the future is not to the white races, — not to the Anglo-Saxon. I think this almost certain. I think of the awful cost of life to the white races, — the more awful cost of character. I think of the vast races of creatures — behemoths and megatheriums and ichthyosaurians — which have disappeared from the earth simply because of the cost of their physical structure. But what is the physical cost of even the structure of an ichthyosaurus to the cost of the structure of a master of applied mathematics! It costs one educated European, — receiving, say, a salary of $100 a month, — exactly as much as it costs twenty educated Orientals to live — each with a family of at least three persons, — or in other words 1 European = 120 Orientals. There is an instinctive knowledge, perhaps, of the future, in the instinctive hatred of the Chinese in America. There is an instinctive sense of the same kind in the feeling which prompts the Oriental to exclude Europeans. The latter *over*live the former; the former underlive the latter. But in all this there are complicated physiological questions extraordinary.

Ever affectionately,
LAFCADIO HEARN.

TO ELLWOOD HENDRICK

KUMAMOTO, 1893.

DEAR HENDRICK, — . . . "Thou shalt not love" is of Buddha. "He who hath wife and child hath taken upon him fear. Such a fear is greater than that which the man should feel who, unarmed and alone, entering a cavern, meets a tiger face to face." It is true, the greatest of all fear is the fear for another, — the pity for another, — the frightful imaginings of sorrow or want or despair for another. But there might be perfect conditions. That is true; — but then, — beware the jealousy of the gods. A Rossetti finds his Ideal Maiden, weds, loses, maddens, and passes the rest of his nights in tears of regret, and his days in writing epitaphs. Children may console and they may shame, — and they may die just when they have become charming, — and they may ruin us; and at best, in the world of the West, they separate from us, and we can keep only memories of them. Some woman or some man gets hold of their heart and bites it, and the poison spreads a veil between parents and offspring for all time. Finally, in any conditions, the burthen of life is enormously increased. How much more must a man bear, and how much less can he assert himself, when he has ever to remember that he has ceased to belong to himself. Such is a Buddhist view of the thing. It is not all wrong. . . .

L. H.

TO ELLWOOD HENDRICK

AUGUST, 1893.

DEAR HENDRICK, — What you wrote about the charming person "*flirting* with her maternal instincts" is delicious. I recognized the portrait in a most fantastic past experience, — but of that anon. The thought sent me off into a reverie about — adulteration.

There is a philosophy about adulteration I don't know much about. I have not sufficiently learned the main facts about the practical and utilitarian side of adulteration, — though I read the "petit dictionnaire des falsifications," and other things. However, let's try. Most of what we sell now is adulteration. We used to feel angry, when I was a boy, at the mere thought that leather-composition should be sold for genuine leather, — shoddy for wool, — cotton mixed with silk for pure silk, etc. We wanted our spoons to be genuine silver, and our claret quite trustworthy. Since then we have had to resign ourselves to margarine, glucose, and other products which have become vast staples of commerce. In some cases the genuine has been altogether supplanted by the false; and the false has been universally accepted with full knowledge of its origin. There have been advantages enormous to industry and manufacture, of course; and the public health has not been ruined, according to prediction. On the contrary it has been improving, and the nervous system developing.

Now may not the same thing be going on in our morals? Or rather, must it not go on? We are substituting the sham for the real. It is very sorrowful and excites awful surmises; but nevertheless the sham seems to do very well. The trouble with the original article was its cost and its enormous solidity. It was not malleable. It resisted pressure. It was not adapted at all to the new life of cities and science. For example, absolute veracity interfered with business, — absolute love became a nuisance, took up too much space, and proved too incompressible. Just as we have become too sensitive to bear the rawness of pure colour, so have we become too sensitive to bear the rawness of pure affection. We consider persons vulgar who wear blood-red, grass-green, burning yellows and blues — persons of undeveloped feeling and taste. So also we begin to think people vulgar who are prone to live by any simple emotions. We hold them undeveloped. We don't want the real thing. No: we want shades, tones, — imperceptible tones, ethereal shades. Even in books the raw emotion has become distasteful, savage. Pure passion is penny-theatrical. Isn't all this a suggestion of fact? And isn't the fact founded upon necessary physiological changes? Existing life is too complex for pure emotions. We want mixed tonics, — delicately flavoured and tinted.

All of which means that the primal sources of life are becoming forgotten. Love, honour, idealism, etc., these can no longer be supreme or absorbing motives. They interfere with more serious necessities, and with pleasure. We have first to learn how to live inside the eight-day clock of modern life without getting caught in the cogs. This learned, — and it is no easy lesson, — we may venture to indulge in some falsifications of emotion, some shot-silk colours of love. Such seems to me the drift. The most serious necessity of life is not to take the moral side of it seriously. We must play with it, as with an *hetaira*.

The genuine is only good for the agricultural districts.

And is this progress in a durable sense, or morbidness in evolution? Really I am not sure.

Ever affectionately,

LAFCADIO HEARN.

TO SENTARŌ NISHIDA

KUMAMOTO, August, 1893.

DEAR NISHIDA, — I have missed you very much this long vacation; but, as I anticipated, it could not be helped. Another bundle of proofs has been keeping me at work; and I find the book promises to be bigger than I told you in my last letter. They are using type that will spread it out to probably

750 pp. I send you one specimen proof — just to show you the size of the type.

The man who has been sent for to fill the place in Kyōto, will not, I imagine, be able to keep it. He is a rabid proselytizer; in Kumamoto, years ago, he formed a society of Christians, called the Christian Band (I forget the Japanese name): that is why the Kyūshū folk nearly killed him. Privately — between you and me — I think there will be great changes in the Kyōto middle school next year; *and I think that I shall get there*. But there is nothing sure. I will not go to Tōkyō as long as I can help it.

Many thanks for your splendid letter about the legends of the ballads. I have put it away carefully to use in a future essay. — You say, if you were to tell me about the noble things the common people do, you would never get done. Indeed, *one* strong fact would give me work for two or three months. The publishers wrote me to say they want stories of the life of the common people *to-day*, — showing the influence of moral teaching on *conduct*: that is, Buddhist, Shintō, and ancestor-teaching. I have been trying to get the facts about the poor girl who killed herself in Kyōto because the Emperor "augustly mourned" after the crazy action of Tsuda Sanzo; but I have not yet succeeded. By the way, I think Tsuda Sanzo will be more kindly judged by a future generation. His crime was only "loyalty-run-mad." He was insane for the moment with an insanity which would have been of the highest value in a good cause and time. He saw before him the

living representative of the awful Power which
makes even England tremble; — the power against
which Western Europe has mustered an army of
more than 15,000,000 of men. He saw, or thought
he saw (perhaps he really *did* see: time only can
show) the Enemy of Japan. Then he struck — out
of his heart, without consulting his head. He did
very wrong; — he made a sad mistake; but I think
that man's heart was noble and true, in spite of all
his foolishness. He would have been a hero under
happier circumstances. . . .

I have just heard that the name of one kind of
those horrid beetles in Kumamoto is *gane-bun-bun*,
and the *hyakushō* call them
gane-bu; and people throw
them out of the window, saying, "Come back the
day-before-yesterday."
Then they never come
back at all.

I have made a mis-
take again. The *gane-bun-bun* is not the greatest
plague I was complaining of, — but the *fu-mushi*.
There is yet another small one, I
have not found out the name of.
They make a whole room smell horribly. Some,
however, call both the big *fu-mushi* and the small
creature by the same name — distinguishing them
only as the green and the black. By the way, I will
put a *fu-mushi* in this letter, because they keep
coming on the table so that I think it may be well to
send one to Izumo, in the hopes of inducing the rest
to emigrate.

All send kindest regards to you, and pray you to take good care of your health.

With every best wish, believe me ever,

Most faithfully,

LAFCADIO HEARN.

TO SENTARŌ NISHIDA

KUMAMOTO, 1893.

DEAR NISHIDA, — It gave me much pleasure to get your last kind letter. There was much depth in your statement of the present instability being consequent upon the stagnation of three hundred years. As to the consequence, however, only two theories are possible. The instability means — however it end — disintegration. Is the disintegration to be permanent? — or is there to be a re-integration? That is what nobody can say. There is this, however. Usually a movement of disintegration represents something like this line, — the undulations

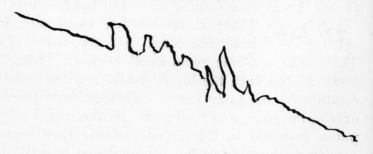

signifying waves of reaction. This movement is downward, and ends in ruin. However, so far,

the undulations in Japan have been, I think, of a
very different character, — something like this: —

which would mean restoration of national solidity
upon a much higher plane than before. The doubt
is whether a much larger movement of disintegration is not going on, — whose undulations are too
large to be seen in a space of thirty years.

You have noticed that under all the surface waves
of a sea, far vaster waves move — too large to be
seen. They are only *felt* — upon *long* voyages.

Mr. Senke has sent me a letter which I think is
the most wonderfully kind and gracious letter anybody ever received in this whole world, and how to
answer it at all, I don't know. He has also promised to send some souvenir; I am not quite sure
what it is: I must *try* to write him a nice letter when
it comes. But Mr. Senke writes as an Emperor
would write — with a grace for which there is no
equivalent in Western speech at all; and whatever
I try to do, it must seem vulgar and common beside the splendid courtesy of Mr. Senke's style.

LAFCADIO HEARN.

TO OCHIAI

KUMAMOTO, November, 1893.

DEAR OCHIAI, — I was very glad indeed to get your letter. It came while the school was closed — all the students having gone upon an excursion to Ōita, so that I did not receive it until to-day (the 11th), when I went to the school to see if there were any letters for me.

Don't think any more about any mistakes you may have made; — everybody will forget them quickly: only think about what makes you happy. But as for Christianity, of course that is a matter for your own conscience; and I would not advise you at all unless you are in doubt. I can only tell you this, — that there are a great many different forms of what is called the Christian religion — a very great many. But what is called the "higher Christianity" is a pure code of ethics; and that code of ethics recognizes that in all civilized religions,— whether of Japan, India, China, Persia, or Arabia, — there is *some* eternal truth; because all religions agree in the deepest teaching about duty and conduct to one's fellow men; and therefore all are entitled to the respect of good men. But in all religions also there are some things which even very good men cannot approve: that is not the fault of the true part of religion, but only the fault of social conditions— that is, the state of society. No state of society is yet perfect; and there can be no perfect religious system until all men become perfectly good. How to become good is, nevertheless, taught by all civilized religions. Nearly everything which is eternally true is taught by one as well as by the other; and therefore a society cannot throw away its religion on account of some errors in it. And each religion represents the experience of a nation with right and wrong — its knowledge of morality. But as society is constructed quite differently in different countries, the religion of one country may not be suited to another. That is why the introduction of a foreign religion may often be opposed by a whole people. For some things which are right in one country may not be right in another. It is not right in China or in Japan to leave one's parents, and to neglect them when they are old. But in England and America and other countries, sons and daughters go away from their parents, and do not think it a duty to support them; — and there is no family relation in those countries such as there is in the Orient. And therefore many things in Western religion are not suited to the kinder and more benevolent life of Japan. Also, some religions teach loyalty, and some do not. For Japan to become strong, and to remain independent, it is very necessary that her people should remain very loyal. Her ancient religion teaches loyalty; — therefore it is still very useful to her. And that is why there is anger shown against some Christians who show no respect to that religion. They are not blamed for not believing in dogmas, but only for what seems to be not loyal.

Perhaps it is better that you should not think a great deal about religious questions until you become old enough to study scientific philosophy —

because these questions ought to be studied in relation to society, in relation to history, in relation to law, in relation to national character, and in relation to science. Therefore they are very difficult. But if you should like to read the highest thoughts of Western people about *modern* religious ideas, I can send you some little books which will show you that the highest religion agrees with the highest science. What I mean by the highest religion is the belief in eternal laws of right conduct. However, as I said, to think about these questions at all requires great study and much knowledge. I think the best advice I can give you in a general way is this, — Do not believe a new thing told you because it is told you; but think for yourself, and follow your own heart when you are in doubt. But remember that the *old* things taught you have been valuable to society — and have been useful for thousands of years — so that we cannot despise them.

I send you a book of old Greek stories to read. Perhaps it will interest you. You will see from the stories how different the old Greek life was from modern life in many things. You must tell me, too, what books you like to read — novels, history, etc.; perhaps I shall be able to send you some from time to time.

Study well, and never be discouraged; — think only how to make yourself a noble and perfect man. And remember the best men in public life have generally been those who made plenty of mistakes and got into plenty of trouble when they were boys.

And never, *never* be afraid — except of your own heart. LAFCADIO HEARN.

TO ELLWOOD HENDRICK

Kumamoto, November, 1893.

Dear Hendrick, — I have been waiting several weeks to tell you of an event which occurred later than I expected. Last night my child was born, — a very strong boy, with large black eyes; he looks more like a Japanese, however, than like a foreign boy. He has my nose, but his mother's features in some other respects, curiously blended with mine. There is no fault with him; and the physicians say, from the form of his little bones, that he promises to become very tall. A cross between European and Japanese is nearly always an improvement when both parents are in good condition; and happily the old military caste to which my wife belongs is a strong one. She is quite well. — Still, I had my anxiety, and the new experience brought to me for a moment, with extraordinary force, the knowledge of how sacred and terrible a thing maternity is, and how even religion cannot hedge it about sufficiently with protection. Then I thought with astonishment of the possibility that men could be cruel to women who bore their children; and the world seemed very dark for a moment. When it was all over, I confess I felt very humble and grateful to the Unknowable Power which had treated us so kindly, — and I said a little prayer of thanks, feeling quite sure it was not foolish to do so.

If ever you become a father, I think the strangest and strongest sensation of your life will be hearing for the first time the thin cry of your own child.

For a moment you have the strange feeling of being double; but there is something more, quite impossible to analyze — perhaps the echo in a man's heart of all the sensations felt by all the fathers and mothers of his race at a similar instant in the past. It is a very tender, but also a very ghostly feeling.

Now the kind dull veil that Nature keeps during most of a life stretched between it and such extraordinary glimpses of the Unknown, is drawn again. The world is the same nearly as before; and I can plan. The little man will wear sandals and dress like a Japanese, and become a good little Buddhist if he lives long enough. He will not have to go to church, and listen to stupid sermons, and be perpetually tormented by absurd conventions. He will have what I never had as a child, — natural physical freedom.

Your two late letters were full of interest and beauty, and you are getting most surprising glimpses of life. I have long had in my mind the idea of a chapter on "Morbid Individuality" — taking issue with Lowell's position in "The Soul of the Far East." Instances like those you have cited are very telling as proofs. The story of the father also is wonderful — absolutely wonderful, — a beautiful surprise of human nature.

What also much impressed me in your letter was the feeling of sadness the spectacle of the great Exposition gave you. But I scarcely think it was due to any reminiscences of boyhood — not simply because of its being certainly a feeling infinitely too complex to have sprung out of a single relative experience in the past (your confession of inability to analyze it, and the statement of others who had the same feeling, would show that), — but also because, if you reflect on other experiences of a totally different kind, you will find they give the same sensation. The first sight of a colossal range of mountains; the awful beauty of a peak like Chimborazo or Fuji; the majesty of an enormous river; the vision of the sea in speaking motion; and, among human spectacles, a military sight, such as the passing-by of a corps of fifty thousand men, will give also a feeling of sadness. You will feel something like it standing in the choir of the Cathedral of Cologne; and you will feel something like it while watching in the night, from some mighty railroad centre, the rushing of glimmering trains, — bearing away human lives to unknown destinies beyond the darkness.

Probably, as Schopenhauer said, the vision of mountains has the effect of producing sadness, because the sense of their antiquity awakens sudden recognition of the shortness of human life. But I do not think it is a mere individual feeling. It is a feeling we share with countless dead who live in us, and who saw the same mountains, — perhaps felt the same way. Besides, there should be a religious ancestral feeling there — since mountains have ever been the abode of gods, and the earliest places of worship and of burial. And I think there is. You do not laugh when you look at mountains — nor when you look at the sea.

What effect does the sudden sight of an extraor-

dinarily beautiful person have upon you? I mean
the very *first*. Is it not an effect of sadness? Analyze
it; and perhaps you will find yourself involuntarily
thinking of *death*.

What has the effect of any great beauty — of art,
or poetry or utterance — no matter what the subject? Is it cheerful? No, it is very sad. But why?
Perhaps partly because of the consciousness of the
exceptional character of that beauty, — therefore
the sudden contrast between the tender dream-
world of art and goodness, and the hideous goblin
realities of the world we know. At all events the
sadness is certainly the ancient sadness, — the
sadness of life, which must, for reasons we cannot
learn, begin and end with an agony.

Now at the Exposition you had all the elements
for what Clifford would call a "cosmic emotion" of
sadness. Vastness, which forced the knowledge of
individual weakness; beauty, compelling the memory
of impermanency; force, suggesting weakness also;
and prodigious effort, — calling for the largest
possible exertion of human sympathy, and love, and
pity, and sorrow. That you should feel like crying
then, does you honour: that is the tribute of all that
is noblest in you to the eternal Religion of Human
Suffering.

Dear H., I have not slept last night: I am going
to rest a little; — good-bye for a short time, with
love to you.

                                    LAFCADIO HEARN.

TO SENTARŌ NISHIDA

KUMAMOTO, November, 1893.

DEAR NISHIDA, — A few days ago there came from Kizuki a little box addressed to me, — from Mr. Senke; and opening it, I found therein the robe of a *Kokuzō* — all black silk with the sacred *mon* of the temple worked into the silk. Accompanying the robe were two poems, very beautifully written upon vari-coloured paper. The robe was very curious in itself, and of course most precious as a souvenir. I hesitated to write at once; for I could not answer Mr. Senke's magnificent letter in a worthy way at all. It was a very long letter, written on fine paper and in large handsome characters. I have now tried to reply, but my answer reads very shabbily compared with Mr. Senke's gracious style.

I found I had forgotten, in writing you the other day, to speak about Kompira, as you asked me. What a pity I had not known about the real temple of Kompira, which I did not see at all. Yes, I did find the place interesting and very beautiful. But it was interesting because of the quaint shops and streets and customs; and it was beautiful *because the day happened to be very beautiful.* The vast blue light coloured everything, — walls, timbers, awnings, draperies, dresses of pilgrims; and the cherry-trees were one blaze of snowy blossoms; and the horizon was clear as crystal. In the distance towered San-uki-Fuji, — a cone of amethyst in the light. I wished I could teach in some school at Kompira *uchi-machi,* and stay there always.

I like little towns. To live at Tadotsu, or at Hishi-ura in Oki, or at Yunotsu in Iwami, or at Daikon-shimain Naka-umi, would fill my soul with joy. I cannot like the new Japan. I dislike the officials, the imitation of foreign ways, the airs, the conceits, the contempt for Tempō, etc. Now to my poor mind, all that was good and noble and true was Old Japan: I wish I could fly out of Meiji forever, back against the stream of Time, into Tempō, or into the age of the Mikado Yūriaku, — fourteen hundred years ago. The life of the old fans, the old *byōbu*, the tiny villages — that is the *real* Japan I love. Somehow or other, Kumamoto doesn't seem to me Japan at all. I hate it.

Ever with best regards,

LAFCADIO HEARN.

TO SENTARŌ NISHIDA

KUMAMOTO, November, 1893.

DEAR NISHIDA, — Both of your letters were as interesting as they were kind. They revealed to me much more than I had been able to learn from the newspapers. I am more than sorry for that terrible destruction and suffering in the *Ken;* but when I think of Okayama, again, I cannot help thinking that the good fortune, which seems especially to belong to Matsue, has not yet deserted her. And the Governor seems to be a first-class man. I like that story of his action with the rice-dealers. But really, the people are very patient. In some Western countries, notably in parts of America, it would have been more than dangerous for men to have acted so selfishly; and they would be in any case afterwards "boycotted," and obliged perhaps to leave the city. It is a great pity they were not made to suffer for such atrocious meanness. When I think of the chrysanthemums in your garden, and read your extraordinary story about catching fish in it, I can realize what a tremendous loss there must have been through all the rice-country. Certainly Matsue is fortunate to have escaped as she did.

Almost at the same time there came to me news from the Gulf of Mexico. Perhaps you will remember that I wrote a novel about some islands there. I used to pass my summers in those islands. They were about sixty miles from the city of New Orleans. Well, on October 4th, a storm burst over that coast, killing more than 2000 people. The island of Grand Isle was covered by the sea in the night; and everything — houses, trees, and people — carried away. Hundreds I used to know are dead. It is a year of storms and calamities, surely, in all parts of the world.

I will write a better letter later: I am writing now to answer your questions about those sentences:—

(i) "Choppy"—"chopped" or "chapped" by cold: "chapped hands"— hands of which the skin is *cracked* by frost. "His hands are all chapped"— that is, all *roughened* by frost. "Choppy" is not so often used as "chapped:" it is a poetical use of the word.

(ii) "He had torn the cataracts from the hills." You must remember here Winter is personified as a

monstrous giant. "Cataracts" is used in the sense
of "waterfalls." The waterfalls are frozen into solid
masses of ice. Winter, the giant, breaks them off,
and hangs them round his waist.

(iii) "And they clanked at his girdle like
manacles (from Latin *manus*, "hand") (you spelled
the word wrong: it is "manacles"). "Manacles," ⌒ ⌒ iron fetters for the hands; — handcuffs. ⊖ ⊖ They are made in pairs, fastened
together by a chain, and closed by a key. They
clank when they strike together, — (i. e.) make a
ringing metallic noise — because they are of fine
steel usually. The sound made by iron is "clank" —
"*to* clank" (verb), "*a* clank" (noun). Why does
Shelley use such a simile? Because Winter is
like a jailer, like the keeper of a prison. He
fastens up, or imprisons, the rivers, lakes, and
ponds with ice. So he is described as a keeper of
prisoners, — with manacles or handcuffs hanging
to his waist, ready for use. Ice striking against ice
makes a ringing noise, very much like iron — sometimes. The comparison is very strong.

And why does he put his chapped finger to his lip?
To put the first finger on the lips is a sign for "Be
silent!" "Do not speak!" In winter the world
becomes silent. The birds are gone; the insects are
dead.

P. S.

DEAR NISHIDA, — I waited over last night to hunt
up the quotation for you; and during the night my
child was born. A very strong boy, — dark eyes and
hair; he has some of my features, some of Setsu's.

Setsu is well enough to send kind words, and to tell you what I was intending to tell you myself, — how delighted we have all been to hear of your good health this year.

I intended to write more, but I am too tired for the moment, — as I have not been in bed for more than 24 hours. So for a little, good-bye, — best regards to you and yours always from

LAFCADIO HEARN.

TO SENTARŌ NISHIDA

KUMAMOTO, November, 1893.

DEAR NISHIDA, — Everybody is well up to date: the little boy looks prettier every day, and gives very little trouble. He scarcely cries at all. Many people come to look at him, and express surprise that he looks so much like a Japanese. But he is going to have a nose something like mine, certainly, when he grows up.

Setsu advises me to write you about another matter. I wanted, and tried several times since coming to Kumamoto, to have Setsu registered as my lawfully married wife, but the answer was always the same — that it was a difficult matter, and would have to be arranged in Tōkyō, if at all. The day before yesterday, I made another attempt when registering the birth of the boy. The registry people said that as the parties came from Matsue, Izumo, they would only make the statement of the marriage by Matsue authority, — and that I had better write to Matsue. But at the same time, they said words

to this effect: "The law is difficult for you. If you
wish the boy to remain a Japanese citizen, you must
register him in the mother's name only. If you
register him in the father's name, he becomes a
foreigner."

Of course we all want the child to be a Japanese
citizen, as he will be the heir and stay of the old folks
after I am dead — whether he goes abroad for a few
years' study or no. Prudence seems to dictate the
latter course. Yet the whole thing is a puzzle. By
becoming myself a Japanese citizen, everything
would be settled. Even that, however, is more
difficult than it at first seemed. Again, I believe
that I could become a Japanese citizen by making
direct application to the Government; — but at the
present time the result might not be for the best.
An Englishman in Yokohama, who became a Japanese citizen, had his salary immediately reduced to
a very small figure, with the observation: "Having
become a Japanese citizen, you must now be content
to live like one." I don't quite see the morality of
the reduction; for services should be paid according
to the market-value at least; — but there is no doubt
it would be made. As for America, and my relatives
in England, I am married: that has been duly
announced. Perhaps I had better wait a few years,
and then become a citizen. Being a Japanese citizen
would, of course, make no difference whatever as to
my relations in any civilized countries abroad. It
would only make some difference in an uncivilized
country, — such as revolutionary South America,
where English or French or American protection is

a good thing to have. But the long and the short of the matter is that I am anxious only about Setsu's and the boy's interests; my own being concerned only at that point where their injury would be Setsu's injury. I suppose I must trust to fate and the gods. If you can suggest anything good to do, however, I will be very grateful.

Every day, it strikes me more and more how little I shall ever know of the Japanese. I have been working hard at a new book, which is now half-finished, and consists of philosophical sketches chiefly: It will be a very different book from the "Glimpses," and will show you how much the Japanese world has changed for me. I imagine that sympathy and friendship are almost impossible for any foreigner to obtain, — because of the amazing difference in the psychology of the two races. We only guess at each other without understanding; and it is only a very keen guesser, indeed, of large experience, who can ever guess correctly. I have met no one else like you. Nothing is so curious as to sit down and talk for hours with a Japanese of the ordinary Tōkyō modernized class. You understand all he says, and he understands all you say, — but neither understands more than the words. The ideas behind the words are so different, that the more we talk the less we know each other. In the case of the students, I found myself obliged to invent a new method of teaching. I now teach my higher classes psychologically. I give them lectures and dictations on various difficulties of the pre-position, for example, starting out with the announcement that they must not allow themselves to think of the Japanese preposition at all. . . .

I have followed this plan with great success in teaching the articles, the value of English idioms, etc., and the comparative force of verbs. But it shows how hopeless for a stranger to see deeply into the Japanese mind. I am taking almost exactly the opposite ground to that of Lowell.

Faithfully ever,

LAFCADIO HEARN.

TO OCHIAI

KUMAMOTO, January, 1894.

DEAR OCHIAI, — Many thanks for your kind letter, with its kind wishes, — and many happy New Years to you.

I have been very glad to hear of your success at school, and all the news about your reading. I think Mr. Nishida's plan is very wise and good. It is true that the lives of such men as Clive and Hastings — and above all Napoleon — are full of interest and romance, because they show the wonderful things that can be achieved by force of character united with great intellect, — Clive being the best man, morally, of the three. But, on the other hand, it is sadly true that the genius and the courage of those three wonderful men were not employed in the noblest way, but most often in a bad cause. Strong characters are very attractive, because those who read about them take pleasure in imagining what they would do if they had the same power and opportunity. But strong characters are only really admirable when they are employed in a good, just, noble cause. And of such characters, the number in Western history is few. Pericles, Miltiades, Epaminondas, were nobler than Alexander; yet people like to read about Alexander, who was not a good man. Marcus Aurelius was nobler than Cæsar; but people like to read more about Cæsar, because he was a great conqueror. And so on through all Western history. There is splendour and honour in brave fighting for what is right; but I do not think we ought to allow ourselves to praise brave fighting for what is wrong. Bravery is noble only when the object is noble. As a quality, it is not peculiar to man at all; — a wild bull is braver than any general. It is very noble to sacrifice one's life for a good cause — for love of parents, country, duty; but we ought not to admire the throwing away of life for an unjust cause. The real rule by which to measure what is admirable and what is despicable is the rule of Duty.

That is why I admire very, very much, all that was noble in the old Japanese life, — its moral code, its household religion, and its unselfishness. Everything is now passing away. By the time you are as old as I now am, all Japan will have been changed; and I think you will remember with regret the kindness and the simplicity of heart and the pleasant manners of the Old Japan, that used to be all about you. The New Japan will be richer and stronger and in many things wiser; but it will neither be so happy nor so kindly as the old.

Well, I trust you will have all possible success, — not only in your school-life, but in all your life to come. I have hopes you will do great and good things, and that I will hear of them.

Ever affectionately yours,

LAFCADIO HEARN.

TO MASANOBU ŌTANI

KUMAMOTO, March, 1894.

MY DEAR ŌTANI, — To study philology, with the idea of becoming a philologist, scarcely seems to me a hopeful undertaking for you. Philology means a great deal, including the comparative study of languages; and it requires a very special natural gift in acquiring languages, to be of any very practical value to you. It would also require, I think, years of study in foreign universities. I am not quite sure what you mean by philology, and what your purpose in following that course would be. You might, of course, do as many do — take the literary and philological course at the university. But the question, to my mind, seems to be this: "What would be the practical value of such studies afterwards?" Do you wish to become a Professor of Philology? Do you wish to give your life to the scientific study of languages? If you do, are you quite sure you have the particular kind of talent required (for, remember, everybody cannot become a philologist any more than everybody can become a mathematician)?

The truth is, I do not know enough about your

A GROUP OF GRADUATES OF THE MIDDLE SCHOOL

1 Mr. Hearn   2 Mr. Nishida   3 The old teacher of Chinese Classics

circumstances and intentions and abilities to advise you well. I can only tell you *in a general way* what I think.

I think you ought not to study what would not be of *practical* use to you in after-life. I am always glad to hear of a student studying engineering, architecture, medicine (if he has the particular moral character which medicine requires), or any branch of applied science. I do not like to see all the fine boys turning to the study of law, instead of to the study of science or technology. Of course much depends upon the mathematical faculty. If you have that faculty, I would strongly advise you to direct all your studies toward a scientific profession — something really practical, — engineering, architecture, electricity, chemistry, etc. If you should ask which, I could not tell you, because I do not know your own highest capacities in such directions. I would only say, — "Whatever you are most sure of loving as a practical profession."

Japan wants no more lawyers now; and I think the professions of literature and of teaching give small promise. What Japan needs are scientific men; and she will need more and more of them every year. To-day you are fortunate; but nothing in this world is sure. Suppose you were obliged suddenly to depend entirely on your own unassisted power to make money, — would it not then be necessary to do something practical? Certainly it would. And *according to the rarity of your abilities* would be your remuneration, — your money-making power. Even

the Queen of England obliged her children to learn
professions.

Now scientific men are still comparatively rare
in Japan. The science-classes in the colleges are
small. Many students begin the study, — but they
find it hard for them, and give it up. Nevertheless,
it is *just because it is hard* that it is so important
and of such high value to the person who masters
it. If you were my son, or brother, I would say to
you, "Study science, — applied science; study for
a practical profession." As for languages and other
subjects, you can study them whenever you please.
The practical knowledge is the only important
knowledge now, — and your whole life will depend
upon your present studies.

You asked whether philology was difficult.
Science *is* difficult, — really difficult; but everything worth having in this world is difficult to get,
exactly in proportion to its value. The only question, I think, should be, "What study will be most
useful to me all through life?" But not whether it
is difficult. What is important to know is always
difficult to learn. Philology is difficult; practical
science is difficult; — both are very difficult. But
philology would never be of much use to you, unless
you have a natural genius for language-study. And
science would be of immense value to you, whether
you have any genius or not. You will need, however,
as I said before, mathematical study to fit you for
that. And I would also remind you of this: —

Hundreds of students leave the university without
any real profession, and without any practical

ability to make themselves useful. All cannot become teachers, or lawyers, or clerks. They become *soshi*, or they become officials, or they do nothing of any consequence. Their whole education has been of no real use to them, because it has not been *practical*. Men can succeed in life only by their ability to *do* something, and three fourths of the university students can *do* nothing. Their education has been only *ornamental*.

Faithfully yours,

LAFCADIO HEARN.

TO SENTARŌ NISHIDA

KUMAMOTO, April, 1894.

DEAR NISHIDA, — You are becoming a very *indifferent* correspondent, if one should judge by scarcity of letters, — so I suppose I am not to hear from you again until something extraordinary happens. So runs the world away from a man. But never shall I be able to understand the people of "the most Eastern East."

Well, I have been to Kompira, — in a *fune-fune* to Tadotsu, thence by rail to the wonderful, quaint old town. We took Kaji along. He never cries now, and behaved so well that on all the railroads and steamers people fell in love with him and played with him. He made the acquaintance of many politicians, of surveyors, of some silk merchants, of two captains, of a naval surgeon, of many gentle women, of the *miko* at Kompira, and — I am sorry to say — of some geisha. However, that was because he was very young, and did not know. I hope when he gets bigger he will be more reserved with his smiles. One thing showed his good taste: he was especially attracted by the two young *miko*, who were really very sweet and pretty, — the prettiest I ever saw, and he made one of them smile even during her dance. I have sent a better picture of him.

I should much rather be in a country-school again. However, so far as I can see, the same trouble is going to find its way into all the public schools, and stay there, until some means be devised of removing schools altogether from the domain of politics by something like the American system. The American system is imperfect; but it has at least this merit, — that the leading citizens and merchants of a place can act as boards of directors, and that the temporary officials proper cannot meddle directly in school matters at all. Thus the school interests are taken care of by those most directly concerned in their welfare, and not by strangers. Each community supports its own school by a general tax. Of course in so corrupt a country as America the pecuniary side of the question is attended with some ugly stealing; but that is done before the money is placed in the hands of the directors, and is done at a serious risk. In some American States, too, the text-books are meddled with by politicians. But I think it might be quite possible in Japan to adopt a system of school-support, which, while removing the schools from the power of the Kenchō to meddle with them, would also establish something like permanency in their management and method. At present everything is so unpermanent and unsteady that one feels the tendency is to dissolution rather than integration.

Ever very truly yours,
LAFCADIO HEARN.

P. S. I forgot your question about the summer vacation. I have not yet been able to decide exactly what to do, but it is at least certain that I go to Tōkyō, and that I hope to meet you there. Should anything prevent you from going, I may try to meet you elsewhere. I should like to see you, and hear some more of the same wonderful things you used to tell me, — which you will read in that much-delayed book. By the way, I did not tell you that the publishers concluded to delay it again, on account of what they call the trade-season. I suppose they are right, but it is very provoking. Including the index the book makes about 700 pages, in two volumes. Meantime I have half written a philosophical book about Japanese life.

Ever faithfully,
LAFCADIO HEARN.

TO ELLWOOD HENDRICK

KUMAMOTO, Spring, 1894.

DEAR HENDRICK, — . . . Are you reading the *Atlantic* at all? There is a wonderful story by Mrs. Deland, "Philip and his Wife." Philip's wife makes me think always of E. B.

The problem of merely being able to live. What a plague it is! And the pain of life isn't hunger, isn't want, isn't cold, isn't sickness, isn't physical misery of any kind: it is simply moral pain caused by the damnable meanness of those who try to injure others for their own personal benefit or interest. That is really all the pain of the struggle of life.

Ever faithfully,

LAFCADIO HEARN.

TO ELLWOOD HENDRICK

KUMAMOTO, May, 1894.

DEAR HENDRICK, — . . . I think there was one mistake in the story of Œdipus and the Sphinx. It was the sweeping statement about the Sphinx's alternative. It isn't true that she devoured every one who couldn't answer her riddles. Everybody meets the Sphinx in life; — so I can speak from authority. She doesn't kill people like me, — she only bites and scratches them; and I've got the marks of her teeth in a number of places on my soul. She meets me every few years and asks the same tiresome question, — and I have latterly contented myself with simply telling her, "I don't know."

It now seems to me that I was partly wrong in a former letter to you about business morality: I took much too narrow a view of the case, perhaps. The comparison between the Western and Oriental brain — which everybody is forced to make after a few years' sojourn here — now appears to me

appalling in its results. The Western business man
is really a very terrible and wonderful person. He
is the outcome, perhaps, of a mediæval wish. For
types are created by men's wishes — just as men
themselves are created. The greatest teaching of
science is that no Body made us, — but we made
ourselves under the smart stimulus of pain. Well,
as I was saying, the business man is an answer to a
wish. (You know about the frogs who asked Jupiter
for a King.) In the age of robber-barons, racks,
swordmills, and *droit de cuissage*, — men prayed
Jupiter for Law, Order, System. Jupiter (in the
shape of a very, very earnest desire) produced the
Business man. He represents insatiate thirst of
dominion, supreme intellectual aggressive capacity,
faultless practical perceptivity, and the art of hand-
ling men exactly like pawns. But he represents also
Order, System, Law. He is Organization, and is
King of the Earth. The pawns cry out, "We are
not pawns." But he always politely answers, "I
am sorry to disagree with you, but I find it expedient
for our mutual interest to consider you pawns; besides, I have no time to argue the matter. If you
think you are not pawns, you must show the faculty
of Organization."

The tyranny of the future must be that of Organization: the monopoly, the trust, the combination,
the associated company — representing supremely
perfect mathematical unification of Law, Order,
and System. Much more powerful than the robber-
baron, or Charlemagne, or Barbarossa, these are
infinitely less human, — having no souls, etc.

(What would be the use of souls! — souls only waste time.) Business is exact and dangerous and power- ful like a colossal dynamo: it is the extreme of every- thing men used to pray for, — and it is *not* what they did *not* pray for. Perhaps they would like the robber-baron better.

We little petty outsiders — the gnats hovering about life — feel the world is changing too quickly: all becoming methodical as an abacus. There is n't any more room for us. Competition is of no use. Law, Order, and System fill the places without consulting us, — the editorial desks, the clerkships, the Government posts, the publishers' offices, the pulpits, the professorships, the sinecures as well as the tough jobs. Where a worker is unnecessary, a pawn is preferred. (Oh, for a lodge in some vast wilderness! — provided with a good table and a regular supply of reading from Murray's circulating library!) One thing is dead sure: in another genera- tion there can be no living by dreaming and scheming of art: only those having wealth can indulge in the luxury of writing books for their own pleasure. . . .

Faithfully ever,

LAFCADIO HEARN.

TO ELLWOOD HENDRICK

KUMAMOTO, May, 1894.

DEAR HENDRICK, — So far from your letters not being interesting, they are always full of inter- est — first, simply because they are *your* letters; secondly, because they tell the evolution of you —

showing how, after all, we are made by the eternal
forces. That you become a business man, in every
sense of the word, is inevitable. It would be wrong
if you did not. It would be wrong not to love your
profession. The evil of becoming a business man
exists only for small men — dries small men up.
Surely you are not small! There is nothing to
regret — except perhaps a temporary darkness
which may yield to enormous light later on. Some
would say to you, "Always keep one little place in
your heart from hardening." I would say nothing
of the kind now: I think you are too large to be
talked to in that way.

Suppose I try to illustrate by reference to the
scope of human thinking in general. Ethical
theology might be represented then as an inverted
pyramid, — thus   ▽ ; hard, skeptical science
by a larger figure, pressing it
down; the highest philosophy by a
circle, — something like this figure.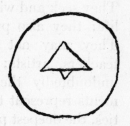
The largest thought accepts all,
surrounds all, absorbs all, — like
light itself. The ugly and the
beautiful, the ignorant and the
wise, the virtuous and the vile, — all come within
its recognition; nature and sins as well as societies
and clubs, — prisons and churches, brothels and
houses. The very duties of observation forced upon
you compel two things: the study of all moral and
material details; the study of all combinations and
wholes. And the larger the grasp of the whole
the larger must become your power and value; for

you will have to see eternal laws working down out of the unknown and thereafter ramifying and inter-ramifying into innumerable actions, reactions, dis-integrations, and crystallizations. The horrible thing about business, men say, is that it considers men as pawns. But if your sight becomes large enough, — if your thought widens enough, — you *must* look upon men as pawns. To be a brother to all you cannot. To be a friend to many you cannot. You become the agent — not of the Commercial Union Assurance Co. only, — but the special agent of infinite laws; and if you act efficiently in that capacity, you cannot do very wrong. The Cosmos will be responsible for you.

The business man to-day is the king of the earth; merchants and bankers are the rulers, and will for all time be, while industrialism continues necessary. They seek and win power, and all the good things of life; they also prevent others from getting either. They may not be poets, philosophers, didactic teachers, artists; but their mental organization is undoubtedly the highest, — because its achieve-ments represent the mastery of the highest difficul-ties, the deepest problems, the most intricate riddles. Certainly this higher organization is obtained at a heavy cost in the majority of cases. The emotions dry up in the evolution of it, and the moral sense weakens. But because this must happen in the majority of cases when any *new* faculty is being developed, it is far from happening in all. The man whose vision is vast enough can scarcely do more evil than a god. He cannot injure his world voluntarily without suffering from his own action. He must study his world as a naturalist his ant-hill. And even as a God he must feel the ultimate evil and good is not of him; but is being forever viewlessly woven in Shadow by the Fates of the Infinite, — whose distaff twists the thread of his own life, and whose will guides his own courses.

The great desire would be for the combination of emotion with knowledge, of philosophy with mathematics, of Plato with a Napoleon, or Spinoza with a Gould. This will come. Now it is very rare. . . .

You might reply, "In the present order of things the combination would ruin the working-power of the man. The Gould could not act the Gould if combined with the Spinoza, — nor could the Napoleon *se foule de la vie d'un million d'hommes* if crossed with a Plato."

I would answer, "Not in the elder generation, but why not to-day? If the moral laws that in a Spinoza would have checked a Gould, or in a Plato checked a Napoleon, were essentially limited in other years, are they so to-day? If the two philosophers had had larger horizons of thinking, would they have recognized a tether, — or would they not rather have viewed themselves as mere force-atoms in an infinite electric stream? Are there not now recognitions of laws transcending all human ethics? — laws of which Goethe threw out such weird suggestions? —and must not business, from its very nature, drift into the knowledge of these laws?"

To-day, it is true, the highest possible type of

business man would have to follow the small policy of the majority. But certainly he can be like one of those compound double-engines, — whereof the best half is kept idle in reserve, — always oiled and speckless and ready for rare emergencies or opportunities. If something within you regrets something else that is passing away, that need not be any alarming sign. The mere fact that the regret exists, indicates higher possibilities. Don't you remember Emerson's extraordinary lines, —

> "Though thou love her as thyself—
> As a self of purer clay, —
> Though her parting dim the day
> Stealing grace from all alive, —
> *Heartily know,*
> *When half-gods go*
> *The Gods arrive!*"

The dear little psyche is going? Well, let her go! Regret her a little — that is sweet and good. Feel lonesome for her awhile. Wait. Then make yourself a new soul, large enough to wrap round the whole world, like the Æther.

Faithfully ever,

LAFCADIO HEARN.

TO PAGE M. BAKER

KUMAMOTO, 1894.

DEAR PAGE, — Though I never hear from you directly, the *T.-D.* brings me occasionally very emphatic proof that I am not forgotten, and am perhaps forgiven. So I venture a line or two, hoping you will not show the letter to anybody.

I told you some years ago I was married; but I did not tell you I had a son, — who is, of course, dearer than my own life to me. Curiously, he is neither like his mother nor like me: he takes after some English ancestor, — for he is grey-eyed, fair-haired (curly chestnut), and wonderfully strong: he is going, if he lives, to be a remarkably powerful man; and, I hope, a more sensible man than his foolish dad.

Well, now two perils menace me. First, the immense reaction of Japan, — reasserting her individuality against all foreign influence, which has resulted in the discharge of most of the high-paid foreign employees; secondly, the war with China. The Japanese — essentially a fighting race, as Bantams are — will probably win the battles every time; but if China be in dead, bitter earnest, *she* will win the war. (Probably her chances will be snatched from her by foreign intervention.) But whatever be the end of this enormous complication, Japan is going to empty her treasury. The chances for Government employees are dwindling: my contract runs only till March, and the chances are 0.

Of course, I can peg along somehow, — getting odd jobs from newspapers, etc., doing a little teaching of English, French, or Spanish. I can't help thinking I would do better to go abroad—especially at a time when every American 100 cents is worth nearly 200 Japanese cents.

Here goes. Could you get me anything to do if

I started in the spring for America? I mean something good enough to save money at. I am past all nonsense now, and for myself only would need very little. But it would not be for myself that I should go. I should want to be sure of being able to send money to Japan, by confining my own wants to good living and an occasional book or two. If you could get me something anywhere south of Mason and Dixon's line, I should try to be practically grateful in some way. I am not in the least desirous of seeing Boston or New York or Philadelphia — or being obliged to exist by machinery. I would rather infinitely be in Memphis or Charleston or Mobile or — glorious Florida.

Or can you get me anything educational in Spanish-America? I could scarcely take my people to the U.S., — but to South America I might try later on. I am now 44, and all grey as a badger. Unless I can make enough to educate my boy well, I don't know what I am worth, — but I feel that I shall have precious little time to do it in. Add 20 to 44, — and how much is left of a man?

Perhaps you will think — if I am worth thinking about at all: "Well, why were you such a d—d fool as to go and have a son?" Ask the gods! Really *I* don't know.

Ever faithfully — or, as the Japanese would say, *un*faithfully, — yours,

LAFCADIO HEARN.

TO ELLWOOD HENDRICK

KUMAMOTO, June, 1894.

DEAR HENDRICK,— . . . We were chatting last time about the morality of business. Now let me tell you how the question strikes an intelligent Japanese student.

"Sir, what was your opinion when you first came to our country about the old-fashioned Japanese? Please be frank with me."

"You mean the old men, who still preserve the old customs and courtesy, — men like Mr. Akizuki, the Chinese teacher?"

"Yes."

"I think they were much better men than the Japanese of to-day. They seemed to me like the ideals of their own gods realized. They seemed to me all that was good and noble."

"And do you still think as well of them?"

"I think better of them, if anything. The more I see the Japanese of the new generation, the more I admire the men of the old."

"But you must have, as a foreigner, also observed their defects."

"What defects?"

"Such weaknesses or faults as foreigners would observe."

"No. According as a man is more or less perfectly adapted to the society to which he belongs, so is he to be judged as a citizen and as a man. To judge a man by the standards of a society totally different to his own would not be just."

"That is true."

"Well, judged by that standard, the old-fashioned Japanese were perfect men. They represented fully all the virtues of their society. And that society was morally better than ours."

"In what respect?"

"In kindness, in benevolence, in generosity, in courtesy, in heroism, in self-sacrifice, in simple faith, in loyalty, in self-control, — in the capacity to be contented with a little, — in filial piety."

"But would those qualities you admire in the old Japanese suffice for success in Western life — practical success?"

"Why, no."

"The qualities required for practical success in a Western country are just those qualities which the old Japanese did not possess, are they not?"

"I am sorry to say they are."

"And the old Japanese society cultivated those qualities of unselfishness and courtesy and benevolence which you admire at the sacrifice of the individual. But Western society cultivates the individual by a competition in mere powers — intellectual power, power of calculating and of acting?"

"Yes."

"But in order that Japan may be able to keep her place among nations, she *must* adopt the industrial and financial methods of the West. Her future depends upon industry and commerce; and these cannot be developed if we continue to follow our ancient morals and manners."

"Why?"

"Not to be able to compete with the West means ruin; yet in order to compete with the West, we must follow the methods of the West, — and these are contrary to the old morality."

"Perhaps — "

"I do not think there is any 'perhaps.' To do any business on a large scale, we must not be checked by the idea that we should never take any advantage if another be injured by it. Those who are checked by emotional feeling, where no check is placed upon competition, must fail. The law of what you call the struggle for existence is that the strong and clever succeed, and the weak and foolish fail. But the old morality condemned such competition."

"That is true."

"Then, sir, no matter how good the old morality may seem to be, we can neither make any great progress in industry or commerce or finance, nor even preserve our national independence, by following it. We must forsake our past, and substitute law for morality."

"But it is not a good substitute."

"It seems to me that it has proved a good substitute in Western countries — England especially — if we are to judge by material progress. We will have to learn to be moral by reason, not by emotion. Knowledge of law, and the reasons for obeying law, must teach a rational morality of some sort at last."

Pretty good reasoning for a Japanese boy, was n't it? He goes to the university next month, — a splendid fellow.   Later the Government is to send him abroad.

Ever faithfully,
LAFCADIO HEARN.

TO SENTARŌ NISHIDA

KUMAMOTO, August, 1894.

DEAR NISHIDA, — Many, many best thanks for the excellent photograph of yourself, and your kindest letter. The photograph brought so vividly before me again the kind eyes that saw so much for me, and the kind lips that told me so many wise, good things, and advised me and helped me so much, — that I could not but feel more sorry than ever at having missed you.

Mr. Senke has sent me the most beautiful letter, which I hope to answer by this same mail. What a divine thing the old Japanese courtesy was ! and how like *Kami sama* the dear old men who remember it, and preserve it. Of course Mr. Senke is a young man, but *his* courtesy is the old courtesy. The high schools seem to me to be ruining Japanese manners, and therefore morals — because morals are manners to a certain extent. Those who lose the old ways never replace them; they cannot learn foreign courtesy, which is largely a matter of tone, — tone of voice, address, touch of minds, and benevolence in small things, which is our politeness. So they remain without any manners at all, and their hearts get hardened in some queer way. They cease to be lovable, and often become unbearable. I hope the great reaction will bring back, among other things, some of the knightly old ways.

I send a reprint of my last Japanese story. Hope my book will reach you soon, and will not displease you. Of course, you will find in it many mistakes — as any book written by a foreigner must be rich in errors. But the general effect of the book will not be bad, I think. I am now trying to write a sketch about Yuko Hatakeyama, the girl who killed herself at Kyōto in May, 1891, for loyalty's sake. The fact is full of wonderful meaning — as indicating a national sentiment.

Kazuo is crawling about, opening drawers, and causing much trouble. His eyes have again changed colour, — from blue to brown, like my own; but his hair remains chestnut. His upper teeth are well out, and everybody wonders how strong he is. He has one Japanese virtue: he does not cry, and keeps his self-control even when hurt. I hope he will keep all these traits. My whole anxiety is now about him: I must send him, or, if possible, take him abroad — for a scientific education, if he prove to have a good head. That will be expensive. But I hope to do it. I do not think a father should leave his son alone in a foreign school, if it can be helped: he ought to be always near him, until manhood. And Setsu would feel at home soon in France or in Italy, — at least at home enough to bear the life until Kazuo could get through a course or two.

The foreign community sorrows about the war, — naturally. Business is paralyzed. Every one feels the Japanese will win the fights. But who will win the war? That might be a question of money. Japan is daring to do what the richest country in Europe fears to do — because it costs so much to fight China. And some of the Izumo boys are out there in the rice-fields of Chosön. I trust they will pass safely through all perils. Please send me any news of them you can.

LAFCADIO HEARN.

TO ELLWOOD HENDRICK

MATSUE, September, 1894.

DEAR HENDRICK, — If ever I must go to America, I hope I can keep out of New York. The great nightmare of it always dwells with me, — moos at me in the night, especially in the time of earthquakes. Of London I should be much less afraid. But in such great cities I do not think a literary man can write any literature. Certainly not if he has to stay in the heart of the clockwork. Society withers him up — unless he have been born into the manner of it; and the complexities of the vast life about him he never could learn. Fancy a good romance about Wall Street, — so written that the public could understand it! There is, of course, a tremendous romance there; but only a financier can really know the machinery, and his knowledge is technical. But what can the mere littérateur do, walled up to heaven in a world of mathematical mystery and machinery! Your own city of Albany is a paradise compared to the metropolis: you are really very fortunate — very, very happy to be able to live at home.

Of course, there is a philosophy of good manners — too much of it, eh? There is Emerson, all suggestive, — but touching eternal truths in his essays on conduct, behaviour, etc.; and there is Spencer, who traces back the history of nearly all good manners to the earliest period of savagery and perpetual war. (You know about the origin of the bow, of our forms of address, and of the forms of prayer.) Politeness survives longest and develops most elaborately under militant conditions, and diminishes in exact proportion as militancy decreases. That there should be less politeness in America than in other countries, and less in the Northern States than in the Southern, might be expected. This was true as to both conditions: it is now true probably only as to the first. With the growth of industrialism, — the sense of equal chances, at least of equal rights before the law, — the abolition of class distinctions, — fine manners vanish more or less. Nevertheless I fancy that under all the American roughness and lack of delicacy, or of that politeness which means "benevolence in small things," there is growing up a vast, deep feeling of human brotherhood, — of genuine kindliness, which may show itself later under stabler conditions. All now is unsettled. It is said that nearly all our *formal* politeness must eventually disappear under conditions of industrialism, and be replaced by something more real and more agreeable, — kindly consideration, and natural desire to please. But that will be in ages and ages only after we are dead. There must be an end of all fighting first, — of cruelty in competition, and this cannot happen

until with intellectual expansion, population ceases
to so increase as to enforce competition without
mercy.

The tendency now (referring to what you said
about trusts) seems to point indeed to what Spencer calls "The Coming Slavery." Monopolies and
trusts must continue to grow and multiply, — must
eventually tend to coalesce, — must ultimately hold
all. Bellamy's ideas will be partly carried out, but
in no paradisaical manner. The State itself will
become the one monstrous trust. Socialism will be
promised all, and be compelled to work against its
own ends unconsciously. The edifice is even now
being reared in which every man will be a veritable
slave to the State, — the State itself a universal monopoly, or trust. Then every life will be regulated to
infinitesimal details, and the working population of
the whole West find themselves situated just as men
in factories or on railroads are situated. The trust
will be nominally for the universal benefit, and must
for a time so seem to be. But just so surely as human
nature is not perfect, just so surely will the directing
class eventually exploit the wonderful situation, —
just as some Roman rulers exploited the world. Assuredly anarchy will eventuate; but first, — in spite
of all that human wisdom can do, — nations will
pass under the most fearful tyranny ever known.
And perhaps centuries of persistent effort will
scarcely suffice to burst the fetters which Socialism
now seeks to impose on human society; — the machinery will be too frightfully perfect, too harmonious
in operation, too absolutely exact and of one piece, —

to be easily attacked. As well try with naked hands
to pierce the side of an iron-clad. The law, the
police, the military power, religious influence, commercial and industrial interests, — all will be as One,
working to preserve the form of the new socialism.
To seek redress, to demand change, were then sheer
madness. And even the power to flee away out of
the land, to dwell among beasts and birds, might
be denied. Liberty of opinion, which we all boast of
now, would be then less possible than in the time of
the sway of Torquemada. . . .

You have heard of the Japanese facile victories
by land and sea. I should not be surprised to hear
of their winning every engagement, and capturing
Pekin. But what the end will be for the country, who
can say? The whole thing is the last huge effort of
the race for national independence. Under the steady
torturing pressure of our industrial civilization, —
being robbed every year by unjust treaties, — Japan
has determined to show her military power to the
world by attacking her old teacher, China. At the
same time she has asked and obtained from England
such revision of the treaty as would not only protect
her against the danger of large fresh investments of
foreign capital, but would probably result in driving
existing capital away. I cannot think that the United
States will be short-sighted enough to grant the
same terms. For instance, though the country is to
be opened to foreign settlement, no Englishman can
hold land except on lease; and the lease, by Japanese
law, expires with the death of the lessor. So that if
I build a stone house, and my landlord die in twenty

years after, I must be at the mercy of his heir, or carry away my house on my back.

It is an ugly business, this war. It may leave Japan absolutely independent, as in the days of Ieyasu. But will that be best for her? I am no longer sure. The people are still good. The upper classes are becoming corrupt. The old courtesy, the old faith, the old kindness are vanishing like snow in sun. Ever affectionately,

LAFCADIO HEARN.

TO OCHIAI

KUMAMOTO, September, 1894.

DEAR MR. OCHIAI, — . . . I was much interested in what your letter related about the doves leaving Kizuki, and about the *O mamori*. It is a curious fact that nearly the same story is told in Kumamoto, in regard to Katō Kiyomasa. At the Nichiren temple of Hommyōji the helmet, armour, and sword of the great Captain were always preserved. Lately they disappeared, and some say they were sent to Korea, — to stimulate the zeal of the army. But some of the people say that in the night horse-hoofs were heard in the temple court; and that a great shadowy horseman, in full armour, was seen to pass. So it is whispered that Kiyomasa rose up from his grave, and buckled on his armour, and departed to lead the Imperial Armies to glory and conquest.

Thanks also for the very interesting note about the Emperor Go-Daigo. You know I visited the

place where he lived at Oki, and the little village —
Chiburi-mura — from which he made his escape in
the fishermen's boat.

What you said about the *mamori* of the soldier
reminds me that at the *ujigami* here little charms are
being given to thousands of soldiers. They are very
narrow, and contrived so as to be slipped into the
lining (*ura*) of a uniform.

Thanks for your two kindest letters. I shall
write you again another day, — this is only my
answer to one of your two letters; the other I still
owe you for.

Best wishes and regards to you always.

                              LAFCADIO HEARN.

                    TO ELLWOOD HENDRICK

                              KōBE, December, 1894.

DEAR HENDRICK, — So it was *you* that sent me
"Trilby" — the magical thing! I never knew till
the Spencer came, and Kipling's "Jungle Book."
And the joke is that I thanked another man for the
gift of "Trilby," and the beast never let on. And
I wrote a two and one-half column review of
"Trilby" to please *him*. Oh! you rascal! why
did n't you tell me? Love to you for "Trilby." . . .

Glad you liked my first book on Japan. The
Tribune essay vexed me. . . . The curious fact of
the article was the statement about the influence
of the *decadents* and of Verlaine being "apparent."
Never read a line of Verlaine in my life, — and
only know enough of the decadent school to con-

vince me that the principle is scientifically wrong,
and that to study the stuff is mere waste of time.

I am writing one article a day for 100 yen a
month. Exchange is so low now that the 100
represents something less than 50 in American
money. And my eyes, or eye, giving out. Curious! — cold seriously affects my remnant of sight.
If I had a few thousand I should go to a hot climate during the winter months. Heat gives me
good vision. Even a Japanese hot bath temporarily restores clearness of sight. . . .

Of course, we shall never see each other again
in this world. And what is the use of being unkind — after all? Life to us literary folk — small
and great — is so short, and we are never in competition, like business men who *must* compete —
what is the use of meanness? I suppose there must
be some use. The effect is certainly to convince
a man of "fourty-four" that the less he has to do
with his fellow men the better, — or, at least, that
the less he has to do with the so-called "cultured"
the better. . . .

The other day you told me of some queer changes
in your inner life wrought by the influences of the
outer. In my case the changes are very unpleasant. I can't feel towards men generally any longer
as I used to — I feel, in short, a little misanthropic.
The general facts seem to be that all realities of relations between men are of self-interest in the main;
that the pleasures of those relations are illusions
— dependent upon youth, power, position, etc., for
degree of intensity. No man, as a general rule,

shows his soul to another man; he shows it only
to a woman, — and then only with the assurance
that she won't give him away. As a matter of
fact, she can't: — the Holy Ghost takes care of
that! No woman unveils herself to another woman
— only to a man; and what she unveils he cannot
betray. He can only talk of her body, if he is
brute enough to wish to: the inner being, of which
he has had some glimpses, can be pictured only in a
language which he cannot use. But what a fighting masked-ball the whole thing is!

Have you read Huxley's views on Ethics and
Evolution? They have been a great revelation to
me. They make it perfectly plain why men cannot
be good to one another on general principles without causing trouble in the order of the universe.
They also explain the immorality of Nature. Cosmic principles afford explanations of — but not
consolations for — individual experiences.

L. H.

TO ELLWOOD HENDRICK

Kumamoto, December, 1894.

Dear Hendrick, — Of course I shall teach the
"Jungle Book" to the little fellow, when he gets big
enough. How pretty of you to send it. I sent
some little prints — don't know if you like them;
in an album they would perhaps interest your
friends who have not been in Japan. I shall look
out for seeds for you regularly hereafter.

About Emerson. Last spring I got a pretty edi-

tion of him from H. M. & Co. and I digested him.
He is only suggestive, but wondrously so at times,
as in his poems. As a suggester he will always be
great. The talk about his truisms must depend
upon the knowledge of the speaker. Emerson will
be large or small, — commonplace or profound, —
according to the reader's knowledge of the thought
of the age.

My reading out here has been pretty heavy. I
have had to digest a good deal of Buddhist and
Chinese stuff, of course. My philosophical favourites are still Spencer and Huxley, Lewes and Fiske
and Clifford. I made Kipling's acquaintance out
here (I mean his books), and told you what I
think of him. Next to Kipling I like Stevenson.
But I have really read very little of anything new.
Browning is a pet study still. Somehow I have
tired of Tennyson — don't exactly know why.

The labour of a mother is something which, I
imagine, no man without a child can understand.
We big folks forget what our own mothers did for
us, — and we have no real chance to see all that
other mothers do. My whole family are always
caring for the boy: his interest and necessities rule
the whole house, — but the mother ! ! for a single
hour she has no rest with him (Japanese give
the breast for two years) — no sleep except when
he allows it, — and yet it all is joy for her. How
they have already taught him Japanese politeness,
how to prostrate himself before his father the first
thing in the morning and last at night, — to ask
for things, putting his hands in the proper way, —

to smile, — to know the names of things before
he can pronounce them, — I can't understand.
Angel-patience and love alone could have done it.
I want her to wean him — but she won't hear of
it; and the old grandmother gets angry at the mere
idea. It is only in home-relation that people are
true enough to each other, — show what human
nature is — the beauty of it, the divinity of it. We
are otherwise all on our guard against each other.
I cannot say how happy I think you are — you
can see Souls without armour or mail, — loving
you. That is the joy of life, after all — is n't it?

LAFCADIO HEARN.

TO SENTARŌ NISHIDA

KŌBE, January, 1895.

DEAR NISHIDA, — I have just written to Mr.
Senke, to apologize for delay in sending my annual
contribution — which I had hoped to be able to do
as a Japanese citizen. But this may give me a
chance to write again, when I get naturalized.

The Governor of Hyōgo did a very strange thing
— informed the British Consul that I was to make
a declaration in writing, presumably before the
Consul, that I intended to be faithful to the Emperor of Japan, and to obey the laws. I did make
the declaration; and the Consul is kind enough to
forward it. But I believe he is doing this out of
personal kindness; for I do not think it is according to English ideas, much less English laws, for
a Consul to accept such a declaration at all. In-

deed, what was asked was equivalent to requesting
the English Consul to accept an English subject's
renunciation of allegiance to Queen Victoria, — and
I am astonished that the Consul, who is a rigid
disciplinarian, in this case allowed me to submit
to him any declaration on the subject. One
thing is sure, that others who want to become
Japanese subjects are going to have plenty of
trouble. These measures are entirely new, and
quite different to anything ever before exacted —
for example, in the case of Warburton and other
Kōbe residents who became Japanese subjects, perhaps for business reasons.

I am thinking of building Setsu a house, either
in Kōbe or Kyōto. When I say Kōbe, I mean
Hyōgo, really; for I cannot well afford to buy land
at $40 to $70 per *tsubo* in the back streets of
Kōbe. In Hyōgo, I can do better. Setsu and I
both agree that Kōbe is warmer than Kyōto; but,
except for the winter months, I should rather live
in Kyōto than in any part of Japan. Tōkyō is the
most horrible place in Japan, and I want to live in
it just as short a time as possible. The weather is
atrocious; — the earthquakes are fearsome; — the
foreign element and the Japanese officialism of
Tōkyō must be dreadful. I want to feel and see
Japan: there is no Japan in Tōkyō. But in spite
of all I say, Setsu thinks of Tōkyō just as a French
lady thinks of Paris. After she has passed a winter there, perhaps she will not like Tōkyō so much.
I imagine that she thinks the Tōkyō, — the really
beautiful Tōkyō — of the old picture-books, and

LAFCADIO HEARN'S FAVOURITE DWELLING-HOUSE

the bank-bills, still exists. Then she knows all
the famous names — the names of the bridges and
streets and temples, — and these are associated in
her mind with the dramas and the famous stories
and legends of Japan. Perhaps I should love
Tōkyō just as much as she does, if I knew the history and the traditions of the country as well.

You will be pleased to hear that my books are
attracting considerable attention now in England.
It is very hard to win attention there, but much
more important than to win it in America. "Out
of the East" has made more impression in England than my first book did. I don't know what
will be said of "Kokoro:" it is a terribly "radical"
book — at variance with all English conventions
and beliefs. However, if you and my few Japanese
friends like it, I shall be happy.

I wish you were here to eat some plum-pud-
ding with me.

Oh! I forgot to tell you that Finck, who wrote
that book about Japan, is rather celebrated (perhaps celebrated is too strong a word — *well known*
is better) as the author of a book called "Romantic Love and Personal Beauty."

Ever faithfully,

LAFCADIO HEARN.

TO ELLWOOD HENDRICK

Kōbe, January, 1895.

DEAR HENDRICK: — Three books and a catalogue reached me — Mallock, Kipling, and a vol-

ume by Morris — for which more than thanks
the value much exceeding, I fear, the slight difference between us.

It now seems to me that time is the most
precious of all things conceivable. I can't waste
it by going out to hear people talk nonsense, — or
by going to see pretty girls whom I can't marry,
being married already, — or by playing games of
cards, etc., to kill time, — or by answering letters
written me by people who have neither real fine
feeling nor real things to say. Of course I might on
occasion do some one of these things, — but, having done it, I feel that so much of my life has been
wasted — sinfully wasted. There are rich natures
who can afford the waste; but I can't, because the
best part of my life has been wasted in wrong
directions and I shall have to work like thunder till
I die to make up for it. I shall never do anything
remarkable; but I think I have caught sight of a
few truths on the way.

I might say that I have become indifferent to personal pleasures of any sort, — except sympathy and
sympathetic converse; but this might represent a
somewhat morbid state. What is more significant,
I think, is the feeling that the greatest pleasure is to
work for others, — for those who take it as a matter
of course that I should do so, and would be as much
amazed to find me selfish about it as if an earthquake
had shaken the house down. Really I am not affect-
ing to think this; I feel it so much that it has become
a part of me.

Then of course, I like a little success and praise, —

though a big success and big praise would scare me; but I find that even the little praise I have been getting has occasionally unhinged my judgement. And I have to be very careful.

Next, I have to acknowledge to feeling a sort of resentment against certain things in which I used to take pleasure. I can't look at a number of the *Petit Journal pour Rire* or the *Charivari* without vexation, almost anger. I can't find pleasure in a French novel written for the obvious purpose of appealing to instincts that interfere with perception of higher things than instincts. I would not go to see the Paris opera if it were next door and I had a free ticket — or, if I did go, it would be for the sake of observing the pleasure given to somebody else. I should not like to visit the most beautiful lady and be received in evening dress. You see how absurd I have become — and this without any idea of principle about the matter, except the knowledge that I ought to avoid everything which does not help the best of myself — small as it may be. Whenever by chance I happen to make a deviation from this general rule, work suffers in consequence.

I think that on the whole I am gaining a little in the path; but I have regular fits of despondency and disgust about my work, of course. One day I think I have done well; the next that I am a hideous ass and fool. Much is a question of nervous condition. But I feel sure that a long-continued period of self-contentment would be extremely injurious to me; and that checks and failures and mockeries are indispensable medicine.

I read the books you sent me — Mallock only because *you* wished me to read it.   I suppose it is the
very best thing he ever did.   How immensely clever
and keen and — immoral !   It is a wonderful thing.
"The Wood beyond the World" astounded me.
Its value is in the study of the quaint English; but
you know that such a thing could not be written in
modern English prose very well; and I must say
that I feel like disputing the *raison d'être* thereof.
It is simply a very naughty story.

Kipling is priceless, — the single story of Purim
Bagat is worth a kingdom; and the suggestive moral
of human life is such a miracle !   I can't tell you
what pleasure it gave me.   Indeed the three books
— as representing three totally distinct fields of literary work — were a great treat.

My boy is quite well again, though we were very
frightened about him.   He suffers from the cold
every winter (you know the Japanese never have
fire in winter), but he is getting hardier, I trust.   He
is very fond of pictures and says funny things about
the pictures in the "Jungle Book."   I am off to the
Southern Islands shortly, — so you may not hear
from me for some weeks.

Ever affectionately,

LAFCADIO HEARN.

TO ELLWOOD HENDRICK

KŌBE, January, 1895.

Since I wrote you last, you dear old fellow, I've
been through some trouble.   Indeed, the very *day*
after writing you, I broke down, and had to remain

three weeks with compresses over my eyes in a dark room. I am now over it — able to write and read for a short time every day, but have been warned to leave routine newspaper work alone. Which I must do.

Your letter was — well, I don't just know what to call its quality: — there was a bracing tenderness in it that reminded me of a college friendship. Really, in this world there is nothing quite so holy as a college friendship. Two lads, — absolutely innocent of everything wrong in the world or in life, — living in ideals of duty and dreams of future miracles, and telling each other all their troubles, and bracing each other up. I had such a friend once. We were both about fifteen when separated, but had been together from ten. Our friendship began with a fight, of which I got the worst; — then my friend became for me a sort of ideal, which still lives. I should be almost afraid to ask where he is now (men grow away from each other so): but your letter brought his voice and face back, — just as if his very ghost had come in to lay a hand on my shoulder. . . .

Kōbe is a nice little place. The effect on me is not pleasant, however. I have become too accustomed to the interior. The sight of foreign women — the sound of their voices — jars upon me harshly after long living among purely natural women with soundless steps and softer speech. (I fear the foreign women here, too, are nearly all of the savagely *bourgeoise* style — affected English and affected American ways prevail.) Carpets, — dirty shoes, — absurd fashions, — wickedly expensive living, — airs, — vanities, — gossip: how much sweeter the Japanese life on the soft mats, — with its ever dearer courtesy and pretty, pure simplicity. Yet my boy can never be a Japanese. Perhaps, if he grows old, there will some day come back to him memories of his mother's dainty little world, — the *hibachi*, — the *toko*, — the garden, — the lights of the household shrine, — the voices and hands that shaped his thought and guided every little tottering step. Then he will feel very, very lonesome, — and be sorry he did not follow after those who loved him into some shadowy resting-place where the Buddhas still smile under their moss. . . .

Ever affectionately,

LAFCADIO.

TO BASIL HALL CHAMBERLAIN

KŌBE, January, 1895.

DEAR CHAMBERLAIN, — I'm able now to write and read a little every day — not much, as to reading: writing tires the eyes less. Glad you like "Glimpses," as I see by your last kind letter. Of course it is full of faults: any work written in absolute isolation must be. It's taking, though: the publishers announce a third edition already, and the notices have been good — in America, enthusiastic. *The Athenæum* praised it fervidly; but a few English papers abuse it. The mixture of blame and praise means literary success generally.

The earthquakes are really horrible. I can sympathize with you.

The sensation of foreign life here is very unpleasant, after life in the interior. A foreign interior is a horror to me; and the voices of the foreign women — China-Coast tall women — jar upon the comfort of existence. Can't agree with you about the "genuine men and women" in the open ports. There are some — very, very few. (Thank the Gods I shall never have to live among them!) The number of Germans here makes life more tolerable, I fancy. They are plain, but homely, which is a virtue, and liberal, which commercial English or Americans (the former especially) seldom are. They have their own club and a good library. But life in Yunotsu or Hino-misaki, or Oki, with only the bare means for Japanese comfort, were better and cleaner and higher in every way than the best open ports can offer.

The Japanese peasant is ten times more of a gentleman than a foreign merchant could ever learn to be. Unfortunately the Japanese official, with all his civility and morality rubbed off, is something a good deal lower than a savage and meaner than the straight-out Western rough (who always has a kernel of good in him) by an inexpressible per cent. Carpets — pianos — windows — curtains — brass bands — churches! how I hate them!! And white shirts! — and *yōfuku!* Would I had been born savage ; the curse of civilized cities is on me — and I suppose I can't get away permanently from them. You like all these things, I know. I'm not expecting any sympathy — but thought you might like to know about the effect on me of a half-return to Western life. How much I could hate all that we call civilization I never knew before. How ugly it is I never could have conceived without a long sojourn in old Japan — the only civilized country that existed since antiquity. Them's my sentiments!

I have not yet been able to read Lowell's new book through. But he must have worked tremendously to write it. It is a very clever book — though disfigured by absolutely shameless puns. It touches truths to the quick, — with a light sharp sting peculiar to Lowell's art. It is painfully unsympathetic — Mephistophelian in a way that chills me. It is scientific — but the fault of it strikes me as being that the study is applicable equally to Europe or America as to Japan. The same psychical phenomena may be studied out anywhere, with the same result. The race difference in persons, like the difference between life and not-life in biology, is only one of degree, not of kind. Still, it is a wonderful book.

Ever truly,
LAFCADIO HEARN.

TO BASIL HALL CHAMBERLAIN

KŌBE, January, 1895.

DEAR CHAMBERLAIN, — To-day is a spring day and I can add a little to my screed. The weather brightens up my eyes.

I was thinking just now about the difference

between the Japanese *hyakushō* and the English merchant.

My servant girl from Imaichi — who cannot read or write — saw you at Kumamoto and said words to this effect: "He speaks Japanese like a great man. And he is so gentle and so kind." Vaguely something of the intellectual and moral side of you had reached and touched her simple mind. The other day a merchant said of you: "Chamberlain — Oh, yes. Met him at Miyanoshita. Tell you, he's a gentleman — plays a good game of whist!" There's appreciation for you. Which is the best soul of the two — my servant girl's or that merchant's?

A merchant, however, has inspired me with the idea of a sketch, to be entitled "His Josses"! . . .

On the other hand it strikes me that in another twenty years, or perhaps thirty, after a brief artificial expansion, all the ports will shrink. The foreign commerce will be all reduced to agencies. A system of small persecutions will be inaugurated and maintained to drive away all the foreigners who can be driven away. After the war there will be a strong anti-foreign reaction — outrages — police-repressions — temporary stillness and peace: then a new crusade. Life will be made wretched for Occidentals — in business — just as it is being made in the schools — by all sorts of little tricky plans which cannot be brought under law-provisions, or even so defined as to appear to justify resentment — tricks at which the Japanese are as elaborately ingenious as they are in matters of etiquette and forms of other kinds. The nation will show its ugly side to us — after a manner unexpected, but irresistible.

The future looks worse than black. As for me, I am in a perpetual quandary. I suppose I 'll have to travel West, — and console myself with the hope of visiting Japan at long intervals.

Well, there's no use in worrying — one must face the music,

I am sorry your eyes are weak, too. What the devil of a trouble physical trouble is! — a dead weight check on will! Still, you have good luck in other ways, and after all, eye-trouble is only a warning in both our cases.

Ever truly,

LAFCADIO HEARN.

TO BASIL HALL CHAMBERLAIN

KŌBE, February, 1895.

DEAR CHAMBERLAIN, — I had mailed you the American letter before your own most kind enclosure came, with the note from Makino. Of course this is beyond thanks, — and I can't say very much about it. Since then I received from you also Lowell's six papers on Mars, — which I have read, and return by this mail, — and your friendly lines from Atami.

Just as you suggested in the Atami letter, I was feeling about matters. There would be special conditions in New Orleans, on the paper of which I was ten years a staff-writer. I should have to

work only a couple of hours a day in my own room,
and would have opportunities of money-making
and travel. There are risks, too, — yellow fever,
lawlessness, and personal enemies. But to leave
Japan now would, of course, be like tearing one's self
in two, — and I am not sure but the ultimate nervous result would destroy my capacity for literary
work. The best thing, I imagine, will be to ask my
friend to keep the gate open for me, in case I have
to go. The great thing for me is not to worry:
worry and literary work will not harmonize. The
work always betrays the strain afterward.

You say my friend writes nicely. He is about
the most lovable man I ever met, — an old-time
Southerner, very tall and slight, with a singular
face. He is so exactly an ideal Mephistopheles
that he would never get his photograph taken. The
face does not altogether belie the character, — but
the mockery is very tender play, and queerly original. It never offends. The real Mephistopheles
appears only when there are ugly obstacles to overcome. Then the diabolical keenness with which
motives are read and disclosed, and the lightning
moves by which a plot is checkmated, or made a
net for the plotter himself, usually startle people.
He is a man of immense force — it takes such a one
to rule in that community, but as a gentleman I
never saw his superior in grace or consideration.
I always loved him — but like all whom I like, never
could get quite enough of his company for myself.

The papers on Mars are quite weirdly suggestive — are they not? Just how much of the theories

and the discoveries were Lowell's very own, I can't make out — though the papers are things to be thankful for. You know the physiological side of his psychology in "Occult Japan" is no more original than the "Miscellany" of a medical weekly.

By the way, I must point out a serious mistake he makes on page 293, — when he says that the absence of the belief in possession by other living men is a proof of the absence of personality in Japan. As a matter of fact there is no such absence. I alone know of three different forms of such belief — and know that one is extremely common. So that all the metaphysical structure of argument built upon the supposed absence of that belief vanishes into nothingness!

As Huxley says, that man who goes about the world "unlabelled" is sure to be punished for it. So I can't help thinking that I ought to have a label. Fancy the man who makes his bear drink champagne seeking my company on the ground that "Neither of us are Christians." The Ama-terasu-Ōmi-kami business first aroused my suspicions, but the phrase itself was so raw!

> Compañia de uno
> 1 Compañia de ninguno;
> Compañia de dos
> 2 Compañia de Dios;
> Compañia de tres
> 3 Compañia es (but never for me);
> Compañia de cuatro
> 4 Compañia del diablo.

This old Spanish hymn might have been made expressly about me, — except in No. 3. I should feel more at home with you if I knew you would share my letters with nobody.   This is all for yourself only.   Ever gratefully, with more than regards,

LAFCADIO HEARN.

TO BASIL HALL CHAMBERLAIN

KŌBE, February, 1895.

DEAR CHAMBERLAIN, — I never liked any letter I got from you more than the last — which brings us closer together. I suppose I have often misread you — being more supersensitive than I ought to be, — and also finding certain of my best friends so differently soul-toned that I am often at a loss to understand hows and whys. But it is curious that we are absolutely at one, after all, on sociological questions, as your letter shows. Undoubtedly the "coming slavery," predicted by Spencer, will come upon us. A democracy more brutal than any Spartan oligarchy will control life. Men may not be obliged to eat at a public table; but every item of their existence will be regulated by law. The world will be sickened for all time of democracy as now preached. The future tyranny will be worse than any of old, — for it will be a régime of moral rather than physical pain, and there will be no refuge from it — except among savages. But, for all that, the people are good. They will be trapped through their ignorance, and held in slavery by their ignorance; and made, I suppose, in the eternal order, to develop a still higher goodness before they can reach freedom again.

I believe there is no point of your letter in which
we are not thoroughly at accord. I have also been
inclined to many schools of belief in these matters:
I have been at heart everything by turns. It is like
the history of one's religious experiences. And just
as when, after emancipating one's self from the last
mesh of the net of creeds, one sees for the first time
the value-social and meaning of all, and the moral
worth of many, — so in sociological questions, it is
by emancipation from faiths in politics that one
learns what lies behind all politics, — the necessity
of the Conservative vs. the Radical, of the pleb. vs.
the aristo. Then, if sympathetic with popular needs
one still recognizes the æsthetic and moral value of
ranks and orders; or, if belonging to the latter, one
learns also to understand that the great, good, unhappy, moral, immoral, vicious, virtuous people are
the real soil of all future hope, — the field of the
divine in Man.

But for all that, when conditions jar on me, I
sometimes grumble and see only evil. What matter?
I never look for it as a study. My work — though
"no great shakes" — must show you that. At the
end of all experiences, bitter and pleasant, I try to
sum up good only.

What I said about the Germans you may not have
understood. I did not explain. There is, I think,
a particular German characteristic which has its
charm. Accustomed for generations to a communal
form of life — totally different from that of the
English — there has been developed among them
a certain spirit of tolerance and a social inclination

essentially German. Also the poverty of their country has nourished a tendency to sobriety of life,
while the causes developing their educational system
on a wonderful level of economy have brought the
race, I believe, to a higher general plane than others.
I don't mean that the top-shoots are higher than
French or English; but I think the middle growth
educationally is. At all events a German community
in America or in Japan, while it remains German —
has a peculiar charm — an independence of conventions, as distinguished from the religious and
social codes, — and an exterior affability, — quite
different from the individualism of other commun-
ities. Perhaps, however, the friendship never goes
quite as deep as in those isolated natures so much
harder to win.

The essay by Spencer you will find in a volume
sent you by mail, and sent to me by my American
friend. It did not appear in the old editions.
Perhaps I may try the feat some day of a Japanese
study on those lines, — though I must acknowledge
that I now perceive several of my views entirely
wrong. I also perceive how closely Lowell reached
the neighbourhood of truth without being able,
nevertheless, (or willing?) to actually touch it. My
conclusion is that the charm of Japanese life is
largely the charm of childhood, and that the most
beautiful of all race childhoods is passing into an
adolescence which threatens to prove repulsive.
Perhaps the manhood may redeem all, — as with
English "bad boys" it oftens does.

I fear I can scarcely finish "Occult Japan," and

that I praised it too much in my late letter, after
hasty examination. It strikes me only as a mood
of the man, an ugly, supercilious one, verging on
the wickedness of a wish to hurt. When my eyes
improve, I should like better to see his work on Mars.
I don't wish to say that my work is as good as
Lowell's "Soul of the Far East;" but it is a curious
fact that in at least a majority of the favourable
criticisms I have been spoken of as far more successful than Lowell. Why? Certainly not because
I am his equal, either as a thinker or an observer.
The reason is simply that the world considers the
sympathetic mood more just than the analytical or
critical. And except when the critic is a giant like
Spencer or his peers, — I fear the merely critical
mood will always be blind to the most vital side of
any human question. For the more vital side is
feeling, — not reason. This, indeed, Spencer showed
long ago. But there was in the "Soul of the Far
East" an exquisite approach to playful tenderness —
utterly banished from "Occult Japan."

Ever yours,
Lafcadio Hearn.

TO BASIL HALL CHAMBERLAIN

Kōbe, February, 1895.

Dear Chamberlain, — Thanks for the curious
historical envelopes. My eyes are nearly well:
there is still one small black spot in the centre of the
field of vision; but I trust it will go away as soon as
the weather becomes warm.

I am delighted to know you like the book. A curious fact is that out of fifty criticisms sent me, in which the critics select "favourites," I find that almost every article in the book has been selected by somebody. It thus seems to appeal to persons of totally different temperament in different ways, and this fact suggests itself, — that perhaps no book written entirely in one key can please so well as a book written in many keys. However, the work must be unconscious. If you are curious about any of the "inside facts," I shall be glad to tell you. The "Teacher's Diary" is, of course, strictly true as to means and facts; and the artistic work is simply one of "grouping." The cruiser at Mionoseki was the Takachiho, — since become famous. Hino-misaki and Yaegaki ought to contain something you would like, — so I trust you will peep at them some time. The Gūji of Hino-misaki is my wife's relative, and the story of his ancestor is quite true.

As for Japanese words, you might like "Out of the East" better. I don't think there are five Japanese words in the book. But it is chiefly reverie — contains little about facts or places. Perhaps you will be less pleased with it in another way.

As for changing my conclusions, — well, I have had to change a good many. The tone of "Glimpses" is true in being the feeling of a place and time. Since then I've seen how thoroughly detestable Japanese can be, and that revelation assisted in illuminating things. I am now convinced, for example, that the deficiency of the sexual instinct (using the term philosophically) in the race is a serious defect rather than a merit, and is very probably connected with the absence of the musical sense and the incapacity for abstract reasoning. It does not follow, however, that the same instinct may not have been overdeveloped in our own case. To an Englishman, it would appear that such overdevelopment among Latin races would account for the artistic superiority as well as the moral weakness of French and Italians in special directions; — and the fact that even certain classes of music are now called sensual (not sensuous), and that there is a tendency to abjure Italian music in favour of the more aspirational German music, — would seem to show that the largest-brained races are reaching a stage in abstract æsthetics still higher than the highest possible development of the æsthetics based on the sexual feeling. That the Japanese can ever reach our æsthetic stage seems to me utterly impossible, but assuredly what they lack in certain directions they may prove splendidly capable of making up in others. Indeed the development of the mathematical faculty in the race — unchecked and unmollified by our class of æsthetics and idealisms — ought to prove a serious danger to Western civilization at last. At least it seems to me that here is a danger. Japan ought to produce scientific, political, and military haters of "ideologists," — Napoleons of practical applications of science. All that is tender and manly and considerate and heroic in Northern character has certainly grown out of the sexual sentiment: but the same class of feelings in the far East would seem to have been evolved out of a different class of emotional habits, and a class bound to disappear. Imagine a civilization on Western lines with cold calculation universally substituted for ethical principle! The suggestion is very terrible and very ugly. One would prefer even the society of the later Roman Empire.

I am sorry your eyes are not all you could wish. Do you not think it may be the weather? The doctor tells me my eyes will be all right in summer, but that I have to be careful in cold weather. And the tropics did me wonderful good. I want to get to the warm zones occasionally — perhaps shall be able to. There are some tropics bad for the eyes, — lacking verdure. I have been unable to get facts about tropical conditions on this side of the world, — except through Wallace. Ceram suggests possibilities. But one must be well informed before going. Then there are the French Marquesas. A French colony ought to be full of romance, and void of missionaries. But all these are dreams.

Ever faithfully,
LAFCADIO HEARN.

TO BASIL HALL CHAMBERLAIN

KŌBE, March, 1895.

DEAR CHAMBERLAIN, — It was very comforting to get a letter from you; for I wanted an impulse to write. I have been blue — by reason partly of the weather; and partly because of those reactions which follow all accomplished work in some men's cases. Everything done then seems like an Elle-woman, —

a mere delusive shell; and one marvels why anybody should have been charmed.

Of course I did not ask point-blank for criticisms, because you told me long ago, "Every man should make his own book," — and, although it is the literary custom in America to consult friends, I could see justice in the suggestion. The title "Out of the East" was selected from a number. It was suggested only by the motto of the Oriental Society, "Ex Oriente lux." The "Far East" has been so monopolized by others that I did not like to use the phrase. "Out of the Uttermost East" would sound cacophonously, — besides suggesting a straining for effect. I thought of Tennyson's "most eastern east," but the publishers didn't approve it. The simpler the title, and the vaguer — in my case — the better: the vagueness touches curiosity. Besides, the book is a vague thing. Sound has much to do with the value of a title. If it had n't, you would have written "Japanese Things" instead of "Things Japanese" — which is entirely different, and so pretty that your admirers and imitators snapped it up at once. So we have "Things Chinese" by an imitator, and "Things Japanese" is a phrase which has found its recognized place in the vocabulary of critics of both worlds. Your criticism on "Out of the East," though, would have strongly influenced me, if you had sent it early enough. I noticed the very same suggestion in the *Athenæum* regarding the use of the word "Orient" and the phrase "Far East" by Americans. For our "Orient" is, as you say, still the Orient of Kinglake, of De Nerval, etc.

But why should it be? To Milton it was the Indian East with kings barbaric sitting under a rain of pearls and gold.

Manila was long my dream. But, although my capacity for sympathy with the beliefs of Catholic peasantry anywhere is very large, — the ugly possibility exists that the Inquisition survives in Manila, and I have had the ill-fortune to make the Jesuits pay some attention to me. You know about the young Spaniard who had his property confiscated, and who disappeared some years ago, — and was restored to liberty only after heaven and earth had been moved by his friends in Spain. I don't know that I should disappear; but I should certainly have obstacles thrown in my way. Mexico would be a safer country for the same class of studies, — Ceram ought to be interesting: in Wallace's time the cost of life per individual was only about 8s. 6d. a year! A moist, hot tropical climate I like best. The heat is weakening, I know, but that moisture means the verdure that is a delight to the eyes, and palms, and parrots, and butterflies of enormous size; — and no possibility of establishing Western conditions of life. I should like very much to see the book you kindly offered to lend me. It might create new aspirations: I am always at night dreaming of islands in undiscovered seas, where all the people are gods and fairies.

Of course I cannot know much about it now, but I am almost sure of having been in Malta as a child. At a later time my father, who was long there, told me queer things about the old palaces of the knights,

and a story about a monk who, on the coming of
the French, had the presence of mind to paint the
gold chancel-railing with green paint. Southern
Italy and the Mediterranean islands are especially
fitted for classical scholars, like Symonds; but what
a world of folk-lore also is there still ungathered!
I should think that, next to Venice, Malta must be
the most romantic spot in Europe.

I see your paper on Loochoo must have been
much more than what you said of it, — viz., that
only some snuffy German would read it. Or was
the London report about the paper on Loochoo
which I have? (There must be a wonderful ghost-
world in those islands, — though it would be quite
hard to get at: probably three years' work.)

You can't imagine my feeling of reaction in the
matter of Japanese psychology. It seems as if
everything had quite suddenly become clear to me,
and utterly void of emotional interest: a race primitive as the Etruscan before Rome was, or more so,
adopting the practices of a larger civilization under
compulsion, — five thousand years at least emotionally behind us, — yet able to suggest to us the existence of feelings and ideals which do not exist,
but are simulated by something infinitely simpler.
Wonder if our own highest things have not grown up
out of equally simple things. The compulsion first —
then the sense of duty become habit, automatic,
the conviction expanding into knowledge of ethical
habit, — then the habit creating conviction, — then
relations, — then the capacity for general ideas.
But all the educational system now seems to me

farcical and wrong, — except in mere dealing with facts apparent to common sense. There are no depths to stir, no race-profundities to explore: all is like a Japanese river-bed, through which the stones and rocks show up all the year round, — and is never filled but in time of cataclysm and destruction.

Ever faithfully,
LAFCADIO HEARN.

TO BASIL HALL CHAMBERLAIN

KŌBE, March, 1895.

DEAR CHAMBERLAIN, — Of course send back the Taylor and Pater — if you don't care for them. I myself was very much disappointed in Pater. Perhaps my liking for Taylor is connected with boyish recollections of his facile charm: even Longfellow cannot greatly thrill me now. And may I make a confession? — I can't endure any more of Wordsworth, Keats, and Shelley — having learned the gems of them by heart. I really prefer Dobson and Watson and Lang. Of Wordsworth Watson sings, —

"It may be thought has broadened since he died!"

Well, I should smile! His deepest truths have become platitudes.

This reminds me that I have wanted to talk to you about a magical bit of Hugo's, "Chant de Sophocle à Salamine." It is such a striking instance of Hugo's greatness and littleness. You know it, I suppose. It opens thus: —

> Me voila! Je suis un Ephèbe, —
> Mes seize ans sont d'azur baignés,
> Guerre, Déesse de l'Erèbe, —
> Sombre Guerre *aux cris indignes*.

The italicized words make me mad. It is a bathos,
the fourth line — shrieking bathos; while the first
part of the verse is like a Greek frieze. But let us
go on: —

> Je viens à toi, la nuit est noire!
> Puisque Xercès est le plus fort,
> Prends-moi pour la lutte et la gloire,
> Et pour la tombe, — mais d'abord, —

(Now for the magnificence!)

> Toi dont le glaive est le ministre,
> Toi que l'Eclair suit dans les cieux,
> Choisis-moi de ta main sinistre
> Une belle fille aux doux yeux.

What makes the splendour of this verse? Not
only the tremendous contrast, — apocalyptic. It
is especially, I think, the magnificent dual use of
"sinistre." How Hugoish the whole thing is! . . .

I fear that what I said long ago is likely to come
true: the first fire is burnt out, — the zeal is dead,
— the educational effort (one of the most colossal
in all history, surely) having served its immediate
purpose (the recovery of national autonomy) is
dead. Hence there is a prospect of decay.

Now I should like to protest against this danger
in a review-article: say, "History of the Decline
and Fall of Education in Japan;" or, "History of
Foreign Teaching in Japan." Could I get documents? — just a skeleton at least, of statistics, rules,

details, numbers. The article has been in my mind
for two years. And I notice the Japanese don't
object to healthy criticisms at all, — rather like
them. They hate petting-talk, however, — and
stupid misinterpretations. I should like to try the
thing.

I think it is Amenomori who is writing rather
savage things in the *Chronicle* just now, about the
Mombushō, and threatens to write more. There is
a something unpleasant in the tone of Japanese
satire to me, — however clever, it shows that they
have not yet reached the same perception of sensibility as we have. Of course I refer only to the
best of them — masters. The sympathetic touch is
always absent. I feel unhappy at being in the company of a cultivated Japanese for more than an hour
at a time. After the first charm of formality is over,
the man becomes ice — or else suddenly drifts away
from you into his own world, far from ours as the
star Rephan.

You will be pleased to hear that I have not yet
dropped money. I have made nothing to speak of,
but have lost none so far. By fall I suppose I shall
have made something, though no fortune, out of
"Glimpses." If I can clear enough to justify a
tropical trip, I shall be satisfied.

Malta must be delightful. But I am not enough
of a scholar to use such an opportunity as Malta
would give. I should do better with Spain and
gipsies, or Pondicherry and Klings.

By the way, my child-tongue was Italian. I spoke
Romaic and Italian by turns. In New Orleans I

hired a teacher to teach me, — thinking memory
would come back again. But it didn't come at all,
and I quarrelled with the teacher, who looked
exactly like a murderer and never smiled. So I
know not Italian.

Ever faithfully,
LAFCADIO HEARN.

TO BASIL HALL CHAMBERLAIN

KŌBE, March, 1895.

DEAR CHAMBERLAIN, — About three days ago
came the welcome books. "The Cruise of the Marchesa" it would be difficult to praise too highly.
There are a few touches here and there slightly
priggish, or snobbish, — but the fine taste of the
writer as a rule, his modesty as a man of science,
his compact force of expression, his appreciation
of nature, his astonishing capacity for saying a
vast deal in a few words, are indubitable, and give
the book a very high literary place. The engrav-
ings are lovely. The other book is an amazement.
How any man could seriously make such a book I
can't possibly imagine. It is the most disgraceful
attempt of the sort I ever saw, — absolutely unread-
able as a whole: an almanac is a romance by comparison. Still I found a lot of interesting facts by
groping through it. I should scarcely like to trust
myself in Manila.

The Marchesa book is a delight, and will bear
many readings. The general impression is that both
Sulu and the Celebes are paradises; but that Dutch

order is highly preferable to the condition of the isles under Spanish domination (in theory). The necessity of dress-coats and *de rigueur* habits is the chief drawback, I should imagine, at a place like Macassar. But the Malayan Dutch colonies must be delightful places. I fear, however, that as in Java, the Christianization of the natives has spoiled the field for folk-lore work.

The Ryūkyū chapters, with the illumination of your own pamphlet, make a very pleasant, dreamy, gentle sensation. Half-China and half-Japan under tropical conditions should create a particular queerness quite different from our Dai Nippon queerness. I hardly believe that the conditions will change so rapidly as those of Japan proper. In such latitudes and such isolation changes do not come quickly. There are little places on the west coast I know of where the conditions must be still pretty near the same as they were a thousand years ago.

I fear, however, my travelling days (except for business and monotonous work) are nearly over. I'm not going to get rich. Some day I may hit the public; but that will probably be when I shall have become ancient. I feel just now empty and useless and a dead failure. Perhaps I shall feel better next season. At all events I have learned that, beyond all doubt and question, it is absolutely useless for me to try to "force work." If the feeling does not come of itself from outside, one had better do nothing.

I had a sensation the other day, though, which I want to talk to you about. I felt as if I hated Japan unspeakably, and the whole world seemed not worth living in, when there came two women to the house, to sell ballads. One took her *samisen* and sang; and people crowded into the tiny yard to hear. Never did I listen to anything sweeter. All the sorrow and beauty, all the pain and the sweetness of life thrilled and quivered in that voice; and the old first love of Japan and of things Japanese came back, and a great tenderness seemed to fill the place like a haunting. I looked at the people, and I saw they were nearly all weeping, and snuffing; and though I could not understand the words, I could feel the pathos and the beauty of things. Then, too, for the first time, I noticed that the singer was blind. Both women were almost surprisingly ugly, but the voice of the one that sang was indescribably beautiful; and she sang as peasants and birds and *semi* sing, which is nature and is divine. They were wanderers both. I called them in, and treated them well, and heard their story. It was not romantic at all, — small-pox, blindness, a sick husband (paralyzed) and children to care for. I got two copies of the ballad, and enclose one. I should be very glad to pay for having it translated literally: — if you think it could be used, I wish you would some day, when opportunity offers, give it to a Japanese translator. As for price, I should say five yen would be a fair limit.

Would you not like me to return some day your version of the Kumamoto Rōjō, and admirable translation? I preserve it carefully; and have used some of the lines for a sketch in the forthcoming book. I rendered nearly the whole into loose verse, but in spite of my utmost efforts, I could do nothing with the best part of it; I could put no spirit into the lines. My suggestion about it is because it is a very curious if not a very poetical thing; and should you ever make an essay upon modern Japanese military songs, it would be a pity not to include it. So it is always carefully kept, not only for its own sake, but also in view of such possible use.

I find it is still the custom when a *shinjū* occurs to make a ballad about it, and sing the same, and sell it. This reminds one of London. Ballad customs seem to be the same in all parts of the world.

I shall soon return the books, with a copy of the next *Atlantic*. What could I send you that you would like ? I should suggest Rossetti, if you do not know him well — for I think he ranks as high as Tennyson. I have only Wallace among travellers. I have all of Fiske and Huxley and Spencer and Clifford and the philosophy of Lewes. By the way, have you read "Trilby"? I have read it several times over. It is a wonderful book. The art of it escapes one at first reading, when one reads only for the story.

LAFCADIO HEARN.

TO BASIL HALL CHAMBERLAIN

KŌBE, 1895.

DEAR CHAMBERLAIN, — I warned you not to get Gautier's complete works — so you have been disappointed against my desire. Gautier's own opinion was adverse to the publication of his com-

plete poems in this shape. He selected and published separately those which satisfied him, in the
"Emaux et Camées." (I once translated "Les
Taches Jaunes,"— is n't it ? — in the other volume;
a bit of weird sensualism quite in the Romantic
spirit.) Gautier's work is often uneven. He was
a journalist, and lived by the newspaper. His life's
complaint was that he could never find time for
perfect work: the effort merely to live finally worried
him to death during the siege, I think. Still, writing
merely for a newspaper, — in haste, — without a
chance to think and polish,—his feuilletons remain
treasures of French literature. (You are very
unjust to his prose; for it is the finest of all French
prose.) His complete works are worth having —
they run to about 60 vols., but they cannot all be had
from one publisher. So he has become a subject
for book-collectors. Sainte-Beuve, like Gautier, existed as a journalist. In France a journalist used to
have literary chances. In English-speaking countries literary work is still outside of the newspapers;
and our would-be littérateurs have therefore a still
harder struggle. (See that article in the *Revue*.
No English prose could accomplish those feats of
colour and sensation — delicate sensation the most
difficult to produce. English as an artistic tongue is
immeasurably inferior to French.)

"Philip and His Wife" was finished in the
October number. I know I sent all the numbers
containing it. Mrs. Deland is a great genius, I
think. Her "Story of a Child" was one of the
daintiest bits of psychology I ever read.

Sorry you deny hereditary sensation. The idea of the experimentalists that the mind of the newly born child is a *tabula rasa*, and that all sensations are based on individual experiences, is no longer recognized — not at least by the evolutional school of psychology, the only purely scientific school. Spencer especially has denied this idea. In the life about us we see every day proofs of inherited capacity for pleasures we know nothing of, and incapacity for pleasures normal to us and to our whole race. Indeed, I can prove the fact to you at any time. . . .

Faithfully,
LAFCADIO HEARN.

P. S. I have been out for a walk. As usual the little boys cried "Ijin," "Tōjin,"— and, although I don't go out alone, the changed feeling of even the adult population toward a foreigner wandering through their streets was strongly visible.

A sadness, such as I never felt before in Japan, came over me. Perhaps your pencilled comments on the decrease of filial piety, and the erroneous impressions of national character in "Glimpses," had something to do with it. I felt, as never before, how utterly dead Old Japan is, and how ugly New Japan is becoming. I thought how useless to write about things which have ceased to exist. Only on reaching a little shrine, filled with popular *ex-voto*, — innocent foolish things, — it seemed to me something of the old heart was beating still, — but far away from me, and out of reach. And I thought I would like to be in the old Buddhist cemetery at Gesshōji, which is in Matsue, in the Land of Izumo,—the dead are so much better off than the living, and were so much greater.

TO BASIL HALL CHAMBERLAIN

KŌBE, March, 1895.

DEAR CHAMBERLAIN, — You will scarcely be able to believe me, I imagine; but I must confess that your letter on "shall" and "will" is a sort of revelation in one sense — it convinces me that some people, and I suppose all people of fine English culture, really feel a sharp distinction of meaning in the sight and sound of the words "will" and "shall." I confess, also, that I never have felt such a distinction, and cannot feel it now. I have been guided chiefly by euphony, and the sensation of "will" as softer and gentler than "shall." The word "shall" in the second person especially has for me a queer identification with English harshness and menace, — memories of school, perhaps. I shall study the differences by your teaching, and try to avoid mistakes, but I think I shall never be able to feel the distinction. The tone to me is everything — the word nothing. For example, the Western cowboy says "Yes, you will, Mister," in a tone that means something much more terrible than the angry educated Englishman's "you shall." I know this confession is horrid — but there's the truth of the matter; and I feel angry with conventional forms of language of which I cannot understand the real spirit. I trust the tendency to substitute "will" for "shall" which you have noticed, and which I have always felt, is going eventually to render the use of "shall" with the first person obsolete. I am "colour blind" to the values you assert; and I suspect that the majority of the English-speaking races — the raw people — are also blind thereunto. It is the people, after all, who make the language in the end, and in the direction of least resistance.

You did not quite catch my meaning on the subject of inherited feeling. I did not hint you denied heredity (though your last letter embodies several strong denials of it, I think). I believe it is an accepted general rule, for example, that only a child having parents of different races can learn even two languages equally well: in other cases, one language gains at the expense of the other. Creoles exemplify this rule. Toys are related to the æsthetic faculty, to the play-impulse, to the imaginative capacity. These differ really in different races; and represent, not individual education at all, but the sum of racial experiences under certain conditions. I cannot believe for a moment that an English child born in Japan could feel the same sensation on looking at a Japanese picture as the sensation felt by a Japanese child when looking at the same picture. (With food, the matter is different: English children in many cases disliking greasy cooking, and in other cases showing a decided preference for fat. Only a very large number of instances—many thousand—could really show any

general rule in the case of English children born
in Japan. The evidence you cite seems to me a
contradiction, or exception to general tendencies.)
The psychical fact about feelings and emotions is
that they are inheritances, just as much as the
colour of hair, or the size of limbs; and tastes — such
as a taste for music or painting — are similarly
inherited. They are outside of the individual
experience as much as a birthmark. To explain
fully why, would involve a lot of neurological
scribbling, — but it is sufficient to say that as all
feelings are the result of motions in nervous structure, the volume and character and kind of feeling
is predetermined in each individual by the character
of nerve-tissue and its arrangement and complexity.
In no two individuals are the nervous structures
exactly the same; and the differences in races or
individuals are consequent upon the differences in
quality, variety, and volume of ancestral experience
shaping each life.

"The experience-hypothesis," says Spencer, "is
inadequate to account for emotional phenomena.
It is even more at fault in respect to the emotions
than in respect to the cognitions. The doctrine that
all the desires, all the sentiments, are generated by
the experiences of the individual, is so glaringly at
variance with facts that I wonder how any one
should ever have entertained it." And he cites
"the multiform passions of the infant, displayed
before there has been any such amount of experience
as could possibly account for them."

In short, there is no possible room for argument

as to whether each particular character — with all its possibilities, intellectual or emotional — is not predetermined by the character of nervous structure, slowly evolved by millions of billions of experiences in the past. As the differences in the ancestral sums of experiences, so the differences in the psychical life. Varying enormously in races so widely removed as English and Japanese, it is impossible to believe that any feeling in one race is exactly parallelled by any feeling in the other. It is equally impossible to think that the feelings of a Japanese child can be the same as those of an English child born in Japan. Amazing physical proof to the contrary would be afforded by a comparative study of the two nervous structures.

To say, therefore, that the sight of a toy — adjusted exactly by the experience of the race to the experience of the individual — produces on the mind of a Japanese child the same impression it would produce on the mind of an English child born in Japan and brought up by Japanese only, would be to deny all our modern knowledge of biology, psychology, and even physiology. The pleasure of the Japanese child in its toy is the pleasure of the dead.   Ever faithfully,

LAFCADIO HEARN.

TO BASIL HALL CHAMBERLAIN

KŌBE, April, 1895.

DEAR CHAMBERLAIN, — "The law of heredity is unlimited in its application" (Spencer, "Biology,"

vol. I, chapter "Heredity"). "Some naturalists
seem to entertain a vague belief [like yours?] that
the law of heredity applies only to main characters
of structure, and not to details; or that though it
applies to such details as constitute differences of
species, it does not apply to smaller details. The
circumstance that the tendency to repetition is in
a slight degree qualified by the tendency to variation (which . . . is but an indirect result of the
tendency to repetition) leads some to doubt whether
heredity is unlimited. A careful weighing of the
evidence . . . will remove the ground for this
skepticism." ("Biology," vol. I, p. 239.)

Your statement that the "weak person will always
remain weak," but that "the manifestations of his
weakness will surely depend on the nature of the
obstacles in his way," is a proof that you do not
perceive the full reach of the explanation. The
manifestations of weakness may be evoked by
obstacles, but the nature of those manifestations
cannot possibly have anything in common with
the nature of the obstacles. The weakness being
hereditary, the nature of the obstacle cannot change
it.

The case of the Northern nations seems to me
direct proof of the contrary to what you suggest.
Olaf Trygvesson and others never really changed
the national religion, except in name, — no such
rapid change would have been possible. The
worship of Odin and Thor continued under the
name of Christ and the Saints, — and still continues
to some extent to influence English life. The

shaking-off of ecclesiastical power at a later day, — the protestantizing of the Northern races, — is certainly the manifestation in history of the same fierce love of freedom that founded the Icelandic Republic. So with English limitation of monarchical power, the history of the constitution, etc. So with the superiority of English and Norse seamanship to-day, — Vikings still command our fleet. The changes you cite as evidence of the non-influence of heredity really prove it: they are, moreover, mere surface-shiftings of colour, and do not reach down into the national life. Variations are the result of heredity, not the exceptions to it. The explanation of this fact would necessitate, however, a long discussion on the deepening or weakening of those channels of nerve-force which are the river-courses of life and thought. Similarly, growth — of brain and thought as well as of body—is the consequence, not the contradiction, of inheritance. So with instinct, — which is organized memory, — and with genius, which represents accumulations of capacity (often at the expense of other growths).

I fear you think of Galton only when you limit the word heredity. Universal life and growth is touched by the larger meaning: Galton's wonderful books represent merely a domestic paragraph of the subject. The underlying principles of evolution — the deep laws of physiological growth and development — involve far vaster and profounder consideration of the subject. Inheritance is no "fad:" it means you and me and the world and our central sun.

My text was plain, — but you have forgotten it.
I spoke of "ancestral pleasure," "hereditary delight." You deny their possibility. The toys are
not ancestral, of course, nor did I say they were, —
but they appealed to ancestral feeling. Why? All
pleasure is hereditary — every feeling is inherited.
Why, then, say so? Because in this case we are
considering race-feelings widely differentiated from
our own.

But all this is surface, — the ghostly side of the
question is the beautiful one, and one which you
would not deny without examining the evidence?
Perhaps you think that the first time you saw Fuji
or Miyanoshita, you had really a new sensation.
But you had nothing of the kind. The sensations of
that new experience in your own life were millions
of years old! Far from simple is the commonest of
our pleasures, but a layer, infinitely multiple, of
myriads of millions of ancestral impressions. Try
to analyze the sensation of pleasure in a sunrise, or
the smell of hay, and how soon we are lost. We can
only classify the elements of such a pleasure "by
bundles," so to speak.

It might at first sight shock a strong soul to
perceive itself not individual and original, but an
infinite compound. But I think one's pride in one's
good should subsequently expand. The thought
that one's strength is the strength of one's ancestors — of a host innumerable and ancient as the
race — has its larger consolation. And here is the
poetry of the thing. You are my friend B. H. C.
But you are much more — you are also Captain

B. H., and a host of others — doubtless Viking and Norman and Danish — a procession reaching back into the weird twilight of the Northern gods.

So much for the fun of our discussion. I won't send the long screed: it is too full of dry stuff, and on reading it over I find that my enthusiasm betrayed me into several wild misstatements.

I am sorry about your cold, and I can sympathize; for I also have been ill, and my boy, and I find spring very trying. I am all right to-day, and so are we all.

Wish I were nineteen years old, and, like Ben, going to sea. As a boy, I cried and made a great fuss because they told me, "You can't go to sea: you are too near-sighted." Perhaps I was saved from disillusions.

You know Frederick Soulié's "Si jeunesse savait, si vieillesse pouvait." There was an unconscious recognition of heredity, — before modern biology had been synthetized.

Ever with best wishes and regards,

LAFCADIO HEARN.

TO BASIL HALL CHAMBERLAIN

KŌBE, April, 1895.

DEAR CHAMBERLAIN, — On re-reading your letter I find it necessary to assure you positively (pardon me if I am rude) that you have no conception whatever, not the least, of the scientific opinions as to psychological evolution held by Spencer. It is necessary I should say this, — otherwise the mere discussion of details would leave you under the impression that I recognize your understanding of the subject. It is quite obvious that you do not understand evolution at all. You do understand natural selection, — but that is quite another matter.

To comprehend psychological evolution, it is first necessary to banish absolutely from the mind every speck of belief that the individual can be changed in character, or intrinsically added to, by any influence whatever, to any perceptible degree. There may be modifications or increments, just as there may be decrements, but these remain imperceptible. The race is visibly modified in the course of centuries — not the individual, whether by education, environment or anything else. The millions of years required for the development of a body are much more required for the development of a mind. Could the individual be really changed to the degree imagined by the soul-theory, a few generations would suffice to form a perfectly evolved race.

Education and other influences only develop or stimulate the preëxisting. There is an unfolding (possibly also a very slight increment of neural structure), but the unfolding is of that formed before birth. There are no changes such as seriously affect character. The evolution of the race is perceptible, — not that of the individual, except as the individual life is that of the race in epitome.

Besides emotions, passions, etc., certain ideas are necessarily inherited. Otherwise mental development in the individual even could not take place. Such is the idea of Space, and other ideas which form the canvas and stage of thought. Simple as they seem, they are complicated enough to have required millions of years to form.

Evolution includes not merely the shaping and modification of existing matter, but the development of visible matter itself out of the invisible. The evidence of chemistry is that all substances we call elements have been evolved by tendencies out of something infinitely simpler and massless.

LAFCADIO HEARN.

Precisely for the same reason that the majority of men in all countries live more by feeling than by reason, and that the emotions, which are inheritances, play a greater part in the individual life than the reasoning faculties, which need training and experience for their development and use, — so is the study of heredity of larger importance in the study of emotional life. And therefore your suggestion that one factor should not be dwelt on rather than others would be bad to follow, — first, because all are not equal either in importance or interest, and secondly because the circumstance related or studied must be considered especially in relation to the principal factor of the psychological state which that circumstance has evoked.

TO BASIL HALL CHAMBERLAIN

KŌBE, April, 1895.

DEAR CHAMBERLAIN, — The factors of evolution are multitudinous beyond enumeration, and no one with a ghost of knowledge of the modern scientific researches on the subject could hold (as you suggest I do) that heredity is a first cause and "exclusive" (!) Heredity is a result, and the vehicle of transmission, as well as the "Karma" (which Huxley calls it). Degeneration, atrophy, atavism, are quite as much factors in evolution as variation and natural selection and development; — but the flowing of the eternal stream, the river of life, is heredity, — whatever form the ripples take. As I have given some twenty years' study to these subjects, I am not likely to overlook any such thing as environment or climate or diet. You cannot, however, get a grasp of the system by reading only a digest of results — a study of biology and physiology is absolutely necessary before the psychology of the thing can be clearly perceived. Now you say you will accept anything Spencer writes on the subject. Well, he writes that "a child" playing with its "toys" experiences "presentative-representative feelings." What are presentative-representative feelings? They are feelings chiefly "deeper than individual experience." What are feelings deeper than individual experience? Mr. Spencer tells us they are "inherited feelings," — the sum of ancestral experiences, — the aggregates of race-experience. Therefore when I said the child's delight in its toys was "hereditary-ancestral," I said precisely what Spencer says, but what you would never acknowledge so long as "only I" said it.

On this subject of emotions inherited as distinguished from others, and from those changes in states of conciousness generally which we call reasoning or constructive imagination, the definite utterances of

Spencer as physiologist are electrically reënforced by the startling theory of Schopenhauer, by the system of Hartmann, and by the views of Janet and his rapidly growing school. Indeed, the mere fact that a child cries at the sight of a frowning face and laughs at a smiling one could be explained in no other manner.

You are not quite correct in saying that Spencer could not obtain a hearing before Darwin. Before Darwin, Spencer had already been recognized by Lewes as the mightiest of all English thinkers, with the remarkable observation that he was too large and near to be justly estimated even in his lifetime. Darwin did much, of course, to illuminate one factor of evolution; but I need hardly say that one factor, though the most commonly identified with evolution, is but one of myriads. Natural selection can explain but a very small part of the thing. The colossal brain which first detected the necessity of evolution as a cosmic law, — governing the growth of a solar system as well as the growth of a gnat, — the brain of Spencer, discerned that law by pure mathematical study of the laws of force. And the work of the Darwins and Huxleys and Tyndalls is but detail — small detail — in that tremendous system which has abolished all preëxisting philosophy and transformed all science and education.

I need scarcely say, however, that I should not be able, as a literary dreamer, to derive the inspiration needed from Spencer alone: he is best illuminated, I think, by the aid of Schopenhauer and the new French school which considers the so-called individ-

ual as really an infinite multiple. These men have
said nothing of value which Spencer has not said
much better scientifically, — but they are infinitely
suggestive when they happen to coincide with him.
So, after a fashion, is the Vedantic philosophy (much
more so than Buddhism), and so also some few
dreams of the old Greek schools.

Your criticisms also show that you take me as
confusing changes of relation of integrated states of
conciousness with inherited integrations of emotional
feeling. These are absolutely distinct. But don't
think that I pretend to be invariably a state of facts:
without theory, a very large part of life's poetry
could never be adequately uttered.

I knew that the music of the "*Kimi ga yo*" was
new, — though I did not know the story of the
German bandmaster. But I did not know that the
words once had no reference to the Emperor. I was
more careful, however, than you give me credit for,
— since I wrote only "the syllables made sacred by
the reverential love of a century of generations,"
which, allowing for poetical exaggeration, seems to
be all right anyhow, even if the words did not refer
to the Emperor. Of course the implication to the
foreign reader would, however, be wrong.

Still, on the subject of loyalty, I cannot see that
the existence of the feeling as inborn is invalidated
by the fact of transference. The feeling is the thing,
— not the object, not the Emperor nor the Daimyō,
— which, I imagine, must have survived all the
changes. Trained from the time of the gods to
obedience and loyalty to somebody, the feeling of the

military classes would not have been instantly dissipated or annihilated by the change of government, but simply transferred. Indeed, that strikes me as having been what the Government worked for. It could not afford to ignore or throw away so enormous a source of power as the inherited feeling of the race offered, and attempted (I think very successfully) to transfer it to the Emperor. The fact in no way affects the truth or falsehood of the sketch "Yūho."

Your criticism is only a re-denial of inherited feeling as a possibility.

Ever very truly,

LAFCADIO HEARN.

TO BASIL HALL CHAMBERLAIN

APRIL, 1895.

DEAR CHAMBERLAIN, — Excuse me if I don't reply more fully to your letter, because my eyes are a little tired. I can only say I wish I were sick, somewhere near you: then perhaps you would come and see me, and talk more of these queer things. You would not find the time heavy. For the subject is a romance.

In order to convey by a diagram any picture-idea of what heredity means, one should have to draw a series of inverted cone-figures representing a reticulation of millions of cross-lines. This could only be done well under a microscope, and on a very limited scale. Because the thing goes by arithmetical progression. The individual is the product of 2, the 2 of

4, the 4 of 8, the 8 of 16 — well, you know the tale
of the smith who offered to shoe a horse with 32 nails,
to receive 1 cent on the first nail, and to double the
sum upon every nail! The enormity of inheritance
is at once apparent. But to produce another individual, another life is needed, which represents the
superimposition in the child of another infinitely
complex inheritance. The fact is only worth stating
as suggesting that under normal circumstances the
child would necessarily represent an increment. He
should receive not only the experience of his father's
race, but all that of his mother's race superimposed
upon it. The fact that he does very nearly do so is
evidenced by the reappearance in his descendants
of parental traits always invisible in himself. Mere
multiplication ought therefore to account for a
larger mental growth and progress than exists or
could ever exist.

Why does n't it? Simply because in the brain the
same selective process goes on as in the vegetable
world. As out of 10,000,000 seeds scarcely one survives: so out of a million mental impressions scarcely
one survives. Indeed, not so many. For the inheritance is of repetitions, — rarely of single impressions.
It is only when an impression has been repeated
times innumerable that it becomes transmissible, —
that it affects the cerebral structure so as to become
organic memory. The inheritance is of a very compound nature, therefore, — requiring either enormous time for development, or enormous experience.
There is reason to believe, however, that in the case
of very highly organized brains, — such as those of

the modern musician, linguist, or mathematician,—
the multiple experiences of even one lifetime may produce structural modifications capable of transmission. This is not the case except in men as much
larger than common men as Fuji is larger than an
ant-hill. And the reason is that such a brain can
daily receive billions of impressions that common
minds cannot receive in a whole lifetime. The thinking is of the constructive character,—the most
highly complex form possible; and the extreme
sensitiveness of the structures renders habitual conceptions which represent combinations of conscious
states never entered into before. Measured by mere
difference of force, the brain of the mathematician
is to the brain of the ordinary man as the most
powerful dynamo to the muscles of an ant.

Happily for mankind, not only is inheritance
something more than repetition, it is also something
less than repetition. Between these two extremes
of plus and minus the physiology of mental activities
in any lifetime represents a fierce struggle for the
survival of the best or worst. Here is where the
environment comes in,.— determining which of a
million tendencies shall have freest play or least play.
According to circumstances the impulses of the dead
are used or neglected. The more used, the more
powerful their active potentialities, and the more
apt to increase by transmission. But their vitality
is racial — measurable only by millions of years.
They may lie dormant for twenty centuries, and be
suddenly called into being again — sinister and
monstrous-seeming, because no longer in harmony

with the age. (Here is the point of the selective process.)

Here comes in the consideration of a very terrible possibility. Suppose we use integers instead of quintillions or centillions, and say that an individual represents by inheritance a total of 10 — 5 of impulses favourable to social life, 5 of the reverse. (Such a balance would really occur in many cases.) The child inherits, under favourable conditions, the father's balance plus the maternal balance of 9, — four of the number being favourable. We have then a total which becomes odd, and the single odd number gives preponderance to an accumulation of ancestral impulse incalculable for evil. It would be like a pair of scales, each holding a mass as large as Fuji. If the balance were absolutely perfect, the weight of one hair would be enough to move a mass of millions of tons. Here is your antique Nemesis awfully magnified. Let the individual descend below a certain level, and countless dead suddenly seize and destroy him, — like the Furies.

In all cases, however, except those of the very highest forms of mental activity, the psychological life consists of repetitions, — not of originalities. And environment, chance, etc., simply influence the extent and volume of the repetitions. In the case of constructive imagination, on the other hand, there are totally new combinations made independently of environment or circumstances: there is almost creation, and in certain cases absolute faculty of prediction. Instance the case of the mathematician who, without having ever seen the Iceland Spar, but knowing its qualities, said: "Cut it at such an angle, and you will see a coloured circle." They cut it, and the circle was seen for the first time by human eyes.

Properly, however, there is no such thing as an individual, but only a combination, — one balance of an infinite sum. The charm of a very superior man or woman is the ghostliest of all conceivable experiences. For the man or woman in question can in a single evening become fifty, a hundred, two hundred different people — not in fancy, but in actual fact. Here the character of the ancestral experience has been so high and rare that a different part of the race's mental life is instantly resurrected at will to welcome and charm, or to master and repel, the various sorts of character encountered, haphazard, in the salon of the aristocratic milieu.

It would be natural to ask: If the emotions and passions are inheritances, why are not these higher faculties inherited en masse as well? Because feeling is infinitely older than thinking, developed millions of years before thinking. Also because the reasoning powers have been grown out of the feelings — as trees from soil. Those forms of consciousness most connected with the animal life of the race are, of course, the first to develop, and the first to become transmissible. But the time may come when higher faculties will be also similarly transmissible.

Taking the highest possible form of human thought, — a mathematical concept, — and analyzing it, we find a whole volume is required for the mere statement of the analysis. The flash of the thought took less than a second; to write all the thinking it involved requires years. We take it to pieces by bundles of concepts and bundles of experiences, — which are changes in relations of compound states of consciousness. The relations of those states of consciousness are resolvable into simpler ones, and those into simpler, and at last we come down to mere perceptions, and the perceptions are separated into ideas, and the ideas into compound sensations, and the compound sensations into sensations simple as those of the amœba, or the humblest protozoa.

Thus we can also trace up the history of any thought from the state of mere animalcular sensation. The highest thought is resolvable into infinite compounds of such sensations. Beyond that we cannot go. The Universe may be sentient, but we don't know it. All we know is sensation and combinations of sensations in the brain. The highest spiritual sentiment is based upon the lowest animal sensations. But what is sensation? No one can tell. On this subject very awful discoveries are perhaps awaiting us.

Now heredity is the most wonderful thing of all things, because it is utterly incomprehensible.

A mathematical calculation has established beyond all question the fact that the number of ultimate units in a sperm-cell and germ-cell combined is totally insufficient to account for the number of impressions and tendencies transmitted—supposing a change in the ultimate units possible. Therefore in order to have a working theory, we are obliged to

use the term polarity, — which only means physical
tendency to relationships. But the mystery of the
transmission of the impulse remains just as far
away as ever.

Of course I can't agree with you as to the statement of culture from outside, except in the poetical
sense. Scientifically the culture movement is internal, — the responses of innumerable dead to exterior influence, — the weirdest resurrections of buried
faculties.

As for evolution being caused by outer influences,
I think the idea leads to misconception of an intelligent power working and watching things. We have
no need of such a theory. Pain is the chief mental
factor. The elements of life are remarkable in being
chemically unstable, — astonishingly unstable, and
the mere working of the universal forces on such
elements quite sufficiently accounts for all changes.
But the fact that there is no line between life and
not-life, no line between the animal and vegetable
world, no line between the visible and invisible, no
assurance that matter has any existence in itself —
that is a very awful truth. It is otherwise incorrect
to think of evolution being caused by outer influences,
because the inner forces are the really direct ones, —
answering to the outer. Moreover, the thing evolved,
and the power evolving, and the forces internal and
external, — the visible and the non-visible, — are
(so far as human reason permits us to judge) all
one and the same. We know only phenomena; and
modern thought recognizes more and more the
Indian thought that the Supreme Brahma is only

playing a chess game with himself. Absolutely we
know only forces — pure ghostliness. The individual substance is but a force combination, — its
changes are force combinations, — the powers outside are but force combinations, — the universe is
a force combination — and we can know nothing
more than vibrations.

Ever,

LAFCADIO HEARN.

P. S. I forgot to notice your statement — "not
through the physical fact of nerve-tissue," etc.

All thinking — all, without exception — is alteration of nerve-substance; either temporary motion
or motion making by countless repetition alterations
that are permanent. Physiologically, "thought"
is a very complex vibration in nerve-tissue. There
is no other meaning whatever in science for
"thought." For "thought" is a perception of relations in preëxisting states of consciousness, and
those are bundles of sensations. What "sensation" is, no man knows. That is the dark spot in
the retina of consciousness. But there is no proof
that sensation exists apart from cell-substance.

To speak of an "ideal process" outside of vibration in nervous substance is therefore like saying
that 5 times 5 = 918. It is a total denial of all
science on the subject. An idea is a bundle of
sensations, and a sensation is coincident with a
movement in cerebral cells. Without the movement there is no sensation, — not at least in the
brain. We do not know the ultimate of sensation,

but thoughts and ideas only mean complex combinations of sensations impossible outside of nerve-substance so far as we know.

Of course if you mean by culture from outside the transmission of civilization from one race to another, — then there has been enormous alteration of cerebral structure. Such alteration is even now going on in Japan, and causes yearly hundreds of deaths.

The brain of the civilized man is 30 p. c. heavier than that of the savage; and the brain of the 19th century much larger than that of the 16th (see Broca). A striking fact of evolution is brain-growth. The early mammals were remarkable for the smallness of their brains. Man's nervous structure is, of course, the most powerful of all. Cut out of the body, it is found to weigh, as a total, double that of a horse. For mind signifies motion, force, — the more powerful the mind the greater the forces evolved. Perhaps the nervous system of a whale might weigh more than that of a man as a total mass, but not nearly so much in parts corresponding with mental differences. Nevertheless the changes effected by progress in the brain are chiefly visible in the direction of increasing complexity rather than in bulk. The study of brain-casts promises to develop some interesting facts.

TO BASIL HALL CHAMBERLAIN

KŌBE, April, 1895.

DEAR CHAMBERLAIN, — In one of your recent letters, which charmed me by its kindness, — though I did not dwell on the pleasure given me, because I was so immediately occupied in discussing my psychical hobby, — you asked me: "How could I expect to hit the public more than I have done?"

Well, not with a book on Japan, perhaps; but I must do better some day with something, or acknowledge myself a dead failure. I really think I have stored away in me somewhere powers larger than those I have yet been able to use. Of course I don't mean that I have any hidden wisdom, or anything of that sort; but I believe I have some power to reach the public emotionally, if conditions allow.

One little story which would never die, might suffice, — or a volume of little stories. Stories, fiction: that is all the public care about. Not essays, however clever, — nor vagaries, nor travels, — but stories about something common to all life under the sun. And this is just the very hardest of all earthly things to do. I might write an essay on some topic of which I am now quite ignorant, — by studying the subject for the necessary time. But a story cannot be written by the help of study at all: it must come from outside. It must be a "sensation" in one's own life, — and not peculiar to any life or any place or time.

I have been studying the "will" and "shall" carefully, and think that I shall be able to avoid serious mistakes hereafter. It is difficult, however, for me to get the "instantaneous sense" — so to speak — of their correct use. The line between "intention" and "future sequence" I can't well define.

I can't help fearing that what you mean by "justice and temperateness" in writing means that you want me to write as if I were you, or at least to measure sentence or thought by your standard. This, of course, would render frank correspondence impossible, — as it does even now to some extent. If I write well of a thing one day, and badly another — I expect my friend to discern that both impressions are true, and solve the contradiction — that is, if my letters are really wanted. For absolute "justice and temperateness," one can find them in the pages of Herbert Spencer — but you would then discern that even *la raison peut fatiguer à la longue.* I should suppose the interest of letters not to be in the text, but in the writer. Am I wrong?

L. H.

TO BASIL HALL CHAMBERLAIN

Kōbe, April, 1895.

DEAR CHAMBERLAIN, — In writing to you, of course, I've not been writing a book — but simply setting down the thoughts and feelings of the moment as they come. I write a book exactly the same way; but all this has to be smoothed, ordinated, corrected, toned over twenty times before a page is ready. It strikes me, however, that the first raw emotion or fancy, which is the base of all, has its value between men who understand each other. You, on the other hand, — differently constituted, — write a letter as you would write a book. You collect and mould the thought instinctively and perhaps unconsciously before setting it on paper.

I'm not quite such an American radical as you think in consequence; for I confess to a belief in the value of aristocracies — a very strong belief. On the other hand, the reality of the thing to the man is its relation to him personally. Don't you think your comfort in all sorts and conditions may be due to your personal independence of those sorts and conditions? It is like Rufz's statement that "the first relations between men are delicious"— so long as you are in nobody's way, and have capacity to please, you have the bright side turned to you. (Again, there is this question: Are you sure the side you see and like is not the artificial side? I don't say it is, but there are possibilities.) My own dislike of mercantile people in all countries is based upon experiences of the contrary sort. But how can men, trained from childhood to watch for and to take all possible advantage of human weakness, remain a morally superior class. That they don't, needs no argument; and that the poorest people in all countries are the most moral and self-sacrificing needs no argument either. Both are acknowledged and indisputable facts in sociology, — in the study of civilized races, at least. When to this marrow-bred sense of morality is superadded the courtesy you yourself in a former letter declared without parallel, I see nothing extravagant in the statement that a Japanese *hyakushō* is more of a gentleman than an English merchant can be — if gentleness means delicate consideration for others, by means of which virtue no man can succeed in life.

I should like to know any story of heroism — sorry not to be near you to coax you for an outline of it. Every fact of goodness makes one better, and an author richer, to know it. There are good heroes and heroines in all walks of life, indeed,— though all walks of life do not necessarily lead to goodness. Indeed, there are some which teach that goodness is foolishness, — but all won't believe it is true.

The extraordinary wastefulness of foreign life is a fact that strikes one hard after life in the interior. Men work like slaves for no other earthly reason than that conventions require them to live beyond their means; and those who are free to live as they wish live on a scale that seems extravagant in the extreme. All goes right in the end, but I have not yet escaped the sensation of imagining one life devouring a hundred for mere amusement. Here is a man who spends, to my knowledge, more than $500 a week for mere amusement. He lives, therefore, at the rate of more than 1000 Japanese lives. I'm not disputing his right; but in the eternal order of things the whirligig of time must bring in strange revenges. . . .

A paper read by Spencer before the Anthropological Society, on the subject of the Method of Comparative Psychology, came into my hands the other day. It was only four or five pages — so

I could read it. What a magnificent teaching for
an essay on Japanese psychology! I may try to take
up the theme some day. There are some terrible
suggestions, however — such as that the Japanese
indifference to abstract ideas is not indifference, but
incapacity to form general ideas. The language
would seem to confirm the suggestion.

P. S. I should like to discuss the "heredity and
evolution" topic of child-feeling, but fear to weary
you with my scribble. Indeed I wrote a long letter,
but concluded not to send to-day. You are quite
right about the inherited feeling of the impulse to
martial play: the new toy would represent subject-
ively some slight modifications of inherited pleasure as regards colour, form, and noise, — but the
inherited feeling remains the chief factor in the
matter. A mask of *o tafuku* as a toy would not
effect modifications in the quality of certain inherited impressions, but only accentuate them, and
accentuate others innumerable faintly connected
with them.

Ever, with regret that I cannot write more for
the moment, yours faithfully,

LAFCADIO HEARN.

TO BASIL HALL CHAMBERLAIN

KŌBE, 1895.

DEAR CHAMBERLAIN, — I might one of these days
get a job in Loochoo, when the country becomes
richer, — and explore ghostology. The ghost-busi-
ness must be simply immense: it must be immense

anywhere that the dead are better housed than the living. Of old I felt sure that if the Egyptian demotic texts were translated, the ghostly side of that literature would be amazing — for just the same reason. Well, they have been translated; and the ghost-stories are without parallel. Assyrian ghost-ology is also very awful; but we don't know much about their necropoles, — for whatever those were, they were of perishable stuff.

As I told the Houghton firm I had a volume of philosophical fairy-tales in mind, and wanted to read Andersen again, they sent me four volumes; . . . the old charm comes back with tenfold force, and makes me despair. How great the art of the man! — the immense volume of fancy, — the magical simplicity — the astounding force of compression! This is n't mere literary art; it is a soul photographed and phonographed and put, like electricity, in storage. To write like Andersen, one must be Andersen. But the fountain of his inspiration is unexhausted, and I hope to gain by drinking from it. I read, and let the result set up disturbances interiorly. Disturbances emotional I need. I have had no sensations since leaving Kyūshū.

LAFCADIO HEARN.

TO ELLWOOD HENDRICK

KŌBE, April, 1895.

DEAR HENDRICK, — . . . Apparently the war is over; and we are glad, — with due apprehension. Possibilities are ugly. The doom of foreign trade in

Japan has, I think, begun to be knelled. In twenty-five years more the foreign merchants will be represented here by agents chiefly. The anti-foreign feeling is strong. I am not sure but it is just. Only — the innocent pay, not the guilty.

As for me, I must confess that I am only happy out of the sight of foreign faces and the hearing of English voices. Not quite happy, though — I am always worried for the future. I drew the lots of the gods: they replied yesterday at Kiyomizu in Holy Kyōto: "All you wish you shall have, but not until you are very old." H'm! Is that Delphic? Can I become very old?

No: Kazuo is not a Japanese rendering of Lafcadio. It signifies only "First of the Excellent," or "Best of the Peerless Ones," but it does serve for both purposes to the imagination.

As I watch the little fellow playing, all the dim vague sensations of my own childhood seem to come back to me. I comprehend by unexpected retrospection!

My eye is not yet quite well. But I expect it will last for some years more.

Best thanks for that admirable and timely letter of advice. Of course I shall follow it absolutely. Wish I had the advantage of being closer to my loved adviser, — for more reasons than one.

L. H.

TO PAGE M. BAKER

KŌBE, April, 1895.

DEAR PAGE, — I paid 35c. postage the other day on a huge envelope the superscription whereof filled my soul with joy. I know it is mean to mention the 35c.; but I do this on purpose, — that I may be properly revenged. Opening the envelope I found a very dear letter, for which I am more than grateful, — *and two pieces of pasteboard, for which I am not grateful at all.* The promised photo had never been put into the envelope, — only the envelope, — only the pasteboards. The two envelopes had never been opened. And the why and the wherefore of the thing I am at a loss to discern. But as you did not stop sending the paper to Kumamoto for eight months after I had vainly prayed for a change of address, I suppose that you simply forgot in both cases. . . .

About the little Japanese dress. Now the matter of a little girl's dress is much more complicated than I can tell you — if you want the real thing. Do you wish for a winter, spring, summer, or autumn dress? — for these are quite necessary distinctions. Do you wish for a holiday dress? — a ceremonial dress? — an every-day dress? The winter ceremonial dress for a girl of good family is very expensive, for it consists of silk skirt, *koshimaki* (body under-petticoat), and four or five heavily wadded silk robes one over the other, — with *obi*, etc. The *obi* is the most costly part of the dress — may run to 30 or even 50 yen: it ought to cost at least 20. The summer dress is light, and much cheaper. I think you ought to get a suit for about (yen) 60–70. Of course, no suits are ready-made. The dress must be made to order; and even the girdle worked up. To tie the girdle will be difficult, — unless a Japanese shows you the method.

If you want only a common cotton suit, which is very, very pretty, it would be quite cheap. But I suppose you want the fashionable dress, and that is as dear as you care to pay. Prices may range up into the hundreds. Boys' dresses — even winter dresses — are not so dear, but my little fellow's ceremonial dress, — the overdress alone, — cost $27 without counting the adjuncts. Boys' soft *obi* cost, however, only 3 or 4 yen; and girls' *obi* five or six times as much. Shoes (sandals) and stockings are cheap. The *geta* could scarcely be managed by a Western child. The straw sandal (*zōri*), with velvet thong, is easy and pleasant to wear. I have heard of *silk tabi*, but never saw any, and I think they are worn only by *geisha*, etc. White cotton *tabi* are the prettiest; and I have heard that white silk *tabi* never look really white, — so the coloured *tabi* would be better in silk. But everybody wears the white cotton *tabi*, and nothing could be prettier than a little foot in this cleft envelope.

The colours of the dress of a girl are much brighter than those of boys' dresses; but they change every additional year of the girl's life. They are covered with designs, generally symbolical, — full of meanings, but meaningless to Western eyes. The finest textures used — crape — silk, etc. — shrink and suffer immensely by washing; for such dresses as you would want are not worn every day — nor at school or in play.

You see the subject is really very complex, and requires years to learn much about. Only a native in any case can be relied on for choice, etc. The suits of "Japanese clothes" usually bought by foreigners in Japan, to take home to their friends, are made to order just to sell to foreigners, and are not Japanese at all — no Japanese would wear them. For the man as for the woman the rules of dress are very strict, and vary precisely according to the age of the wearer.

For a little girl two years old, you would not need a *hakama*, — divided skirt. Such *hakama* are worn by little school-girls, and are usually sky-blue. They are not, like the men's fashionable *hakama*, made of Sendai silk. The *hakama* of a high official may be very expensive.

I think what you want could be got for about $40 (American money, including all costs), unless you want a winter dress. It would be very heavy, and likely to make the little one too warm, for this climate is not like that of New Orleans. The chief cost is the *obi*, — the broad stiff heavy silk girdle.

Thanks for the sweet things you said about my little boy. He was born November 16th, '93; — so he is younger than your little angel by four or five months. Mrs. Baker was right. Trust a mother's eye to decide all such problems! And say all the kindest and wisest and prettiest things you can to Mrs. Baker for her kindest message. . . .

LAFCADIO HEARN.

P. S. What you wrote about Constance is very beautiful. No man can possibly know what life means, what the world means, what anything means, until he has a child and loves it. And then the whole universe changes, — and nothing will ever again seem exactly as it seemed before.

TO BASIL HALL CHAMBERLAIN

Kōbe, May, 1895.

Dear Chamberlain, — I received your kind letter shortly after returning from Kyōto, where I have been living in an old samurai *yashiki* transformed into a hotel.

I am quite sorry your eyes are troubling you; and indeed I should sincerely advise you to get away from all temptation to reading or writing for some months. Considering how much your translation of that ballad signified in the matter of personal kindness under such circumstances, I cannot but feel pain, — though you will not be sorry to hear that you made a sketch possible, entitled "A Street-Singer," sent to H. M. & Co. towards the construction of a new book now under way.

I have not written you before because feeling under the weather — hungry for sympathy I cannot get, and have no reason really to expect. It is only long after one gets credit as a writer that one wins any recognition as a thinker. My critics are careful to discriminate. One assures me that as a poet I am impeccable, and "a great man," but that I must remember my theories can only be decided by the "serious student." Or in other words that I am never to be taken seriously. The men taken seriously get $10,000 a year for trying to do what I could do much better. Poor myself must try to live on "dream-stuff."

I am sorry you cannot read. But still you are fortunate, because you are able to live without being at the mercy of cads and clerks. That alone is a great happiness. I am pestered with requests to do vulgar work for fools at prices they would not dare to offer, if they did not imagine me an object of charity. Happily I can get away from them all, and keep the door locked.

What a privilege to live in Kyōto. I should be glad of a very small post there. The Exhibition is marvellous — showing how Japan will revenge herself on the West. Artistically it is very disappointing. There are funny things — a naked woman (not a "nude study," but simply a naked woman in oil) for which the artist insolently asks $3000. It is worth about three rin. The Japanese don't like it, and they are right. But I fear they do not know why they are right.

Ever with best regards,
LAFCADIO HEARN.

TO PAGE M. BAKER

KŌBE, May, 1895.

DEAR PAGE, — It was *almost* unkind, after all to have sent the very dear picture, because it brought back too vividly hours of pleasant talk and kind

words and great projects and all sorts of things
which have forever passed away. But there was a
pleasure in the pain too, — for it is quite a help in
life to feel that ever so far away there is somebody
who loves you, and whom Time will not quickly
change. You look just the same. I — I should
scare you were I to send you a picture — you would
think Time was much faster than he is. For I am
very ancient to behold.

Well, love to you for the picture. . . .

Of news little to tell you that you do not get
from other sources. Japan has yielded the Liao-tung
Peninsula; but the nation is full of sullen anger
against Russia and the interference-powers. The
press is officially muzzled; but there is no mistaking
the popular feeling. Even an overthrow of the existing Government is not impossible, and a return to
that military autocracy which is really the natural
government of an essentially military race. If the
Japanese house of representatives had not interfered
seriously and idiotically with naval expansion,
Russian interference would have been almost impossible.

I was on the Matsushima yesterday, the flag-
ship. She has few scars outside; but she must have
been half torn to pieces inside. Her decks were
covered only a few months back with blood and
brains. She is only 4280 tons; and she had to fight
with two 7400 ton battle-ships and European gun-
ners. She lost half her crew, but won gloriously.
(The Japanese really never lost one ship — only a
torpedo-boat that got run aground.) The people are

only playful spite; for I should be glad to get letters
from you upon those conditions. The Japanese
P.O. people don't seem to do things after our
fashion just now, since discharging all their foreign
employés. The new clerks get about $10.00 a
month ($4.50 American money), and most of them
are married on that!

No: I do not see the newspapers. The clubs
have them; but I take infinite care to avoid the
vicinity of clubs. Sometimes a friend sends me a
paper (the *Herald*, for example); and the publishers
sent me only a few notices this time, — about
three, I think. That *Herald* I saw, through kindness
of a man whom I don't even know.

I don't know that you are wrong about not
ordering the dress just now. The taller the little
Constance gets, the better she will look in one. I
fancy that the summer dress will be best, — it
shows the figure a little: the winter dress, for a
cold day, makes one look a little bit roly-poly.
Perhaps a little school-girl's dress would please

you; — though it is not very dear, but rather very cheap, it is pretty, — quite pretty and of many colours. The Japanese robes bought in Japan by foreign ladies are especially made for them; — they are not the real thing. No pretty grown-up American girl would feel comfortable in the Japanese girdle, which is not tied round the waist, but round the hips, — so that Japanese women, well dressed, look shorter-limbed then they really are, and they are short of limb compared with the women of Northern races. Much stuff has been written, however, about the short-legged Japanese. I have seen as well-limbed men as one could care to see: — they are shorter of stature than Northern Europeans or Americans, but they would make a very good comparison with French, Spanish, or Italians — the dark types. They are heavily built, too, sometimes. The Kumamoto troops are very sturdy; and the weight of the men surprised me. But the finest men, except labourers, that I have seen in Japan are the men-of-war's-men, — the blue-jackets. They are picked from the sturdiest fishing population of Southern Japan, where the men grow big, and I have seen several over six feet.

But I have been digressing. It was very sweet, — your little picture of home life with the darling *fillette*. She is much more advanced than my boy. He is younger, of course; but girls mature intellectually so much quicker than boys. He is puzzled, too, by having to learn two languages, — each totally different in thought construction; but he knows, when the postman gives him a letter, which language it is written in. I think, though it is not for me to say it, that the whole street loves him; — for everybody brings him presents and pets him. At first he worried me a little by calling out to every foreigner, — some rough ones into the bargain, — "Hei, papa!" But the old sea-captains and the mercantile folk thus addressed would take him up in their arms and pet him; and there is a big captain with a red face who watches for him regularly, to give him candies, etc. We are going soon to another house; and we shall miss the good kind captain.

I 'm still out of work, and going to stay out of it. I think I can live by my pen. I am not sure, of course; but I can hang out here a couple of years more, anyhow, — and trust to luck. My publishers seem to be all right.

Infinite thanks about the syndicate project. I can certainly undertake the matter for the figure named, — for I won't be away more than six months. I have written my publishers to ask if I can get certain proofs of a new book (not quite finished yet — so please don't mention it) early enough to start about October. I should like one provision, — that I may choose another point, such as Java, in preference to Manila or Ryūkyū, — supposing ugly circumstances, such as cholera, intervene. I might try a French colony, — Tonkin, Noumea, or Pondicherry. At all events this would not hurt the syndicate's interests. I should hope to be back in spring; and I would not disappoint you as to quality. Perhaps the more queer places I go to, the better for the syndicate.

I don't know what to tell you about war-matters. The unjust interference of the three powers has to be considered, though, from two points of view. The first is, that the anger of the nation may create such a feeling in the next Diet as to provoke a temporary suspension of the constitution. The second is that most of us feel the check to Japan was rather in the interest of foreign residents. The feeling against foreigners had been very strong, not without reason, as the foreign newspapers, excepting the *Mail* and the *Kōbe Chronicle*, had mostly opposed the new treaties, and criticized the war in an unkindly spirit. Besides, there never had been any really good feeling between foreigners and Japanese in the open ports. Now there was really danger that after a roaring triumph, without check, over China, the previous feeling against foreigners would take more violent form. The sympathetic action of England improved the feeling very much; and really I think the check will in the end benefit Japan. She will be obliged to double or triple her naval strength, and wait a generation. In the meantime she will gain much in other power, military and industrial. Then she will be able to tackle Russia, — if she feels as she now does. The army and navy were furiously eager to fight Russia. But Russia has enormous staying power; and the fleets of three nations stood between the 150,000 men abroad and the shores of Japan. Of course it was a risk. England might have settled the naval side of the matter in Japan's favour. But war would have had sad consequences to industry and commerce. The Japanese statesmen were right. Besides, what does Japan lose? — Nothing, except a position; for the retrocession must be heavily paid for. The anger of the people is only a question of national vanity wounded; — and though they would sacrifice everything for war, it is better that they were not suffered by the few wise heads to do so.

I was sorry about your having to slap that fellow. But you will always be the old-style Knight — preferring to give a straight-out blow, than simply to sit down at a desk and score a man every day, unwearyingly, as Northern editors do.

I am glad to hear of Matas. I used to love him very much. . . .

As to kissing in Japan, there is no kissing. Kissing is not "forbidden" at all; — there is simply no impulse to kiss among the Turanian races. All Aryan races have the impulse, as an affectionate greeting. Children do not kiss their parents; — but the pressing of cheek to cheek is nearly the same thing — as a demonstration. Mothers lip their little ones; — but — how shall I explain? The kiss, as we understand it in the Occident, is considered not as an affectionate, but as a *sexual* impulse, or as of kin to such an impulse. Now this is absolutely true. Undoubtedly the modern kiss of the cultivated West may have no such meaning in 99,997 cases out of 99,998. But the original primitive signification of pressing lip to lip, as Aryan races do, or even lip to cheek, is physiologically traceable to the love which is too often called

l'amour, but which has little to do with the higher
sense of affection. With us the impulse of a child
to kiss is absolutely *instinctive*. The Japanese
child has no such impulse whatever; but his way
of caressing is none the less delicious.

On the other hand, it is significant that the Japanese word for "dear," "lovable" is also used to
signify "sweetness" of the material saccharine kind.
But perhaps this is offset by the fact that Japanese
confectionery, though delicious, never nauseates
through over-sweetness; and that the quantity of
sugar used is very much less than with us. One
never gets tired of *kwashi;* but plumcake and
bonbons in the West need to be sparingly used.
Perhaps we want too much sweetness of all kinds.
The Japanese are in all things essentially temperate
and self-restrained—as a people. Of course, Western notions and examples begin to spoil them a
little.

It is possible by the time this reaches you that
I shall have become a Japanese citizen, — for legal
reasons. (Say nothing yet about it.) If I marry
my wife before the consul, then she becomes
English, and loses the right to hold property in her
own country. Marrying her by Japanese custom
will not be acknowledged as legal, without special
permission of the minister of foreign affairs, — but
if I get the permission, then she becomes English,
and the *boy* too. So my marriage, though legal
according to every moral code, and according to
the old law, becomes illegal by new law, and the
wife and family—as I really follow the Japanese

code, supporting father, mother, and grandparents
— have no rights except through a will, which
relatives can dispute. I therefore cut the puzzle by
changing nationality, and becoming a Japanese.
Then I lose all chance of Government employ at
a living salary; for the Englishman who becomes a
Japanese is only paid by the Japanese scale. Also
I lose the really powerful protection given to Englishmen by their own nation. Finally I have to pay
taxes much bigger than consular fees, and my
boy becomes liable to military service. (But that
won't hurt him.) I hope in any case to give him
a scientific education abroad. The trouble is I am
now forty-five. I'll be sleeping in some Buddhist
cemetery before I can see him quite independent. . . .

I have lost friends because their wives did n't like
me — more than once; — as Chamberlain says,
"No: you'll never be a ladies' man." But the
kindly spirit of Mrs. Baker shows even through
your own letters; — and if I can ever see you again,
I know that, although not a ladies' man, I won't
be disliked in one friend's home as a fugitive visitor.
Say everything grateful to her for me that you can.

Good-bye, with love to your pretty gold-head, —
and regards to all friends.

LAFCADIO HEARN.

TO BASIL HALL CHAMBERLAIN

KōBE, July, 1895.

DEAR CHAMBERLAIN, — In reading Schopenhauer (I believe you have the splendid Haldane & Kemp version in three volumes: it is said to preserve even the remarkable sonority of the German original), you may notice where Schopenhauer failed, only through want of knowledge undeveloped in his time. While highly appreciating Lamarck, — the greatest of the evolutionists before Darwin, greater even than Goethe, — he finds fault with his theory as not showing proof of the prototype formless animal from which all organic forms existing are derived. Therefore Schopenhauer insisted on the potential prototype existing in the Will only. But since Schopenhauer's day, the material formless prototypal animal has been found; and the theory of Schopenhauer as to forms falls back into a region of pure metaphysics. He is none the less valuable on that account. He represents the soul (psyche) of an enormous fact, or at least a soul which can be fitted to the body of science for the time being. He has been justly called a German Buddhist; and his philosophy is entirely based on the study of Brahmanic and Buddhist texts. The only absolutely novel theory in his book is the essay on sexual love, — vol. 3 in your edition. There is one defect in it, but that does not hurt the value of the whole. And then the splendour of style, of self-assertion, of imagery Huxley equalled only, I think twice, in all of his essays. Of course Schopenhauer belongs to the evolutional school; that is the reason why he has been taken up to-day after long neglect. His work gives new force to evolutional psychology of the new school. The most remarkable popular effect of the newer school has not, I think, yet been noticed. It is in fiction; and the success of a work taken in this line recently has made a fortune for publishers and author. Unfortunately, poor I have not the constructive art necessary to attempt anything of the kind — not yet! Perhaps in twenty years more.

Very faithfully,

LAFCADIO HEARN.

TO BASIL HALL CHAMBERLAIN

KŌBE, August, 1895.

DEAR CHAMBERLAIN, — A delicious surprise, — though one that gave some pain; for I suffered to think you should have used your eyes to such an extent for my sake. Mason, too, one day actually wrote me that he would copy something for me if I needed it (which luckily I had got from another source): I should be pained to have either of you try your eyes for my poor vagaries. Please don't think me too selfish; — it was simply lovable of you, but don't do it again.

I think I may be able to use a fragment or two effectively: what I want now to get is the rhythm used in the singing, — and that none of my people can remember. They said it was very wonderful, but very difficult to catch: so that it would seem some melodies are as hard for the Japanese themselves to learn by ear, as they are for us to so learn. I had the same curious experience at Sakai and in Kizuki; yet I asked persons who had been listening to the singing for several hours, and were natives of the place. They all said, "Ah! that is very difficult. So a good *ondo tori* is hard to find; and they are paid well to come to our festivals." But when the woman comes again I shall try to syllabify the measure on paper.

I can feel the popular mind in the peasant songs: in the military songs I cannot. But there is a queer variation in tone used in military singing which is very effective. The leader suddenly turns down his voice nearly a full octave, and all the chorus follow: it is like a sudden and terrible menace, — then all go back to high tenor notes again. What you tell me about Ryūkyū priests' songs surprised me. You must have got everything that could be got there in an astonishingly short time. I sent you the Nara *miko*-songs, — mystical hymns about sowing, etc., — very artless. The Nara and Kompira *miko* are really virgins. *Entre nous* I am sorry to say that the *miko* of Kizuki are not: but, as they ought to be, there is no use specifying in any public way. It would be like denying the virtue of nuns in general, because one or two sisters fall from grace. While the ideal lives anywhere it strikes me as wrong to insist too much on realism.

I know you make a collection of everything relating to Japan, so I must send you a photo of Yuko Hatakeyama. I had it copied from a badly faded one — so it does not come out well. You are

not of those who refuse to see beyond the visible;
and though there is nothing beautiful or ideal in this
figure, it was certainly the earthly chrysalis of a very
precious and beautiful soul, which I have tried to
make the West love a little bit. So you may prize it.

Some one, thinking to please me, sent me by this
mail a large French periodical, full of gravures
porno- or semi-pornographiques, Saint Anthony and
French courtesans and angels mixed up together.
I burned the thing, — astonished at the revulsion
of feeling it produced in myself. (The work was
beautiful in its way, of course, but the way!) After
all, it seems to me that Japanese life is essentially
chaste: its ideals are chaste. I can feel now exactly
how a Japanese feels about certain foreign tendencies. I know all about Japanese picture-books of a
certain class — innocent things in their very frankness: there is more real evil, or at least more moral
weakness in any number of certain French public
prints. It strikes me also that the charm even of
the *jōro* to the Japanese mind is quite different from
any corresponding Western feeling. She figures
simply as an ideal lady of old time, and the graces
cultivated in her, and the costume donned, are those
of an ideal past. The animalism of half-exposures
and suggestions of whole exposures is not any more
Japanese than it was old-Persian. Even the naughty
picture-books were intended for imitations, catechism.

Talking of catechism, I have been thinking of
making a Buddhist catechism of a somewhat fantastic sort.

"How old are you?"

"I am millions of millions of years old, as a phenomenon. As absolute I am eternal and older than the universe," etc.

Faithfully ever,

LAFCADIO HEARN.

TO ELLWOOD HENDRICK

KŌBE, September, 1895.

DEAR HENDRICK, — . . . I am waiting every day for the sanction of the minister to change my name; and I think it will come soon. This will make me Koizumi Yakumo, or, — arranging the personal and family names in English order, — "Y. Koizumi." "Eight clouds" is the meaning of "Yakumo," and is the first part of the most ancient poem extant in the Japanese language. (You will find the whole story in "Glimpses" — article "Yaegaki.") Well, "Yakumo" is a poetical alternative for Izumo, my beloved province, "the Place of the Issuing of Clouds." You will understand how the name was chosen.

If all goes well, and I am not obliged to return to America, I shall next year probably return to Izumo, and make a permanent home there. So long as I can travel in winter, I need not care about the weather. When my boy grows big enough, if I live, I shall take him abroad, and try to give him a purely scientific education — modern languages if possible, no waste of time on Latin, Greek, and stupidities. (Literature and history can be best learned at home;

and the greatest men are not the products of schools, not in England or America, at least: Germany is an exception.) He might turn out to be very commonplace, in which case all plans must be changed; but I suspect he will not be stupid. He says, by the way, that he was a doctor in his former birth. It is quite possible, for he has my father's eyes.

In regard to what you asked me about the English literature business, I think there is no way of teaching English literature except by selections, — joined together with an evolutional study of English emotional life, illustrated after the manner of Taine's "Art in Italy," etc. But such work, combining history with literature, would involve the use of an immense library, and would be very costly to the teacher. By the way, I *hate* English literature. French literature is much more interesting. What I should most like would be to make a study of comparative literature—including Sanscrit, Finnish, Arabic, Persian, — systematizing the best specimens of each into kindred groupings on the evolutional plan. That *would* be worth doing; for it means a study of the evolutional development of all mankind. But such undertakings, I fear, are for the extremely rich. LAFCADIO HEARN.

TO ELLWOOD HENDRICK

KŌBE, Autumn, 1895.

DEAR HENDRICK, — . . . It has often occurred to me to ask whether you think other men feel as I do about some things—you yourself, for example.

Work with me is a pain—no pleasure till it is done.
It is not voluntary; it is not agreeable. It is forced
by necessity. The necessity is a curious one. The
mind, in my case, eats itself when unemployed.
Reading, you might suggest, would employ it. No:
my thoughts wander, and the gnawing goes on just
the same. What kind of gnawing? Vexation and
anger and imaginings and recollections of unpleasant things said or done. *Unless somebody does or
says something horribly mean to me, I can't do certain
kinds of work,* — the tiresome kinds, that compel
a great deal of thinking. The exact force of a hurt
I can measure at the time of receiving it: "This
will be over in six months;" "This I shall have to
fight for two years;" "This will be remembered
longer." When I begin to think about the matter
afterwards, then I rush to work. I write page after
page of vagaries, metaphysical, emotional, romantic,
— throw them aside. Then next day, I go to work
rewriting them. I rewrite and rewrite them till
they begin to define and arrange themselves into a
whole, — and the result is an essay; and the editor
of the *Atlantic* writes, "It is a veritable illumination,"
— and no mortal man knows why, or how it was
written, — not even I myself, — or what it cost to
write it. Pain is therefore to me of exceeding value
betimes; and everybody who does me a wrong
indirectly does me a right. I wonder if anybody else
works on this plan. The benefit of it is that a *habit*
is forming, — a habit of studying and thinking in a
way I should otherwise have been too lazy-minded
to do. But whenever I begin to forget one burn,

new caustic from some unexpected quarter is poured into my brain: then the new pain forces other work. It strikes me as being possibly a peculiar morbid condition. If it is, I trust that some day the power will come to do something really extraordinary — I mean very unique. What is the good of having a morbid sensitive spot, if it cannot be utilized to some purpose worth achieving?

There was a funny suicide here the other day. A boy of seventeen threw himself on the railroad track and was cut to pieces by a train. He left a letter to his employer, saying that the death of the employer's little son had made the world dark for him. The child would have nobody to play with: so, he said, "I shall go to play with him. But I have a little sister of six; — I pray you to take care of her."

Ever affectionately,
LAFCADIO HEARN.

TO BASIL HALL CHAMBERLAIN

SEPTEMBER, 1895.

MY DEAR CHAMBERLAIN, — Your paper on Luchu gave me more pleasure, I am sure, than it even did to the president of the society before whom it was read; and I was delighted with the nice things said of you. Of course this paper — being a much more elaborate monograph than the other — differs from its predecessor in the matter of suggestiveness. To me it is like a graded anthropological map, — shading off the direction of character-tendencies, language, customs, to the uttermost limit of the subject. I had no idea how much you had been doing in the Archipelago — your own field of research by unquestionable right. If I ever go down there I shall certainly attempt nothing out of the much humbler line which I can follow: there is really nothing left for another man to do in the way of gathering general knowledge about an unfamiliar region.

There is one expression of opinion in the monograph which I may venture a remark about. The idea is growing upon me, more and more each day I live, that the supposed indifferentism of the Japanese in religious matters is affected indifferentism — that it is put on like *yofuku*, only for foreigners. I see too much of the real life, even here in Kōbe, to think the indifferentism real. And I believe the Jesuits, who are better judges far than our comfortable modern proselytizers, never accused the Japanese of indifference. However, this is but suggestive: I think that should you ever find time to watch the incidents of common life minutely, you will recognize the Jesuits as the keenest observers. As for the educated classes, I have also reason to know that in most cases the indifference is feigned. This will show you how my own opinions have changed in five years' time.

Very truly yours,

LAFCADIO HEARN.

TO SENTARŌ NISHIDA

KŌBE, October, 1895.

DEAR NISHIDA, — Kazuo knows your picture, always hanging on the wall by my desk, and your name — so that if you see him soon, he will not think you a stranger. He talks well now, but is getting naughty, like his father used to be — very naughty. I see my own childish naughtiness all over again. I think he will be cleverer than his father. If he shows real talent, I shall try to take him to France or to Italy, later on in life. English schools I don't like: they are too rough. New England schools are better; especially for the earlier teaching. The systems of Spencer and others have been much better followed out in Eastern Massachusetts than in England, where religious conservatism persists in loading the minds with perfectly useless acquirements. The future demands scientific education — not ornamented; and the thoroughly trained man never needs help. I remember a friend in the United States Army, — engineer and graduate of West Point (a splendid institution): he was coaxed out of the army by an electrical company because of his knowledge of applied mathematics. What wonderful men one meets among the scientifically educated to-day one must go abroad to know. Such men, unfortunately, do not come to Japan. If *they* had been chosen for teachers, I fancy that education would have felt their influence. It does not feel the influence of common foreign teachers. But, a student said to me, "We must cultivate our own

powers through our own language hereafter,"— and
I think he expressed the sensible general feeling of
the day.

Ever with kindest hopes and wishes for you,

LAFCADIO HEARN.

TO BASIL HALL CHAMBERLAIN

KŌBÉ, November, 1895.

DEAR CHAMBERLAIN,—Your more than gracious
flying visit, having set in motion the machinery of
converse, left me long continuing a phantom talk
with a phantom professor across a real table, —
which I touched to make sure.

Then my wife's delight with her Miyako-miyage,
and the boy's with the pictures, you can imagine, —
though not perhaps my own feeling of mingled
pleasure and sorrow. Whatever you do is done so
delicately and finely that I fear I could show no
appreciation of it in writing.

It was lucky that we had returned from Kyōto
just so as to be here for your visit. What pleased
me most of all, perhaps, was your seeing my boy.
I have often thought if I can realize my dream of
taking him to Europe, which now seems quite
possible, I might some day have the pleasure of
presenting him as a man.

You wanted a thinking book; and I must confess
that is now my own want: I care only for a novel
when it illustrates some new philosophical idea, or
when it possesses such art that it can be studied for
the art alone. Perhaps Lombroso would interest

(and revolt) you at the same time: Nordau is only a new edition of Lombroso, I think — a journalistic one. I detest his generalizations, so far as I know them through extracts: all being false that I have seen. Progress depends on variation; and the morale of Nordau would lead to, or accentuate, already existing Chinese notions in the conventional world, that all departures from formality and humbug are to be explained by degeneration. Without having read it, I should judge the book a shallow one, — much at variance with Spencer's views on eccentricity and its values. Of the Italian school, Mantegazza most appeals to me, and would, I think to you — though he is sentimental as Michelet in "L'Amour." . . .

You think me too dissatisfied, don't you? It is true I am not satisfied, and already unable to look at my former work. But the moment a man can feel satisfied with himself, progress stops. He can only move along a level afterwards; and I hope the level is still some years off. (I see a possibility to strive for; but I am afraid even to speak of it — so well out of reach it now is.) But what you will be glad to hear is that my publishers are treating me well enough. I have up to September made about 2000 yen (Japanese money), and prospects of making about 4000 in 1896. It is now largely a question of eyes.

I visited the grave of Yuko Hatakeyama last week at Kyōto, — and saw all the touching relics of her, and of her suicide: also secured copies of her letters, etc. A nice monument has been erected over her resting-place by public subscription; and there was a little cup of tea before the *sekito* when I arrived.

Needless to say that I am asked to send messages which could only be spoiled by putting them into English, and my wife is ashamed, or at least shy, of writing what she would like to write if possessing more self-confidence in matters epistolary. But you will understand without more words.

Most gratefully,

LAFCADIO HEARN.

TO SENTARŌ NISHIDA

KŌBE, December, 1895.

DEAR NISHIDA, — I suppose we have both been very busy — you with the winter school-term, and I with my new book. I trust you got my last letter, and that you know how grateful we feel to you for the advice and help given to Mr. Takaki, and for smoothing matters. We are also anxious to hear that you are well, and are hoping to see you this coming summer.

As for the naturalization business, it seems to hang fire.[1] A couple of months ago, there came to the house an official, who asked us many questions. What he asked me was not important or interesting; but his questions to Setsu were amusing. He enquired how long we had been together — whether I had always been kind — whether she thought I would always be good to her — whether she would

[1] I am not sure if you know this expression; — it is said of a gun or pistol which does not go off when the trigger is pulled.

be content always to have such a husband — whether she was in earnest — whether she had made the application of her own free will, or under pressure from relations — whether I had not forced her to make such an application — whether she held any property in my name. Afterwards she had to go to some office where she was asked the same questions over again. Since that time we have heard nothing. I am wondering if my request (or her request, I should say) will be refused. I suppose it could be; and I have not been over-prudent, for I did not reply respectfully to the offer of a place of some sort in the university — what kind of place I don't know — made through Kano, — and I think Saionji has charge of the foreign business just now. Perhaps it is all right; — the delay, however, has its legal vexations: — money-orders having been made out, for example, in a Japanese name, — a little too soon. What a funny thing it all is.

I made the acquaintance some ten days ago of Wadamori Kikujirō, — the memory-man. He is a native of Shimane. I did all I could to please him, and hope to do more. He gave me an exhibition of his wonderful power, — and another exhibition to a small circle of foreigners to whom I was able to introduce him. They were very much pleased.

I think I told you that "Kokoro" is printed, — that is, in type. I am waiting only for the proofs. I think you will get a copy in March or April. Half of another Japanese book has been written, and part of another book (not on Japanese subjects) — so you will see how hard I have been working. Also my eyes are very much better. It seems to have been a case of blood to the eyes; and a doctor told me that if I took violent exercise I should get well. I did so, — and got quite well. I have only now to be careful.

Exercise was difficult at first; but now I am used to it. By exercising every day, I have kept quite well.

Kazuo, except for a cold, is all a father can imagine. He talks very well now, and tries to draw a little. I must get rich for his sake if I have any brains to make money. My friends in America and England predict good fortune for me. I am not too hopeful; but I think it is much better that I hereafter devote all my efforts to writing — until I find whether I can do well by it. Should I succeed I can travel everywhere, and Kazuo's education abroad would not be a cause of anxiety.

Ever with warmest regards,
LAFCADIO HEARN.

TO ELLWOOD HENDRICK

KŌBE, December, 1895.

DEAR HENDRICK, — Eyes a little better, and courage reviving. Moreover I enclose letter showing prospects in a better light. The book is to be out in spring.

My boy is beginning to talk, and to look better. He walks now. He has much changed, — always growing fairer. I shall send a photo of him as soon as I think the difference from his first chubby aspect becomes apparent enough to interest you. . . .

What succeeds like force? — eh? See what Japan has now become in the eyes of the world! Yet that war was unjust, unnecessary. It was forced upon Japan. She knew her strength. Her people wished to turn that strength against European powers. Her rulers, more wisely, turned the storm against China, — just to show the West what she could do, if necessary. Thus she has secured her autonomy. But let no man believe Japan hates China. China is her teacher and her Palestine. I anticipate a reaction against Occidental influence after this war, of a very serious kind. Japan has always hated the West — Western ideas, Western religion. She has always loved China. Free of European pressure, she will assert her old Oriental soul again. There will be no conversion to Christianity. No! not till the sun rises in the West. And I hope to see a United Orient yet bound into one strong alliance against our cruel Western civilization. If I have been able to do nothing else in my life, I have been able at least to help a little — as a teacher and as a writer, and as an editor — in opposing the growth of what is called society and what is called civilization. It is very little, of course, — but the gods ought to love me for it. They ought to make me rich enough to go every year for six months to uncivilized lands — such as Java, Borneo, etc. If I have good luck with my books, I 'll make a tropical trip next spring.

Love to you,
LAFCADIO.

TO ELLWOOD HENDRICK

TŌKYŌ, January, 1896.

DEAR HENDRICK, — It is really queer, you know
— this university. It is imposing to look at, — with
its relics of feudalism, to suggest the picturesque
past, surrounding a structure that might be in the
city of Boston, or in Philadelphia, or in London,
without appearing at all out of place. There is even
a large, deserted, wood-shadowed Buddhist temple
in the grounds!

The students have uniforms and peculiar caps
with Chinese letters on them; but only a small per-
centage regularly wear the uniform. The old discipline has been relaxed; and there is a general
return to sandals and robes and *hakama*, — the cap
alone marking the university man.

About seventy-five per cent of the students ought
not to be allowed in the university at all for
certain branches. Some who know no European
language but French attend German lectures on
philosophy; some who know nothing of any European language attend lectures on philology. What is
the university, then ? — is it only a mask to impose
upon the intellectual West ? No: it is the best Japan
can do, but it has the fault of being a gate to public
office. Get through the university, and you have
a post — a start in life. Fancy the outside Oriental
pressure to force lads through — the influences inter-
crossing and fulminating ! Accordingly, the power
within is little more than nominal. Who rules in
fact ? Nobody exactly. Certainly the Directing

MR. HEARN'S GARDEN IN TŌKYŌ

President does not, — nor do the heads of colleges, except in minor matters of discipline. All, or nearly all, are graduates of German, English, or French or American universities; — they know what ought to be — but they do only what they can. Something nameless and invisible, much stronger than they, — political perhaps, certainly social, — overawes the whole business.

I ought not to say anything, and won't *except to you*. No foreign professor says much, — even after returning home. None have had just cause to complain of treatment received. Besides, if things were as they are in the West, I would n't be allowed to teach (there would be a demand for a "Christian" *and* gentleman). I lecture on subjects which I do not understand; and yet without remorse, because I know just enough to steer those who know much less. After a year or two I shall probably be more fit for the position.

Studying in one class, for a university text, Tennyson's "Princess" (my selection); in another, "Paradise Lost," — the students wanted it, because they heard it was difficult. They are beginning to perceive that it is unspeakably difficult for them. (Remember, they know nothing of Christian mythology or history.) I lecture on the Victorian poets, etc., and on special themes, — depending a good deal on dictation.

Only two and one half miles from the university. Seas of mud between. One hour daily to go, and one to return by jinrikisha ! — agony unspeakable. But I have one joy. No one ever dreams of com-

ing to see me. To do so one should have webbed
feet and be able to croak and to spawn, — or else
one should become a bird. It has rained for three
months almost steadily; — some of the city is under
water: the rest is partly under mud. And to increase
the amphibious joy, half the streets are torn open
to put down Western water-mains. They will yawn
thus, probably, for years to come.

The professors I have seen few of. I send you
two books; notice the charming pictures to "Ino-
shima." Florenz is a Magister Artium Liberalium
of Heidelberg, I think, — fat and good-natured and
a little — odd. There is a Russian professor of
philosophy, Von Koeber, — a charming man and
a divine pianist. There is a go-and-be-damned-
to-you American professor of law. . . . There
is a Jesuit priest, Emile Heck, — professor of
French literature. There is a Buddhist priest,
professor of Buddhism. There is an anti-Chris-
tian thinker and really great philosopher, Inoue
Tetsujirō, — lectures against Western Christianity,
and on Buddhism. There is an infidel, — a ren-
egade, — a man lost to all sense of shame and
decency, called Lafcadio Hearn, professing atheism
and English Literature and various villainous notions
of his own.

The Jesuit I did not want to know. I am afraid
of Jesuits. Out of the corner of mine cyclops-eye
I looked upon him. Elegantly dressed, — with a
beard enormous, bushy, majestic, black as hell, —
and a small keen bright black caressing demoniac
eye. The Director, who knows not, introduced

me ! — oh ! ah ! Embarrassed at the thought of
my own thoughts contrasted with the perfect courtesy of the man. Blundered; — spoke atrocious
French; gave myself away; got questioned without
receiving any idea in return except an idea of admiration for generous courtesy and very quick piercing
keenness. Felt uncomfortable all day after—talked
to myself as if I had still before me the half-shut
Jesuit eye and the vast and voluminous beard. *Et
le fin au prochain numéro, — ou plus tard.*

L. H.

TO PAGE M. BAKER

Kōbe, January, 1896.

DEAR PAGE, — What a pleasure your letter was —
in spite of the typewriting ! How shall I answer it ?
From the end backwards, — as the last was the
most pleasant.

Of course it was *really* long ago that we used to sit
together — sometimes in your office, sometimes upon
a doorstep, sometimes at a little marble-topped
table somewhere over a glass of something, — and
talk such talk as I never talked since. It is very
nearly ten years ago. That is quite true. But you
say that my flitting has been my gain, and that I have
made myriads of friends by my books. That is not
quite so true as you think. You think so only because
you have still the heart of the old Southern gentleman, — the real aristo. and soldier, — the man
who said exactly what he thought, and expected
other people to do the same, and lived in a world

where people did so. That is why also you remain
for me quite distinct and different from other men:
you have never lost your ideals — therefore you can
remain ideal to others, as you will always do to me.
But you are enormously mistaken in supposing that
I have made myriads of friends, or gained anything
— except what one gains by disillusion, and the
change that comes with the care and love of others:
this, of course, is gain. But book-success ! No: it
seems to me just the reverse. The slightest success
has to be very dearly paid for. It brings no friends
at all, but many enemies and ill-wishers. It brings
letters from autograph-hunters, and letters enclosing
malicious criticisms, and letters requesting subscriptions to all sorts of shams, and letters of in-
vitation to join respectable-humbug societies, and
requests to call on people who merely want to gratify
the meanest sort of curiosity, — that which views
a fellow creature *only* as a curiosity. Then, of
course, there are uncounted little tricks and adver-
tising dodges to be avoided like pitfalls, — and extravagant pretences of sympathy, often so clever
as to seem really genuine, made for utilitarian purposes. Then there are all sorts of little snobberies
and patronizings and disappointments. And after
the work is done, it soon begins to get shabby and
threadbare in memory; and I pick it up and wonder
how I could have written it, and marvel how anybody
could have bought it, and find that the criticisms
which I did n't like were nearly all true. Sometimes
I feel good, and think I have really done well; but
that very soon passes, and in a day or two I find I

have been all wrong, and sure never to write anything quite right.

The fact seems to be that when ideals go away, writing becomes mere downright hard work; and the reward of the pleasure of finishing it is not for me, because I have nobody to talk to about it, and nobody to take it up, and read it infinitely better than I could do myself. The most delightful criticisms I ever had were your own readings aloud of my vagaries in the *T.-D.* office, after the proofs came down. How I should like to have that experience once more — just to hear you read something of mine quite fresh from the composition-room, — with the wet sharp inky smell still on the paper !

But I suppose I have gained otherwise. You also. For there is something in everybody — the best of him, too, is n't it ? — which only unfolds in him when he has to think about his double, — the other self to which he has given existence; and then he sees things differently. I suppose you do. I imagine you must now be ever so much more lovable than you used to be — but that you have less of yourself proportionately to give away. If I were in New Orleans I don't think that I could coax you to talk after a fixed hour: you would say, "— ! it 's after twelve o'clock: I must be off!"

What you write about little Miss Constance is very sweet. I hope soon to send her some Japanese fairy-tales written by your humble servant; — that is, I *hope;* for the Tōkyō publisher is awfully slow in getting them out. You have had anxiety, I find. But the delicacy that causes it means a highly

complex nervous organization; and the anxieties will
be well compensated, I fancy, later on. She will
become, judging from the suggestion of that gold-
head in the photograph, almost too beautiful: I hope
to see another photograph later on. I shall send one
of Kazuo in a few days. We were terribly frightened
about him, — for he caught a serious cold on the
lungs; but after a few weeks he picked up well. He
gets taller, and every day surprises us with some new
observation. He seems to get fairer always instead
of darker — nobody now ever takes him to be a Japanese boy. He is very jealous of his mother, — won't
allow me to monopolize her for even five minutes;
and I am no longer master in my own house. Servants and relatives and grandparents, they all obey
him, — and pay no attention at all to my wishes
unless they happen to be in harmony with his own.
Certainly Japanese people are kinder to children
than any other people in the world, — too good altogether. Still, they do not spoil children, — for as
a general rule they manage to make them grow up
strangely, incomprehensibly obedient. I don't understand it, — except as heredity: indeed, I may as
well frankly say that the longer I live in Japan, the
less I know about the Japanese. "That is a sign,"
says one Oriental friend, "that you are beginning to
understand. It is only when a foreigner confesses
he knows nothing about us that there is some reason
to expect he will understand us later on."

About the letters, I need only say, perhaps, that
I shall give you the best of what I write this year
(excepting, of course, essays on Buddhist philosophy,

or stuff of that sort, which would be out of place,
no doubt, in a newspaper). I may include a few
little stories. . . .

"Kokoro" ought to reach you next March. It is
rather a crazy book; but I wish I could hear you *read*
one or two pages in it. . . .

Ever affectionately,

LAFCADIO HEARN.

TO OCHIAI

KŌBE, February, 1896.

DEAR OCHIAI, — I am delighted that you have
taken up medicine, for two reasons. First, it will
assure your independence — your ability to maintain yourself, and to help your people. Secondly,
it will change all your ideas about the world we live
in, and will make you large-minded in many ways,
if you study well. For in these days, you cannot
study medicine without studying many different
branches of science — chemistry, which will oblige
you to understand something of the nature of the
great mystery of matter, — physiology, which will
show you that the most ordinary human body is full
of machinery more wonderful than any genius
ever invented, — biology, which will give you perceptions of the eternal laws which shape all form
and regulate all motion, — histology, which will
show you that all life is shaped, after methods that
no man can understand, out of one substance into
millions of different forms, — embryology, which
will teach you how the whole history of a species
or a race is shown in the development of the indi-

vidual, as organ after organ unfolds and develops in the wonderful process of growth. The study of medicine is, to a large extent, the study of the universe and of universal laws, — and makes a better man of any one who is intelligent enough to master its principles. Of course you must learn to love it, — because no man can do anything really great with a subject that he does not like. There are many very horrible things in it which you will have to face; but you must not be repelled by these, because the facts behind them are very beautiful and wonderful. There is so much in medicine — such a variety of subjects, that you will have a wide choice before you in case some particular branch should not be attractive to you.

Also do not forget that your knowledge of English will be of great use to you in medicine, and that, if you love literature, medicine will give you plenty of chance to indulge that love. (Some of our best foreign authors, you know, have been practising physicians.) In Kōbe I find that some of the best Japanese doctors find English very useful to them, not only in their practice, but also in their private studies. But you will also have to learn German; and that language will open to you a very wonderful literature, if you like literature—not to speak of the scientific advantages of German, which are unrivalled.

Well, I trust to hear good news from you later on. Take great care of your health, I beg of you, and believe me ever anxious for your success.

Very truly always,

LAFCADIO HEARN.

TO SENTARŌ NISHIDA

KŌBE, February, 1896.

DEAR NISHIDA, — I should have answered your kindest letter before now but for illness, — so I only sent a photo of Kazuo, as I had a cold in my eyes, nose, chest, back; a most atrocious and damnable cold, which rendered any work out of the question.

Mr. Katayama — dear Mr. Katayama — wrote a charming little poem. I am going to have a large copy made of it, and have it mounted as a little *kakemono*, for a souvenir. I love all these funny little things: they are the real Japan — the humour and the kindness and the grace of it. As for the so-called New Japan, — with its appearance of Occidentalism, and its utter loss of the old poetry and the old courtesy — well, however necessary it may be, it is certainly as much of a moral loss as it is a material advance. I wish I could live somewhere out of the sight and the sound of all that is new.

I had a letter from Ochiai, which I shall answer in a day or so; — for the moment I am behind with all my correspondence. What can be the matter with the lad? He did not tell me the nature of his sickness. I am really sorry for him. Strangely enough, on the very same day, I had a letter from one of the cleverest of the Kumamoto students, who seemed a tower of strength, but who has broken down after a year at the university. Some students I liked have gone mad; numbers have died; numbers have had to give up. The strain is too great because the hardship is too great, — the cold, the poor cheap food, the poor thin clothes. "Hardy" the lads claim to be. So naturally they are — much hardier than Europeans in certain respects. But some knowledge of physiology seems to be needed in Government schools. No man — however strong — can keep hardy while the heavy strain of study is unsupported by good living. I think most of the lads I know who died or went mad would never have even fallen sick if they had had only hard physical labour. Physical labour is not dangerous, but strengthening. And in the Government schools there is no feeling for the lads: everybody has to do the best he can for himself. Those who do get through the mill are not always the best — though they may be the strongest.

Ever, with best regards of all of us,

LAFCADIO HEARN (KOIZUMI YAKUMO).

TO PAGE M. BAKER

KŌBE, March, 1896.

DEAR PAGE, — I have your exquisite photo of Constance — like a bit of marble it is. . . . And I have your letter — a very dear letter, though — excuse me — I cannot help hating the typewriter!

I have been very sick with inflammation of the lungs, and unable to move until recently. But I shall soon, I hope, be able to send you something. . . .

About my name. Koizumi is a family name: I take my wife's name as her husband by adoption—

the only way in which I could become a Japanese citizen. Koizumi means "little spring" or "little source." The other name means "many clouds," and is an alternate poetical name for Izumo, the "Place of the Issuing of Clouds." For I became a citizen of the province of Izumo, where I am officially registered. The word is also the first word of the most ancient poem in the Japanese language — referring to a legend of the sacred records. *Please do not publish this!* it is a little private matter, and the whole explanation, though read at a glance by a Japanese, would require many pages to make clear. As to your other question, I always wear the Japanese dress at home or in the interior. In Kōbe or the large cities I wear Western clothes when I go on the street; because it does not do there for a man with a long nose to be too "Japanesey" — there has been a surplus of "Japanesey" display on the part of foreigners of the jocose class. I am Japanese only among Japanese. . . .

And you have been very sick too. Do you know that I am often worried by the fear that one of us might die before we meet again? I very often think about you. Please take every care of yourself, — all the outing you can. I think, though, you are a long-lived tough race — you Bakers; and that Page M. Baker will be writing some day an obituary of Lafcadio Hearn that was, — with many pleasant observations which the said Lafcadio never deserved and never will deserve.

You think I am misanthropic — no, not exactly; but I do feel an intense hatred for the business class

of Northern mankind. You know I never could
learn much about them till I was ass enough to go
North. . . . And you will remember that settled
dislikes or likes come to this creature at intervals —
never thereafter to depart. My last horror — one
that I can scarcely bear — is what is called "business
correspondence." That is why I say that I dislike
the sight of typewriting — though I assure you,
dear Page, I am glad to get a line from you written
or printed in any way, shape, or form.

Ghosts! After getting your letter last night I
dreamed. Do you remember that splendid Creole
who used to be your city editor — whose voice
seemed to come up from a well, a lover of music
and poetry and everything nice? John ——? Is it
not a sin that I have forgotten his name? Next to
yourself I see him, however, more distinctly than
any other figure of the old days. He recited "The
Portrait" of Owen Meredith in that caressing
abysmal voice of his. Last night I was talking to
him. He sat in a big chair in the old office, and
told me wonderful things, — which I could not
recall on waking; but I was vaguely annoyed by
the fact that he "avoided the point." So I interrupted, and said: "But you do not tell me — you
are dead — is there . . ." I only remember saying that. Then the light in his eyes went out, and
there was nothing. I woke up in the dark and
wondered.

For six years in Japan I have been walking up and
down — over matted floors — by myself, just as I
used to do in that room you wrote me from. Curi-

ously, my little boy has the same habit. It is very
difficult to make him keep still at meal-time. He
likes to take a nibble or sup of something, then
walk up and down, or run, then another nibble, etc.
— I hope the gods will save him from adopting
other former habits of mine, which are less innocent,
when he grows up: — for example, if he should take
a foolish fancy to every damozel in his path. However, I expect that his mother's strong common-
sense, which he seems to inherit, will counterbalance
the fantasticalities bequeathed him by me. . . . It
has only been since his entrance into this world that
I fully realize what a "disgraceful person" I used
to be.

I live pretty much alone — have no foreign
friends and very few Japanese friends outside of
my family, which numbers, however, a good many
dear souls. How isolated I have managed to be
you can imagine from the fact that sometimes for
months no one sees me except home-folks. I work
when I can; and when I cannot I bury myself in
studies — philosophical studies: you can scarcely
believe how they interest me now, and I find worlds
of inspiration in them — new perceptions of commonplace fact. I try not to worry, and let things
take their course. Probably next year I shall be
leading a busier life; but I don't know whether
Japanese officialism can be endured for any great
length of time. I had one dose of it too much
already. The people are the best in the world; the
military and naval men are *men*, and generally
braves garçons. . . .

The old men are divine: I do not know any other word to express what they are. When you meet a horrid Japanese, though, there is a distorted quality about him that makes him a unique monster — he is like an awry caricature of a Western mean fellow, without the vim and push — solid contemptibility *in petto*. You can scarcely imagine what he may be. Every transition period has its peculiar monsters.

I wonder, wonder, wonder whether I shall see you again, — and walk up and down on that cocoanut matting, — and make noises through the speaking-tube leading to the composing-room. Perhaps I could make some sketches of American life better now — after having looked back at it from this distance of eight thousand odd miles. . . .

LAFCADIO HEARN (Y. KOIZUMI).

TO SENTARŌ NISHIDA

KŌBE, April, 1896.

DEAR NISHIDA, — It made me happy to get your letter, and to hear from you that you think I am beginning to understand the Japanese a little better. My other books have had success in Europe as well as America; — the leading French review (*Revue des Deux Mondes*) had a long article about me; and the *Spectator*, the *Athenæum*, the *Times* and other English journals have been kind. Still, I am not foolish enough to take the praise for praise of fact, — feeling my own ignorance more and more every day, and being more pleased with the approval of a Japanese friend than with the verdict of a foreign reviewer, who, necessarily, knows nothing to speak of about Japan. But one thing *is* encouraging, — namely, that whatever I write about Japan hereafter will be widely read in Europe and elsewhere, — so that I may be able to do good. My first book is being translated into German.

I got a beautiful letter from Mr. Senke the other day, to which he has, I trust, by this time the answer, — in which I told him that I hope to see Matsue and Kizuki again in about another month. Setsu, mother, and the boy come with me. Kazuo is now much better — except morally; — he is more mischievous than ever. I want him to have as much of the sea this summer as he can bear. And I want to swim at Kizuki and Mionoseki, and to talk to you all I can — without tiring you.

I have been away. I have been at Ise, Futami, and nearly a week in Ōsaka. Ise disappointed me a little. The scenery is superb; but I like Kizuki better. At Ise there is so much money, — such enormous hotels, — such modernization: the place did not *feel* holy to me, as Kizuki did. Even the *miko* won't show their faces for less than five yen. Besides, it was bitterly cold, and hurt my lungs. I came back sick. Ōsaka delighted me beyond words. Excepting Kyōto, it is certainly the most interesting city on this side of Japan. And I could never tell you how Tennōji delighted me — what a queer, dear old temple. I went to Sakai, of course, — and bought a sword, and saw the grave of the eleven samurai of Tosa who had to commit *seppuku* for killing some foreigners, — and told them I wished they could come back again to kill a few more who are writing extraordinary lies about Japan at this present moment. I would rather live a month in Ōsaka than ten years free of rent in Tōkyō.

Speaking of Tōkyō reminds me to tell you that my engagement with the university is not yet assured. Day before yesterday I had a letter from Professor Toyama that my becoming a Japanese citizen had raised a difficulty "which," he wrote, "we must manage to get over somehow." I wrote him that I was not worried about the matter, and had never allowed myself to consider it very seriously, — hinting also that I would not accept any low salary. What he will next write I don't know, and don't very much care. If Matsue were a little warmer in winter I should rather be teaching there. Indeed I think that even after a few years in Tōkyō, I should be asking to get back to Matsue; and in any event I hope to make a home there. If I can get such a *yashiki* as I had — I mean buy one for my own home — Matsue would be a very happy place to work and study in. Besides, if my health keeps fair, I can hope eventually to be able to travel in the coldest winter months, and then the Matsue climate would make no difference for me. In summer it is delicious. Even Setsu now thinks it better to live in the interior; and I shall be glad to escape from the open ports. I have seen enough of the foreigners here, and like them less than ever.

I should certainly like Mr. Asai very much, from your charming account of him; and, at any rate, I expect to see both you and him within forty days

from this writing. If you think he would like a copy
of "Kokoro" it will make me very happy to send
him one. As he has studied philosophy, however,
I don't know what he will think of the chapters on
the Idea of Preëxistence and the Worship of Ancestors. You know the school of thought that I follow
is bitterly opposed; and I believe it is not honestly
taught in any English establishment. In one or
two American universities it is partly taught; but
only the French have given it really fair attention
abroad.

LAFCADIO HEARN (Y. KOIZUMI).

P. S.   It made me feel queer to be addressed by
Prof. Toyama as "Mr. Yakumo Koizumi"!

TO ELLWOOD HENDRICK

TŌKYŌ, May, 1896.

DEAR HENDRICK, — . . . Somebody (who, I do
not know) has been sending me books. Did you send
me a book by Richard Le Gallienne? I thought Mrs.
Rollins had sent it, and I wrote to her nice things
about it, which vexed her into sending me a very
sharp criticism of it (she *is* a critic), and proving
me to have praised a worthless book out of liking
for the sender! Where am I? I am certainly wrong.
I did think the book nice because of my belief that
she sent it; and I am now equally convinced that it
is n't nice at all, because she proved that it was not.
I should certainly make a bad critic if I were
acquainted with authors and their friends. One

sees what does not exist wherever one loves or hates.
As I am rather a creature of extremes, I should be
an extremely crooked-visioned judge of work. I
have not tried to answer Mrs. Rollins's letter—fact
is, I *can't*.

No: the head on the title-page of "Kokoro" is
not Kazuo, but the head of a little boy called Takaki.
The photograph was soft and beautiful, and showed
an uncommonly intellectual type of Japanese head.
The woodcut is rather coarse and hard. — But I
enclose a third edition of Kazuo: he is growing a
little better-looking, but is not so strong as I could
wish; and he is so sensitive that I am very much
worried about his future. Physical pain he bears
well enough; but a mere look, a careless word, a
moment of unconscious indifference is fire to his
little soul. I don't know what to do with him. If
he shows the artistic temperament I shall try to
educate him in Italy or France. With an emotional
nature one is happier among Latins. I confess that
I can only bear the uncommon types of Englishmen,
Germans, and Americans, — the conventional types
simply drive me wild. On the other hand, I can
feel at home with even a villain, if he be Spaniard, Italian, or French. According to evolutionary
doctrine, however, it seems not unlikely that the
Latin races will be squeezed out of existence in the
future pressure of civilization. They cannot hold
their own against the superior massiveness of the
Northern races, — who, unfortunately, have no
art-feeling at all. They will be absorbed, I suppose.
In the industrial invasion of the barbarians, the

men will be quietly starved to death, and the women taken by the conquerors. History will repeat itself without blood and shrieks.

What is the present matter with American civilization? Nearly all the clever American authors seem to be women, and most of them have to go "out of town" for their studies of life. American city-life seems to wither and burn up everything. There is something of the same sort noticeable in England — the authors have to go out of England. Of course, there are some great exceptions — like James and Mallock. But how many great writers deal with civilized life as it is? They go to the Highlands, like Black and Barrie, — or to Italy, like Crawford, — or to strange countries, like Kipling; — but who to-day would write "A London Romance"? This brings up another question. What is the meaning of English literary superiority? It is all very well to howl about the copyright question, and the shameful treatment of American authors; but what American authors have we to compare with the English? Excepting women like Mrs. Deland and Miss Jewett and Mrs. Phelps, etc., — what American writers can touch English methods? James is certainly our best; — so London steals him; but he stands alone. America has no one like a dozen, — nay, a score of English writers that might be named. It certainly is not a question of remuneration; for real high ability is always sooner or later able to get all it asks for. It must be an effect of American city-life, and American training, and American environment; — perhaps

over-education has something to do with it. Again
— English work is so massive — even at its worst:
the effort made is always so much *larger*. Perhaps
we do things too *fast*. The English are slow and
exact. I am told that the other Northern races are
still somewhat behind — always excepting great
Russia. But in the France of 1896, what is doing?
The greatest writers of the age are dead or silent.
Is not our horrible competitive civilization at last
going to choke all aspirational life into silence?
After the Du Maurier school, what will even England be able to do? Alfred Austin after Alfred
Tennyson!

These are my thoughts sometimes; — then, again,
I think of a possible new idealism, — a new prodigious burst of faith and passion and song greater
than anything Victorian; — and I remember that
all progress is rhythmical. But if this comes, it
will be only, I fear, after we have been dust for a
century.

I feel this is an awfully stupid letter. But I'll
write a better one soon. My best wishes for your
big, big, *big* success. They will be realized, I think.

Ever affectionately,

LAFCADIO HEARN.

TO ELLWOOD HENDRICK

MIONOSEKI, IZUMO, July, 1896.

DEAR HENDRICK, — I have just had a most
delightful letter from you. Your letters are full of
witty flashes and curious observation. As they

contain personal portraits, I make it a duty to burn them; but I regret it — like a destruction of the artistic. The rapid sketches they give of the most extraordinary bits of character, in the midst of the most extraordinary and complicated life of the century, are such as only one having your own most peculiar opportunities could make.

Do you ever reflect how much more of life you are able to see in one month than the ordinary mortal in twenty-five years? You belong to a purely modern school of travelling observers. Fifty years ago such experiences were not possible — at least upon any scale to speak of.

But why is it that the most extraordinary experiences of business men are never written? Is it because, like the scholarly specialist who knows too much about literature to make any literature, they see too much of the wonderful to feel it? The astounding for others is for them the commonplace, — perhaps. Or perhaps they are not sympathetic like your friend Macy, — have no inclination to apply the philosophy of relations to what they see and study?

I have been sick — eyes and lungs; — and now I am in an Izumo fishing-village to recruit. I swim in the harbour every day for about five hours, and am burnt all over in all colours, and getting thinner and stronger. There are no tables here, and I have to write on the floor.

With best love and felicitations,
LAFCADIO HEARN.

TO SENTARŌ NISHIDA

AUGUST, 1896.

DEAR NISHIDA,—We got back on the night of the twenty-third. We had to wait a couple of days at Sakai; and I had some more swimming. Dr. Takahashi was very much surprised at my condition. He said that my lungs had become perfectly well, and that the swimming had brought out all the chest-muscles again in an extraordinary way — considering the time in which it had happened. He tells me to go to the sea whenever I feel pulled down again.

Sakai is a queer place for swimming. The currents change three times every day, and twice at least become very strong. One who cannot swim far has to be careful. Straws in the water show the way of the current near shore; but in the middle there are cross-currents going the other way.

There were eight foreign officers on the Meiji Maru. They were very kind to us. The captain (his name is Poole) was decorated with the 3d Order of the Rising Sun (I think) and got a present of $2000 for services during the war,—the transport-service, of course. He told me some very interesting things about the behaviour of the soldiery, — very nice things.

I felt unhappy at the Ōhashi, because you waited so long, and I had no power to coax you to go home. I can still see you sitting there so kindly and patiently, — in the great heat of that afternoon. Write soon, — if only a line in Japanese, — to tell us how you are.

Kaji-*chan* remembers you, and sends his little greeting to Nishida-San no Oji-San. We all hope to have another summer with you next year.

Ever faithfully, with warmest regards of all,

LAFCADIO HEARN.

I still see you sitting at the wharf to watch us go. I think I shall always see you there.

小泉八雲

TO ELLWOOD HENDRICK

TŌKYŌ, 1896.

DEAR HENDRICK, — I am in immediate and awful need of books, and am going to ask you to put me into communication with a *general book-dealer* to whom I can send P. O. orders, and who will mail me books directly on receipt of cash. It is hopeless ordering through local book-dealers, — not simply because of charges and errors, but because of enormous delays. On a separate sheet I enclose some titles of what I badly want for the moment; and I am sending some cash. This said, I promise not to trouble you further *except when I can't help it.* See what a nuisance I am!

You may well believe me in a hurry when I send a letter with such a beginning. Imagine my position: — a professor of literature without books, improvising lectures to students without books. I reached Tōkyō about seven days ago, and have not yet got a house, — but am living in a hotel. At present I can give you no valid impressions: — every-

thing is a blur. But so far the position does not
seem disagreeable — rather the reverse. In fact I
am afraid to express my satisfaction, — remembering Polyxenes. The salary is 400 yen, — and in
Japan, a yen is a dollar though it is only fifty-odd
cents in America. Old pupils of Izumo and elsewhere gather round me, welcoming me, delighted —
some needing help and winning it — some needing
only sympathy. Professors far off, moving in separate and never-colliding orbits. I can teach for years
— if I please — without ever seeing any of my col-
leagues. But Government favour, you know, is
uncertain. The chances are that I shall hold on for
three years at least.

When I heard last from you I was in Izumo.
There I became very strong by constant swimming
and starving, — Japanese diet takes all the loose
flesh from a man in short order. My lungs got quite
sound, and my miserable eye *nearly* well.

I suppose that I partly owe this place to my
books, and partly to Professor Chamberlain's kind
recommendation. The Japanese seldom notice
literary work, — but they have paid considerable
attention to mine, considering that I am a foreigner.
My ambition, though, is independence in my own
home, — an old-fashioned *yashiki*, full of surprises
of colour and beauty and quaintness and peace. And
a few years abroad with my boy, — who is very mischievous now, and beats his father occasionally. —
Curious, how much better the Japanese understand
children than we do. You remember as a boy the
obligatory morning *dip* in the sea, no doubt. This

no Japanese parents would inflict on their child. I
tried it with mine, but the folks said, "That is wrong:
it will only make him afraid of the water." Which
proved true. Moreover, he would not allow me to
come near him any more in the sea, — but used
to order me to keep away. "Go away, and don't
come back any more." Then the grandmother took
him in charge; and in a week he was as fond of the
water as I, — had overcome his fear of it. But it
requires great patience to treat children Japanese-
style, — by leaving them *almost* free to follow their
natural impulses, and coaxing courage by little and
little.

Awful weather, — floods, wreckings, ruinings,
drownings. I think the deforestation of the country
is probably the cause of these terrible visitations. In
Kōbe just before I left, the river, usually a dry sand-
bed, burst its banks after rain, swept away whole
streets, wrecked hundreds of houses, and drowned
about a hundred people. Then you know the tidal
wave in the north — it was *only* 200 miles long —
destroyed some 30,000 lives. A considerable part
of East Central Japan is still under water at this
moment — river water. Lake Biwa rose and
drowned the city of Ōtsu.

Is n't it almost wicked of me to have fought for
a foreign salary under such circumstances? — especially while students come to tell me: "My father
and mother have educated me thus far by selling all
their property, — piece by piece, — even mother's
dresses and our lacquer-ware had to be sold. And
now we have nothing, and my education is unfinished

— and unless it is finished I cannot even hope for a
position. Teacher, I shall work six years to pay the
money back, if you will help me." Poor fellows ! —
their whole expense is only about $120 (Japanese)
a year. But if I did not take the salary, another
foreigner would ask even more; and I am working
for a Japanese community of my own. Buying
books is rather extravagant, but my literary work
pays for that.

Well, here 's love to you. (If the book-business
does not bother you too much, please tell the book-
dealer to mail *everything*, — not to send by express.)

Ever faithfully,

LAFCADIO HEARN.

(Y. KOIZUMI.)

TO ELLWOOD HENDRICK

OCTOBER, 1896.

DEAR HENDRICK, — I have two unanswered
letters from you — delayed in reaching me because
of my change of residence. One is only a glorious
shout of joy and sympathy; — the other describes
charmingly the incidents and sensations of your
Nova Scotia days. It struck me while reading it
that the great pleasure each of you had was in watching the display of the powers and the graces of the
other, in the new field, — and from thinking about
that I began to think of my own experiences. I
believe that my happiest glows of sympathetic admiration have been felt under somewhat like circumstances. If one's friend is a fine keen man, and one

is proud of him, what greater enjoyment than to see him face the unfamiliar and watch him dealing with it *en maître*, — turning it this way and that with symmetrical ease, — and winning all he wants with a smile or a bright jest? The pleasure of watching a play is nothing to it. And again, what *novel* (it is always new, you know) — what novel delight that of seeing a soldier, a man of business, or even a "man of God," turning into a boy under the mere joyous bath of air and sun and summer air out of town! It gives one a larger sense of humanity, and a sort of awe at the omnipotent magic of Nature.

Well, I have a house, — a large, but, I regret to say, not beautiful house in Tōkyō. There is no garden, — no surprises, — no delicacies, — no chromatic contrasts: a large bald utilitarian house, belonging to a man who owns eight hundred Japanese houses, and looks after them all at seventy-eight years of age. He was a sake-brewer: he is now good to the poor, — buries free of charge the head of any family unable to pay the expenses of a Buddhist funeral. He looked at my boy and played with him and said: "You are too pretty, — you ought to have been a girl. When you get a little older you will be studying things you ought not to study, — pulling girls about, and doing mischief." (Because he used to be an old rascal himself.) But he set me thinking. I don't think K. will be very handsome; but if he feels like his father about pretty girls, — what shall I do with him? Marry him at 17 or 19? Or send him to grim and ferocious Puritans that he may be taught the Way of the Lord? I am now beginning to think that really much of ecclesiastical education (bad and cruel as I used to imagine it) is founded upon the best experience of man under civilization; and I understand lots of things which I used to think superstitious bosh, and now think solid wisdom. Don't have children (Punch's advice is the same, you know) unless you want to discover new Americas. . . .

In haste to give a lecture on *ballad* literature (!).

Affectionately,

LAFCADIO.

TO ELLWOOD HENDRICK

TŌKYŌ, October, 1896.

DEAR HENDRICK, — I have had several delightful letters from you, some of which were not answered in detail, though deserving to be. Let me see about my deficiencies in acknowledging your letters during recent hurry and flurry: — That sermon, belonging to the 13th — or perhaps the 10th century — was really an amazement. Thanks for kindly note about Lowell's words of praise. . . .

As for the university. Because the shadow of the Jesuit, broadening back through the centuries, is very black, and because I saw stake-fires in it, I didn't relish the idea of his acquaintance. But that *had* to come, you know. There was a weary matriculation ceremony at which all of us had to be present; and it was purely Japanese, so that we could not understand it. We had to sit for three hours and listen. So I and the Jesuit, for want of anything else to do, got into a religious discussion; and I found him charming. Of course, he said that every thought which I thought was heresy, — that all the philosophy of the 19th century was false, — that everything accomplished by free thought and Protestantism was folly leading to ruin. But we had sympathies in common, — the contempt of religion as convention, scorn of the missionaries, and just recognition of the sincerely and profoundly religious character of the Japanese, — denied, of course, by the ordinary class of missionary jackasses. Then we were both amused by the architecture of the university. It is ecclesiastical, of course, — and the pinnacles and angles are tipped with cruciform ornaments. "C'est tout-a-fait comme un monastère," said my comrade of the beard; — "et ceçi, — on en fera une assez jolie église. *Et pourtant ce n'est pas l'esprit Chrétien qui,*" etc. His irony was delicious, and the laughter broke the ice.

Now comes a queer fact. The existing group of professors in the Library college who keep a little together are the Professor of Philosophy (Heidelberg), the Professor of Sanscrit and Philology (Leipsig), the Professor of French Literature (Lyons), and the Professor of English Literature — from the devil knows where. There is little affiliation outside. Now all this group is — including myself — Roman Catholic by training. Why it is, I can't say, except the Jesuit, we are not believers, — but there is a human something separating us from the *froid protestantisme,* or the hard materialism of the other foreign professors, — something warmer and more

natural. Is it not the *Latin* feeling surviving in
Catholicism, — and humanizing paganly what it
touches? — penetrating all of us — the Russian,
the German, the Frenchman, and L. H., through
early association? Really there is neither art nor
warm feeling nor the spirit of human love in the
stock Protestantism of to-day. — I regret to say,
however, that I have no Spencerian sympathizer.
In my beliefs and tendencies I stand alone; and
the Jesuit marvels at the astounding insanity of my
notions. He, like all of his tribe, does not quite
know how to take the American. The American
Professor of Law — enormously self-sufficient, and
aggressive — rather embarrasses him. I saw him
wilt a little before him; and I like him all the better
for it, — as he is certainly very delicate, and his
shrinking was largely due to this delicacy. But
all these are only impressions of the moment.

As a member of the faculty, I have to sometimes attend faculty meetings, called for various
purposes. One of the purposes was to decide the
fate of a certain German Professor of History — not
nominally for the purpose, but really. I could not
help the professor, and I felt that he was really
unnecessary — not to speak of $500 per mensem.
I do not think his contract will be renewed. I did
not like the man very much: he is a worshipper of
Virchow and an enemy of English psychology, etc.,
ipso facto. We could have no sympathies. But I
was startled by the fashion in which those who
professed to be his friends suddenly went back upon
him, when they saw the drift of things. The drift

was given by the Japanese Professor of Philosophy (Buddhist and other), — a fine, lean, keen, soft-spoken, persistent champion of Japanese national conservatism, and a good honest hater of sham Christianity. I like him: his name is Inoue Tetsujirō. He very sensibly observed that he saw no reason why foreign professors should forever teach *history* in a Japanese university, — or why students should be obliged to listen to lectures not in their native tongue. I felt he was right; but it meant the doom of nearly all foreign teaching. (Perhaps I shall last for some years more, and the professors of foreign *languages* — but the rest will certainly go before long.)

I said to my little self: "Don't expect any love from those quarters, old fellow: the Japanese themselves will treat you more frankly, even if they get to hate you." I have no doubt whatever that there will be as much said against *me* as *dare* be said. Happily, however, my engagement is based on Japanese *policy* — kindly policy — with a strong man behind it; and mere tongue-thrusts will do me no harm at all in the present order of things.

"Sufficient for the day is," etc.

LAFCADIO HEARN.

TO ELLWOOD HENDRICK

TŌKYŌ, November, 1896.

DEAR HENDRICK, — I fear — I suspect that this position has been given unto me for a combination of reasons, among which the dominant is that I may write at ease many books about Japan. This has two unfortunate aspects. Firstly, the people who do not know what labour literary work is imagine that books can be written by the page as quickly as letters, and keep asking me why I don't get out another book — that means the Influence of Hurry-Scurry. Secondly, I am plunged into a world of which the highest possible effort in poetry seems to be this: —

> *"Sometimes I hear your flute,*
> *But I never can see your face,*
> *O beautiful Oiterupé!"*

Who is Oiterupé? Euterpe, of course. And this represents, I do assure you, the very highest possible result of a Western education at Göttingen, etc., upon the mind of the modern Japanese poet. Formerly he would have said something. Now he is struck dumb by — Heidelberg or Göttingen.

I have only twelve hours a week in which to teach; but, as I told you before, there are no text-books, and the university will not buy any; and the general standard of English is so low that I am sure not half of my classes understand what I say. Worst of all, there is no discipline. The students are virtually the masters in certain matters: the authorities fear their displeasure, and they do things extraordinary which fill European professors with amazement and rage — such as *ordering* different hours for their lectures, and demanding after a menacing fashion subscriptions for their various undertakings. Fancy the following colloquy: —

Professor — "But this is not a case of distress: I don't think a professor should be asked for money where money is not needed — and then—"

Student — "The question is simply, will you pay or will you not?"

Professor — "I have told you my ideas about—"

Student —"I am not interested in your ideas. Will you or will you not?"

Professor (flushing with anger, like Sigurd the Bishop) —"No."

Student turns his back upon professor, and walks away with the air of one going to prepare for a vendetta.

I have told you before that the first, second, and third year classes are mixed together. But that makes no matter. The matter is that the students can change the subjects of their studies when they please, and do so occasionally by way of showing their disapproval of the professor. "You must not teach that subject: I wish you to teach us about Greek mythology instead" is a specimen observation.

I cannot write to you about such delightful friends as the one described in your last letter, for the simple reason that I haven't any. (You know that it is very difficult for me to find sympathizers in such a frogpond as the foreign community of an open port.) The Russian professor of philosophy, although boasting a Heidelberg degree, acknowledges to me that he believes heretics ought to be burnt alive ("for the saving of their souls"), and that he hopes to see the whole world under Catholic dom-

ination. I fancy he dreams of the Russian conquest
to come; and the Panslavic dream is not impossible! He is a queer man, — about fifty at least, —
a bachelor. Soft and cold — snowy in fact. The
Jesuit improves on acquaintance — gentle, courteous, half-sympathetic, but always on guard, like a
man afraid of being struck by some human affection.
The American lawyer, hard and grim, has a rough
plain goodness about him — providing that he be put
to no trouble. . . . And the German, Dr. R——,
of whom I spoke rather unsympathetically before,
seems to me now the finest man of the lot. There can
be no question of his learning, and his dogmatism;
but he gives me the solid feeling of a man honest like
a great rock of black basalt — huge, hard, direct —
one of those rare German types with eyes and hair
blacker than a coal. His hand is broad, hard, warm
always, and has something electrical in its grasp.
I think I shall get fond of him, if he doesn't talk
Virchow to me. (For Virchow is my *bête noir!* I
hate his name with unspeakable hatred.) At all
events, to my great surprise, I find this grim dark
German takes absolute pleasure in doing a kindness,
and in speaking well of others. Wherefore I feel that
I am unreasonable and wrong to feel repelled by his
liking for Virchow.

Of course, we must all go some day, if the
university doesn't go first. But as all have big
salaries, all prepare for the rainy day. I shall not
complain if allowed to finish my three years —
though I should prefer six. But you can imagine
how unstable everything looks — with changes

in the ministry of education about every twelve months, — and the political influences behind the students. I am reposing upon the safety-valves of a steam-boiler, — much cracked, with many of the rivets loose, — and the engineers studying how to be out of the way when the great whang-bang comes around.

And when it does come, may it blow me, for a moment at least, in the immediate vicinity of Ellwood Hendrick.

Ever affectionately,
LAFCADIO HEARN.

TO ELLWOOD HENDRICK

TŌKYŌ, December, 1896.

DEAR OLD FELLOW, — . . . The Emperor paid us a visit the other day; and I had to don a frock-coat and a thing which inspired the Mohammedan curse, — "May God put a HAT on you!" We stood in sleet and snow — horribly cold (no overcoats allowed) and were twice permitted to bow down before His Majesty. I confess I saw only *les bottes de S. M.* He has a deep commanding voice — is above the average in height. Most of us got cold, I think — nothing more for the nonce. Lowell discovered one delicious thing in the Far East — "The Gate of Everlasting Ceremony." But the ancient ceremony was beautiful. Swallow-tails and plugs are not beautiful. My little wife tells me: "Don't talk like that: even if a robber were listening to you upon the roof of the house, he would get angry." So I am only saying this to you: "I don't see why I should be obliged to take cold, merely for the privilege of bowing to H. M." Of course this is half-jest, half-earnest. There is a reason for things—for anything except — a plug-hat! . . .

Affectionately,
LAFCADIO HEARN.

TO ELLWOOD HENDRICK

Tōkyō, January, 1897.

DEAR HENDRICK, — "Sentimental Tommy" is marvellous. Gives me a very great idea of Barrie. The question with me is whether such a *milieu* and such a suggested ancestry could produce such types as Grizel and Tommy. I am not quite sure of it: I am still under the impression that blood *will* tell, and that children of drunkards and whores are not apt to prove angels — though there must be exceptions when the better inheritance dominates. However, the book has a good meaning as well as a great art, and the tendency is to recognitions of truths deeper than those of "Philistia." You were awfully good to send it; but I feel rather small — my last sending being so poor a sprat to your salmon.

Never mind. I'll send you my own book sometime this year — I *think*. It ought to be in the printer's hands by the time you get this letter. It will probably be called "A Living God, and Other Studies"— or something of that sort. But only the gods exactly know.

Half of my psychological book — or nearly half
— is also written. I shall dedicate it probably to
the Lady of a Myriad Souls — whose photo in a
black frame decorates my Japanese alcove. Provided — I don't die or worse before it is finished.
Any suggestions? I'm trying to explain all mysterious things which philosophers, etc., call *inex-
plicable* feelings. Have you any? Please turn some
over to me, and let me digest them. I've managed
the *frisson* (woman's touch), some colour-sensations,
sublimities, etc. I want some mysterious feelings
— some exquisitenesses, — normal only. *Parfum
de jeunesse* suggests experiences. Do you know
any? . . .

Ever faithfully,

LAFCADIO.

TO ELLWOOD HENDRICK

KōBE, February, 1897.

DEAR HENDRICK, — . . . Oh! have you read
those two marvellous things of Kipling's last —
"McAndrews' Hymn," and "The Mary Gloster"?
Especially the "Mary Gloster." I have no more
qualified ideas about Kipling. He is to my fixed
conviction the greatest of living English poets, and
greater than all before him in the line he has taken.
As for England, he is her modern Saga-man, —
skald, scôp, whatever you like: lineal descendants
of those fellows to whom the Berserker used to say:
"Now you just stand right here, and see us fight
so that you can make a song about it."
Meanwhile the Holy Ghost has become tempo-

rarily (perhaps) disgusted with me; and I am doing
nothing for three days past. Simply can't — no
feelings. I can *grind;* but what's the use? I want
to do something remarkable, unique, extraordinary,
audacious; and I haven't the qualifications. I want
sensations — dreams — glimpses. Nothing! Will
I ever get another good idea? Don't know. Will
I ever have any literary success? — So swings the
pendulum! I fear my next book won't be as good
as it ought to be. . . .

After all, the Jesuit *is* really the most interesting
person. We are close to each other because we are
so enormously far away, — just as in Wundt's colour-theory the red and violet ends of the spectrum
overlap after a fashion. . . .

Ever faithfully,
LAFCADIO HEARN.
(Y. KOIZUMI.)

TO ELLWOOD HENDRICK

TŌKYŌ, May, 1897.

DEAR E. H., — I have been reading your last
over and over again — because it is very pretty
indeed, one of the very prettiest letters I ever read.
There is altogether something so deliciously *assured*
about it — so full of happy confidence, that I feel
quite comfortable and jolly about you . . . notwithstanding the fact that I am tolerably sure you
will be taken utterly away from me in the end. For
this shall a man leave not only his friend, but his
father and his mother, — saith the Sacred Book.

You know that particular passage makes the Japanese mad, — but not quite so mad as the observation: "Unless a man shall hate his father and his mother," etc., which has knocked the wind out of much missionary enterprise.

I can't write much more about yourself, because I don't know anything yet. So I shall talk about Tōkyō.

As you know, I have been somewhat idle — for a month at least. And the loneliness thickens. And certain gentlemen make it a rule to spit upon the ground with a loud noise when I pass by. I believe the trick is not confined to the Occident, having found Japanese skilful at it; but these be nevertheless manners of Heidelberg doctors! Nevertheless, it won't work.

But really the conditions are very queer. I felt instinctively before going to Tōkyō, that I was going into a world of intrigue; but what a world I had no conception. The foreign element appears to live in a condition of perpetual panic. Everybody is infinitely afraid of everybody else, afraid to speak not only their minds, but to speak about anything except irrelevant matters, and then only in a certain formal tone sanctioned by custom. They huddle together sometimes at parties, and talk all together loudly about nothing, — like people in the expectation of a possible catastrophe, or like folks making a noise to drive away ghosts, or fear of ghosts. Somebody, quite accidentally, observes— or rather drops an observation about facts. Instantly there is a scattering away from that man as from dynamite.

He is isolated for several weeks by common consent. Then he goes to work to reform a group of his own. Gradually he collects one — and rival groups are formed. But presently some one in another party or chat talks about something as it ought to be. Bang-fizz — chaos and confusion. Then all the groups unite to isolate that wicked tongue. The man is dangerous — an intriguer — ha! And so on — *ad lib.*

This is panic, pure and simple, and the selfishness of panic. But there is some reason for it — considering the class of minds. We are all in Japan living over earthquakes. Nothing is stable. All Japanese officialdom is perpetually in flux, — nothing but the throne is even temporarily fixed; and the direction of the currents depends much upon force of intrigue. They shift, like currents in the sea, off a coast of tides. But the side currents penetrate everywhere, and *clapotent* all comers, and swirl round the writing-stool of the smallest clerk, — whose pen trembles with continual fear for his wife's and babies' rice. Being good or clever or generous or popular or the best man for the place counts for very little. Intrigue has nothing at all to do with qualities. Popularity in the biggest sense has, of course, some value, but only the value depending upon certain alternations of the rhythm of outs-and-ins. That 's all.

In the Orient intrigue has been cultivated as an art for ages, and it has been cultivated as an art in every country, no doubt. But the result of the adoption of constitutional government by a race accustomed to autocracy and caste, enabled intrigue to spread like a ferment, in new forms, through every condition of society, — and almost into every household. It has become an infinite net—unbreakable, because elastic as air, though strong enough to upset ministers as readily as to oust clerks.

Future prospects— ? *Dégringolade.*

I feel sorry to say that I think I have been wrong about a good many of my sincere hopes and glowing predictions. Tōkyō takes out of me all power to hope for a great Japanese future. You know how easily a society in such a state can be manipulated by shrewd foreign influence. The race must give evidence of some tremendous self-purifying and self-solidifying power, before my hopes can be restored to their former rainbow hues. At present I think it can truthfully be said that every official branch of service shows the rapidly growing weakness that means demoralization. The causes are numerous — too numerous to mention, — inadequate pay being a large one, as the best men will not take positions at $15 or $20 a month. But the great cause is utter instability and discouragement. The P. O., the telegraph-service, the railroads, etc., all are in a queer state.

And I — am as a flea in a wash-bowl. My best chance is to lie quiet and wait the coming of events. I hope to see Europe, with my boy, some day.

Well, this is only private history to amuse E. H., to make Western by contrast to Eastern life seem more beautiful to him. Affectionately,

LAFCADIO.

TO ELLWOOD HENDRICK

TŌKYŌ, May, 1897.

DEAR E. H., — I am still alive in alternations of
gloom and sun. I anticipate now chiefly a national
bankruptcy, or a war with Russia to upset my bank-
account. There is a Buddhist text (Saddharma-
Pundarika, chap. III, verse 125): — "The man
whom they happen to serve is unwilling to give
them much, and what he gives is soon lost. Such
is the fruit of sinfulness." It would be impossible, I imagine, that I should escape some future
extraordinary experience of calamity. It is simply
ridiculous, — can't help seeing the absurdity of it.
Otherwise I have sorrow.

For my friends have been dying quickly. Some
years ago, one said to me: "You will outlive us:
foreigners live longer than Japanese." This I did
not think true, as I know many Japanese over eighty,
and the longevity of the western farmers is sometimes extraordinary — 110 years being not very rare,
and 100 plentiful, as examples. But my friend was
doubtless referring to the more delicate classes —
the hot-house plants, conservatory-growths, moulded
by etiquette and classical culture and home-law.
And I fear he was right. Nearly all my Japanese
friends are dead. The last case was three or four
days ago, — the sweetest of little women, — a
creature not seemingly of flesh and blood, but made
of silk embroidery mixed with soul. She was highly
accomplished — one of my wife's school friends.
Married to a good man, but a man unable to care

for her as she ought to have been cared for. No force to bear children: the pretty creature had never been too strong, and over-education had strained her nerves. She ought never to have been married at all. She knew she was dying, and came to bid us good-bye, laughing and lying bravely. "I must go home," she said, "but I 'll soon be well and come back." She must have suffered terribly for more than a year — but she never complained, never ceased to smile, never broke down. Died soon after reaching home.

Another friend, a man, dying, tells his wife: "Open the windows (shōji) wide, that my friend may see the chrysanthemums in the garden." And he watches my face, laughing, while I pretend to be pleased. The beauty of his soul is finer than any chrysanthemum, and it is flitting. He wakes up in the night and calls: "Mother, did you hear from my friend? is his son well?" Then he goes to sleep again — his last words — for he is dead at sunrise. These lives are too fine and frail for the brutal civilization that is going to crush them all out — every one of them, — and prove to the future that sweetness is immoral à la Nietzsche: that to be unselfish is to sentence one's self to death and one's beloved to misery and probable extermination.

But then imagine beings who never, in their lives, did anything which was not — I will not say "right," that is commonplace — any single thing which was not beautiful! Should I write this the world would, of course, call me a liar, as it has become accustomed to do. But I could not now even write of them except to you — the wounds are raw.

I am thinking about Velvet Souls in general, and all ever known by me in particular. Almost in every place where I lived long, it was given me to meet a velvet soul or two — presences (male or female mattered nothing) which with a word or look wrapped all your being round in a softness and warmth of emotional caress inexpressible. "Velvet" isn't a good word. The effect is more like the bath of tropical light and warmth to the body of a sick voyager from lands of consumption and rheumatism. These souls are intellectual in many cases, but that is not the interest of them — the interest is purely emotional. A purely intellectual person is unpleasant; and I fancy our religion is chiefly hateful because it makes its gods of the intellectual kind now-a-days. I should like to write about such souls — but how difficult. A queer thing for me is that in memory *they unite*, without distinction of sex, into one divine type of perfect tenderness and sympathy and knowledge, — like those Living Creatures of Dante's Paradise composed of many different persons. I have found such souls also in Japan — but only Japanese souls. But they are melting into the night.

LAFCADIO.

P. S. A very sad but curious story. A charming person, of high rank, bore twins. A Western woman would be proud and pleased. Shame struck the Japanese mother down. She became insane for

shame. All Japanese life is not beautiful, you see.
Imagine the cruelty of such a popular idea, — a
peasant would have borne the trouble well, — but
a daughter of princes — no!

TO SENTARŌ NISHIDA

TŌKYŌ, 1897.

DEAR NISHIDA, — Your last kind letter came just
after I had posted mine to you. Since then I have
been horribly busy, and upset, and confused, — and
even now I write rather because feeling ashamed
at having been so long silent, than because I have
time to write a good letter. We got a house only
on the 29th, and are only half-settled now. The
house is large — two-storied, and new — but not
pretty, and there is no garden (at least nothing
which deserves to be called a garden). We moved
into it *before it was finished,* so as to make sure of it.
It is all Japanese, of course — ten rooms. It belongs
to a man who owns seven hundred and eighty
houses! — a very old man, a *Sakeya,* named
Masumoto Kihei. (Somebody tells me I am wrong,
— that he has more than eight hundred houses.)
He buries poor people free of charge — that is one
of his ways of showing charity. He has one super-
intendent who, with many assistants, manages the
renting of the houses. The house is very far from
the university — forty-five minutes by *kuruma* — in
Ushigomé, and almost at the very end of Tōkyō.
But it was a case of *Shikata ga nai.*

I teach only twelve hours. I have no text-books

except for two classes, — one of which studies Milton's "Paradise Lost" and the other Tennyson's "Princess" (at my suggestion). I did not suggest "Paradise Lost;" but as the students wanted in different divisions of the class to study different books, made them vote, and, out of seventy-eight, sixty-three voted for "Paradise Lost"! Curious! (Just because it was hard for them, I suppose.) My other classes are special, and receive lectures on special branches of English literature (such as Ballad Literature, Ancient and Modern; Victorian Literature, etc.); — the professor being left free to do as he pleases. Of course, the position, as I try to fill it, will be an expensive one. I shall probably have to buy $1000 worth of books before next summer. Ultimately everything will be less expensive. The classes are very badly arranged (*badly* is a gentle word); for the 1st, 2d and 3d years of literature make one class; — the 2d and 3d together another class; — the 3d by itself a third class. You will see at once how difficult to try to establish a systematic three-years' course. I am doing it, however, — with Professor Toyama's approval; — hoping that the classes may be changed next year.

The students have been very kind and pleasant. My old Kumamoto pupils invited me to a meeting, and I made a speech to them. They meet in the same temple where Yaoya-O-Shichi used to meet Kichizo Sama, — her acolyte-lover. It is called Kichijōji. — I met some of my old pupils who had become judges, others who were professors, others engineers. I felt rather happy.

Professor Toyama I like more and more. He is a curious man,—really a *solid* man and a man of the world, — but not at all unkind, and extremely straightforward. He *can* be very sarcastic, and is very skilful at making jokes. Some of the foreign professors are rather afraid of his jokes: I have heard him make some sharp ones. But he does not joke yet with me directly — seems to understand me very well indeed. He knows a great deal about English authors and their values, — but says very little about his own studies. I do not understand how he found time to learn as much about the English and American authors as he seems to know. He gave me some kind hints about the students — told me exactly what they liked, and how far to humour them. I had only one long talk with him, — that was at the house of Dr. Florenz one evening. The doctor had invited five of us to dinner.

What else is there to tell you? I must not say too much about the mud, the bad roads, the horrible confusion caused by the laying-down of those new water-pipes. The weather is vile, and Tōkyō is hideous in Ushigome. But Setsu is happy — like a bird making its nest. She is fixing up her new home, and has not yet had time to notice what ugly weather it is.

In Tōkyō we find everything *very* cheap, — except house-rent. And even house-rent is much lower than in Kōbe, — very much lower. I pay only $25 for a very big house; but I expect to do even better than that. Affectionate regards,

LAFCADIO HEARN (Y. KOIZUMI).

TO SENTARŌ NISHIDA

TŌKYŌ, 1897.

DEAR NISHIDA, — This morning (the 17th) Mr.
Takahashi came with your letter of introduction.
He is a charming gentleman, and I felt unhappy at
not being able to talk Japanese to him. He brought
a most beautiful present — a tea-set of a sort I had
never even seen before, — "crackled" porcelain
inside to the eye, and outside a chocolate-coloured
clay etched with pretty designs of houses and groves
and lakes with boats upon them. The cups were a
great surprise and delight — especially as they were
made in Matsue. Mr. Takahashi gave me better
news of you than your last letter brought me: he
thought you were getting stronger, — so I have
hopes of pleasant chats with you. He told us many
things about Matsue. He is a very correct, courteous
gentleman; and I felt quite clumsy, as I always do
when I meet a real gentleman of the Japanese
school. I think I should like any of your friends.
Mr. Takahashi had something about him which
brought back to me the happy feeling of my pleasant
time in Izumo.

I don't feel to-day, though, like I used to feel in
Izumo. I have become very grey, and much queerer
looking; and as I never make any visits or acquaintances outside of my quiet little neighbourhood, I
have become also rather *henjin*. But I have written
half a new book. I am not able to say now what it
will be like: for the things I most wish to put into
it — stories of real life — have not yet been written.

I have finished only the philosophical chapters. One subject is "Nirvana," and another the study of matter in itself as unreality, — or at least as a temporary apparition only. Then I have taken up the defence of Japanese methods of drawing, under the title of "Faces in the Old Picture-Books." My public, however, is not all composed of thinkers; and I have to please the majority by telling them stories sometimes. After all, every public more or less resembles a school-class. They say, just like my students always used to say when they felt very tired or sleepy, hot days, — "Teacher, we are tired: please tell us some extraordinary story."

I can't just now remember when — at Matsue — a man came into the classroom to watch my teaching. He came from some little island. I have quite forgotten the name. He looked a little like Mr. Takahashi; — but there was something different in his face, — a little sad, perhaps. When the class was over he came to me and said something very good and kind, and pressed my hand and went away to his island. It is a queer thing that experiences of this kind are often among the most vivid of one's life — though they are so short. I have often dreamed of that man. Often and often. And the dream is always the same. He is the director of a beautiful little school in a very large garden, surrounded by high white walls. I go into that garden by an iron gate. It is always summer. I teach for that man; and everything is gentle and earnest and pleasant and beautiful, just as it used to be in Matsue, — and he always repeats the nice things

he said long ago. If I can ever find that school,
with the white walls and the iron gate, — I shall
want to teach there, even if the salary be only the
nice things said at the end of the class. But I fear
the school is made of mist, and that teacher and
pupils are only ghosts. Or perhaps it is in *Hōrai*.
Ever with best regards from all of us, faithfully,

LAFCADIO HEARN.

TO ELLWOOD HENDRICK

Tōkyō, August, 1897.

DEAR HENDRICK, — As for Miss Josephine's letter, I believe that I cannot answer it at all: it was
so sweet that I could only sit down quietly and think
about it, — and I feel that any attempt to answer
it on paper would be no use. There is only one way
that it ought to be adequately answered, and that
way I hope that you will adopt for my sake.

It was a more than happy little romance — that
which you told me of, and makes one feel new
things about the great complex life of your greater
world. The poetry of the story makes a singular
appeal to me now — possibly because in this Far
East such loving sympathy is non-existent (at least
outside of the household). Artistic life depends
a great deal upon such friendships: I doubt whether
it can exist without them, any more than butterflies
or bees could exist without flowers. The ideal is
created by the heart, no doubt; but it is nourished
only by others' faith and love for it. In all this
great Tōkyō I doubt if there is a man with an ideal —

or a woman (I mean any one not a Japanese); and so far as I have been able to hear and see there are consequently no friendships. Can there possibly be friendships where there is no aspirational life? I doubt it very much.

I must eat some humble pie. My work during the past ten months has been rather poor. Why, I cannot quite understand — because it costs me more effort. Anyhow I have had to rewrite ten essays: they greatly improved under the process. I am trying now to get a Buddhist commentary for them — mostly to be composed of texts dealing with preëxistence and memory of former lives. I took for subjects the following: — Beauty is Memory; — why beautiful things bring sadness; — the riddle of touch — i. e., the *thrill* that a touch gives; — the perfume of youth; — the reason of the pleasure of the feeling evoked by bright blue; — the pain caused by certain kinds of red; — mystery of certain musical effects; — fear of darkness and the feeling of dreams. Queer subjects, are they not? I think of calling the collection "Retrospectives." It might be dedicated to "E. B. W.," — I fancy that I should do well to use the initials only; for some of the essays might be found a little startling. But when the work will be finished I cannot tell.

In this Tōkyō, this detestable Tōkyō, there are no Japanese impressions to be had except at rare intervals. To describe to you the place would be utterly impossible, — more easy to describe a province. Here the quarter of the foreign embassies, looking like a well-painted American suburb; —

near by an estate with quaint Chinese gates several
centuries old; a little further square miles of inde-
scribable squalor; — then miles of military parade-
ground trampled into a waste of dust, and bounded
by hideous barracks; — then a great park, full of
really weird beauty, the shadows all black as ink;
— then square miles of streets of shops, which burn
down once a year; — then more squalor; — then
rice-fields and bamboo groves; — then more streets.

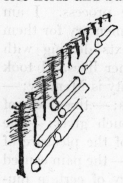

All this not flat, but hilly, — a
city of undulations. Immense
silences — green and romantic —
alternate with quarters of tur-
moil and factories and railroad
stations. Miles of telegraph-
poles, looking at a distance like
enormous fine-tooth combs, make
a horrid impression. Miles of
water-pipes — miles and miles
and miles of them — interrupt the traffic of the
principal streets: they have been trying to put
them underground for seven years, — and what
with official trickery, etc., the work makes slow
progress. Gigantic reservoirs are ready; but no
water in them yet. City being sued by the foreign
engineer (once a university professor) for $138,000
odd commission on plans! Streets melt under rain,
water-pipes sink, water-pipe holes drown spreeing
men and swallow up playful children; frogs sing
amazing songs in the street. — To think of art or
time or eternity in the dead waste and muddle of
this mess is difficult. The Holy Ghost of the poets

is not in Tōkyō. I am going to try to find him by
the seashore.

The other night I got into a little-known part of
Tōkyō, — a street all ablaze with lanterns about
thirty feet high, painted with
weird devices. And I was interested especially by the insect-
sellers. I bought a number of
cages full of night-singing in-
sects, and am now trying to make a study of the
subjects. The noise made by these creatures is very
much more extraordinary than you could imagine;
but the habit of keeping them is not merely due to
a love of the noise in itself. No: it is because these
little orchestras give to city-dwellers the *feeling* of
the delight of being in the country, — the sense of
woods and hills and flowing water and starry nights
and sweet air. Fireflies are caged for the same
reason.

This is a refinement of sensation, is it not? —
only a poetical people could have imagined the
luxury of buying summer-voices to make for them
the illusion of nature where there is only dust and
mud. Notice also that the singers are *night-singers*.
It is no use to cage the cicadæ: they remain silent
in a cage, and die.

In this horrid Tōkyō I feel like a cicada: — I am
caged, and can't sing. Sometimes I wonder whether
I shall ever be able to sing any more, — except at
night? — like a bell-insect which has only *one* note.

What more and more impresses me every year
is the degree to which the writer is a creature of

circumstance. If he can make the circumstance, like
a Kipling or a Stevenson, he can go on forever.
Otherwise he is likely to exhaust every motive in
short order, to the same extent that he depends on
outer influence.

There was a little under-ripple of premonition in
that very sweet letter from Miss Josephine, — just
the faintest suggestion of a thought that the future
might hold troubles in its shadow. Now I suppose
that for none can the future be only luminous; but
that you will have a smooth and steady current to
bear you along to the great sea appears to me a
matter of course. I do not imagine there will be
rocks and reefs and whirlpools for you. You have
both such large experience of life as it is, and of
the laws and the arts of navigating that water, that
I have no anxiety about you at all. Such little disillusions as you may have should only draw you nearer
together. But there is the sensation of being
afraid for somebody else — one has to face that;
and the more boldly, perhaps, the less the terror
becomes. It is worse in the case where one would be
helpless without the other. But I imagine that
your union is one of two strong independent spirits
— each skilled in self-guidance. That makes everything so much easier.

One thing you *will* have to do, — that is, to take
extremely good care of yourself for somebody else's
sake. Which redounds to my benefit; for I really
don't know what I should do without that occasional
wind of sympathy wherewith your letters refresh
me. I keep telling my wife that it would be ever so

much better to leave Tōkyō, and dwell in the country, at a very much smaller salary, and have peace of mind. She says that nowhere could I have any peace of mind until I become a Buddha, and that with patience we can become independent. This is good; and my few Japanese friends tell me the same thing. But perhaps the influence from 40 Kilby Street, Boston, is the most powerful and saving of all.

An earthquake and several other things (I *hate* earthquakes) interrupted this letter. It is awfully dull, I know — forgive its flatness. . . .

Ever, dear H., your

LAFCADIO.

TO ELLWOOD HENDRICK

TŌKYŌ, 1897.

DEAR HENDRICK, — . . . You speak about that feeling of fulness of the heart with which we look at a thing, — half angered by inability to analyze within ourselves the delight of the vision. I think the feeling is unanalyzable, simply because, as Kipling says in that wonderful narrative, "The Finest Story in the World," "the doors have been shut behind us." The pleasure you felt in looking at that tree, at that lawn, — all the pleasure of the quaint summer in that charming old city, — was it only *your* pleasure? There is really no singular, — no "I." "I" is surely collective. Otherwise we never could explain fully those movements within us caused by the scent of hay, — by moonlight on summer waters, —

by certain voice tones that make the heart beat
quicker, — by certain colours and touches and long-
ings. The law that inherited memory becomes
transmuted into intuitions or instincts is not absolute.
Only some memories, or rather parts of them, are
so transformed. Others remain — will not die.
When you felt the charm of that tree and that lawn,
— many who would have loved you were they able
to live as in other days, were looking through you
and remembering happy things. At least I think
it must have been so. The different ways in which
different places and things thus make appeal would
be partly explained; — the supreme charm referring
to reminiscences reaching through the longest
chain of life, and the highest. But no pleasure of
this sort can have so ghostly a sweetness as that
which belongs to the charm of an ancestral home —
in which happy generations have been. Then how
much dead love lives again, and how many ecstasies
of the childhoods of a hundred years must revive!
We do not *all* die, — said the ancient wise man.
How much of us dies is an unutterable mystery.

Science is rather provoking here. She tells us
we are advancing toward equilibration, to be followed by dissolution, to be succeeded by another
evolution, to end in another disintegration — and
so on forever. Why a cosmos must be dissipated
into a nebula, and the nebula again resolved into
a sun-swarm, she confesses that she does not know.
There is no comfort in her except the comfort of
doubt, — and that is wholesome. But she says
one encouraging thing. No thought can utterly

perish. As all life is force, the record of everything must pass into the infinite. Now what is this force that shapes and unshapes universes? Might it be old thoughts and words and passions of men? The ancient East so declares. There can be rest eternal only when — not in one petty world, but throughout all the cosmos—the Good only lives. Here all is, of course, theory and ignorance, — for all we know. Still the faith ought to have value. How would the well-balanced man try to live if once fully persuaded that his every thought would affect not only the future of himself, but of the universe! The other day something queer happened. I was vexed about something wrong that had been done at a distance. Some days after, one said to me: "The other day, while you were so angry, people were killed" — mentioning the place. "I know that," I said.   "But do you not feel sorry?" "Why should I feel sorry? — I did not kill anybody." "*How do you know you did not? Your anger might have been added to the measure of the anger that caused the wrong.*" Unto this I could not reply. Thinking over the matter, indeed, who can say what his life may be to the life of the unseen about him?   Ever very affectionately,

                              LAFCADIO HEARN.

TO ELLWOOD HENDRICK

1897.

DEAR HENDRICK, — . . . The idea of a set of philosophical fairy-tales often haunts me. One doesn't need to go to the Orient for the material. It is everywhere. The Elle-woman is real. So are the Sirens, Circe, and the Sphinx and Herakles and Admetos and Alkestis. So are the Harpies, and Medusa, and the Fates who measure and cut and spin. But when I try, I find myself unable to create for want of a knowledge of every-day life, — that life which is the only life the general reader understands or cares about.

Then the philosophical fairy-tales might deal with personal experiences common to all men, — impulse and sorrow and loss and hope and discovery of the hollowness of things. But the inclination only is with me, — the pushing sensation, — the vague cloud-feeling of the thing. Can you help — suggest — define — develop by a flash or two? If you can, be sweet, and tell me; and the fairy-tales shall be dedicated unto you. Indeed they shall in any case, if I can ever write them. In haste, with love,

LAFCADIO HEARN.

TO MITCHELL McDONALD

TŌKYŌ, November, 1897.

DEAR McDONALD, — I can only very poorly express my real feeling at the true goodness shown me, not only in coming out to my miserable little shanty, over that muddy chaos of street, — but in making me feel so free-and-easy with you, in the charming way you accepted the horrid attempt at entertainment, and in the hundred ways by which you showed your interest and sympathy. It was more than nice — that is all I can say.

But you set some mental machinery at work too. I believe almost your first remark was your desire that I should write fiction, — and I believe I understand why you wish this. It is because you wish me to make some profit out of my pen; and, being well informed on all business matters, you know, just as well as we literary men do, that fiction is about the only material that really pays. And now I am going, after a little thinking about the matter, to answer you in kind.

Why do not men like myself write more fiction? For two reasons. The first is because they have little knowledge of life, little *savoir-vivre*, to help them in the study of the artificial and complex growth of modern society. The second is that, unless very exceptionally situated, they are debarred, by this very want of knowledge and skill, from mixing with that life which alone can furnish the material. Society everywhere suspects them; common life repels them. They can *divine*, but they must have rare chances to do that. Men like the genius Kipling belong to the great life-struggle, understand it, reflect it, and the world worships them. But dreamers who talk about preëxistence, and who think differently from common-sense folk, are quite outside of social existence. But — I can do this: You know all about the foreign life of these parts, — the shadows and the lights. You can give me, perhaps, in the course of three years, *suggestions* for six little stories — based upon the relations between foreigners and Japanese in this era of Meiji: studies of the life of the "open ports."

I should need only real facts — not names or dates — real facts of beauty or pathos or tragedy. There are hosts of these. All the life of the open ports is not commonplace: there are heroisms and romances in it; and there is nothing in this world nearly as wonderful as life itself. All real life is a marvel — but in Japan a marvel that is hidden as much as possible — especially hidden from dangerous chatterers like Lafcadio Hearn.

Of course I could not make a book in a few months, — not in less than two or three years; but I *could* make one, with the mere help of hints from a man who knows. And if that book of short stories (six would be enough to make a book) should ever be so written, I should certainly make a dedication of it to M. McD. as prettily as I could.

There is an answer to your wish so far as I can make one for the present. I shall be down to see you the next month, probably, and we can chat over matters if you have time. And I shall take care not to come when you are *too* busy.

Faithfully, with affectionate regards and thanks,
LAFCADIO HEARN.

TO MASANOBU ŌTANI

Tōkyō, December, 1897.

DEAR ŌTANI, — I have your very nice letter, which gave me much pleasure. This is just a line before I go away, in regard to the subject for January, and relevant matters.

First let me tell you that you are very, very much mistaken — extraordinarily mistaken — in thinking that I do not care for what you call "vulgar" songs. They are just what I care *most* about. In all the poems that you translated for me this month, I could find but *one* that I liked very much; and that was a *dodoitsu*.

Now I am going to shock you by saying something that may surprise you; but if I do not say it, you will *never* understand what I want. In all the great mass of student poetry that you collected for me, I found only seventeen pieces that I could call poetry, — and on submitting those seventeen pieces to higher tests, I found that nearly all were reflections of thoughts and feelings from older poets. As for the book that you translated, I could find no true poetry in it at all, and scarcely anything original.

And now let me tell you my honest opinion about this whole matter. The *refined* poetry of this era, and most of the poetry that you collected for me of other eras, is of little or no value. On the other hand, the "vulgar" songs sung by coolies and fishermen and sailors and farmers and artisans, are very true and beautiful poetry; and would be admired by great poets in England, in France, in Italy, in Germany, or in Russia.

You will think, of course, that this only shows my ignorance and my stupidity. But please reflect a little about the matter. A great poem by Heine, by Shakespeare, by Calderon, by Petrarch, by Hafiz, by Saadi, remains a great poem *even when it is translated into the prose of another language*. It touches the emotion or the imagination in every language. But poetry which cannot be translated is of no value whatever in world-literature; and it is not even true poetry. It is a mere playing with values of words. True poetry has nothing to do with mere word-values. It is fancy, it is emotion, it is passion, or it is thought. Therefore it has power and truth. Poetry that depends for existence on the peculiarities of *one language* is waste of time, and can never live in people's hearts. For this reason there is more value in the English ballad of "Childe Waters" or of "Tamlane," than in the whole of the verse of Pope.

Of course, I know there are some beautiful things in Japanese classical poetry — I have translations from the *Manyōshū* and *Kokinshū* which are beautiful enough to live forever in any language. But these are beautiful because they do *not* depend on word-values, but upon sentiment and feeling.

I fear you will think all this very foolish and barbarous; but perhaps it will help you to understand what I want. "Vulgar" poetry is supremely valuable, in my humble opinion.

Please this month collect for me, if you can, some poems on the *Sound of the Sea and the Sound of the Wind*. If there are not many poems on these subjects, then you might add poems on the Sea and the Wind in any other connection. What I want to get is the *feeling* that the sound and the mystery of Wind and Sea have inspired in Japanese Song.

With best wishes ever, faithfully yours,

Y. KOIZUMI.

WRITING-ROOM IN MR. HEARN'S TŌKYŌ HOUSE

His three sons on the verandah

TO MASANOBU ŌTANI

Tōkyō, June, 1898.

MY DEAR ŌTANI, — I am pleased to hear that the incident was imaginary, — because this gives me a higher idea of your sense of art. True literary art consists very largely in skilful combination of real or possible facts in an imaginary succession. Literature artistic never can be raw truth, any more than a photograph can be compared with a painting. Here is a little sentence from one of the greatest of modern French writers: —

"*L'art n'a pas la vérité pour objet.* Il faut demander la vérité aux Sciences, parce qu'elle est leur objet; — il ne faut pas la demander a la littérature, *qui n'a et ne peut avoir d'objet* que le beau." (Anatole France.)

Of course this must not be taken *too* literally; but it is substantially the most important of truths for a writer to keep in mind. I would suggest this addition: "Remember that nothing can be beautiful which does not contain truth, and that making an imagination beautiful means also to make it partly true."

Your English is poor still; but your composition was *artistic*, and gave me both surprise and pleasure. You understand something about the grouping of facts in the dramatic sense, and how to appeal by natural and simple incidents to the reader's emotion. The basis of art is there; the rest can only come with years of practice, — I mean the secret of compressed power and high polish. I would suggest

that when writing in your own language, you aim
hereafter somewhat in the direction of compression.
You are now somewhat inclined to diffuseness;
and a great deal is gained in strength by understanding how much of detail can be sacrificed. . . .

Yours faithfully,
Y. KOIZUMI.

TO MITCHELL McDONALD

TŌKYŌ, January, 1898.

DEAR McDONALD, — I believe those three days
of mine in Yokohama were the most pleasurable
in a pilgrimage of forty-seven years. I can venture
to say little more about them *per se*. Such experience will not do for me except at vast intervals.
It sends me back to work with much too good an
opinion of myself, — and that is bad for literary
self-judgement. The beneficial result is an offsetting
of that morbid condition, — that utter want of self-
confidence. On the whole, I feel "toned-up" —
full of new energy; that will not be displeasing
to you. I not only feel that I ought to do something
good, but I am going to do it, — with the permission
of the gods.

How nice of you to have invited Amenomori to
our tiffin, — and the trip to Ōmori! I look forward in the future to a Kamakura day, under like
circumstances, when time and tide permit. I believe
A. can surprise us at Kamakura, which he knows
better than any man living. He does not give his
knowledge to many people.

I am sending you Knapp's book, as I promised, and that volume of mine which you have not read. Excuse the shabbiness of the volumes. I think Dr. Hall knows much about the curious dialect which I have used, — the Creole. Please say to him for me what you feel ought to be said.

I won't write any more now — and I settle down forthwith to work with fresh vim and hope.

With more than grateful remembrance,

Affectionately yours,

LAFCADIO HEARN.

TO MITCHELL McDONALD

Tōkyō, January, 1898.

DEAR McDONALD, — I have both of your kindest letters. It gave me no small pleasure to find that you liked "Youma:" you will not like it less knowing that the story is substantially true. You can see the ruins of the old house in the Quartier du Fort if you ever visit Saint-Pierre, and perhaps meet my old friend Arnoux, a survivor of the time. The girl really died under the heroic conditions described — refusing the help of the blacks, and the ladder. Of course I may have idealized her, but not her act. The incident of the serpent occurred also; but the heroine was a different person, — a plantation girl, celebrated by the historian Rufz de Lavison. I wrote the story under wretched circumstances in Martinique, near the scenes described, and under the cross with the black Christ. As for the "Sylvestre Bonnard" I believe I told you that that was

translated in about ten days and published in two
weeks from the time of beginning — at the wish of
the Harpers.   Price $115, if I remember rightly, —
and no commission on sales, — but the work suffers
in consequence of the haste.

How to answer your kind suggestion about pulling
me "out of my shell," I don't well know.   I like
to be out of the shell — but much of that kind of
thing could only result in the blue devils.   After
seeing men like you and the other Guardsman, —
the dear doctor, — one is beset with a foolish wish
to get back into the world which produced you both,
back to the U. S. A., — out of Government grind,
out of the unspeakable abomination and dulness
and selfishness and stupidity of mere officialism.
And I can't afford that feeling often — not *yet*.   I
have too many little butterfly-lives to love and take
care of.   Some day, I know, I must get back for a
time.   Meanwhile I must face the enemy and stand
the music.

Now I want you to tell me that Highbinder
romance when I next meet you.   Perhaps your
solitary experience could give me more than one
good story.   Every good man's life is full of romances.
The trouble is to get him to tell them, and to understand them properly when told.   Your "Prussian
officer" is delicious; but I fear my talent is not quite
up to the mark of telling it as it ought to be told.
Maupassant — Kipling — they would delight the
world with such a thing.   Never mind ! — I am
sure, *if* you want me to write stories, that you can
give me all the material you want or that I need.   I

shall sit again at the table, supporting that beautiful cap with its silver-eagle, — and I shall talk and talk and talk until you tell me more stories.

Won't you be glad to hear that my new book will be finished this month, — perhaps this week? Then for the "Stories from Many Lips" — or something of that kind.

Ever affectionately yours,

LAFCADIO HEARN.

TO MITCHELL McDONALD

Tōkyō, January, 1898.

DEAR McDONALD, — I got your kindest reply to my note of the other day, — actually apologizing for not writing sooner. But I told you never to bother yourself about writing me when you do not feel like it or when you are in the least busy; and I shall never feel neglected if you be silent, but only think that you have business on hand, and hope that you will have good luck in the undertaking.

Why, yes: I must get down some Saturday, or Friday afternoon — that would be still better — so as to return to Tōkyō Sunday night: for my Saturdays are free. But not *too* soon. It is only about two weeks since I was with you — though I acknowledge that it seems to me like three months. I wish I could see you more often; — then again, I think, you would be tired of my chatter soon. (I know what you would protest; but it does n't matter.) Well, not to argue too much, I promise to make a visit during February, — though I shall scarcely be able to name an exact day in advance.

I have never been in San Francisco, unfortunately. But that matters little, if I can ask all the questions I want. The value in a literary way of the scenes would be less the scenes themselves than the impression which they made upon your own memory. I anticipate much pleasure in asking you about it, as well as delight in hearing the story itself.

What will you think of my wickedness? I am going to tell you a bad story about myself. The other day (I mustn't try to pretend it was long ago, like I did about the Club-Hotel story in your carriage, for fear of being questioned as to direct facts) my publishers sent me some rather nasty newspaper clippings, together with what affected to be a manuscript history of my personal eccentricities and weaknesses. They suggested that I should correct, amend, or reject, but that they should be glad to publish it with my approval. (About 19 pp. I think.) Having read it with considerable anger, I laid it aside for a couple of days, — during which time I effectually restrained the first impulse to write a furious letter. Then I most effectually amended that MS.; I corrected it as thoroughly as it could possibly be corrected — but not with pencil or pen: such instruments being quite inadequate for the purpose. In short, I corrected, amended, and rejected it all at the same time — with the assistance of a red-hot stove. They shall never know; but as murder will out, I must tell somebody, and that somebody shall be you. With best regards to the doctor, — ever with hopes to see you *soon*,

LAFCADIO HEARN.

TO MITCHELL McDONALD

Tōkyō, January, 1898.

DEAR McDONALD, — It would do me a great deal of harm if I could believe your appreciations and predictions; but I am quite sure you are mistaken about both. As to success, I think my greatest good fortune would consist in being able occasionally to travel for about six months, — just to pick up strange or beautiful literary material. If I can ever manage that much — or even if I can manage to get so far independent that I can escape from officialdom — I shall be very fortunate indeed. Want to get to Europe for a time, in any case, to put my boy there. But all this is dream and shadow, perhaps.

Literary success of any enduring kind is made only by refusing to do what publishers want, by refusing to write what the public want, by refusing to accept any popular standard, by refusing to write anything to order. I grant it is not the way to make money quickly; but it is the way — and the only way — to win what sincerity in literary effort ought to obtain. My publishers have frankly gone over to the Philistines. I could not write for them further even if they paid me $100 per line.

What a selfish letter I am writing! You are making me talk too much about my own affairs, and you would really spoil me, if you could. Talking to me of fame and hundreds of thousands of dollars! Of course I should like to have hundreds of thousands, and to hold them at your disposal; but I should also like to live in the realization of the life

of the Arabian Nights. About the truth of life
seems to be this: You can get what you wish for
only when you have stopped wishing for it, and do
not care about keeping it.

I see your name in the papers often now, and
in connections that fill me with gladness. You are
a power again in the land — wish you could be here
for longer than you are going to stay. But, after all,
that would not be best for you — would it?

Affectionately ever,
LAFCADIO.

TO MITCHELL McDONALD

Tōkyō, January, 1898.

DEAR McDONALD, — *After all*, instinct is n't a
bad thing. Your just-received excellent advice is
precisely what my "blind instinct" — as scientific
men call it — told me. No: I shall do nothing without consulting you.

Well, I imagine that not *next* Friday, but the
Friday after will be most convenient to you. I 'll
try the later date, therefore. (Friday need not be
a Black Friday in Japan — I used to hate to do anything on that day — landed in Japan on Good
Friday (!) but now I belong to the Oriental gods.)

Wonder if you know that the *Revue des Deux
Mondes* has sent a poet here to write up Japan —
M. André Bellesort. He is a man of big literary
calibre, and has a rare wife — who speaks Persian.
About as charming a Frenchwoman as one could
wish to know. She speaks English, Italian, and

Spanish besides. Trying to get them interested in Amenomori. They are at the Hotel Metropole, — perhaps on account of the Legation.

Faithfully and affectionately yours,

LAFCADIO HEARN.

TO MITCHELL McDONALD

TŌKYŌ, February, 1898.

DEAR McDONALD, — I *ought* to have answered you about the subject of investment the other day; but I thought it would be better to wait. However, now I think (I have just received your telegram, and I confess it made me uncomfortable) that I had better write my feelings frankly. I suppose that, being naturally born to bad luck, I shall lose my small savings in the ordinary course of the world's events; but I would prefer this prospect to the worry of mind that I should have about any investment. In fact, rather than stand that worry again (I have had it once) I should prefer to lose everything now. The mere idea of business is a horror, a nightmare, a torture unspeakable. The moment I think about business I wish that I had never been born. I can assure you truthfully that I would rather burn a five hundred dollar bill than invest it, — because, having burned it, I could forget all about it, and trust myself to the mercy of the gods. Even if I had Jay Gould behind me, to pull me up every time I fell, I should not have anything to do with business. Even to have to write you this letter makes me wish that all the business in the world could be instantly

destroyed. I am afraid to explain more. I think
I won't go to Yokohama on Friday next — but
later, — well, what 's the use of writing more — you
will understand how I feel. Ever most faithfully,
                                    LAFCADIO HEARN.

TO MITCHELL McDONALD

TŌKYŌ, February, 1898.

DEAR McDONALD, — When I saw that big envelope, I thought to myself, "Lord! what a *lot* of
h—l I am going to get!" You see my conscience
was bad. I was wrong not to have told you long ago
of my peculiar 'phobia. And inside that envelope
there was only the kindest of kind letters, — proving
that you understood me perfectly well, and forthwith
putting me at ease.

I read the prospectus with great interest (by the
way, I am returning it, because, as it is still in the
state of a private document, I think it is better
that I do not keep it); and I am proud of my friend.
He can do things! "Canst thou play with Leviathan like a bird? Or canst thou bind him for thy
handmaidens?" No, I can't, and I am not going to
try; but I have a friend in Yokohama — an officer
of the U. S. Navy — *he* plays with Leviathan, and
makes him "talk soft, soft words"— indeed he even
"presses down his tongue with a cord." Well, I
should like you to be as rich as you could be made
rich, without having worry. But as for *me!* — the
greatest favour you can ever do me is to take off my
hands even the business that I have — contracts,

and the like, — so that I need never again remember them. Besides, if I were dead, you are the one I should want to be profiting by my labours. Then every time you set your jaw square, and made them "fork over," my ghost would squeak and chipper for delight, — and you would look around to see where the bats came from.

Well, next week I'll try to get down. In fact I feel that I must go to Yokohama, for various reasons besides imposing upon a certain friend there. To-day I have been packing up my book all the time from morning until now — so as to send by registered letter.

About "the best." You are a dreadful man! How could you think that I had got even halfway to the bottom. I have only drunk three bottles yet; but that is a shameful "only." Three bottles in one month is simply outrageous; and I look into the glass often to observe the end of my nose. That "best" is too seductive.

With affectionate thanks for kindest letter,

Faithfully ever,

LAFCADIO.

TO MITCHELL McDONALD

Tōkyō, February, 1898.

DEAR McDONALD, — Your telegram made me feel comfortable. I had been a little uneasy, — especially because you never told me what really was the matter; — and when a man like you cannot bend his back, the matter could not have been a joke. Also the telegram convinced me that you were really thinking about coming up, and possibly might come up during the spring or the summer or the coming autumn season, and that I could squat on the floor and talk to you — which made me comparatively happy.

I have been otherwise disgracefully blue. When I want to feel properly humble, I read "Glimpses of Unfamiliar Japan"— about half a page; — then I howl, and wonder how I could ever have written so badly, — and find that I am really only a very twenty-fifth-rate workman and that I ought to be kicked. Then the weather has been trying; — the mails are behind; — the afflictions of Tōkyō manifold. Also I have been provoked to think that there is no other person like you known to me in the entire world, — and that you are by no means immortal, — and that, even as it is, you think ever so much more of me than I deserve. Also I have been meditating on the unpermanency of the universe, and considering the possible folly of making books at all. — This must be the darkness before the dawn: at least I ought to think so.

I have partly in mind the plan for making the best part of number eight out of stories adapted from the Japanese. Not sure that I can carry the plan out satisfactorily; — but I am resolved that number eight must be worthy of your hopes for me, — and that it shall prove an atonement for the faults of the first book dedicated to you.

Take all care of yourself, and believe me most grateful for that telegram.

Affectionately,

LAFCADIO.

TO MITCHELL McDONALD

TŌKYŌ, February, 1898.

DEAR FRIEND, — Two or three mornings ago I woke up with a vague feeling of pleasure — a dim notion that something very pleasant had occurred the day before. Then I remembered that the pleasure had come from your unanswered letter. I kept putting off writing, nevertheless, day after day, in consequence partly of the conviction that such a letter should not be answered in a dull mood, and partly because some of my college work this past week has been more than usually complicated — involving a study of subjects that I thoroughly hate, but must try to make interesting — the literature and spirit of the eighteenth century.

Well, even now, I do not quite know what to say about your letter. To tell me that I have something of your father's spirit more than pleased me — not because I could quite believe it, but because you did. Your father must have been a very fine man, without any pettiness, — and I have more smallness in me than you can suspect. How could it be otherwise! If a man lives like a rat for twenty or twenty-five years, he must have acquired something of the disposition peculiar to house-rodents, — must n't he? Anyhow, I could never agree to let you take all the trouble you propose to take for me merely as a matter of "thank you." I must contrive ways and means to better your proposal — not to cancel the obligation, for that could not be done, but at least to make you quite sure that I appreciate the extreme rarity of such friendship.

I am writing with hesitation to-day (chiefly, indeed, through a sense of duty to you), — for I fear that you are in trouble, and that my letter is going to reach you at the worst possible time. However, I hope you have not lost any very dear friends by that terrible accident at Havana. I think you told me that you were once on that ship, nevertheless; and I fear that you must receive some bad news. My sympathies are with you in any event.

My Boston friend is lost to me, certainly. I got a letter yesterday from him — showing the serious effect upon friendship of taking to one's self a wife, — a fashionable wife. It was meant to be exactly like the old letters; — but it was n't. Paymaster M. M. must also some day take a wife, and . . . Oh! I know what you are going to say; — they all say that! They all assure you that they *both* love you, and that their house will be always open to you, etc., etc., and then — they forget all about you — purposely or otherwise. Still, one ought to be grateful, — the dropping is so gently and softly done.

Affectionately ever,

LAFCADIO HEARN.

TO MR. AND MRS. JOHN ALBEE

Tōkyō, February, 1898.

MY DEAR FRIENDS, — I am going to address you together, as that will save me from the attempt to write in two keys corresponding to the differing charm of your two letters. Certainly it gave me, as you surmised, sincere pleasure to hear from you. Mrs. Albee surprised me at the same time by a most agreeable, though I fear somewhat *generous*, reference to a forgotten letter. I think I must have penned many extravagances in those days. I *know* it — in certain cases: anyhow I should be afraid to read my own letters to Mr. Albee over again. As for my old ambition then expressed, I don't quite know what to say. The attempt referred to led me far at one time in the wrong direction — though whatever I have learned of style has certainly been due rather to French and Spanish studies than to English ones. I have now dropped theories, nevertheless; and I simply try to do the best I can, without reference to schools.

Do you know that I had a dim notion always that Mr. Albee was a millionaire, — or at least a very wealthy dilettante? — which would be the best of reasons for never sending him a book, notwithstanding my grateful remembrance of his first generous encouragement. (*Here* I use "generous" in the strongest meaning possible.) I am, *selfishly*, rather pleased to hear that the price of a book is sometimes for him, as for me, a question worth thinking over — because the fact permits me to offer him a volume occasionally. Otherwise indeed I wish he were rich as my fancy painted him.

You say that you have not read "all my books on Japan." Any that you particularly care to read, I can send you — though I should not recommend the "Glimpses," except for reference. "Kokoro" would probably best please Mrs. Albee, and after

it, "Out of the East." Hereafter I shall send a copy
of every "new book" to you. Of course I shall be
glad to have the pleasure of seeing Mr. Albee's
"Prose Idyls"— many sincere thanks for the kind
remembrance!

With kindest and best regards, faithfully ever,

LAFCADIO HEARN.

TO JOHN ALBEE

TŌKYŌ, May, 1898.

DEAR MR. ALBEE, — My best thanks for the
"Prose Idyls." The book leaves on the mind an
impression of quiet brightness like that of a New
England summer sky thinly veiled. Three idyls
especially linger in my imagination, — each for a
reason all its own. Hawthorne might have written
"The Devil's Bargain:" it is a powerful moral
fancy, and the touch of grotesque humour in it is
just enough to keep it from being out of tone in the
gallery of optimist studies. "The Family Mirror"
is haunting: the whole effect, to my notion, being
brought out by that charming reference to the
damaged spot at the back. Then "A Mountain
Maid" much appealed to me by its suggestion of
that beautiful and mysterious *sauvagerie*, as the
French call it, — that wholly instinctive shrinking
from caress, which develops with the earliest bud-
ding of womanhood, but which the girl could not
herself possibly explain. Indeed I fancy that only
evolutional philosophy can explain it at all. Ana-
logous conditions in the boy of fourteen or fifteen

TO MITCHELL McDONALD

a little sketch on this subject, which *may* be printed
some day or other: "A Pair of Eyes."

My next volume will have a series of what I
might call *metaphysical idyls*, perhaps, at its latter
end. I fear you will think them too sombre, — now
that I have felt something of the sunshine of your
soul. However, each of us can only give his own
tone to the thread which he contributes to the
infinite warp and woof of human thought and
emotion. Is it not so? With kindest regards to Mrs.
Albee, very gratefully yours,

LAFCADIO HEARN (Y. KOIZUMI).

TO MITCHELL McDONALD

TŌKYŌ, February, 1898.

DEAR McDONALD, — I must try to forget some
of your beautiful letter for fear that it should give
me much too good an opinion of myself. A reverse
state of mind is, on the whole, much better for the
writer, — I mean for any professional writer.

I believe all that you wish me to believe about
your generous call — but, if friend McDonald does
not think my house a poor rat-trap, that is because
friend McDonald has not yet discovered what a
beautiful Japanese house is like. Let me assure
him, therefore, that it is something so dainty, so
wonderful, that only by custom can one cease to be
afraid to walk about in it.

Yes, as you surmised, one of your suggestions is
wrong. The professional writer, however small

his own powers may be, generally knows the
range of literary possibilities; and I *know* that what
you wish cannot be done by any Western writer
with the least hope of success. It has been exten-
sively tried — always with the result of failure.
The best attempt, perhaps, was the effort of Judith
Gautier, — a very delicate French writer; but it
did not succeed. As for "A Muramasa Blade,"
"Mito Yashiki," etc., the less said the better. In
any case, it is not so much that the subject itself is
immensely difficult for a foreigner, as that even
supposing this difficulty mastered, the Western
public would not care twopence about the result.
Material is everywhere at hand. Yearly, from the
Japanese press are issued the most wonderful and
thrilling stories of Japanese feudal life; but a master-
translation of these, accompanied with illustrations
of the finest kind, would fall dead in a Western
book-market, and find its way quickly into the ten-
cent boxes of second-hand dealers. And why?
Simply because the Occidental reader could not
feel interested in the poetry or romance of a life so
remote.

No: the public want in fiction things taken raw
and palpitating out of life itself, — the life they
know, — the life everybody knows, — not that which
is known only to a few. Stories from Japan (or
India or China, for that matter) must be stories
about Western people among alien surroundings.
And the people must not be difficult to understand;
they must be people like the owner of the "Mary
Gloster" in Kipling's "Seven Seas." (You ought to

buy that book — and love it.) Of course, I don't
mean to say that I could ever do anything of Kipling's kind — I should have to do much humbler
work, — but I am indicating what I mean by "raw
out of life."

As for the other suggestion, — who ever was such
a pretty maker of compliments! — I can only say
that I am happy to have a friend who thus thinks
of me.

Gratefully, with much thanks for your charming
letter,   LAFCADIO HEARN.

TO MITCHELL McDONALD

TŌKYŌ, March, 1898.

DEAR McDONALD, — I did not think much of
the title of Morrow's book; but your judgement of
the stories interested me, and the selfsame evening
I began the volume — in bed. I read three quarters
at a run, and the rest early in the morning. They
are queer and sometimes powerful little stories —
not less interesting because they are, most of them,
improbable. They have the charm of the now old-
fashioned stories of 1850–70, — perhaps not finished
to the same extent as the *Atlantic* stories used to
be; but they make me think of them a little. (The
literary centres clamour for realism to-day; but I
fancy that the taste for the romantic will live a good
while longer.) Then again there is a little of the
old-time gold light of California days here — that
will always have a charm for readers. I wonder if
Morrow is a young man: if he is, I should believe

him likely to do still better in the future. If he writes for money, he need not do much finer work; but if just for love of the thing, I should say that he could finish his work better than he does, — as in the study of the emotions of the man who finds his wife untrue to him, and solves a moral problem after quite an ideal fashion. The subject was splendid: it might have been made more of. — But not to criticize things — especially things which I could not do myself — I must say that I enjoyed the tales, and that they ought to have a very good sale.

Somehow your own story — the "Highbinder story"— kept riding on the back of that gold dragon all the while I was reading. The real dominated the romantic, and yet betimes made the romantic seem possible. I could feel everything to be just as it was — my experience as a police-reporter gave verisimilitude to the least detail. You are after all a knight-errant in soul, — a real knight, tilting, not against shadows and windmills, but against the dragons of corrupted law and the giants of fraud who haunt the nineteenth century. You are a survival, I fear—there are few like you: you ride alone: all the more reason that you should take every care of yourself — care of your health; I fear you are not exercising enough, keeping too confined. If you are really, as I believe, fond of your little friend, don't forget his prayer that you make health your No. 1 consideration.

Hope to be down Friday about 2 p. m. or 2.30 at latest. Affectionately,

LAFCADIO.

TO MITCHELL McDONALD

MARCH, 1898.

DEAR McDONALD, — I do not feel pleased at
your returning to me the money and giving me your
own copy of the book. I feel mean over it. But
what can one do with a man who deliberately takes
off his own coat to cover his friend during a nine
minutes' drive? I shall remember the *feeling* of
that coat — warmth of friendship must also have
been electrical in it — until I die.

Affectionately and somewhat reproachfully, — in
haste,

LAFCADIO HEARN.

I write *in haste*, so as not to keep your man
waiting.

TO MITCHELL McDONALD

TŌKYŌ, March, 1898.

DEAR McDONALD, — Just got your letter, —
your more than kind letter. Happily there is no
occasion to send the telegram. I am getting well
fast, and think I shall be lecturing on Monday.
No: I did not minimize things. I have been laid
up, but it was more painful than serious. Can't
tell what it was — a painful swelling of one side of
the face, and nose. My picturesque nose suffered
most. That a square mile of solid pain could be
concentrated into one square inch of nose was a
revelation! Anyhow, it felt just like a severe case

of frost-bite; but I suppose it was only some sort of a cold. Going to Yokohama had nothing to do with it; but the weather must have had. It was rather trying, you know, last Tuesday.

You are the one who tries to minimize things, my dear friend, by assuring me that there are thousands of . . . people like yourself. I am glad to think that you *can* believe thus well of the world; but I can't, and I should not be glad to think you were right. I prefer the exceptional. Then you will remember my philosophical theory that no two living beings have even the same voice, and that it is the uniqueness of each that has value. I should have to abandon my theories to accept your opinion of things in general, and I am prejudiced in favour of my theories.

Perhaps next week I can run down, and if that be not a good time for you, the week following. Anyhow the term will be over in about two weeks more, and — I hope — the cold. Tuesday deceived even the creatures of the spring. Hundreds of little frogs began to chant their song of birth, and flowers were opening everywhere. Now there is no sound of a frog. They woke up too soon, the creatures, — and the flowers look as if they were dying of consumption. In your hotel you don't know all this — because you keep up the atmosphere of the Bermudas under that roof. In Ushigome we are practically in the country, and observe the seasons.

Affectionately,

LAFCADIO.

TO MITCHELL McDONALD

TōKYō, March, 1898.

DEAR McDONALD, — Was n't I lucky in deciding
to get back early last night? It would have been no
easy matter getting back this morning — everything is drowned in snow! That was the reason of
yesterday's atrocious cold. Verily I was inspired by
the gods — both as to going and returning.

This morning I woke up with an extreme feeling
of comfort and lightness — which reminded me
that something very pleasant must have happened
the day before, — and I heard the U. S. C. cynically
observing with a Mephistophelian smile, "Well,
I guess our friend here will pull your chestnuts out
of the fire for you!" And then I thanked all the
host of heaven for that which had been, and also
for that which would never again be. After all, I
am rather a lucky fellow, — a most peculiarly lucky
fellow. Principally owing to the note written some
eight years ago by a certain sweet young lady whose
portrait now looks down on me from the ceiling
of No. 21 Tomihisa-chō, Ichigaya, Ushigome-ku,
in the city of Tōkyō, Japan.

I send with this "Some Chinese Ghosts" in
awfully bad condition. Early work of a man who
tried to understand the Far East from books, —
and could n't; but then, the real purpose of the
stories was only artistic. Should I ever reprint the
thing, I would change nothing, — but only preface
the new edition with a proper apology.

You remember my anecdote yesterday of the

Memphis man — "What! a d—d nigger? I'd as soon shoot a nigger as I'd shoot a rat!" He was a very pretty boy, too. I forgot to tell you something also about him that occurs to me this morning. He was walking lame in a pair of top-boots one morning, and I asked him what was the matter. "Only these d—d boots," he said; "they've taken all the skin off my feet." "Have n't you another pair?" I asked. "Lots of 'em," he answered; "but I'm not going to *give in* to these: I won't let 'em get the better of *me!* — I won't let them get the better of *me!*" I rather admired this vengeful and foolish pluck; and I am thinking now that I'd better follow the example. Spite of all conditions I'm getting No. 6 book under way; and I won't *give in* either to publishers or to public.

Loving thanks for yesterday's extraordinary enjoyableness and for all things. In haste.

Affectionately ever,
LAFCADIO HEARN.

TO MITCHELL McDONALD

Tōkyō, March, 1898.

DEAR McDONALD, — I am looking and looking for your last kind letter; but for the moment I cannot find it. So I must give it up for to-night, if I am to write you.

I'm through with the university; and I must get down to Yokohama, either to-morrow or Monday, and try to bore you, and to coax that story from Mrs. Burns (is that the name?), — but I shall make

another visit later, if the weather allows. This will
be only an expedition — partly in search of literary
material. I feel I must get a few stories, to keep on
the surface. Otherwise I 'll get heavy and sink. I
have been rather heavy lately. My dog-sketch has
developed into such a nightmare that I myself am
afraid of it, and don't want to think about it for a
few days. Then I have just finished a short sketch,
"In a Pair of Eyes" — considerably metaphysical.
Such things may interest; but they will not touch
hearts; and an author must try to get loved by his
readers. So I shall forage.

Consul General Gowey gave me an agreeable
start the other day by sending me a number of
"The Philistine" — you know the little thing, very
clever — with a pretended quotation from one of
my books. The quotation, however, hit what I
think, — though I never put the matter in just that
shape. It was nice of the consul to send it — made
me feel jolly. I must some day send him something
to amuse him. Not to like him is impossible.

I think you must have hosts of friends now calling
on you, — since the battle-powers of the great
Republic are gathering out this way. I hope you
won't have to get yourself killed for Uncle Sam;
but if you have, I want to be in the conning-tower
about the same time. I fancy, however, that Manila
would not be a mouthful if the navy is ordered to
gobble it; and that the chief result of the expedition
to U. S. officers would be an uncommonly large and
fine supply of cigars.

I have last week declined three dinners. It

strikes me that the average university professor is circumstanced about thus: —

1. Twelve to fourteen lectures a week.

2. Average of a hundred official banquets per year.

3. Average of sixty private society-dinners.

4. Average of thirty to fifty invitations to charitable, musical, uncharitable, and non-musical colonial gatherings.

5. Average of a hundred and fifty social afternoon calls.

6. Average of thirty requests for contributions to Japanese publications.

7. Average of a hundred requests for pecuniary contributions from all sources.

8. Average of four requests per month for speeches or outside lectures.

9. Average of a hundred calls from students "wanting" things — chiefly to waste *the professor's* time.

This is only about half the list. I say "No" to *everything* — softly, of course. Otherwise how should I exist, breathe, even have time to think? — much less write books? Oh dear, oh dear! — What a farce it is! When they first started, they wanted the professors to wear a uniform of scarlet and gold. (I am sure about the gold — not quite sure about the scarlet.) The professors kicked at the gold, — luckily for themselves!

Ever affectionately,

LAFCADIO.

TO MITCHELL McDONALD

Tōkyō, March, 1898.

DEAR McDONALD, — Sunshine, warmth, and beauty in the world to-day; and sunshine and warmth of another sort in my heart — beautiful ghostly summer made by words and thoughts in Yokohama. "When the earth is still by reason of the South wind" — that is my mental world.

I am sending the photo of our friend, which reminds me that I was reproached very justly on reaching home last night. "But you did not bring your American friend's picture? . . . Forgot to put it into the valise? . . . Oh! but you *are* queer — always, always dreaming! And don't you feel just a little bit ashamed?" I do feel ashamed, but more than a little bit.

Also I send you a little volume containing "The House and the Brain" — published in other editions under the title "The Haunted and the Haunters." (Usually it is bound up with that tremendous story about the Elixir of Life, — the "Strange Story" of Bulwer Lytton.) Professor Saintsbury calls this the best ghost-story ever written. But you ought to read it at night only — after the hotel becomes silent.

By way of precaution I must make a confession. I shall not be able to eat again until about Tuesday noon, I think. The tiffins, dinners, "irresistibles," and above all that Blue Soul, were too much for me. I am getting old, sure enough, — and when I go down again to Yokohama I must live in the most ascetic manner. I feel constitutionally demoralized by all that luxurious living. Still, I must say that I suspect the sudden change of the weather is partly responsible for the feeling.

Now, really — don't you feel tired of all this talk? Of course I know — but the conditions are so much like those of old college friendships that they seem more of dreams than of reality.

Ever affectionately,

LAFCADIO.

TO MITCHELL McDONALD

TŌKYŌ, April, 1898.

DEAR McDONALD, — Your kindest letter came last night. I must confess to a feeling of remorse for transferring all my troubles to your broader shoulders, — a remorse tempered somewhat, of course, by the certainty that you find a pleasure in helping your friend, but nevertheless, a remorse. So pray do not do anything more than you find it pleasant and inexpensive to do.

We are under the weather for the moment. We shall not be able to profit by the holidays. I have escaped cold and all other troubles; but I could not escape the generally depressing influence of this chilly, sunless, muddy, slimy season. In other words, I feel too stupid to do anything. Probably the sight of the sun will make us all feel happy again.

Of course I shall be unhappy till I get your photos, — both military and civilian. I fear to ask too many; but all I can get, I want. Don't hurry; but

— don't forget me, if you think I deserve to be remembered.

I am a little anxious lest war take you away from Japan, which would leave me less satisfied with this world than I now am. But I should like indeed to accompany you in a descent on Manila, and to chronicle events picturesquely.

I should never be able, however, to do anything so wonderful as did Loti in describing the French attack on the coast of Annam. It was the greatest literary feat ever done by a naval officer; but it nearly cost him his place in the navy, and did in fact suppress him for several years. In his reissue of the narrative I see that he was obliged to suppress the terrible notes on the killing.

Ever affectionately,

LAFCADIO HEARN.

TO MITCHELL McDONALD

TŌKYŌ, April, 1898.

DEAR FRIEND, — The holidays are over; and the winter is still dying hard. We are all feeling pretty well now notwithstanding, — and my imp was down yesterday to Ueno, in the sea of people, trying to get a glimpse of things. Because he had a naval uniform on, he became quite angry at the *kurumaya* for proposing to lift him up to look over the heads of the people. The K. wisely answered: "I know you are a man — but then you must think that I am a horse only, and ride on my back. Even military men ride horses, you know !" Subsequently, the imp

had to submit to circumstances, — swallowed his
pride, — and got on the man's back. I liked the
pride, though: it was the first flash of the man-spirit
in him.

I wonder if you are ever tired simply of living!
That is what the weather made me for a time.
Glimpses of sun now seem quite delicious. Well,
it is the same way with my Yokohama friend. If
I saw him too often, I should not feel quite so warm
in the sunshine that he can make — should begin to
think the light a normal and usual, instead of a most
extraordinary condition. There is one thing, however, that I hope to live to see: M. McD. in a private residence of his own, and a beautiful young Mrs.
McD. therein.

If the quarrel with Spain does nothing else, perhaps it will stir up the American people to make
a good-sized navy in short order. With so many
thousand miles of coast to defend they are at a big
disadvantage compared with most European powers.
I see that Captain Mahan has been getting out a new
book on the subject, just at the right time. What a
lucky author he has been on the whole; and all circumstances seem to have actually bent themselves
in his favour.

Affectionately, with regards to the doctor and all
friends,

LAFCADIO.

TO MITCHELL McDONALD

Tōkyō, April, 1898.

DEAR McDONALD, — Just after having posted my letter (dated 11th, but mailed 14th) yours came, together with the most precious photographs. My warmest thanks, not only for them, but also for the friend's inscription upon them, which adds to their preciousness. But — see how mean I am! — I hope for *at least* one more, — the one with the full-dress hat *on*. You don't like it; but I just love it, and I hope you will save one for me. The two you sent are admirable: I am going to put the large one in a frame.

Shall I climb Fuji? Perhaps; but I know that at this blessed moment I could not do it. I am too soft now. Must harden up first in the sea; and then, please the gods, I 'll climb with you. The climb is simply horrid; but the view is a compensation.

I don't know what to do with you — after that remark about Loti. Unless I can manage in the next three years to write something very extraordinary indeed, I fear you will be horribly disappointed some day. You should try to consider me as a *tenth-rate* author, until the literary world shall have fixed my place. And don't for a moment imagine me modest in literary matters. I am Satanically proud — not modest at all. If I tell you that much of my work is very bad, I tell you so, not because I am modest, but because, as a professional writer, I can see bad execution where you would not see it unless I pointed it out to you. It is like an honest carpenter, who knows his trade, and will tell his customer: "That is n't going to cost you much, because the work is bad. See! this is backed with cheap wood underneath! It looks all right only because you don't know how we patch up these things."

Ever most affectionately,

LAFCADIO HEARN.

TO MITCHELL McDONALD

Tōkyō, April, 1898.

DEAR McDONALD, — Your letter came this morning (Sunday), and it rejoiced me to find that you are not yet in likelihood of being allowed to attend the Asiatic side of the smash; while, as you suggest, before you could join . . . on the other side, the serious part of the campaign would be over. That torpedo squadron at Porto Rico is apparently stronger than any force of the same kind possessed by the U. S.; and although Northern seamanship must tell in a fight, machinery in itself is a formidable thing, even without anything more than mere pluck behind it. But just think how a literary narrative of a battle would sell in America! Would n't L. B. & Co. make money!

How kind of you to send photo of Amenomori ! (Yes; you returned the little one.) This will not fade, and is a decided improvement. I need scarcely tell you that out of a million Japanese heads, you could not find another like this. It represents the cream of the race at its intellectual best.

In writing hurriedly the other day, I forgot to

answer your question about the *Athenæum* paper.
Yes: the notice was hostile, — but not directly so;
for a literary work the book was highly praised. The
critic simply took the ground of denying that what I
wrote about existed. I was braced with a missionary,
and while the missionary's book was accepted as
unquestionable fact, mine was pronounced a volume
from Laputa. The *Saturday Review* knew better
than that.

As to the royalties given to Kipling, they are
fancy rates, of course, and probably never twice the
same. Publishers bid against each other for the
right of issuing even a limited edition. Macmillan
& Co. hold the ultimate right in all cases; but they
do not often print the first edition. Jas. Lane Allen
probably gets only ten per cent. He may get more;
but not much more — there is no American to compare with Kipling in the market, except Henry James
and Marion Crawford. Kipling probably outsells
both together. James is too fine and delicate a
writer — a psychological analogist of the most complex society — ever to become popular. In short,
any writer's chances of good terms, in England or
America, must depend upon his popularity, — his
general market value. Once that he makes a big
success — that is, a sale of 20,000 copies of a book
within a year and a half, suppose — he can get
fancy terms for his next book.

. . . As to when I shall have another MS. I don't
know. To-day, I am hesitating whether I ought
or ought not to burn some MS. My work has lately
been a little horrible, a little morbid perhaps. Every-

thing depends upon exterior influence,—inspiration; and Tōkyō is the very worst place in all Japan for that. Perhaps within a year from now, I shall have a new book ready; perhaps in six months — according to what comes up, — suggestions from Nature, books, or mankind. At the very latest, I ought to have a new book ready by next spring.

But there is just one possibility. In case that during this year, or any year, there should come to me a good idea for such a story as I have been long hoping to write, — a single short powerful philosophical story, of the most emotional and romantic sort, — then I shall abandon everything else for the time being, and write it. If I can ever write *that*, there will be money in it, long after I have been planted in one of these old Buddhist cemeteries. I do not mean that it will pay *because* I write it, but because it will touch something in the new thought of the age, in the tendencies of the time. All thought is changing; and I feel within myself the sense of such a story — vaguely, like the sense of a perfume, or the smell of a spring wind, which you cannot describe or define. What divine luck such an inspiration would be ! But the chances are that a more powerful mind than mine will catch the inspiration first, — as the highest peak most quickly takes the sun. Whatever comes, I 'll just hand or send the MS. to you, and say, "Now just do whatever you please — only see that I get the proofs. The book is yours."

Ever so many thanks for kind advice, and for everything else.

I read that war has begun. Hope it will soon end.
Anyhow Uncle Sam does not lose time: he knows
too well that time is money. And after it is over, he
will probably start to build him the biggest fleet in
creation; for he needs it. Ever affectionately,

LAFCADIO HEARN.

TO MITCHELL McDONALD

TŌKYŌ, April, 1898.

DEAR FRIEND, — Your kindest letter is with me.
I cannot quite understand your faith in my work:
it is a veritable Roman Catholic faith, — for it refuses to hear adverse arguments. I only say that
I can see no reason to suppose or even hope that I
can ever be worth to publishers nearly as much as the
author of a blood-and-thunder detective story contributed to a popular weekly.

About getting killed: — I should like nothing so
much if I had no one but myself in the world to
take care of — which is just why I would not get
killed. You never get what you want in this world.
I used to feel that way in tight places, and say
to myself: "Well, I don't care: *therefore* it can't
happen." It is only what a man cares about that
happens. "That which ye fear exceedingly shall
come upon you." I fear exceedingly being burned
alive slowly, in an earthquake fire, — being eaten
by sharks, — being blinded or maimed so as to
prove of no further use; — but dying is probably a
very good thing indeed, and as much to be desired
for one's self as dreaded for one's friends.

But my work is not done yet: I can't afford luxuries till it is done, I suppose — at least so the gods think.

No: I shall not burn the MS. yet; but if I decided, after deliberation, to burn it, I think I should be right. How much I now wish I had burned things which I printed ten or twelve years ago!

I think with you that the U.S.N. will sweep the Spaniards off the sea; but still I feel slightly uneasy.

I have met a most extraordinary man to whom I gave your address, — in case he should need advice, or wish to see Amenomori. He is going to the hotel, but is now at Nikko. His name is E. T. Sturdy. He has lived in India, — up in the Himalayas for years, — studying Eastern philosophy; and the hotel delicacies will do him no good, because he is a vegetarian. He is a friend of Professor Rhys-Davids, who gave him a letter of introduction to me; and has paid for the publication of several Eastern texts — Pali, etc. Beyond any question, he is the most *remarkable* person I have met in Japan. Fancy a man independent, strong, cultivated, with property in New Zealand and elsewhere, voluntarily haunting the Himalayas in the company of Hindoo pilgrims and ascetics, — in search of the Nameless and the Eternal. Yet he is not a Theosophist exactly, nor a Spiritualist. I did not get very near him — he has that extreme English reserve which deludes under the appearance of almost boyish frankness; but I think we might become fast friends did we live in the same city. He told me some things that I shall never forget, — very strange things. I envy, not

him, but his independence. Think of being able
to live where one pleases, nobody's servant, — able
to choose one's own studies and friends and books.
On the other hand, most authors write because
they are compelled to find occupation for their minds.
Would I, being independent, become idle? I don't
think so; but I know that some of my work has been
done just to keep the mind from eating itself, — as
does the stomach without food. *Ergo*, perhaps, I
ought to be maintained in a condition of "eternal
torment"?

Well, it is not impossible that you may eventually suggest to me something of the great story that
is eventually to be written — let us hope. Assuredly
if I once start in upon it, I shall be asking you questions, and you will be able to help me very much.

Ever affectionately,

LAFCADIO.

TO ERNEST FENOLLOSA

TŌKYŌ, May, 1898.

DEAR PROFESSOR, — It is too bad that I should
twice have missed the pleasure of seeing you, — and
still worse that Mrs. Fenollosa should have come
into my wretched little street to find me absent. But
it were better always when possible to let me know
in advance of any chances for a visit — otherwise
I can seldom be relied upon; especially in these
months, for I am over head and ears in work, —
with the dreadful prospect of examinations and
the agonies of proof-reading to be rolled upon me at

the same moment. You are so far happy to be able
to command your time: I cannot often manage it.

Well, even if I had been free, I do not think I
should have cared to go to the Ukioy-e exhibition
again — except, of course, to hear you talk about it.
I am inclined to agree with one who said that the
catalogue was worth more than the view. It (not
the catalogue) left me cold — partly, perhaps,
because I had just been looking at a set of embroidered screens that almost made me scream with
regret at my inability to purchase them. I remember
only three or four at Ukioy-e, — the interesting
Kappa; Shōki diverting himself; a Listening
Girl — something of that sort: nothing excited in me
any desire to possess it, even as a gift, except the
Kappa and the Shōki. (I know I am hopeless — but
it were hopeless to try to be otherwise.) Verily I
prefer the modern colour-prints, which I can afford
sometimes to buy. What is more, I do not wish to
learn better. While I know nothing I can always
follow the Shintō code and consult my heart about
buying things. Were I to know more, I should
be less happy in buying cheap things. It is like
the Chinese characters on the shop-fronts. Once
you begin to know the meaning of a few, the magical charm — the charm of mystery — evaporates.
There's heresy for you! As for the catalogues
— especially the glorious New York catalogue —
I think them precious things. If they do me no
other good, they serve the purpose of suggesting
the range and unfathomability of my ignorance.
I only regret that you do not use legends, — do not

tell stories. If you did, Andersen would be quickly superseded. We buy him only for the folk-lore and the references.

Now I must thank Mrs. Fenollosa for the exceeding kindness of bringing those books so far for me. I fear I shall have little chance to read within the next couple of weeks; but if I get the least opportunity, I must try to read the "Cardinal" anyhow. I shall, whatever happens, return the volumes safely before very long. As for the Stevenson, it was not worth while thanking me for; besides, I do not candidly think it an example of the writer at his highest. But one reads these things because the times force you to.

As for the Mountain of Skulls — yes: I have written it, — about seven or eight times over; but it still refuses to give the impression I feel, and can't define, — the impression that floated into my brain with the soft-flowing voice of the teller. I shall try again later; but, although I feel tolerably sure about the result, nothing but very hard work will develop the thing. Had I only eleven more stories of such quality, what a book could be made out of them! Still, it is quite impossible that a dozen such tales could exist. I read all the Jatakas to no purpose: one makes such a find only by the rarest and most unexpected chance.

By the way, it puzzled me to imagine how the professor knew of my insignificance having visited the exhibition! But a charming professor who made three long visits there wants very much to make Professor Fenollosa's acquaintance, — E. Foxwell, a fellow of Cambridge, and an authority on economics. Quite a rare fine type of Englishman, — at once sympathetic and severely scientific, — a fine companion and a broad strong thinker.

Faithfully, with best regards and thanks,

LAFCADIO HEARN.

TO MITCHELL McDONALD

TŌKYŌ, June, 1898.

DEAR McDONALD, — I wonder if you are perfectly disgusted with my silence and general invisibility. But perhaps you have been far too busy to think enough about me even to say, "D——n his lying little soul!" (which is what I would have said under like circumstances); for I have been reading about you, — and know that you have had some sad and very important duties to perform, of an unexpected character.

I got by the last steamer only two notices for you; they are amusing, because they represent two entirely different religious points of view in Methodist criticism. Perhaps you will think the favourable notice very kindly under the circumstances.

What to say about the Manila matter I don't know. My notion is that you will not be likely to get the furlough so soon. Events are thickening, and looking very dark as well as strange. What most delights me is the prospect of an Anglo-American alliance. Then will come the world-struggle of races — British and Yankee against the Slav and his allies. Hope we shall not see that — it will be a very awful thing, — a vast earthquake in all the world's markets. And the Latins, curiously enough, are being drawn together by the same sense of their future peril. Their existence is in danger. Loti offers his services to Spain, after having been dropt from the French navy, — not because the moral justice of the question is understood by him, or even felt by him; but because his blood and ancestral feelings naturally attract him to Spain rather than to America. I should be sorry to see the best writer of prose of any country in this world blown to pieces for his chivalrous whim; but he is very likely to get killed if he goes into this mess. All men of letters will feel then very sorry; and a marvellous genius will have been thrown away for nothing — since there is no ghost of a hope for Spain.

I shall get down to Yokohama unexpectedly, I suppose, very soon — if I feel well enough: the weather has been so atrocious that I had fire in my room up to last week. I hope you have not felt any the worse for these abominable changes of temperature. Another such "spring" would drive me wild! In spite of it I have nearly completed a sixth chapter or essay for book Number Six. I am full of projects and suggestions; but cannot yet decide which among the multitude are strong enough to survive and bear development.

Ever affectionately, with faint hopes of forgiveness,

LAFCADIO HEARN.

TO ELLWOOD HENDRICK

Tōkyō, June, 1898.

Dear Wizard, Magician, Thaumaturgist, —
Your letter was wonderful. It made things quite
vivid before me; and I can actually see G. and M.
and the others you speak of (including myself,
under the influence of demophobia). Also you
cannot imagine how much good such a letter does a
fellow in my condition. It is tonicky, — slips ozone
of hope into a consumptive soul. I must now keep
out of blues for at least another seven years.

Anyhow, things are about right. My little wife
is getting strong again; my eyes are all right; the
examinations are over; the vacation begins; Little,
Brown & Company send me heaps of books; and we
go to the seaside as soon as I can manage it, — with
an old pupil of mine, — an officer now of engineers.

Speaking of pupils reminds me that just as you
keep me from follies, or mischief, by a bit of sound
advice at times, — not to say by other means, — so
here I have learned to be guided by K.'s mamma.
Indeed, no Occidental-born could manage a purely
Japanese household, or direct Japanese according to
his own light. Things are so opposite, so eccentric,
so provoking at times, — so impossible to understand. A foreign merchant, for example, cannot
possibly manage his own Japanese clerks — he must
trust their direction to a Japanese head clerk. And
this is the way all through the Orient, — even in
Aryan India. Any attempt to control everything
directly is hopelessly mischievous. By learning to

abstain therefrom, I have been able to keep my
servants from the beginning, and have learned to
prize some of them at their weight in gold.

What I was going to say especially is in reference
to pupils and students. In Tōkyō students do
everything everywhere for or against everybody.
They are legion, — they are ubiquitous. The news-
vender, the hotel-clerk, the porter of a mansion,
the man-servant of any large house is sure to be
a student, struggling to live. (I have had one for a
year — a good boy, and inconceivably useful, who
soon enters the army.) A Tōkyō resident is *obliged*
to have students about him. They are better guards
than police, and better servants than any servants.
If you don't have a student or two, you may look out
for robbers, confidence-men, rowdies, trouble of all
kinds at your house. Students *police* Tōkyō.

Well, I found I could not be familiar with my
students. It spoiled matters. I had to be a little
unpleasant. Then reserved. As a consequence all
is admirable. Direct interference won't do. I have
to leave that to the lady of the house; and she can
manage things without ever getting angry. But
another student, whom I am educating, *did* give me
much heart-burning, until I became simply cruel
with him. I should have dropped him; but I was
told: "You don't understand: have patience, and
wait." "But," I said, "his work is trash — worthless." "Never mind," was the answer, "wait and
see!" At the end of the year, I am surprised by
the improvement and the earnestness. "You see,"
I am told, "that boy was a spoiled child while his

family were rich; but his heart is good. He will do well yet." And I find this quite probable. How the Japanese can manage with perfect gentleness and laughter what we cannot manage by force or fraud or money, ought to be a lesson. And I sympathize with this character — only, my own character is much too impatient and cranky to allow of correct imitation.

I am, or have been, the teacher of men who, although insignificant in English, are literary celebrities in their own tongue. Their portraits are known over Japan; their poems and stories celebrated. Naturally they feel proportionately averse to being treated as mere boys. Still, an appeal to their honour, gently made, will sometimes work wonders. I tried it the other day, by advice of the director, when there had been a refusal to obey. He said: "Don't write to them; don't *order* them: just go and talk to them. You know what to say." And they obeyed — *in spite of the fact that the whole room laughed at them for their change of resolve.* There is hope for this class of men: if the university system were better managed, they would be splendidly earnest. . . .

Affectionately,

Lafcadio Hearn.

TO MITCHELL McDONALD

Tōkyō, July, 1898.

Dear McDonald, — We ran over somebody last night — and the train therefore waited in mourning

upon the track during a decorous period. We did
not see Tōkyō till after eleven considerably. But
the waiting was not unpleasant. Frogs sang as if
nothing had happened, and the breeze from the sea
faintly moved through the cars; — and I meditated
about the sorrows and the joys of life by turns, and
smoked, and thanked the gods for many things, —
including the existence of yourself and Dr. Hall.
I was not unfortunate enough to see what had
been killed, — or the consequences to friends and
acquaintances; and feeling there was no more pain
for that person, I smoked in peace — though not
without a prayer to the gods to pardon my want
of seriousness.

Altogether I felt extremely happy, in spite of the
delay. The day had been so glorious, — especially
subsequent to the removal of a small h—l, containing
several myriads of lost souls, from the left side of
my lower jaw.

Reaching home, I used some of that absolutely
wonderful medicine. It was a great and grateful
surprise. (I am not trying to say much about the
kindness of the gift — that would be no use.) After
having used it, for the first time, I made a tactile
investigation without fear, and found —

What do you think?

Guess!

Well, I found that — *the wrong one had been
pulled*, — No. 3 instead of No. 2.

I don't say that No. 3 didn't deserve its fate. But
it had never been openly aggressive. It had struggled
to perform its duties under disadvantageous cir-

cumstances: its character had been modest and shrinking. No. 2 had been, on the contrary, Mt. Vesuvius, the last great Javanese earthquake, the tidal wave of '96, and the seventh chamber of the Inferno, all in mathematical combination. It — Mt. Vesuvius, etc. — is still with me, and although to-day astonished into quiescence, is far from being extinct. The medicine keeps it still for the time. You will see that I have been destined to experience strange adventures.

Hope I may be able to see you again *soon*, — 4th, if possible. Love to you and all kind wishes to everybody.

LAFCADIO.

TO MITCHELL McDONALD

TŌKYŌ, July, 1898.

DEAR McDONALD, — I mailed you this morning the raw proofs, and the *Revue des Deux Mondes*. I fear you will find the former rather faulty in their present unfinished state. But if you mount Fuji you will be a glorious critic.

I don't know how to tell you about the sense of all the pleasant episodes of yesterday, coupled with the feeling that I must have seemed too sombre toward the close, — instead of showing to you and friend Amenomori the happiest face possible. I was unusually naughty — I suppose; but I was worried a little. However, my sky is only clouded for moments — and my friends know that appearances signify nothing serious.

We had adventures at Shimbashi. I saw a well-dressed fellow getting rather close to my wife while she was counting some small change; and I pushed in between her and him — just in time; for she had found his hand on her girdle, trying to get her watch. Then I had a hand poked in my right side-pocket, and another almost simultaneously into my left breast-pocket. The men got nothing from either of us. What interested me was the style of the work. The man I noticed especially was a delicate-looking young fellow, very genteelly dressed, and wearing spectacles. He pretended to be very hot, and was holding his hat in his left hand before him, and working under it with his right. The touching of the pocket with the fingers reminded me of nothing so much as the motion of a cat's paw in playing. You know the cat does not give a single stroke, but a succession of taps, so quickly following each other that you can scarcely see how it is done. The incident was rather curious and amusing than provoking.

I fear poor Amenomori was disappointed — after all his pains about Haneda.

It was just as well that we made the trip yesterday. To-day the weather is mean, — cloudy, hot, and dusty all at the same time. Yesterday we had clear azure and gold, — and lilac-flashing dragonflies, — and a glorious moon coming home.

After seeing your shoulders I have no doubt about your finding Fuji child's-play — even Fuji could not break such a back as that; but I think that you will do well, on the climb, to eat very lightly.

My experience was that the less eating the easier climbing. I took one drink on the stiff part of the climb, — contrary to the advice of the guides, — and I was sorry for it. The necessity is to reduce rather than stimulate the circulation when you get to the rarefied zone. Perhaps you will find another route better than the Gotemba route; but Ameno-mori would be the best adviser there.

Ever affectionately, with countless thanks,

LAFCADIO.

TO MITCHELL McDONALD

TŌKYŌ, August, 1898.

DEAR McDONALD, — I am sending you two of Zola's books, and a rather complex social novel by Maupassant — not, any of them, to be returned. I recommend "Rome" only; the others will just do to lend to friends, or to read for the sake of the French, when you have nothing better on hand.

What a glorious day we did have! Wonder if I shall ever be able to make a thumbnail literary study thereof, — with philosophical reflections. The naval officer, the Buddhist philosopher, and the wandering evolutionist. The impression is alto-gether too sunny and happy and queer to be forever lost to the world. I must think it up some day.

My back feels to-day as if those little sand-crabs were running over it; but the pain is nearly all gone. I shall be ready for another swim in a day or two.

And that supper at the Grand Hotel! I am awfully demoralized to-day — feeling gloriously well, but not in a working mood. A week more of holidays would ruin me! Discomfort is absolutely necessary for literary inspiration. Make a man perfectly happy, and what has he to work for? Nothing shall disturb my "ancient solitary reign" excepting the friends with whom I yesterday imposed upon the patience of certain crabs, — who suddenly found themselves facing a problem for which all their inherited experience had left them supremely unprepared.

Too soon we shall have winter upon us again; and I shall be struggling with problems of university-student peculiarities; — and I shall be working wonderfully hard at a new book. There will be all kinds of dull, dark, tiresome days; but whenever I want I can call back the summer sun, — simply by closing my eyes. Then, in blue light, between sand and sea-line, I shall discern a U. S. naval officer in Cape May costume, and a Buddhist philosopher, busied making little holes in the beach, — sapping and mining the habitations of small horrified crabs. Also I shall see a lemon yellow sky, with an amethystine Fuji cutting sharply against it. And many other things, — little dreams of gold.

Affectionately ever,

LAFCADIO.

TO MITCHELL McDONALD

Tōkyō, September, 1898.

DEAR McDONALD, — I thought the house would go last night; but we had only two trees blown down

this time, and the fence lifted in a southwesterly
direction. Truly I was wise not to go to Shinano
as I intended: it would have been no easy thing to
get back again. And you did well not to try Fuji.
It might have been all right; and it might have
been very dangerous work indeed. When a typhoon
runs around Fuji, Amenomori tells me that it blows
the big rocks away like a powder-explosion. Judging from the extraordinary "protection-walls" built
about the hut at the mountain-top, and from the
way in which the station-house roofs are purposely
weighted down, I fancy this must be quite true.
A lava-block falling from the upper regions goes
down like a bounding shot from a cannon; and I
should just about as soon stand in front of a 50-lb.
steel shell.

The Japanese papers to-day are denouncing some
rice-speculator who has been praying to the gods
for bad weather! The gods do wisely not to answer
anybody's prayers at all. City-dwellers would pray
for fine weather, while farmers pray for rain; —
fellows like me would pray for eternal heat, while
others would pray for eternal coolness; — and what
would the gods do when begged by peace-lovers
to avert war, and by military ambitions to bring
it about? Think of twenty people praying for
a minister's death; and twenty others pleading for
his life. Think of ten different men praying to the
gods for the same girl! Why, really, the gods
would in any event be obliged to tell us to settle
our own little affairs in our own little way, and
be d—d! One ought to write something some day

about a dilemma of the gods; — Ludovic Halévy
did something of the sort; but he did not exhaust
the subject.

Affectionately,

LAFCADIO.

TO MITCHELL McDONALD

Tōkyō, October, 1898.

DEAR McDONALD, — I have your delightful letter
and throw all else overboard for the moment to send
a few lines of greeting and chatter.

I have sent word to Mr. —— that I can receive
no foreign visitors. I run away from the house
on days of danger from calls, — and nevertheless
I cannot entirely escape. Yet you would have me
enter like Daniel into that lions' den of the Grand
Hotel, because you are the Angel of the Lord.
Well, I suppose I must get down soon, — but I cannot say exactly a day. Better let me come after
the fashion of the Judgement, — when no man
knoweth.

I am right glad to hear you are well again. . . .

Don't know what my book will turn out to be
after a few more months of work. It will be a queer
thing anyhow: the Japanese part will be interesting
enough; but the personal-impression parts do not
develop well. And I must work very hard at it.
You think that a day or two in the Grand Hotel is
good for me once in a while; but you can't imagine
what difficulty it is to find any time while the thing
is still in pupa-condition.

But what most injures an author is not means and leisure: it is *society*, conventions, obligations, waste of time in forms and vanities. There are very few men strong enough to stand the life of society, and to write. I can think of but one of importance, — that is Henry James; — but his special study *is* society.

And now for a lecture. (In haste.)

Affectionately,
LAFCADIO.

TO MITCHELL McDONALD

Tōkyō, October, 1898.

DEAR McDONALD, — I find myself not only at the busiest part of the term, the part when professors of the university don't find time to go anywhere, — but also in the most trying portion of the work of getting out a book, — the last portion, the finishing and rounding off.

And I am going to ask you simply *not* to come and see your friend, and *not* to ask him to come to see you, *for at least three months more.* I know this seems horrid — but such are the only conditions upon which literary work is possible, when combined with the duties of a professor of literature. I don't want to see or hear or feel anything outside of my work till the book is done, — and I therefore have the impudent assurance to ask you to help me stand by my wheel. Of course it would be pleasant to do otherwise; but I can't even think of pleasant things and do decent work at the same time. Please think of a helmsman, off shore, and the ship in rough weather, with breakers in sight.

Hate to send you this letter — but I think you will sympathize with me in spite of it.

Affectionately,

LAFCADIO.

TŌKYŌ, October, 1898.

DEAR McDONALD, — I am very glad that I wrote you that selfish letter, — in spite of the protests of my little wife, who says that I am simply a savage. I am glad, because I felt *quite sure* that you would understand, and that the result would be a very sweet note, which I shall always prize. Of course, I mean three months at the outside: I have vowed to finish by the year's end, and I think I can. As for letters, you can't write too many. It takes me five minutes at most to write a letter (that is, to you); but if it took an hour I could always manage that.

"Like the little crab," — yes, indeed. Thursday, three enemies dug at my hole, but I zigzagged away from them. I go in and out by the back way, now, so as to avoid the risk of being seen from afar off.

Ever most affectionately (with renewed thanks for that delicious letter),

LAFCADIO.

TO ELLWOOD HENDRICK

Tōkyō, 1898.

Dear Hendrick, — Verily I think I ought to be apologizing for my blues. But it is such a relief to write them betimes — when you are sure of a patient hearing. Besides, it may interest you to hear of a small professional scribbler's ups and downs. I used only to pray for opportunity: if I could only get an audience! Now I have one — a small one. An offer of $1200 from a syndicate, which would make for me nearly $3000 here; and plenty of others. *And I can't write.* That is, I can do nothing except what would lower the little reputation I have gained. In such a case the duty is plainly not to try, but to wait for the Holy Ghost, — or (as I am out of his domain) the coming of the gods. I am now in a period of mental drought, but have written half of a book that will probably be dedicated to E. H., — or will certainly unless another incomplete book should be ready first, a book to be called perhaps "Thoughts about Feelings."

I am quite uncertain, however, as to the realization of this latter book. Looking back through my life I find that, with the exception of West-Indian and a few New Orleans experiences, I remember nothing agreeable. It was a rule with me from boyhood to try to forget disagreeable things; and in trying to forget them I made no effort to remember the agreeable, — just because "a sorrow's crown of sorrows is remembering happier things." So the past is nearly a blank. Then another queer thing is my absolute ignorance of realities. Always having lived in hopes and imaginations, the smallest practical matters, that everybody should know, I don't know anything about. Nothing, for example, about a boat, a horse, a farm, an orchard, a watch, a garden. Nothing about what a man ought to do under any possible circumstances. I know nothing but sensations and books, — and most of the sensations are not worth penning. I really ought to have become a monk or something of that kind. Still, I believe I have a new key to the explanation of sensations, — if I can find the incident to peg the essays upon, — the dummies for the new philosophical robes. So far the book of reveries consists of only two little chapters. The better part of my life might just as well never have been lived at all. I am only waking up in the hoariness of age, and my next birth will probably see me a mud-turtle or a serpent, or something else essentially torpid and speechless.

Of course, I can write and write and write; but the moment I begin to write for money, vanishes the little special colour, evaporates the small special flavour, which is ME. And I become nobody again; and the public wonders why it ever paid any attention to so commonplace a fool. So I must sit and wait for the gods.

Yet a little while, I shall be all hope and pride and confidence; and again a little while, up to my ears in the Slough of Despond. And the beautifully milled dollars and exquisitely engraved notes you talk of will stay in the pockets of practical people.

LAFCADIO.

Afterthought

DEAR OLD MAN, — Speaking on the subject of
"Life" — have you read "Amiel's Journal" (*Journal
Intime*) ? If not, I would advise you to, as its fine
delicate analysis of things is in pure harmony with
your own way of thinking, so far as generalities go.
In it there is a paragraph about Germans, of precisely
the same tenor as the paragraph in your letter; and
there is an admirable analysis of "society," with
some severe but just (just at the time written)
animadversions upon American society.

It seems to me, however, that neither Amiel nor
anybody else has exactly told us what society means.
Amiel comes very close to it. I think, however, the
real truth would be more brutal. . . . Is not the charm
(and its display) of womanly presence and power
the real force ? Because it is not really intellectual,
this society. Intellectual societies are societies of
artists, men of letters, philosophers, where absolute
freedom of speech and action and dress are allowed.
The polite society only delicately sniffs or nibbles
at intellectual life, or else subordinates it to its
fairy shows and transformation scenes. I don't suppose for a moment that I am suggesting even the
ghost of anything new, — but I wish only to suggest that I think (in view of all this) that nobody
has ever, in English, dared to say what society
really is as a system or display, — to cut boldly
into the heart of things. I don't mean to say it is
shocking, or wrong, or anything of that sort. It
is quite proper in the existing order of things, or

else it wouldn't be. But there are evolutional illustrations in it. . . .

By the way, a Japanese friend tells me I have
only *one soul*, — confirming the Oxford beast's
revelation. "Why?" I asked. "You have no
patience. Those who have no patience have only
one soul. I have four souls." "How many souls can
one have?" I enquired. "Nine," he said. "Men
who can make other men afraid of them, men of
strong will: they have nine souls, or at least a great
many."

Good-bye, — I think you have several souls.

LAFCADIO.

Tōkyō, November, 1898.

DEAR MRS. FENOLLOSA, — I see that my little
word "sympathy" — used, of course, in the fine
French sense of fellow-feeling in matters *not* of the
common — was as true as I could wish it. . . .

I am the one now to give thanks,—and very earnest
thanks; for I confess that I felt a little nervous
about your opinion. Independently of the personal
quality which makes it so precious for me, I believe
that it must represent, in a general way, the opinion
of a number of cultured ladies whom I never have
seen, and never shall see, but who are much more
important as critics than any editors, — for they
make opinion, not in newspapers or magazines,
but in social circles. And I was a little bit afraid of
my new venture in "Retrospectives." I picked out
the little piece sent you, because it had a Japanese

subject as a hanging-peg, — so that I thought you and the professor would feel more inclined to take the trouble of reading it. . . .

Well, you are one of my Rewards in this world: I don't know that I can expect any better return than your letter for a year's work on a book, — and I certainly do not want anything better. In this particular case too, with a new venture, encouragement is positively a benefit as well as a pleasure. In other cases, it might make me too well satisfied with my work, and tempt me to be careless, or at least less careful. . . .

I see Mr. Edwards has gone; and I am sorry to think that I may never see him again, — for he is in every way a man and a gentleman. Probably we shall have a book from him some day; and it will not be a common book, for that man is incapable of the *common:* he will think hard, work solidly, and put his own square-set Oxford self into every thought. It will certainly be interesting.

My best thanks for that volume of Watson. . . . I have a very strong liking for Watson; and there are bits in that book of delightful worth. I shall venture to impose on your good nature by keeping it just a "weeny" bit longer, — to copy a verse or two.

I sprained my foot nearly two weeks ago, and after a week in bed and bandages, managed to hobble around the university again, but I am now all over the main trouble. Tōkyō roads are dangerous after dark sometimes. The enforced homeing, however, did me good; for my next book is almost ready for the publisher.

And now that you understand my wishes to try to do something new — at least understand them well enough to write me so very pleasant a letter, — I am sure you won't think me too selfish for being so rare a visitor. I am like a setting hen, — afraid to leave my eggs till the hatching is done and the shells are broken. With all best wishes and thanks,

Very truly yours,

LAFCADIO HEARN.

TO MITCHELL McDONALD

TŌKYŌ, November, 1898.

DEAR McDONALD, — I have your precious letter. It came all right. I am very glad that I was mistaken about the registry-business being neglected — but I thought it my duty to make the remark. As one of my students says: "A friend is a man to whom you can tell all your *suspicions.*"

Now I am going to tell you something much more than "suspicions." I think it time; — and I want you to listen, and to think over it.

You do not understand my situation.

One reason that you do not understand is because you are a bachelor. Another reason is because you are a naval officer *and* a bachelor, — consequently to a considerable degree independent of social conventions of the smaller and meaner kind.

I am in a somewhat critical position and time. Don't make any mistake about it. Small as I am, I have mountains to lift; and if you do not realize it, you cannot help it, but can only get your fingers crushed. Only your fingers — mind! but that will hurt more than you think.

Here is my fix: I have "down upon me"—

I. Society. Civilized society conspires to starve certain men to death. It must do so in self-defence. There *are* privileged men; I may become one yet.

II. I have down on me the Church. By Church, you must not think of the Roman, Greek, Episcopalian, etc., persuasions, — but all Christendom supporting missionary societies, and opposing free-thinking in every shape. Do not be deceived by a few kindly notes about my work from religious sources. They are genuine, — but they signify absolutely nothing against the great dead weight of more orthodox opinion. As Professor Huxley says, no man can tell the force of a belief until he has had the experience of fighting it. Good! Church and Society together are pretty vigorous, you will acknowledge.

III. The English and American Press in combination, — the press that represents critical opinion in London as well as in New York. Don't mistake the meaning of notices. All, or nearly all, are managed by the publishers. The policy is to praise the work — because that brings advertisements. Society, Church, Press—that means a big combination, rather. On my side I have a brave American naval officer — and the present good will of the Japanese Government, which has been vaguely aware that my books have been doing some good.

Now you may say, "How important the little mite thinks himself, — the cynosure of the world!"

But that would be hasty thinking. I am pretty much in the position of a book-keeper known to have once embezzled, or of a man who has been in prison, or of a prostitute who has been on the street. These are, none of them, you will confess, *important* persons. But what keeps them in their holes? Society, Church, and public opinion—the Press. No man is too small to get the whole world's attention *if* he does certain things. Talent signifies nothing. Talent starves in the streets, and dies in the ginhouse. Talent helps no one not in some way independent of society. *Temporarily*, I *am* thus independent.

At this moment the pressure is very heavy — perhaps never will be much heavier. Why? Because I have excited some attention, — because there is a danger that I might succeed. You must not think I mean that everybody in general, or anybody in special, *thinks out these thoughts*. Not at all. Society, Church, and Press work blindly, instinctively, — like machinery set in motion to keep a level smooth. The machinery feels the least projection, and tries to flatten it out of existence, — without even considering what it may be. Diamond or dung makes no difference.

But if the obstruction prove *too* hard, it is lifted out of the way of the machinery. That is where my one chance lies — in making something solid that forces this kind of attention.

You might ask me, if I think thus, why dedicate a book to our friend the doctor? That is a different matter. My literary work *cannot* be snubbed; and it goes into drawing-rooms where the author would

be snubbed.   Besides, a doctor can accept what
other people can't.

You see that there are many who come to Japan
that want to see me; and you think this is a proof
of kindly interest.   Not a bit of it.   It is precisely
the same kind of curiosity that impels men to look
at strange animals, — a six-legged calf, for instance.
The interest in the book is in some cases genuine;
the interest in the personality is of the New York
Police Gazette quality.   Don't think I am exaggerating.   When I get my fingers caught in the cogs,
I can feel it.

So much for the ugly side of the question.   Let
us take the cheerful one.

Every man who has new ideas to express, at
variance with the habits of his time, *has to meet the
same sort of opposition.*   It is valuable to him.   It
is valuable *to the world at large.*   Weakness can't
work or burst through it.   Only strength can succeed.   The man who does get through has a right to
be proud, and to say: "I am strong."   With health
and time, I shall get through, — but I do feel afraid
sometimes of physical disaster.   Of course I have
black moments; but they are also foolish moments
— due to disordered nerves.   I must just hammer
on steadily and let money quarrels go to the deuce,
and sacrifice everything to success.   When you are
in the United States you may be able to help me
with the business part of the thing — providing
that you understand exactly the circumstances,
and don't imagine me to be a possible Kipling or
Stevenson.   Not only am I a mere mite in litera-

ture, but a mite that has to be put forward very, very cautiously indeed. "Overestimate" me! well, I should rather say you did.

And now we'll leave theory for practice. I don't think you can do anything now — anything at all. You *might* — but the chances are not worth taking. You will be surprised to hear, I fancy, that the author must see his proofs — not for the purpose of assuring himself that the text is according to the copy, but for the purpose of making it *different* from the MS. Very few writers can perfect their work in MS.; they cannot see the *colour* and line of it, till it gets into type. When a statue is cast, it is cast exactly according to the mould, and shows the lines of the mould, which have to be removed: then the polishing is done, and the last touches are given. Very slight work — but everything depends upon it. So with artistic writing. It is by changes in the printed form that the final effect is obtained. Exactness according to the MS. means nothing at all; that is only the casting, — a matter of course; and another man can no more look after your proofs than he can put on your hat. Did you ever try the experiment of letting a friend try to fit your hat comfortably on your own head? It can't be done.

Health is good; sprain about well; book nearly through — sixteen chapters written. Only, the flavour is not yet quite right.

Finally, dear friend, don't think, because I write this letter, that I am very blue, or despondent, or anything of that sort. I am feeling to-day unusually well, — and remember something said to me ten

years ago by a lady who at once detested me after
our introduction. She said: "A man with a nose
like you should not worry about the future — he
will *bore* his way through the world." I trust in
my nose. With true love to you,   LAFCADIO.

TōKYō, December, 1898.

DEAR McDONALD, — I am very, very sorry that
you had that accident, — and I fear that you are
worse off than you let me know. I must get down
to-morrow (Saturday), and see how you are —
though I fear I can do no more than chatter to you
like an *usots'ki*. Well, we've both had accidents lately
— my foot is n't quite well yet. We must have extra
good luck to make up for these mishaps.

Yes, I should be glad to know your friend Bedloe,
— or any of your naval friends: they are *men* as well
as gentlemen, and I feel quite at home with them.

Ah! I had almost forgotten. I *have* Kipling's
"Day's Work" already. It is great — very great.
Don't mistake him, even if he seems too colloquial
at times. He is the greatest living English poet and
English story-teller. Never in this world will I be
able to write one page to compare with a page of
his. He makes me feel so small, that after reading
him I wonder why I am such an ass as to write at
all. Love to you, all the same, for thinking of me
in that connection.

Term's over — all but a beastly "dinner." D—n
dinners! I'll *see* you presently.   LAFCADIO.

TO MITCHELL McDONALD

TŌKYŌ, December, 1898.

DEAR McDONALD, — Do you know we talked uninterruptedly the other day for ten hours, — for the period that people are wont to qualify when speaking of the enormity of time as "ten *mortal* hours"? What a pity that they could not be made *im*mortal! They will be always with me, — though I really fear that I must have tired you, in spite of protests. Every time I can get such a chat with you, you become much dearer to me — so that I really cannot feel as sorry as I ought for keeping you engaged that long.

Well, I don't quite know what I shall do about the " Ghostly Japan." I shall think a little longer. My duty, I feel, is to sacrifice it: only I don't want to have any tricks played upon me, — just because tricks annoy. Nevertheless I ought to accept the annoyance cheerfully: it is part of the price one must pay for success. Huxley says that one of the things most important for anybody to learn is that a heavy price must be paid for success.

I got a letter from a Yale lad, which I enclose, and a magazine which I am sending you. The wish is for an autograph; but there the case is meritorious and I want the sympathy of boys like that — who must be the writers and thinkers of 1900. So I wrote him as kind a letter as I could, — assuring him, however, that I am not a Buddhist, but still a follower of Herbert Spencer. It is a nice little magazine. I suppose that H. M. & Co.'s advertisement had something to do with the matter; but from the business point of view, it is an excellent idea to try to work a book through the universities. Those lads are thinkers in their own way. See the poem on page 90,—also on page 83: both show thinking. I ventured to advise the writer of "Body and Soul" to make a new construction of the thought. The conditions might be reversed. First the man is the body; the woman the soul. But the woman's soul is withered up by the act of the man; and the body only remains. Then the man gets sorry, and gets a soul through the sorrow of the wrong that he has done. Then *she* becomes the Flesh, and *he* the Ghost. I did not explain all this — only suggested it. A case of vicarious sacrifice. How many women have to lose their own souls in order to give souls to somebody else!

Wish I was with you to-day, and to-morrow, and many days in succession. But if we have plum pudding every day — ! I mean not *you* by the plum pudding, but the circumstantial combination. I wanted to say that pleasure spoils the soul for working purposes, — but I am afraid to attempt to carry the simile further, lest you should turn it round, and hit me with it. I shall see you erelong, anyhow.

Affectionately,
LAFCADIO.

A memory of long ago... I am walking upon a granite pavement that rings like iron, between buildings of granite bathed in the light of a cloudless noon. Shadows are short and sharp: there is no stir in the hot bright air; and the sound of my footsteps, strangely loud, is the only sound in the street... Suddenly an odd feeling comes to me, with a sort of lingering shock, — a feeling, or suspicion, of universal illusion. The pavement, the bulks of hewn stone, the iron rails, and all things visible, are dreams! Light, colour, form, weight, solidity — all sensed existences — are but phantoms of being, manifestation only of one infinite ghostliness for which the language of man has not any word....

MR. HEARN'S LATER HANDWRITING

TO MITCHELL McDONALD

Tōkyō, December, 1898.

DEAR FRIEND, — "I 've gone and been and *done* it." This wise: — You see I kept thinking about things — discounts and money-profits and bargains, and publishers playing into each other's hands, — and the possible worthlessness of the work, — and the necessity of improving it much more before insisting upon high prices, — and the wisdom of recopying half of it, — and the risks of shipment and shipwreck and fire and dishonest post-office clerks — till I got nearly crazy! If I listened much more to the echoes of your suggestions and advice, I should have gone *absolutely* crazy. Therefore in fifteen minutes I had the whole thing perfectly packed and labelled and addressed in various languages, and shot eastward by doubly-registered letter—dedicated to Mrs. Behrens, but entrusted largely to the gods. And to save myself further trouble of mind, I told the publishers just to do whatever they pleased about terms — and not to worry me concerning them. And I feel like a man liberated from prison, — smelling the perfumed air of a perfect spring day. "Ghostly Japan" will concern me no more — unless the ship is wrecked, or the manuscript lost in some way: which must not be thought about. The book is gone, and the illustrations go by next mail. Pray to the gods for the book — that 's all that we can do now.

I hope the foot is not any worse. You are an impatient boy, too, you know — when it comes to sitting still, instead of rushing things. Please take all good care of yourself till I run down, which will be very soon.

Affectionately,

LAFCADIO.

TO ERNEST FENOLLOSA

TŌKYŌ, December, 1898.

MY DEAR PROFESSOR, — I have been meditating, and after the meditation I came to the conclusion not to visit your charming new home again — not at least before the year 1900. I suppose that I am a beast and an ape; but I nevertheless hope to make you understand.

The situation makes me think of Béranger's burthen, — *Vive nos amis les ennemis!* My friends are much more dangerous than my enemies. These latter — with infinite subtlety — spin webs to keep me out of places where I hate to go, — and tell stories of me to people whom it would be vanity and vexation to meet; — and they help me so much by their unconscious aid that I almost love them. They help me to maintain the isolation indispensable to quiet regularity of work, and the solitude which is absolutely essential to thinking upon such subjects as I am now engaged on. Blessed be my enemies, and forever honoured all them that hate me!

But my friends! — ah! my friends! They speak so beautifully of my work; they *believe* in it; they say they want more of it, — and yet they would destroy it! They do not know what it costs, — and

they would break the wings and scatter the feather-
dust, even as the child that only wanted to caress the
butterfly. And they speak of communion and converse and sympathy and friendship, — all of which
are indeed precious things to others, but mortally
deadly to me, — representing the breaking-up of
habits of industry, and the sin of disobedience to
the Holy Ghost, — against whom sin shall not be
forgiven, — either in this life, or in the life to come.

And they say, — Only a day, — just an afternoon
or an evening. But *each* of them says this thing.
And the sum of the days in these holidays — the
days inevitable — are somewhat more than a week
in addition. A week of work dropped forever into
the Abyss of what might-have-been! Therefore
I wish rather that I were lost upon the mountains,
or cast away upon a rock, than in this alarming city
of Tōkyō, — where a visit, and the forced labour of
the university, are made by distance even as one
and the same thing.

Now if I were to go down to your delightful little
house, with my boy, — and see him kindly treated,—
and chat with you about eternal things, — and yield
to the charm of old days (when I must confess that
you fascinated me not a little),—there is no saying
what the consequences to me might eventually
become. Alas! I can afford friends only on
paper, — I can occasionally write, — I can get
letters that give me joy; but visiting is out of the
possible. I must not even *think* about other
people's kind words and kind faces, but work, —
work, — work, — while the Scythe is sharpening

within vision. Blessed again, I say, are those that don't like me, for they do not fill my memory with thoughts and wishes contrary to the purpose of the Æons and the Eternities!

When a day passes in which I have not written — much is my torment. Enjoyment is not for me, — excepting in the completion of work. But I have not been the loser by my visits to you both — did I not get that wonderful story? And so I have given you more time than any other person or persons in Tōkyō. But now — through the seasons — I must again disappear. Perhaps *le jeu ne vaudra pas la chandelle;* nevertheless I have some faith as to ultimate results.

Faithfully, with every most grateful and kindly sentiment,

LAFCADIO HEARN.

TO MASANOBU ŌTANI

Tōkyō, December, 1898.

DEAR ŌTANI, — To-day I received the gift sent from Matsue, — and the very nice letter with which you accompanied it. I think that a better present, or one which could give me sincerer pleasure will never be received. It is a most curious thing, that strange texture, — and a most romantic thing also in its way, — seeing that the black speckling that runs through the whole woof is made by characters of letters or poems or other texts, written long ago. And I must assure you that I shall always prize it — not only because I like it, but particularly because your mother wove it. I am going to have it made into a winter *kimono* for my own use, which I shall always wear, according to season, in my study-room. Surely it is just the kind of texture which a man of letters ought to wear! My best thanks to you and your family, — most of all to your kind mother, — and my earnest wishes for a fortunate year to come.

Your collection of poems this month interested me a great deal in a new way — the songs separately make only a small appeal to imagination; but the tone and feeling *of the mass* are most remarkable, and give me a number of new ideas about the *character of the "folk-work."* . . .

With renewed best wishes for a happy and fortunate New Year to you and yours,

Sincerely,

Y. KOIZUMI.

TO ———

DEAR FRIEND, — I am afraid this letter which I am now writing will not please you altogether. Forgive anything in it which you do not like — for the sake of the friendship behind it.

The matter is difficult; and I cannot at this moment report any progress. I understand something of the matter. It is not any use to try to do anything further until I explain things as well as I can, and have heard your answer. Before I can do anything more, I want you to make some promises to *me*, your friend. After that you can make them to her, if you love her well enough.

To begin with, in regard to explanation, I think you are wrong, and that your wife and her father are quite right. Under the same circumstances, if I were her father, I should take her away from her husband if I could.

You are not wrong by *heart* — you are wrong only because you do not understand, do not know the conditions. Women of different classes cannot be all treated alike. Your wife is a refined, gentle lady — very sensitive and very easily hurt by harsh words or neglect. You cannot expect to treat such a lady like a farm-servant or a peasant-woman. It would kill her. But I have heard (*not* from your wife, but from other persons) that she was allowed by you to work in the garden, under a hot sun, thirty days after childbirth and the loss of her child. This seems to me a *terrible* thing, and you cannot have known what it means to a woman's constitution.

A refined lady will not submit to be treated like a servant — unless she has no spirit at all. Your wife's action shows that she has self-respect and spirit; and you want the mother of your children to be a woman of spirit and self-respect. Do not be angry with her because she shows this honourable pride. It is good.

I do not think that you can expect your wife to act as a daughter to your parents, or to live with them as a daughter exactly in the old way. Meiji has changed many things. Girls who have passed through the new schools are no longer hardy and strong like the Samurai women of old days. Observe how many of them die after a year of marriage.

Then your parents and your wife belong to different eras, — different conditions, — different worlds. If they should expect your wife to be all to them that a daughter-in-law might have been in the old days, I fear that would be impossible. She has not the strength for that; and her whole nature is differently constituted.

I think you could only be happy by living alone with each other in your own house. Perhaps this seems wrong to you, — but that is Meiji. The fault is in the times, not in hearts.

If you marry another educated lady of the new school, you will have exactly the same trouble. The old conditions cannot be maintained under the new system of change.

But the chief trouble, of course, would be your attitude to your wife. You have not, I think, been considerate to her — regarded her too much as one bound to serve and obey. It will not do in *her* case. She has spirit, and she wants different treatment. It is better for a strong man to treat a wife exactly as he would treat a child that he loves. By her weakness and delicacy every educated woman is a child, and must be petted and loved like a child. If she be harshly treated, and have no pleasure — even if she be treated as well as you would treat a *man-friend* — then the result is unfortunate always, and the children born will show the mother's pain.

Your wife is evidently afraid of the future — thinks it impossible that she can get from you the treatment or the consideration she ought to have, and must have in order to be happy. She will not say anything definite; but I am sure of this. She will not tell you her troubles — you should know them without being told. Not to know them *shows* the want of consideration.

The higher you go in society and in educated circles, the more the woman differs from the man. She cannot be judged or understood as a man. She becomes a distinct being with a distinct character, and very, very delicate feelings.

Well, this is enough to give you an idea of how I see the matter. *Can you honestly promise to treat your wife in a completely new way, — with such delicacy as you never did before, and always?* If you can, I *think* we can manage to do something. There is also something important to consider in regard to family matters. Can you not make this matter smooth also? Please answer before three o'clock. Do not come to the house until late this evening, or to-morrow. In haste,

Affectionately, your friend,

Y. KOIZUMI.

TO ———

DEAR FRIEND, — After you bid us good-bye, I began to think about things, and resolved to write you a little letter about my conclusions. Of course, because I am a foreigner, I cannot pretend to make absolutely correct conclusions; but I should like to be of use to you as a friend, and therefore believe that I cannot do any harm by presenting both sides of the question, as they appear to me.

It seems that there is one view of the matter which might not have been fully thought over yet. The woman's side, I mean. It is true she has not' stated it; but I imagine it might be this: —

A woman of cultivation, although seeming very strong, may be very sensitive and delicate — and may suffer more than a strong man can imagine possible, by reason of very little matters. When about to become a mother, her capacity for suffering greatly increases, and after childbirth it remains intense. These are natural conditions; but after the loss of a child, the condition is a very serious one, especially for a lady who has been well educated. I know this chiefly by some knowledge of medical physiology. — Now, what I mean is this: Anything that a wife does during or after pregnancy should, I believe, be not only forgiven, but *lovingly* forgiven, — because *then*, what she suffers no man can really understand. And the more educated she is, the more refined she is, the more she suffers.

Suppose now we look at her view, — or at what might be her view. She has a very affectionate and true husband; but he is very strong, has never been nervous or nervously sick, cannot understand what she suffers. She is ashamed to confess her weakness and her pain. So she does not tell him. She smiles and tries to make it appear that she is strong. The loss of her child is a very great pain to her — more than any man could understand; but she tries to forget it. Still, her husband does not know all this. She is not able to be quick and active and ready, and he does not understand why. Even a woman's

memory weakens during this painful period. Her
mind is not so strong, and can only become as before
after the weaning of her child, or many months after
childbirth. To the strong peasant-woman this is a
small trial; but to the educated lady it is a question
of life and death, and not a few even lose their
reason after losing a child — become insane. The
physiologist knows this; but many do not. And the
wife, in such a case, may seem not to be kind to
the parents — simply because she *cannot* be. She
has the will, — not the physical power. She is in
the position of one who needs a servant — needs all
the help and comfort she can get — all the love she
can obtain. She cannot give help and do service;
because neither body nor mind is strong enough.
And neither is strong enough — *because* she has
been strained to her uttermost by her years of
education. It is the same way the world over.
The lady cannot do or suffer as much as the woman
who has not passed her youth at schools. Mind
and body have been transformed by education.

Now, dear friend, I imagine that this must be
the state of affairs. Your wife and her parents do
not wish to do wrong, in my opinion. She feels
that she is not strong enough to remain your wife
under the same conditions. She cannot bear hardship, or do many things which seem to a man mere
trifles, while in a delicate condition. And she fears
that she would be unhappy and sick and lose
another child. But she will never *tell* you. A woman
will not tell those things. Unless a husband can
understand *without being told,* — the two cannot

live together long. The result must be, for the wife, death!

I think, dear friend, that this is the truth of the matter. Now you can separate good friends, or else — what could you do?

If I were in your place, perhaps I should try to prevent the separation. I should let the wife have her own gentle way. I should try to make her comfortable, and not ask her to help me or my parents in any way, — but only to bear my children and to love me, and to make home happy. But *unless* she has a good heart, I should be wrong.

There is no question, I think, about the good heart. Your wife has that, surely. It seems to me only a case of misunderstanding. Remember, dear friend, that you are a very strong man, and that you can afford to be very considerate to a weak woman, after the torture of childbirth and the loss of the love — the child-love — for which Nature has been changing the whole body. Remember also, that even your parents — not knowing the strain of this new education on the physical system of the girl — might judge her a little severely. Certainly she must love you, and wish that she could be to you all you wish.

Forgive this long letter. What I want to say is this: If it be not too late, let us try whether a reconciliation is not possible. If you can make allowances, and change conditions a little, all would be well, perhaps. If *not*, — if you want a stronger woman for a wife, — perhaps it is better to separate. But it would be a great pity to separate simply

because of a misunderstanding. So let us try to
make things as they were before.

Affectionately your friend,

Y. KOIZUMI.

TO MITCHELL McDONALD

TŌKYŌ, January, 1899.

DEAR McDONALD, — I got home safe and early,
— thanks to your carriage! But I feel a little uneasy
about you; and when you get perfectly right again
in that strong back of yours, I want to hear from
you — *not* before. Don't imagine that I must have
an answer to every scrawl. I don't know what to
say to you and the doctor, — except that you are
both spoiling me. Tōkyō seems unusually tristful
this rainy evening; and I feel that it is because you
and the doctor are both far away, — and that the
world is not really anything like what you make it
appear to be.

I came up with three Americans, all of whom
talked about Manila, Aguinaldo, "the people at
home," Boston, the Pennsylvania Central, Baldwin's
locomotives, the Pacific Coast, — and the com-
manders of the various iron-clads at Manila. It
did me good to hear them. They cocked up their
heels on the seats, home-fashion; and I felt sort of
pulled towards them,—but we didn't get acquainted.
They knew everything about everything in the whole
world; and it did one good to hear them. Wish we
had a few men of that sort in the university.

It will feel lonesome in Japan after you go back:

I think I should like to be one of those small eaglets that you used to supply with fish on the voyage, — and have a hen wander occasionally within reach of my rope.

Only a line before going to sleep. A stupid note — just to show that I am thinking of you. My wife is delighted with the photo, and says it is the best of all by far — in which I agree with her.

Love to you, and *do* take every care of your dear self.

LAFCADIO.

TO MITCHELL McDONALD

Tōkyō, January, 1899.

DEAR McDONALD, — I suppose you have heard of a famous old drama which has for its title, "The Woman Killed with Kindness." Presently, if you do not take care, you will be furnishing the material for a much more modern tragedy, to be called, "The Small Man Killed with Kindness." Here I have been waiting three days to write you, — and have not been able to write, because of the extravagant and very naughty things which you have done. That whiskey! Those cigars! That wonderful beefsteak! Those imperial and sinfully splendid dinners! Those wonderful chats until ghost-time, and beyond it! And all these things — however pleasing in themselves — made like a happy dream by multitudes of little acts and words and thoughts (all observed and treasured up) that created about me an atmosphere not belonging at all to this world

of Iron Facts and Granite Necessities. "Come
soon again" — indeed! Catch me down there
again this winter! Steep a man's soul in azure and
gold like that again, and you will utterly spoil him
for those cold grey atmospheres under which alone
good work can be done. It is all tropical down there
at No. 20 Bund; and I must try to forget the tropics
in order to finish No. 8. The last time I had such
an evening was in 1889, — in a flat of Fifth Avenue,
New York, where a certain divine person and I
sat by a fire of drift-wood, and talked and dreamed
about things. There was this difference, however,
that I never could remember what passed as we
chatted before that extraordinary fire (which burned
blue and red and green — because of sea-ghosts
in it). *That* was largely witchcraft, but at No.
20 Bund, without witchcraft, there is more power
than that. And if I am afraid of it, it is not because
I do not like it even more than the magic of Fifth
Avenue, but because — No. 8 must be done quickly!

You must really promise to be less good to me
if you want to see me again before the Twentieth
Century. I wish I knew how to scold you properly;
— but for the moment I shall drop the subject in
utter despair!

I hope what you say about my being still a boy
may have a grain of truth in it, — so that I can get
mature enough to make you a little bit proud of
encouraging me in this out-of-the-way corner of
the world. But do *you* please take good care of
that health of yours, if you want to see results: I
am just a trifle uneasy about you, and you strong

men have to be more careful than midges and gnats like myself. Please think twice over these little remarks.

I have no news at all for you; — there is no mail, of course, and nothing interesting in this muddy place. I can only "report progress." I have a very curious collection of Japanese songs and ballads, with refrains, unlike any ever published in English; and I expect to make a remarkable paper out of them.

By the way, I must tell you that such enquiries as I tried to make for you on the subject of waterfalls only confirm what I told you. The mere idea of such a thing is horribly shocking to the *true* Japanese nature: it offends both their national and their religious sense. The Japanese love of natural beauty is not artificial, as it is to a large degree with us, but a part of the race-soul; and tens of thousands of people travel every year hundreds of miles merely to enjoy the sight and sound of a little waterfall, and to please their imagination with the old legends and poems concerning it. (The Japanese heart never could understand American willingness to use Niagara for hydraulic or electric machinery — never! And I must confess that I sympathize altogether with them.) But that is not all: the idea of a *foreigner* using a waterfall for such a purpose would seem to millions of very good, lovable people like a national outrage. The bare suggestion would excite *horror*. Of course there are men like ⸺ who have suppressed in themselves all these feelings, — but they represent an almost imperceptible minority. They regard the ruin of Fairy-land as certain; — but the mass are still happy in their dreams of the old beauty and the old gods.

LAFCADIO.

TO MITCHELL McDONALD

Tōkyō, January, 1899.

DEAR McDONALD, — Our scare is pretty nearly over; — the fever was broken to-day, and we had a consultation of doctors. It seems to have been pneumonia of the nasty, sudden kind. The little fellow never lost his senses; but for part of yesterday he lost all power to speak. I think he will get strong from now. The other boy got laid up about the same time, but much less severely. The night they caught cold, the thermometer went down to 26°, and the change was too much for them. By constant care for a few days, I think we shall have them all right again: then I shall hope, either to coax you up here, or go down to see you — if only to shake hands. So far I am lucky; for I have been working like a Turk, and keeping well. Work is an excellent thing to keep a fellow from worrying, and my "self-confidence" is growing in the proper cautious way again.

What a funny, funny episode is that story of Lieutenant Hobson, shipped to Manila to keep him from being kissed to death by pretty girls! Wonder if he would not prefer to face the Santiago forts again? The incident is quite peculiarly American, and pretty in its way: it ought to make heroes

multiply. There is something to be a hero for, —
to have one's pick of the finest girls in the country.
Still I have been thinking that most of us would
feel shy about marrying the woman who would
stand up and ask for a kiss in a theatre. It is the
same sort of enthusiasm that makes women tear
out their earrings, and throw them on the stage
when a Liszt or a Gottschalk is improvising. I see
no reason why heroism should arouse less enthusiasm
and affection than musical skill; but don't you think
that in either case we should prefer the silent admiration of the giver that does n't lose her head, but
remains strongly self-controlled — "all in an *iron
glow*," as Ruskin calls it? When the brave lieutenant wants a wife, I fancy he will be looking for
that kind of woman, rather than the other.

There is no news for me by mail, — but we shall
have another mail next week, I suppose. The university course runs smoothly: this is my third year;
and my subject happens to be the 19th century,
in which I feel more at home than in the other
branches of the subject. Fancy! I am lecturing
now on Swinburne's poetry. They would not
allow me to do this in a Western university perhaps
— yet Swinburne, as to form, is the greatest 19th
century poet of England. But he has offended
the conventions; and they try to d—n him with
silence. I believe you can trust me to do him justice
here, when I get the chance.

Affectionately,

LAFCADIO.

TO MITCHELL McDONALD.

TŌKYŌ, January, 1899.

DEAR McDONALD, — Everything is bright and sunny with us again: we have to keep the boys in a warm room, and nurse them carefully, but they are safe now. I shall never forget your kindest sympathy, and the doctor's generous message. Am I bad for not writing sooner? To tell the truth I was a little tired out myself, and got a touch of cold; but I'm solid and shipshape again, and full of hope to see you. I shall have no more duties until Tuesday morning (31st); so, if you will persist in risking a bad lunch and an uncomfortable room, and the trouble of travelling to Tōkyō, I shall be waiting for you. I think you ought to come up *once* more, anyhow. I want you to see yourself *viv-à-vis* with Elizabeth. I want to chat about things. (No mail yet at this writing.) If you cannot conveniently come this week, come just when you please any *afternoon* between Fridays (inclusive) and Mondays.

Odin said, in the Hávamál, — "*I counsel thee, if thou hast a trusty friend, go and see him often; because a road which is seldom trod gets choked with brambles and high grass.*"

This is a case of "don't-do-as-I-do, — but-do-as-I-tell-you" — is n't it? Besides, I am not worth a d—n as a friend, anyhow. I quote these most ancient verses only because you expressed an interest in them during our last delightful chat; — but whether you come or no, brambles will *never* grow upon the pathway. LAFCADIO.

TO MITCHELL McDONALD

Tōkyō, February, 1899.

DEAR McDONALD, — I have just got your dear letter: don't think me neglectful for not writing to you sooner; — this is the heavy part of the term; and the weather has been trying me.

Well, I am glad to hear that you have read a book called "Exotics and Retrospectives." I have not seen it. Where did it come from? How did you get it? When was it sent? Did the doctor get his copy? (Don't answer these questions by letter in a hurry: I am not asking very seriously, — as I suppose I shall get my copies by the *Doric*.)

I have been doing nothing to speak of lately: too tired after a day's work, — and the literary jobs on hand are mechanical mostly, — uninteresting, — mere ruts of duty. I hate everything mechanical; but romances do not turn up every day.

Thanks for your interest in my lecture-work; but you would be wrong in thinking the lectures worth printing. They are only dictated lectures — dictated out of my head, not from notes even: so the form of them cannot be good. Were I to re-write each of them ten or fifteen times, I might print them. But that would not be worth while. I am not a scholar, nor a competent critic of the best; there are scores of men able to do the same thing incomparably better. The lectures are good for the Tōkyō University, however, — because they have been adapted, by long experience, to the Japanese student's way of thinking and feeling, and are put in the simplest possible language. But when a professor in Japan prints his lectures, the authorities think they have got all that he knows in hand, and are likely to look about for a new man. It is bad policy to print anything of the kind here, and elsewhere the result would be insignificant. I had better reserve my force for work that other people *cannot* do better, — or at least won't do.

Affectionately,

LAFCADIO.

TO MITCHELL McDONALD

February, 1899.

DEAR McDONALD, — You should never take the pains to answer the details of my letters: it is very sweet of you to do it, — but it means the trouble of writing, as it were, with a sense of affectionate obligation, and it also means the trouble of re-reading, line by line, letters which are not worth reading more than once — if even once. Please forget my letters always, and write whatever you like, and don't think that I expect you to take me very seriously. Why, I cannot even take myself always very seriously! — By the way, that was a very pretty simile of yours about the nebula condensing into a sun. But the nucleus, to tell the truth, has not yet begun to integrate: there is a hardening here and there upon the outermost edges only, — which is possibly contrary to the law that makes great suns.

It is pleasant to know that the sickness was not very severe. Still, I am inclined to suspect that you

underrate it. Naval men always call a typhoon
"a gale," or "a smart breeze" — don't they?

I did receive a book and various letters, and I
have had by this mail four requests for autographs —
two from England. The book I would send you if
it were worth it, but it is a very stupid attempt at
an anti-Christian-Spiritist-Theosophico-Buddhist
novel, written anonymously. I don't like this kind
of thing, unless it be extremely well done, and does
not meddle with "astral bodies," "luminiferous
ether," and "sendings." There has been so much
disgusting nonsense written about Buddhism by
Theosophists and Spiritists that ridicule is unjustly
sprinkled upon the efforts of impartial men to explain
the real beauties and truths of Eastern religion.

Affectionately,

LAFCADIO.

TO MITCHELL McDONALD

Tōkyō, February, 1899.

DEAR McDONALD, — Now don't give yourself
all that trouble about coming up to Tōkyō. It
would have been an ugly trip for you last Saturday
or Sunday, anyhow: wait till the fine days, and till
you don't know what else to do. I think I shall
see you before you go to the U. S. anyhow, in Tōkyō;
but I don't think you will be able to manage the
trip very often. If I telegraph, "Dying — quick
— murder:" then I know that you will even quit
your dinner and come; — isn't that pleasant to be
sure of?

I was thinking the other day to ask you if you
ever knew my dead friend, — W. D. O'Connor
(U. S. Signal Service), Washington. He was very
fond of me in his way — got me my first introduction to the Harpers. I believe that he died of
overwork. I have his portrait. He was Whitman's
great friend. Thinking about him and you together, I was wondering how much nationality has
to do with these friendships. Is it only Irish or
Latin people who make friends for friendship's sake?
Or is it that I am getting old — and that, as Balzac
says, men do not make friends after forty-eight?
Coming to think of old times, I believe a man is
better off in a very humble position, with a very
small salary. He has everything then more or less
trustworthy and real in his surroundings. Give
him a thousand dollars a month, and he must live
in a theatre, and never presume to take off his mask.

No, dear friend, I don't want *your* book. I should
not feel comfortable with it in hand: I cannot comfortably read a book belonging to another person,
because I feel all the time afraid of spoiling it. I
feel restrained, and therefore uncomfortable. Besides, *your* book is where it ought to be doing the
most good. Nay! I shall wait even until the crack
of doom, rather than take your book.

There is to be a mail sometime next week, I suppose. Ought to come to-day — but the *City of
Rio de Janeiro* is not likely to fly in a blizzard,
except downward. If she has my book on board
she will certainly sink.

By the way, you did not know that I am fatal to

ships. Every ship on which I journey gets into trouble. Went to America in a steamer that foundered. Came to Japan upon another that went to destruction. Travelled upon a half-dozen Japanese steamers, — every one of which was subsequently lost. Even lake-boats do not escape me. The last on which I journeyed turned over, and drowned everybody on board, — only twenty feet from shore. It was I who ran the *Belgic* on land. The only ship that I could not wreck was the *Saikyō-Maru*, but she went to the Yalu on the next trip after I had been aboard of her, — and got tolerably well smashed up; so I had satisfaction out of her anyhow. If ever I voyage on the Empress boats, there will be a catastrophe. Therefore I fear exceedingly for the *Rio de Janeiro;* she is not strong enough to bear the presence of that book in a typhoon. Affectionately,

LAFCADIO.

TO MITCHELL McDONALD

TŌKYŌ, March, 1899.

DEAR FRIEND, — I really felt badly at not being able to see more of you yesterday, — especially to see you off to Shimbashi: I could not even slip down to the gate without putting on shoes that take a terrible time to lace. On the other hand, you left in the house a sense of warmth and force and sun, — that were like a tonic to me, — or like a South-wind from the sea on a summer's day; and I felt in consequence better satisfied with the world at large.

Do you recognize this pen: a U.S. pen, contributed to my pen-holder by a U. S. N. officer whom I know a little, and like very much.

I hope by this time that the Gordian knot shows some inclination to unravel; and that the worry is diminishing. I remember, with much quiet laughter, your story of the bear. I think I have found nearly as good a simile — in an Indian paper. The fat Baboo got into a post-carriage, with many furious steeds, which the driver was accustomed to drive after the manner of the driving of Jehu, — and the driver was given further to meditation, during which he had no consciousness of the base facts of earth. And the bottom of the carriage fell out; and the Baboo landed feet first, and ran, — with the carriage round him, — and the horses were rushing at a speed not to be calculated. For the Baboo, it was death or run, — because the driver neither heard nor saw; and the exertions made are said to have been stupendous. The Baboo got off with a large amount of hospital, caused — or rather necessitated — by the unusual exercise. . . .

Well, I hope I shall some day again see you. I feel, however, that something has been gained: you have been up; and I can't find fault — even should you never again visit Tomihisa-chō.

By the way, you are a bad, bad boy to have given a present to those *kurumaya*. You spoil them. Talk again to me about ruining the morals of your "boy"! Won't I be revenged! Affectionately,

                                    LAFCADIO.

Boy sends love to Ojisan McDonald.

TO MITCHELL McDONALD

TŌKYŌ, March, 1899.

DEAR McDONALD, — I don't know what to say
about "Cyrano de Bergerac" as a poem, except that
as for fine workmanship, it is what we should expect
the best dramatic French prosody of this sort to
be. The verse-smith is certainly a great craftsman.
But was the subject worth the labour spent upon it?
I have no doubt that upon the French stage the effect
would be glorious, — exciting, — splendid: all that
sort of thing; and the story is "Frenchy," — wrap-
me-up-in-the-flag-of-honour style of extravagance.
It is n't natural — that is a great fault. Why it
should please English and American readers I can't
quite see: I don't believe the approbation is quite
genuine, — any more than the admiration for Bernhardt was genuine on the part of those who went to
see her without knowing a word of her language. I
can understand why Frenchmen should enthusiastic-
ally praise the book, but not why Americans should.
The heroine is a selfish, uninteresting little "chit;"
the other characters are without any sympathetic
quality that I can find. Cyrano wanting to fight with
everybody about his nose — to impose his nose on
the world at the point of the sword, while perpetrat-
ing rhymes the while — surely is not a very grand
person. No poet could make such a nose attractive.
We can forget the nose of Mephistopheles because
his wit and force dazzle us; but Mephistopheles has
no weaknesses — not at least in the first part of
"Faust." Cyrano has many; and one even suspects

that his virtues are the outgrowth of his despair about his nose. But I am glad to have read the wonderful thing; and I shall prize the book as long as I live, — because it came up here in your coat-pocket, and was given me with a smile and a twinkle of the eye that were (in my poor judgement) incomparably more beautiful than the writer's best lines; for these latter are not quite out of the heart, you know.

Speaking of an ugly subject for heroic treatment, I was thinking to-day about something that you would have done better than the man who did it, — the ugly subject being a hairy caterpillar in a salad at a banquet. The lady of the palace had ladled the salad and the caterpillar into the plate of some admiral or commodore, and saw what she had done when it was too late. The seaman caught her horrified eye, held it, and, smiling, swallowed the caterpillar unseen by the other guests. After the banquet, the beauty came to thank him — out of the innermost rosy chamber of her heart — when he is reported to have said: "Why, Madam, did you think that I would permit your pleasure of the evening to be spoiled by a miserable G—d d—d caterpillar!" Yes, you would have consumed the caterpillar; but you would not have "cussed" in the closing scene — though that was a lovable profanity in a man of the older school. Well, I think that commodore, or whatever his title may have been, a better man out and out than Cyrano. He would have done just as much, and made no fuss at all about it. Affectionately, LAFCADIO.

TO MRS. FENOLLOSA

APRIL, 1899.

DEAR MRS. FENOLLOSA, — To say that you have sent me the most beautiful letter that I ever received — certainly the one that most touched me — is not to say anything at all ! Of course I hope to see more of the soul that could utter such a letter, — every word a blossom fragrant like the lovely flower to which the letter was tied.

And yet — strange as it may seem — I feel like reproaching you! It is not *good* for a writer to get such a letter; — he ought to be severely maintained rather in a state of perpetual self-dissatisfaction. You would spoil him! Nevertheless, how pleasant to know that there is somebody to whom I can send a book hereafter with a tolerable certainty of pleasing! I shall not even try to thank you any more now; and I shall not dare to *re*read your letter for at least a month. But I hope that my next publication — which is all new — will not have a less welcome in your heart.

Ever with kindliest sympathies, — and unspoken gratitude for the delicious letter and the delicious flower,   LAFCADIO HEARN.

TO MITCHELL McDONALD

Tōkyō, May, 1899.

DEAR MITCHELL, — I am sending you the address of the great silk house, or rather dry-goods house, in Tōkyō; but a word in addition. If you and the consul are not afraid of taking cold by walking about in stocking-feet awhile, I strongly advise you to visit also the Japanese show-rooms, — just to see the crêpe-silks, spring goods, embroidered screens, etc., — the things made to suit Japanese taste, according to real art principles. You will find them much more interesting, I imagine, than the displays made to please foreigners. Even the *towels* and the *yukata* stuffs ought to tempt you into a trifling purchase or two in spite of yourselves; but nobody will grumble even if you do not buy at all. It is just like a bazaar, you need only go upstairs and walk through, from room to room, looking at the cases.

I was delighted with the little book which good Consul Bedloe so kindly gave me — I read it in the train. Please thank him with the best thanks in your capacity (which is practically unlimited) for the picture: it will be always a souvenir for me of one of the most, if not the absolutely most, delightful days that I passed in Yokohama. If you think he would care for the enclosed shadow of this old owl, please kindly give it him. I would I had at the moment some better way of acknowledging the rare pleasure which his merry good fellowship and his inimitable stories and everything about himself filled me with. I can't help feeling as if I had made a new friend — though that would not do to say, you know, upon such short acquaintance, to him. I only want to tell *you* just how the experience affected me.

I shall not thank you for my happy two days with you, and all the beautiful things that you "so beautifully *did*." But I felt as if the sky had become more blue and the grass more green than could really be the case. You know what that means.

With hope to see you soon again,

LAFCADIO.

TO MITCHELL McDONALD

TŌKYŌ, May, 1899.

DEAR MITCHELL, — I am still, o' nights, holding imaginary conversations with you from the windows of a waiting train, — or listening to wonderful stories from a delightful phantom-consul. In other words, the impressions of my last days in Yokohama are still haunting me, and — I fear — creating too much desire after the flesh-pots of Egypt. But in spite of these moral and intellectual debaucheries, I have been doing fair work, — and have in hand a ghost-story of a new and pathetically penetrating kind.

Speaking of ghosts, the design for the cover is to be plum-blossoms against a grey-blue sky. Can't say this is appropriate — the plum-blossom being the moral emblem of female virtue. A lotus in a golden lake, — a willow in rainy darkness, — would be better. But so long as I am not consulted, exact appropriateness cannot be expected; besides, it would be lost upon the public.

I 've been thinking over all your plans and hopes for me, and I am going to blast them unmercifully. I am quite convinced that you can do nothing at all, until the day when I make a hit on my own spontaneous account. *Then* you can do anything. For the interval, I must be very careful not to seem anxious to want attention of any sort, and do better work than I ever did before. You will only be able to find me a literary agent — or something of that sort, — and to talk nicely about me to personal friends.

Give my most grateful, most sincere, most unchangeable regards to Dr. Bedloe. I think more on his subject than I am going to put on paper just now.

Affectionately,

LAFCADIO.

Beauties of the landscape — scenery between Tōkyō and Yokohama.

TO MRS. FENOLLOSA

Tōkyō, May, 1899.

DEAR MRS. FENOLLOSA, — You will be shocked, I fear, when I tell you that I was careless enough to lose the address given me in your last charming letter. Your letters are too precious to be thus mislaid; and I am ashamed of negligence in this case. But though I forgot the address, I forgot no word of the letter, — nor of the previous charming

letter, with its quotation from that very clever friend
of yours (Miss Very) — the Emerson quotation
from the Brahma-poem. I hope you will tell me
more about your friend some day; for she seems to
be intellectually my friend also. I liked very much
what she said, as quoted by you, — who know
curiously well how to give pleasure, and do it so
generously, notwithstanding such meagre return.

I was struck by the paragraph in your last letter
concerning the *feeling* of understanding a writer
better than anybody else in the whole world. You
seemed to think it presumptuous to make such a
declaration about any writer; but the feeling, I believe, is always *true*. I have it in regard to all my
favourite authors, — especially in regard to certain
pages of French writers, like Anatole France,
Loti, Michelet, Gautier, Hugo. And I know I am
right — though I never can be a critic. The fact
is that the greatest critics, each of them, think
likewise; and their criticisms prove them correct.
No two feel or appreciate an author in exactly the
same way: each discerns a different value in him.
For no two personalities being the same, and no
personal understanding the same, the "equation"
makes the judgement unique in this world, and so
incomparably valuable, when it is a large one. . . .

The missionaries are furthermore wrong in sending women to the old-fashioned districts. The
people do not understand the maiden-missionary,
and if she receives a single foreign visitor not of her
own sex, the most extraordinary stories are set in
circulation. Of course, the people are not malicious

in the matter; but they find such a life contrary to all their own social experience, and they judge it falsely in consequence.

For myself I could sympathize with the individual, — but never with the missionary-cause. Unconsciously, every honest being in the mission-army is a destroyer — and a destroyer only; for nothing can replace what they break down. Unconsciously, too, the missionaries everywhere represent the edge — the *acies*, to use the Roman word — of Occidental aggression. We are face to face here with the spectacle of a powerful and selfish civilization demoralizing and crushing a weaker and, in many ways, a nobler one (if we are to judge by comparative ideals); and the spectacle is not pretty. We must recognize the inevitable, the Cosmic Law, if you like; but one feels and hates the moral wrong, and this perhaps blinds one too much to the sacrifices and pains accepted by the "noble army." . . .

LAFCADIO HEARN.

TO MITCHELL McDONALD

Tōkyō, June, 1899.

DEAR MITCHELL, — I reached my little Japanese house last night, carrying with me a sort of special tropic atmosphere or magnetic cloud — composed of impressions of hearts, hands, and minds dearer and altogether superior to the things of this world. Are you not as Solomon who "made silver to be in Jerusalem as stones, and cedars as the sycamore-trees that are in the lowland for multitude"?

Presently I squatted down before my *hibachi*,
and smoked and viewed the landscape o'er —
inverted in the pocket-lens of Dr. Bedloe, and
invested thereby with iridescences of violet and
crimson and emerald. And it occurred to me that
the prismatic lights in question symbolized those
fairy-tints and illusions which the two of you wove
around me while I remained in the circle of your
power. Spell it must have been — for I cannot yet
assure myself that I left Tōkyō only yesterday
morning, and not a month ago. The riddle reverses
the case of Urashima; — I have been trying to argue
out the question whether happiness does really make
the hours shorter, or does rather stretch time infinitely, like the thread of a spider. No doubt,
however, the true explanation lies in contrasts —
the contrasts of the extraordinary change from real
Japanese existence to the American colonial circle
of the year of grace 1899. It is really, you know,
like taking a single stride of a thousand years in
measure, — and the result is, of course, more bewildering than the striding of Peter Schlemihl. He
could only go from the Pole to the Tropics in an
afternoon—just now you are like old acquaintances
who come back at night to talk to us as if they had
not been under the ground for thirty years and more.
Are you all quite sure down there that you are
alive? I believe *I* am, — though I have to pinch
myself betimes to make sure. Then I have the evidence of that magnifying glass; and my shoes tell
me that I must have been out.

Yet more — I have two letters to send you.

(They need no comment, other than that which I have inscribed upon them.) I enclose them only because I know that you want to see them.

By the way, I feel otherwise displeased with you. I could forgive you for much besides getting off a moving train. *There was a pillar right behind you* as you stepped off. What would the not impossible Mrs. Mitchell McD. of my wishes say to you for that!   Affectionately,

LAFCADIO.

TO MITCHELL McDONALD

TŌKYŌ, June, 1899.

DEAR MITCHELL, — Your delightful letter is with me. I did not get through that examination work till Sunday morning — had about 300 compositions to look through: then I had nearly a day's work packing and sending out prizes which I give myself every year — not for the best English (for that depends upon natural faculty altogether), but for the best *thinking,* which largely depends upon study and observation.

Lo! I am a "bloated bondholder." I am "astonished" and don't know what to say — except that I want to hug you! About the semi-annual meeting, though — fear I shall be far away then. Unless it be absolutely necessary, I don't think I shall be able to come. Can't I vote by letter, or telegraph? If you make out a form, I'll vote everything that you want, just as you want it. (By the way, I *might* be able to come — in case I am not more than fifty miles off. Perhaps I can't get to where I want to go.) We'll take counsel together. Yet, you ought to know that I hate meetings of all kinds with hatred unspeakable.

So it was a Mrs. ——, not a Mr. ——. I am afraid of Scotch people. However, that was a nice letter. Perhaps I ought to send her a copy of "Ghostly Japan." But one never can tell the exact consequences of yielding to these impulses of gratitude and sympathy. My friends are enough for me — they are as rare as they are few; rare like things from the uttermost coasts, — diamonds, emeralds and opals, amethysts, rubies, and topazes from the mines of Golconda. What more could a fellow want? *All* the rest is useless even when it is not sham — which it generally is.

Have n't been idle either. Am working on "The Poetry and Beauty of Japanese Female Names." Got all the common names I want into alphabetical order, and classified. Aristocratic names remain to be done, — an awful job; but I think that I shall manage it before I get away.

Perhaps I shall not finish that dream-work for years, — perhaps I might finish it in a week. Depends upon the Holy Ghost. By the way, a thing that I had never been able to finish since I began it six years ago, and left in a drawer, has suddenly come into my present scheme, — fits the place to a "T." So it may be with other things. I leave them to develop themselves; and if I wait long enough, they always do.

I have heard from the Society of Authors. The American public is good to me. I have only a very small public in England yet. I fancy at present that I shall do well to become only an *associate* of the Authors' Society, — pay the fees, — and wait for fame, in order to take the publishers privately recommended to me. We shall see.

What a tremendous, square, heavy, settled, immoveable, mountainous thing is the English reading public! The man who can bore into the basalt of that mass must have a diamond-drill. I tell you that I feel dreadfully minute, — microscopic, — when I merely read the names of the roll of the Authors' Society. Love to you from all of us,

LAFCADIO.

TO MITCHELL McDONALD

TŌKYŌ, June, 1899.

DEAR McDONALD, — Do you know that I felt a little blue after you went away the other day, — which was ungrateful of me. A little while ago, reading Marcus Aurelius, I found a quotation that partially explains: "One man, when he has done a service to another, is ready to set it down to his account. Another is not ready to do this. . . . A third in a manner does not even know what he has done, but he is like a vine which has produced grapes, and seeks for nothing more after it has once produced fruit." And I feel somewhat displeased at the vine — inasmuch as I know not what to do in regard to my own sense of the obligation of the grapes.

The heat is gorgeous and great. I dream and write. The article on women's names is dry work;

but it develops. I have got it nearly two thirds —
yes, fully two thirds done. I am going to change the
sentence "lentor inexpressible" which you did not
like. It is a kind of old trick word with me. I send
you a copy of the old story in which I first used it,
— years and years ago. Don't return the thing —
it has had its day.

I feel queerly tempted to make a Yokohama trip
some afternoon, towards evening, instead of morning:
am waiting only for that double d—d faculty meeting, and the finishing up of a little business. "Business?" you may bewilderingly exclaim. Well, yes
— business. I have been paying a student's way
through the university — making him work, however, in return for it. And I must settle his little
matters in a day or so — showing him that he has
paid his own way really, and has discharged all
his obligations. Don't think he will be grateful —
but I must try to be like the vine — like Mitchell —
and though I can't be quite so good, I must pretend
to be — act as if I were. The next best thing to
being good is to imitate the acts and the unselfishness of Vines.   LAFCADIO.

YAIDZU, August, 1899.

DEAR MITCHELL, — I am writing to you under
very great difficulties, and on a floor, — and therefore
you must not expect anything very good.

Got to Yaidzu last night, and took a swim in a
phosphorescent sea.

To-day is cold and grey — and not a day for you to enjoy. I saw an immense crowd of pilgrims for Fuji at Gotemba, and wondered if you would go up, as this time you would have plenty of company.

Sorry I did not see dear Dr. Bedloe; but I hope to catch him upon his way back to the Far East.

How I wish you could come down some fine day here — only, I *do* fear that you could not stand the fleas. I must say that it requires patience and perseverance to stand them. But you can have glorious swimming. When I can get that — *fleas* and all other things are of no consequence.

Also I am afraid that you would not like the odours of fish below stairs, of *daikon,* and of other things all mixed up together. *I* don't admire them;—but there is swimming — nothing else makes much difference.

You would wonder if you saw how I am quartered, and how much I like it. I *like* roughing it among the fisher-folk. I love them. I am afraid that you not only could n't stand it, but that you would be somewhat angry if you came down here — would tell me that "I ought to have known better," etc. Nevertheless I want you to come for one day — see if you can stand it. "Play up the Boyne Wather softly till I see if I can stand it." Ask Dr. Bedloe the result of playing the Boyne Wather softly. But I am warning you fairly and fully.

Affectionately,

LAFCADIO.

P. S. I am *sure* that you could not stand it — perfectly sure. But then — think of the value of the *experience*. I had a Japanese officer here last year and *he* liked it.

TO MITCHELL McDONALD

YAIDZU, August, 1899.

DEAR MITCHELL, — Went to that new hotel this afternoon, and discovered that the people are all liars and devils and . . . Therefore it would *never* do for you to go there. Then I went to an ice and fruit seller, who has a good house; and he said that after the fourteenth he could let you have sleeping room. The village festival is now in progress, so that the houses are crowded.

If this essay fails, I have the alternative of a widow's cottage. She is a good old soul — with the best of little boys for a grandson, and sole companion; the old woman and the boy support themselves by helping the fishermen. But there will be fleas.

Oh! d—n it all! what is a flea? Why should a brave man tremble before a nice clean shining flea? You are not afraid of twelve-inch shells or railroad trains or torpedoes — what, then, is a flea? Of course by "a flea" I mean fleas *generically*. I've done my best for you — but the long and the short of it is that if you go anywhere outside of the Grand Hotel you *must* stand fleas — piles, multitudes, *mountains* and *mountain-ranges* of fleas! There! Fleas are a necessary part of human existence.

The iceman offers you a room breezy, cool, — you

eat with me; but by all the gods! you 've *got* to make the acquaintance of some fleas! Just think how many unpleasant acquaintances *I* run away from! yet — I have Buddha's patience with fleas.

At this moment, a beautiful, shining, plump, gathered-up-for-a-jump flea is walking over my hand.

Affectionately,

LAFCADIO.

TO MITCHELL McDONALD

TŌKYŌ, September, 1899.

DEAR MITCHELL, — I am sending you two documents just received — one from Lowder's new company, I suppose; the other, which makes me rather vexed, from that —— woman, who has evidently never seen or known me, and who spells my name "Lefcardio." (Wish you would point out to her somebody who looks small and queer, — and tell her, "That is Mr. Hearn — he is waiting to see you.") At all events, these folks have simply been putting up a job to amuse themselves or to annoy me; —— has apparently been putting up a job to annoy *you.* We are in the same boat; but you can take much better care of yourself than I can. I do wish that you could find out something about those —— people: I am very much ashamed at having left my card at the hotel where they were stopping.

One thing sure is that I shall not go down to the Grand Hotel again for ages to come — I wish I could venture to say "never"—nevermore. It is one more nail in my literary coffin every time I go down. If I am to be tormented by folks in this way, I had better run away from the university and from Tōkyō at once.

That —— woman is a most damnable liar. I wonder who she can be.

Well, so much for an outburst of vexation — which means nothing very real; for I only want to pour my woes into your ear. I can't say how good I think you are, nor how I feel about the pleasure of our last too brief meeting. But I do feel more and more that you do not understand some things, — the immense injury that introductions do to a struggling writer, — the jealousies aroused by attentions paid to him, — the loss to him of creative power that follows upon invitations of any kind. You represent, in a way, the big world of society. It kills every man that it takes notice of — or rather, every man that submits to be noticed by it. Their name is legion; and they are strangled as soon as they begin to make the shadow of a reputation. Solitude and peace of mind only can produce any good work. Attentions numb, paralyze, destroy every vestige of inspiration. I feel that I cannot go to America without hiding — and never can let you know where I go to. I shall have to get away from Tōkyō, — get somewhere where nobody wants to go. You see only one side — what you think, with good reason, are the advantages of being personally known. But the other side, — the disadvantages, — the annoyances, the horrors — you do not know anything about; and you are stirring them up — like a swarm of gnats. A few more visits to Yokohama would utterly smash me — and at this moment, I do wish that I never had written a book.

No: an author's instincts are his best guide. His natural dislike to meet people is not shyness, — not want of self-appreciation: it is empirical knowledge of the conditions necessary to peace of mind and self-cultivation. Introduce him, and you murder his power, — just as you ruin certain solutions by taking out the cork. The germs enter; and the souls of him rot! Snubs are his best medicine. They keep him humble, obscure, and earnest. Solitude is what he needs — what every man of letters knows that an author needs. No decent work was ever done under any other conditions. He wants to be protected from admiration, from kindnesses, from notice, from attentions of any sort: therefore really his ill-wishers are his friends without knowing it.

Yet here I am — smoking a divine cigar — out of my friend's gift-box, — and brutally telling him that he is killing my literary soul or souls. Am I right or wrong? I feel like kicking myself; and yet, I feel that I ought never again in this world to visit the Grand Hotel! I wonder if my friend will stand this declaration with equanimity. He says that he will never "misunderstand." That I *know*. I am only fearing that *understanding* in this case might be even worse than misunderstanding. And I can't make a masterpiece yet. If I could, I should not seem to be putting on airs. That is the worst of it.

Hope you will forgive and sympathize with
LAFCADIO.

TO MITCHELL McDONALD

TōKYō, October, 1899.

DEAR MITCHELL, — No news up here, to interest you.

I am not doing anything much at present. Don't know whether I shall appear in print again for several years. Anyhow, I shall never write again except when the spirit moves me. It does n't pay; and what you call "reputation" is a most damnable, infernal, unmitigated misery and humbug — a nasty smoke — a foretaste of that world of black angels to which the wicked are destined. (Thanks for your promise not to make any more introductions; but I fear the mischief has been done; and Yokohama is now for me a place to be shunned while life lasts.)

Six hundred pages (about) represent my present quota of finished manuscript. But I shall this time let the thing mellow a good deal, and publish only after judicious delay. While every book I write costs me more than I can get for it, it is evident that literature holds no possible rewards for me; — and like a sensible person I am going to try to do something really good, that won't sell.

In the meanwhile, however, I want not to think about publishers and past efforts at all. That is waste of time. I shall prepare to cross the great Pacific instead, — unless I have to cross a greater Pacific in very short order. I should like a chat with you soon; but I am not going down to Yokohama for an age. It is better not. When I keep to myself

up here, things begin to simmer and grow: a sudden
change of milieu invariably stops the fermentation.
Wish you were anywhere else that is pleasant
except — at the G. H.

Affectionately ever,
LAFCADIO.

TO MITCHELL McDONALD

Tōkyō, October, 1899.

DEAR MITCHELL, — I cannot quite tell you how
sorry I felt to part from you on the golden afternoon
of yesterday: like Antæus, who got stronger every
time he touched the solid ground, I feel always so
much more of a man after a little contact with your
reality. Not more of a *literary man*, however; for
I try to shut the ears of my mind against your praise
in that direction, and I close the door of Memory
upon the sound of it. If I did n't, I should be ruined
by self-esteem.

And to think that you will be eight, ten or
twenty thousand miles away, after next year!

Woke up this morning feeling younger — not
quite fifty years of age. Gradually the sense of age
will return: when I feel about sixty again — which
will be soon — I shall run down to see you.

Want to say that those cigars of the doctor's
are too good for me: luxury, luxury, luxury. The
ruin of empires! But I like a little of it — not
too often — once in a year. It makes me buoyant,
imponderable — fly in day dreams.

And I want to see Bedloe. Do not, if you can

help it, fail to come up again, once anyhow, before the good year dies. Only this word of love to you.

In haste,

LAFCADIO.

TO PROFESSOR FOXWELL

TŌKYŌ, October, 1899.

DEAR PROFESSOR, — I had given up all expectation of seeing you again in Japan, — as a letter received from Mr. Edwards gave me to understand that you were on your way back to England. To-day, however, I learned by chance that you were still in Tōkyō, — though no longer an inhabitant of the Palace of Woe. Therefore I must convey to you by this note Mr. Edwards's best regards, and express my own regret that you will not again help me through with a single one of those dreary quarters between classes. However, I suppose that the day of my own emancipation cannot be extremely remote.

I have had a number of pleasant letters from that wonderful American friend of ours. He has been in Siam, — where he sold to the King's people more than two tons of dictionaries without emerging from the awning of his carriage; and I suppose that the books were carried by a white elephant with six tusks. He has been since then in Ceylon, Madras, Calcutta, — all sorts of places, too, ending in "bad," — doing business. But he will not return to Japan — he goes to the Mediterranean. He sent me a box of cigars of Colombo: they are a little "sharp," but very nice — strange in flavour, but fine.

No other news that could interest you. Excuse me for troubling you with this note — but the idea of seeking you at the Metropole would fill me with dismay. If you do go to England, please send me a good-bye card. If you do not go very soon, I shall probably see you somewhere "far from the madding crowd."

Best regards,

LAFCADIO HEARN.

TO PROFESSOR FOXWELL

NOVEMBER, 1899.

DEAR PROFESSOR, — Nay! I return into my shell for another twelve months at least. You see — I thought you were going away, and felt a little sorry, and therefore went to that dreadful hotel and let you hand me over for an afternoon to your American friend who quotes Nordau's "Degeneration," but that was really, for me, supreme heroism of self-sacrifice. . . . (By the way, I have seen too much of that type of man elsewhere to be altogether delighted with him: superficies of bonhomie, studied suggestions of sympathy, core hard as Philadelphia pressed brick: he *swarms* in America; and I much prefer the Gullman brand.) As for a party of four, — "*Compania de cuatro, compania del diablo!*" The only way I can have a friend in these parts is to make this condition: "Never introduce me; and never ask me to meet you in a

crowd." You ought to recognize, surely, that I
could n't afford to be known and liked, even if
that were possible. I can "keep up my end" only
by strictly following the good maxim: *Tachez de
n'avoir besoin de personne.* Now, really, dear Professor, why should I lose an evening of (to me)
precious work, and tire myself, merely to sit down
with Mr. G. and Mr. M.? What do I care for Mr.
G. or Mr. M.? What do I care for the whole foreign
community of Tōkyō? Why should I go two steps
out of my way for the sake of men that I know
nothing about, and do not want to know anything
about? "Life is too short," as the Americans say.
With thanks all the same,

Crankily yours,

LAFCADIO HEARN.

Next time — next two times we meet — it is my
turn to play host, remember.

TO MRS. WETMORE

TŌKYŌ, January, 1900.

DEAR MRS. WETMORE, — Memories of handwriting must have become strong with me; for I
recognized the writing before I opened the letter.
And thereafter I did not do more than verify the
signature — and put the letter away, so that I
might read it in the time of greatest silence and
serenity of mind. During the interval there rose
up reproachfully before me the ghost of letters
written and rewritten and again rewritten to you,
but subsequently — I cannot exactly say why —

posted in the fire! (This letter goes to you in its first spontaneous form — so much the worse for me!)

"Indifferent" you say. But you ought to see my study-room. It is not very pretty — a little Japanese matted room, with glass sliding windows (upstairs), and a table and chair. Above the table there is the portrait of a young American naval officer in uniform — he is not so young now; — that is a very dear picture. On the opposite wall is the shadow of a beautiful and wonderful person, whom I knew long ago in the strange city of New Orleans. (She was sixteen years old, or so, when I first met her; and I remember that not long afterwards she was dangerously ill, and that several people were afraid she would die in that quaint little hotel where she was then stopping.) The two shadows watch me while the light lasts; and I have the comfortable feeling of monopolizing their sympathy — for they have nobody else to look at. The originals would not be able to give me so much of their company.

The lady talks to me about a fire of wreckwood, that used to burn with red and blue lights. I remember that I used to sit long ago by that Rosicrucian glow, and talk to her; but I remember nothing else — only the sound of her voice, — low and clear and at times like a flute. The gods only know what *I* said; for my thoughts in those times were seldom in the room, — but in the future, which was black, without stars. But all that was long ago. Since then I have become grey, and the father of three boys.

The naval officer has been here again in the body, however. Indeed, I expect him here, upstairs, in a day or two, — before he goes away to Cavite, — after which I shall probably never see him again. We have sat up till many a midnight, — talking about things.

Whether I shall ever see the original of the other shadow, I do not know. I must leave the Far East for a couple of years, in order to school a little son of mine, who must early begin to learn languages. Whether I take him to England or America, I do not yet know; but America is not very far from England. Whether the lady of the many-coloured fires would care to let me hear her voice for another evening, sometime in the future, is another question.

Two of the boys are all Japanese, — sturdy and not likely to cause anxiety. But the eldest is almost altogether of another race, — with brown hair and eyes of the fairy-colour, — and a tendency to pronounce with a queer little Irish accent the words of old English poems which he has to learn by heart. He is not very strong; and I must give the rest of my life to looking after him.

I wish that I could make a book to please you more often than once a year. (But I have so much work to do!) Curiously enough, some of the thoughts spoken in your letter have been put into the printer's hands — ghostly anticipation? — for a book which will probably appear next fall. I cannot now judge whether it will please you — but there are reveries in it, and sundry queer stories.

I think that you once asked me for a portrait of

my boy. I send one — but he is now older than
his portrait by some two years. I shall send a better
one later on, if you wish. I should like to interest
you in him — to the simple extent of advising me
about him at a later day; for you represent for
my imagination all the Sibyls, and your wisdom
would be for me as the worth of things precious from
the uttermost coasts.

Perhaps something of *me* lives in that collie you
describe: I think that I can understand exactly
what she feels when the Invisible gathers about, —
that is what she feels in regard to her mistress. A
collie *ought* to recognize the ghostly, anyhow: her
ancestors must have sat at the feet of Thomas of
Ercildoune. By the way, my poor dog *did* get
murdered after all, — killed by men from a strange
village. They were chased by the police; but they
"made good their escape." She left behind her
three weird little white puppies. We fed them and
nursed them, and saved two. It is painful being
attached to birds and dogs and cats and other lovable creatures: they die before us, and they have
so many sorrows which we cannot protect them
from. The old gods, who loved human beings,
must have been very unhappy to see their pets
wither and perish in a little space.

Good-bye for the moment. It was so kind to
write me.

LAFCADIO HEARN.

TO MASANOBU ŌTANI

Tōkyō, January, 1900.

MY DEAR OTANI,—I suppose that, when you ask me to express my "approval" or non-approval of a society for the study of literature, etc., you want a sincere opinion. My sincere opinion will not please you, I fear, but you shall have it.

There is now in Japan a mania, an insane mania, for perfectly useless organizations of every description. Societies are being formed by hundreds, with all kinds of avowed objects, and dissolved as fast as they are made. It is a madness that will pass — like many other mad fashions; but it is doing incomparable mischief. The avowed objects of these societies is to do something useful; the real object is simply to waste time in talking, eating, and drinking. The knowledge of the value of time has not yet even been dreamed of in this country.

The study of literature or art is never accompanied by societies of this kind. The study of literature and of art requires and depends upon individual effort, and original thinking. The great Japanese who wrote famous books and painted famous pictures did not need societies to help them. They worked in solitude and silence.

No good literary work can come out of a society — no original work, at least. Social organization is essentially opposed to individual effort, to original effort, to original thinking, to original feeling. A society for the study of literature means a society

organized so as to render the study of literature, or
the production of literature, absolutely impossible.

A literary society is a proof of weakness— not a
combination of force. The strong worker and
thinker works and thinks by himself. He does not
want help or sympathy or company. His pleasure
in the work is enough. No great work ever came
out of a literary society, — no great original work.

A literary society, for the purpose of studying
literature, is utterly useless. The library is a better
place for the study of literature. The best of all
places is the solitude of one's own room.

I should not say anything against a society organized for the translation and publication of the whole
of Shakespeare's plays, — for example. But translation is a practical matter — not original work, nor
even literary study in the highest sense.

Even in the matter of making a dictionary, no
society, however, can equal the work of the solitary
scholar. The whole French Academy could not
produce a dictionary such as Littré produced by
himself.

I have said that I think these Japanese societies
mean a mischievous waste of time. Think of the
young scholars who go from Japan to Europe for
higher study. They are trained by the most learned
professors in the world, — they are prepared in
every way to become creators, original thinkers,
literary producers. And when they return to Japan,
instead of being encouraged to work, they are asked
to waste their time in societies, to attend banquets,
to edit magazines, to deliver addresses, to give lectures

free of charge, to correct manuscripts, to do everything which can possibly be imagined to prevent
them from working. They cannot do anything;
they are not allowed to do anything; their learning
and their lives are made barren. They are treated,
not like human beings with rights, but like machines
to be used, and brutally used, and worn out as soon
as possible.

While this rage for wasting time in societies goes
on there will be no new Japanese literature, no
new drama, no new poetry — nothing good of any
kind. Production will be made impossible and only
the commonplace translation of foreign ideas. The
meaning of time, the meaning of work, the sacred-
ness of literature are unknown to this generation.

And what is the use of founding a new journal?
There are too many journals now. You can publish
whatever you want without founding a journal. If
you found a journal, you will be obliged to write
for it quickly and badly; and you know that good
literary work cannot be done quickly, — cannot be
made to order within a fixed time. A new journal —
unless you choose to be a journalist, and nothing but
a journalist — would mean not only waste of time,
but waste of money.

I am speaking in this way, because I think that
literature is a very serious and sacred thing — not
an amusement, not a thing to trifle and play with.

Handicapped as you now are, — with an enormous number of class-hours, — you cannot attempt
any literature work at all, without risking your
health and injuring your brains. It is much more

important that you should try to get a position allowing you more leisure.

And finally, I have small sympathy with the mere study of English literature by Japanese students and scholars. I should infinitely prefer to hear of new studies in Japanese literature. Except with the sole purpose of making a new *Japanese* literature, I do not sympathize with English or French or German studies.

There is my opinion for you. I hope you will think about it, — even if you do not like it. Work with a crowd, and you will *never* do anything great.

Many years ago, I advised you to take up a scientific study. It would have given you more leisure for literary work. You would not. You will have future reason to regret this. But if you want advice again, here it is: *Don't* belong to societies, *don't* write anything that comes into your head, *don't* waste the poor little time you have. Take literature seriously, — or leave it alone.

Yours very truly,

Y. Koizumi.

TO YASUKOCHI

Tōkyō, November, 1901.

Dear Mr. Yasukochi, — Not the least of my pleasure in looking at the fine photograph, so kindly sent to my little son, was in observing how very well and strong you appear to be. Let me also have the privilege of thanking you — though my boy, of course, sends his small recognition of the favour.

Your letter of September 3d interested me very
much; for I had not heard anything about you at
all since the last visit you made to my little house
in Tomihisa-chō. For example, I had not heard
of your going to Kumamoto Ken; and although
I often wondered about you, I knew nobody who
could inform me. (I had, indeed, one Kumamoto
pupil, Mr. Gōshō; but I quite forgot about his having been in my class at Kumamoto, until he came
to see me after graduating — to say good-bye.) The
experience of army-life which you have had must
have been somewhat hard as discipline; but I imagine
that, after all those years of severe study and mental
responsibility, the change to another and physical
discipline must have been good from the point of
health. I think that it probably made you stronger;
and I am glad you were in the artillery-corps, —
where one has an opportunity to learn so many things
of lasting value. But I trust that many years will
elapse before Japan again needs your services in a
military capacity.

It was kind of you to remember Numi. A
curious thing happened after the last time we saw
him. One in my household dreamed that he came
back, in his uniform, looking very pale, and speaking
of a matter concerning his family. The next day,
the papers began to print the first accounts of the
ship being missing. The coincidence was curious.
The matter of which he seemed to have spoken was
looked after, as he would have wished.

I have no doubt at all of good things to come
for you, if you keep as strong as your picture now

proves you to be. The rest will be, I think, only
question of time and patience. I look forward wit
pleasure to the probability of seeing you agair
(Except that I have got greyer, I fear you will fin
me the same as of old, — somewhat queer, etc.)
have been working very steadily, rather than hard
but by systematically doing just exactly so muc
every day, neither more nor less, I find that I ar
able to do a good deal in the course of a year.
mean "good deal" in the sense of "quantity"—th
quality, of course, depends upon circumstance
rather than effort.

Thanks, again, for your kindness in sending th
photograph, and for the pleasant letter about your
self. May all good fortune be yours is the earnes
wish of

Y. KOIZUMI.

TO YRJÖ HIRN

TŌKYŌ, January, 1902.

DEAR PROFESSOR, — About a week ago I re
ceived from Messrs. Wahlstrom and Weilstrand —
how strangely impressive these Northern names
— the dainty "Exotica," with its sunrise and flying
swallows-design, and — my name and private ad
dress in Japanese thereon ! . . . I have sent a boo
for Mrs. Hirn. If there are any of my books tha
you do not know, and would like to have, — suc
as "Gleanings in Buddha-Fields" or "Youma
— I shall be glad to have them sent you fror
America.

Thanks indeed for the photograph. I had imagined a face with the same strong, precise lines,
but in a blond setting. Yet some shades of fair hair
come out dark in photographs — so that I am not
yet quite sure how far my intuition miscarried. You
are what I imagined — but a shade or two stronger
in line.

As for myself, I have no decent photograph at
present. . . . I am horribly disfigured by the loss
of the left eye — so get photographed usually in
profile, or looking downward. I am a very small
person; and when young, was very dark, with the
large alarming eyes of a myope.

I imagine that you have been tactfully kind in
your prefatory notice of me. I could only guess;
but your letter confirms a number of my guesses.
The article by Zilliacus, to which you refer, I do not
know: I cannot read German in any event. The
paper by Dr. Varigny in the *Revue des Deux Mondes*
was a mere fantasy,—unjust in the fact that it ac-
credited me with faculties and knowledge which I
do not possess. The mere truth of the matter is that
I have had a rather painful experience of life, for
lack of the very qualities ascribed to me. (In American existence one must either grind or be ground —
I passed most of my time between the grindstones.)

As for the choice of the subjects translated, it
gave me most pleasure to find some of my "Retrospectives" in that stern and sturdy tongue: it was a
bracing experience. The selections from "Glimpses"
I should not have advised; for the book is disfigured
by faults of "journalistic" style, and was written

before I really began to understand, not Japan, but how difficult it is to understand Japan. Nevertheless your judgement in this particular was coincident with the general decision: the story of the Shirabyoshi has, for example, appeared in four languages. It is a story of the painter Bunchō, — and the merit is in no wise mine, as I merely paraphrased a Japanese narrative. Don't think me ungrateful, please, because I express my preferences thus. Really the experience of trying to follow in Swedish the meaning of my "Serenade," etc., was more than a delight, — and I imagined that the translator had successfully aimed at reproducing in Swedish the rhythm of the English sentences.

I am happy in reading your words about the Japanese dances: as you have seen a living example of one kind, you will not judge them all severely hereafter. Of course there are dances and dances. I wish that you could see the dancing of a pair of *miko*, — little Shintō maid-priestesses: it is a simple performance, but as pleasing as a hovering of butterflies.

Your "Origins of Art" is a book that seems to have proved above the range of some small critics; but you have been felt and appreciated in higher spheres, I think. I was amused by the dullardism of some English critics, evidently incapable of perceiving that the sterling value of such a book is suggestive, — that it was intended to make men think, not to furnish some intellectual lazy-bones with ready-made ideas. . . .

Finland I know only through Léouzon Le Duc's

delicious prose-translation. I think of forests of birch, and lakes interminably opening into lakes, and rivers that roar in lonely places, and "liver-coloured earth." Wonder if the earth is really that colour?—the ground of my garden, after a shower, is exactly "liver-colour" — a rich reddish brown.

Please convey my humble thanks to Mrs. Hirn, and believe me

Yours most sincerely,

LAFCADIO HEARN.

TO YRJÖ HIRN

TŌKYŌ, April, 1902.

DEAR PROFESSOR,—Many thanks for the archæological treatise, and for your kindness in sending me the "critical" news. (I think that I can appreciate the good will that can impel so busy a professor to give me so much of his time.) And please to convey my thanks to Mrs. Hirn for her charming letter.

Concerning your project for another volume of "Exotica," kindly assure Mrs. Hirn that she is as fully authorized as I can authorize her to translate whatever she pleases to select from my books.

By the way, you appear to have been deceived by some bookseller; for none of my books are out of print, except "Some Chinese Ghosts," and that by my own will and desire. . . .

Far from being uninterested in the social and political changes of Finland, I feel, as every generous thinker ought to feel, sincere regret at the probable disappearance of a national civilization, and the inevitable loss of intellectual freedom. I think of the "absorption" as a great political crime. . . . Here in Japan, I watch, day by day, the destruction of a wonderful and very beautiful civilization, by industrial pressure. It strikes me that a time is approaching in which intellectual liberty will almost cease to exist, together with every other kind of liberty, — the time when no man will be able to live as he wishes, much less to write what he pleases. The future industrial communism, in its blind dull way, will be much less liberal than Russian rule, and incomparably more cruel. By that time, Russia herself will be getting less conservative; and I imagine that the Englishman and the American of the future may flee to the new Russia in search of intellectual freedom!

At present, however, the United States offers great opportunity to merit, and every latitude to mental liberty. If you should ever have to leave your own beloved country, I think you would be most happy in America.

The Far East is not impossible — if you wish very much to visit it. Government service anywhere is not a bed of roses; and Tōkyō is said to be the most "unsympathetic" place in the world. But salaries are fair; and a three years' sojourn would furnish rich experience. It you ever want *very* much to see Japan, perhaps you may be able to obtain a Government post — especially if you have friends in legations, and "high places." Then I can write more to you about the matter. But at present you are fortunate enough to be envied in a brotherly way. I wish you every happiness on your European journey.

How much I should like to see Europe again! — I have three boys to look after, however, and all things are uncertain. I am glad that you have a bright little son; — you know what hopes and fears the possession involves. His travels with you will be of priceless advantage to him. The best of all education is through Ear and Eye — while the senses are most fresh and plastic.

Sincerely yours,
LAFCADIO HEARN.

TO DR. AND MRS. YRJÖ HIRN

Tōkyō, May, 1902.

DEAR FRIENDS, — I am a little disappointed in being able to send you to-day only "Kokoro" and "Gleanings in Buddha-Fields" — these being the only books of mine, not in your possession, that I could lay hands on. However, they are the best of the earlier lot; and I imagine that you will be interested especially in the latter. Japan is changing so quickly that already some of the essays in "Kokoro" — such as the "Genius of Japanese Civilization" — have become out-of-date. By the way, have you seen Bellesort's "La Société Japonaise?" — a wonderful book, considering that its author passed only about six months in Japan!

A few days ago I had the delightful surprise of your album-gift: I have lived in Finland! It is very strange that some of the pictures are exactly

what I dreamed of — after reading the "Kalewala."
In fact, the book illustrates the "Kalewala" for
me: even the weird expression in the eyes of the old
Kantele-singers seems to me familiar. Of course,
the views of city streets and splendid buildings were
all surprises and revelations; but the hills and woods
and lakes looked like the Finland of my reveries.
Of all the views, that of Tmatia seemed to me most
like the scenery of the Runoia: there was something
in it of *déjà vu*, most ghostly, that gave me particular
delight. My affectionate thanks to you both. I
shall ever treasure the book and remember the kind
givers.

LAFCADIO HEARN.

TO MRS. HIRN

Tōkyō, June, 1902.

DEAR MRS. HIRN, — I have received the copy of
Euterpe, so kindly sent me, containing your translation, — which gave me much pleasure.

What a nice little paper *Euterpe* is! Long ago
we used to have good papers like that—real literary
papers, in nearly the same format — in America.
Now, alas! they have become impossible. The taste
for good literature in America is practically dead:
vulgar fiction has killed the higher fiction; "sensa-
tionalism" and blatant cheap journalism have
murdered the magazines; and poetry is silent. I
wish there could be another paper in America like
Euterpe. . . .

I have been wondering, in reading your translation, whether there is no better word for the English "ghostly" than *mystika* — surely, they are not alike in meaning. The old English name for a priest, you know, is "a *ghostly* father." And I am wondering whether "*ewigt*" really has the sense of "infinitely." The Buddhist thought is that the innermost eternal life in each of us becomes "infinite" by union with the One, when the shell of Karma is broken. Individuality and personality exist only as passing phenomena: the Reality is One *and* infinite.

Please pardon these little observations, which are not intended as criticisms, but only as suggestions.

Believe me ever most sincerely yours,

LAFCADIO HEARN.

TO MRS. WETMORE

Tōkyō, July, 1902.

MY DEAR MRS. WETMORE, — Perhaps you can remember having said, twelve years ago, "I want you to go to Japan, because I want to read the books that you will write about it." As my tenth volume on the subject is now in press, — you ought to be getting satisfied.

I am writing — not without some difficulty — to ask whether you would or could play the part of a fairy god-sister, in helping me to find, for the time of a year or two years, some easy situation in America.

As my eyes are nearly burnt out, I should have to depend upon quality rather than quantity of work. Some post upon a literary weekly — where

I could employ a typewriter — would be good.
I doubt whether the universities would give me a
chance at English literature.

So much for the want. I must bring my boy with
me: it is chiefly for his sake. Once that he learns
to speak English well, the rest of his education
will not disturb me. I am his only teacher and want
to continue to teach him for a few years more.
— South or West I should prefer to East — "where
only a swordfish can swim."

As you are a queen of fairies, you might touch
with your wand the *only* thing that would exactly
help me. England is hopeless, of course: I have
no chance of earning anything in that "awful
orderliness." My family will be well provided for
during my absence; but the provision will leave
me under the necessity of earning something
abroad. . . .

What is worse still, I have been so utterly isolated
here that I have no conception of the actual tone
and state of things abroad. I do not know "how
I stand."

You should try to think of your old acquaintance
as a small grey unpleasant "old man." . . .

Yours very sincerely,

LAFCADIO HEARN.

TO MRS. WETMORE

YAIDZU, August, 1902.

DEAR MRS. WETMORE, — Your kindest letter of
July 23d reached me on the 15th of August, —

at this little fishing-village of Yaidzu, where I am staying with my boy.

What you say about my finding you a "grey-haired woman of forty" is, of course, impossible. Even if my eyes said so, I should say that they were telling untruth. It is quite certain that you are a fairy, — capable of assuming myriad shapes, — but I know the shapes to be each and all — *Maya!* I never really saw any of the magical forms but two — no, three — in photograph; and they were all different persons, belonging to different centuries, and containing different souls. About you I should not even trust the eyes of the X-rays. My memory is of a Voice and a Thought, — multiple, both, exceedingly, — but justifying the imagination of *une jeune fille un peu farouche* (there is no English word that gives the same sense of shyness *and* force) who came into New Orleans from the country, and wrote nice things for a paper there, and was so kind to a particular variety of savage that he could not understand — and was afraid.

I am half-sorry already for not having written you more fully. I fear you think that I am in a very *immediate* hurry. No: if a fair chance can come to me in the course of a year, or even fifteen months, I can easily wait. My people have their own homes now, and I have some little means; and nothing presses. Even if the ——s should find ways and means to poke me out of the Government service (they have tried it — in oh! so many ways — for four years past), I should feel quite easy about matters for a twelvemonth. Please do not think that I would dream of giving you any hurry-scurry trouble. But, perhaps in a year's time, something might offer itself.

I am *afraid* of New York City for my boy's sake. I should not like to let him risk one New York winter. Besides, what exercise can a boy have in New York — no trees, fields, streams. Awful place — New York. If anything were to happen to *him*, the sun would go out. I can't take risks — must be sure what I am doing. . . . Oh, if I were by myself — yes: twenty dollars a month in America would suit me anywhere. I have no longer any wants personal.

Every year there are born some millions of boys cleverer, stronger, handsomer than mine. I may be quite a fool in my estimate of him. I do not find him very clever, quick, or anything of that sort. Perhaps there will prove to be "nothing in him." I cannot tell. All that I am quite sure of is that he naturally likes what is delicate, clean, refined, and kindly, — and that he naturally shrinks from whatever is coarse or selfish. So that he *might* learn easily "the things that are most excellent" — and most useless — in the schooling of civilization. Anyhow, I must do all I can to feed the tiny light, and give it a chance to prove what it is worth. It is ME, in another birth — with renewed forces given by a strange and charming blood from the Period of the Gods. I must not risk the blowing out of the little lamp.

I heard that in the Stanford University in California, there are somewhat romantic conditions, —

KAZUO AND IWAO, MR. HEARN'S OLDER CHILDREN

"no ceremonies," no humbug, — estimates only of
"efficiency." Long ago I wrote the letter of application, and — like many a letter to you — posted
the same in the ravening stove. "Too idyllic," —
I thought to myself, — "in the present state of
evolution, no human institution could be suffered
to realize the ideals of that university!" If I were
wrong or right — I should like to know.

But sufficient for this writing is the perfect selfishness thereof. My dear fairy god-sister, please
do not take any painful trouble for me, *but* — if
you can hit something with your moonshiny wand,
during the next year or so, I shall be so glad! Even
though I be not glad, I shall always be grateful for
the last kind letter.

My best wishes to you in everything that you can
imagine, you will be always sure of. "If wishes"
— but, after all, there *is* some human sweetness in
these conventional phrases. They help one to utter
a mood, or a sense of gratefulness for pleasure
given.   LAFCADIO HEARN.

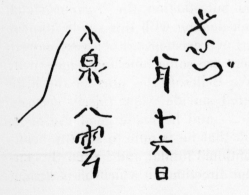

TO YRJÖ HIRN

YAIDZU, August, 1902.

DEAR PROFESSOR, — Your kind letter of July 20th is with me. . . .

I am so glad to hear that you are not likely to be obliged to leave Europe. It is perhaps the greatest possible misfortune for a man of culture to find himself obliged to withdraw from intellectual centres to a new raw country, where the higher mental life is still imperfectly understood. There are certain compensations, indeed, — such as larger freedom, and release from useless conventions, but these do not fully make up for the sterility of that American atmosphere in which the more delicate flowers of thought refuse to grow. I am delighted to think of your prospective pleasure in the Italian paradise.

I am writing to you from the little fishing-village of Yaidzu — where there are no tables or chairs.

Bellesort's book is a surprisingly good book in its way. It describes *only* the disintegration of Japanese society — under the contact of Western ideas — the social putrefaction, the *dégringolade* of things. As a book dealing with this single unpleasant phase of Japanese existence, it is a very powerful book; and there are some touching pages in it. It was I who gave Bellesort the story of the little boy who committed suicide when falsely accused of stealing a cake, — and he made good use of it. . . . I don't think that he is able to see the beautiful out of conventional limits; and he mostly confines himself to the directions in which he is strong.

I am inclined to believe that his sympathies are clerical — that he presents Brunetière and the Jesuit side of things. However, his book is the best thing of its kind yet produced — the critical kind. It requires a special nervous structure, like that of Pierre Loti, to see the strange beauty of Japan. Let me, however, advise you to read many times the charming book of the American, Percival Lowell, — "The Soul of the Far East." It is strange that Lowell should have written the very best book in the English language on the old Japanese life and character, and the most startling *astronomical* book of the period, — "Mars," — more interesting than any romance. . . .   LAFCADIO HEARN.

Tōkyō, September, 1902.

MY DEAR HENDRICK, — I had to wait several days before answering your letter, — as I felt too much pleased to venture writing for that length of time. And now, in answering, I shall have to talk a great deal about myself, and my own affairs, — which seems to me rather graceless.

All that you proposed, except two things, appear to me very good. But to put the question in the best *general* way, I am convinced by long experience that I can do nothing profitable with publishers, except at such serious cost to health and to literary reputation as would be utterly prohibitive. What I have been able to do so far has been done mostly in dead opposition to publishers, and their advisers; and in the few cases where I tried to do what publishers wished I have made very serious mistakes.

Editorial work on a monthly or weekly paper, with a sympathetic head, who would let me have my own way, and use a typewriter — let me agree to furnish at fixed intervals certain material, while free to use the over-time as I pleased — would be good. . . .

Of course, the main trouble about any kind of newspaper work is that it kills all opportunity for original literary work — but I could afford the sacrifice.

Certain branches of teaching admit of opportunity for literary work, — particularly those in which teaching rises to the dignity of the lecture. . . .

The main result of holding a chair of English literature for six years has been to convince me that I know very little about English literature, and never could learn very much. I have learned enough, indeed, to lecture upon the general history of English literature, without the use of notes or books; and I have been able to lecture upon the leading poets and prose-writers of the later periods. But I have not the scholarship needed for the development and exercise of the critical faculty, in the proper sense of the term. I know nothing of Anglo-Saxon: and my knowledge of the relation of English literature to other European literature is limited to the later French and English romantic and realistic periods.

Under these circumstances you might well ask

how I could fill my chair. The fact is that I never made any false pretences, and never applied for the post. I realized my deficiencies; but I soon felt where I might become strong, and I taught literature as the expression of emotion and sentiment, — as the representation of life. In considering a poet I tried to explain the quality and the powers of the emotion that he produces. In short, I based my teaching altogether upon appeals to the imagination and the emotions of my pupils, — and they have been satisfied (though the fact may signify little, because their imagination is so unlike our own).

Should I attempt to lecture on literature in America, I should only follow the same lines—which are commonly held to be illegitimate, but in which I very firmly believe there are great possibilities. Subjects upon which I think that I have been partly successful are such as these: —

The signification of Style and Personality.

Respective values of various styles. Error of the belief that one method is essentially superior to another.

Physiological signification of the true Realism— as illustrated by the Norse writers and, in modern times, by Flaubert and Maupassant. Psychological signification of Romantic methods.

Metaphysical poetry of George Meredith: illustrating the application of the Evolutional Philosophy to Ethics.

D. G. Rossetti and Christina Rossetti.

The Poetical Prose and the Poetry of Charles Kingsley.

Four great masters of modern prose: Carlyle, Ruskin, De Quincey, Froude.

The mystical element in modern lyric verse. (I use the term "mystical" in the meaning of a blending of the religious with the passional emotion.)

Of the truth and the ideal beauty in Tolstoi's Theory of Art.

"Beyond man:"— a chapter upon the morality of insect-communities, — suggesting the probable lines of ethical evolution.

Very heterogeneous, this list; but I have purposely made it so. I have had to lecture upon hundreds of subjects, without ever having had the time to write a lecture. (I have to lecture here twelve hours a week, on four different subjects — and to do one's best is out of the question. The authorities never pay the slightest attention to what the professor does; *but they hold him strictly responsible for the success of his lectures!*) . . .

I think that I have hinted ways in which I might be able to make myself useful — i. e., in the teaching of certain literary values. — There is also the subject of Composition (method, independently of grammatical and rhetorical rules). The hard experience of writing certain kinds of books ought to be of some practical worth. The art of what *not* to say, — the art of focussing effects, — the means of avoiding imitation (even of the unconscious order), and of developing a literary personality; — these can be talked of, I think, without a knowledge of Greek or Sanscrit. I really think that I could do some good by lecturing on these things —

though conscious of having often failed in the very directions that I should recommend.

One thing more, I must not forget to say. I cannot be separated from my boy — not even for twenty-four hours. I have taught him about three hours a day every day for several years. When he becomes a little older, I may be able to let him attend a *day*-school; but at present, I imagine that this would be difficult. I feel handicapped; but it can't be helped, and the race is for him.

Summary: As a cog in a wheel I should probably break off. As a personal equation I might have some worth. And I can wait a full year for a chance.

Your letter was a wonderful event for me — a great and happy surprise. The Fairy Queen also wrote me a beautiful letter (I suppose that all she does is beautiful): I had to read it many times to learn the full charm of it. I have lost all power to write a nice letter of thanks — feel stupid.

We have a nice home a little out of Tōkyō — to which I should not be ashamed to invite you, or even the Fairy Queen: only, you would have to take off your shoes, for it is a Japanese house.

I shall try to atone later on for the great length of this weary scrawl: how tired you must be after reading it! All happiness to you. Be sure that, whether I win or fail, I shall never be able to even tell you how sincerely and deeply I remain grateful for that letter.

Y. KOIZUMI, LAFCADIO HEARN.

TO ELLWOOD HENDRICK

Tōkyō, 1902.

Dear Hendrick, — I am glad to hear that you are a strong and successful swimmer in that awful sea of struggle, and that your home is happy. Having two little ones, you can understand now what the Japanese call *Mono no aware*, — weirdly translated by Aston as "the Ah-ness of things."[1]

Thanks for the Martinique clippings. The Swede's account seems to me possibly apocryphal, — for his localizations are all wrong. The other man did, apparently, visit Saint-Pierre, and explore the vicinity. — I opened and re-read that black day a letter from Saint-Pierre, enclosing a spray of arborescent fern, labelled "From the sunny garden."

The time is approaching in which I must go abroad, for my boy's sake. To Queen Elizabeth I wrote, asking for a possible smoothing of the way; and if you can put a spoke in my wheel any time about next spring, or during the summer, I should be as grateful as I can — which is nothing to brag of, I need scarcely say. I should like some easy post, for about two years. "Easy posts" must be in sharp demand; and I am not sure that I am asking for the possible. New York is, of course, the place where I do not want to go — for my lad's sake; but I shall probably make a flying trip there, — if the gods allow.

For the time being, I am with Macmillan. But I fancy really that all publishers regard authors

---

[1] More literally, "the pity of things."

merely as units in a calculation, — excepting the great guns who, like Kipling, can force strong respect. I need scarcely tell you that my books do not make me rich. In fact, I have given up thinking about the business side of literature, and am quite content to obtain the privilege of having my book produced according to my notion of things. Still, by reason of various translations into Swedish, Danish, German and French, I have some literary encouragements.

I believe you know that I have three boys: they are sturdy lads all — though the eldest is rather too gentle up to date. I live altogether in Old Japan, outside of lecture-hours; and might think myself lucky, but for that "Ah-ness of things." Of course, I have become somewhat old — it is more than twelve years since I saw you! And then I have had to learn a multitude unspeakable of unpleasant things. But, as they say here, *Shikata ga nai!* There's no help for that!

Japan is changing rapidly, as you can imagine; and the changes are not beautiful. I try to keep within fragments of the old atmosphere — that linger here and there, like those bands of morning-coloured mist which you have seen spanning Japanese pictures. Within these wreaths of the lifting mirage, all is Fairy-land still; and my home will always have its atmosphere of thousands of years ago. But in the raw light outside, the changings are ugly and sad.

Ever faithfully,

Y. KOIZUMI.

TO MRS. WETMORE

TŌKYŌ, November, 1902.

DEAR MRS. WETMORE, — . . . I have had your beautiful letter in my drawer for about a week, before daring to re-read it. And I have been thinking in circles, — about how to answer it.

For — O fairy! what have you dared to say? I am quite sure that I do *not* know anything about Japanese art, or literature, or ethnology, or politics, or history. (You did not say "politics" or "history," however, and that seems to be what is wanted.) But perhaps you know *what* I know better than I myself know,—or perhaps you can give me to eat a Fairy Apple of Knowledge. At present I have no acquaintance even with the Japanese language: I cannot read a Japanese newspaper; and I have learned only enough, even of the *kana*, to write a letter home. I cannot lie — to my Fairy: therefore it is essential that I make the following declaration:—

I have learned about Japan only enough to convince me that I know nothing about Japan.

Perhaps your kind professor suspects as much; — for has he not plainly said that no (American) university would hire me to teach English or French literature? That means accurate perception of my range, in one direction. Possibly, therefore, he would not expect from me any attempts at a pretence of exact knowledge.

I have held a chair of English literature here for nearly seven years, by setting all canons at defiance,

and attempting to teach only the emotional side of
literature, in its relations to modern thought; —
playing with philosophy, as a child can play with
the great sea. I have been allowed to do just as
I pleased, — on the condition of being interesting
(which condition the students take care shall be
fulfilled). Should I attempt to lecture about Japan,
I imagine that it would be necessary to allow me
nearly the same liberty in America. I might hope
to be suggestive, — to set minds dreaming or
darkling in new directions. But I could not pretend
to impart exact knowledge. I could not afford to
fail: that would be . . . a great shame to my
good name at home. So I cannot answer "Yes"
without being certain of my ability to perform all
that could be reasonably expected of me, — as a
small "man-of-letters" (not as anything else).

What I could do would be about thus: —

I could attempt a series of lectures upon Japanese
topics, — dealing incidentally with psychological,
religious, social, and artistic impressions, — so as
to produce in the minds of my hearers an idea of
Japan different from that which is given in books.
Something, perhaps, in the manner of Mr. Lowell's
"Soul of the Far East" (incomparably the greatest
of all books on Japan, and the deepest), — but
from a different point of view.

What I could not do would be to put myself forward as an authority upon Japanese history, or any
special Japanese subject. The value of my lectures
would depend altogether upon suggestiveness, —
not upon any crystallizations of fact.

Again, there is a doubt to be solved — concerning
quantity as well as quality. To do my best, I should
hope that quantity were not too strongly insisted
upon. How many lectures would be wanted during
one term — distinct lectures? and how many hours
would be demanded for a lecture? . . . You see,
the conditions in Tōkyō are monstrous: I have to
lecture twelve hours a week on *four* different subjects; — that means for lecturing what reporter's
work means in relation to literature! . . . I
imagine that I could endeavour to do something
about equal to the work of Professor Rhys-Davids
in his American lectures, — as to bulk. The six
lectures represent a volume of about 225 pages.
Lectures to represent, in printed form, a carefully
made book of about 250 or 300 pages would represent my best effort.

For I have reached that time of life at which "the
state of the weather" becomes a topic of enormous
importance.

And the rest of what has to be said I shall put
into a letter, which I pray you to read, and to poke
into the fire if it is not satisfactory.

To fail, after being recommended by you, would
be an unpardonable sin against all the higher
virtues. Can't risk it.

Well, if President Schurman can make good use
of me, and arrange things within my capacity, I
will go straight to your Palace of Faery before going
elsewhere. Only to see you again — even for a
moment, — and to hear you speak (in some one of
the Myriad Voices), would be such a memory for

me. And you would let me "walk about gently, touching things"? . . .

It is an almost divine pleasure and wonder to watch the unfolding of a soul-blossom, as you say, — providing that one is strong enough not to be afraid. I am, or have been, always afraid: the Future-Possible of Nightmare immediately glooms up, — and I flee, and bury myself in work. Absurd?

And your book — of course that will be some opportunity for a delightful chat. You will find me as good as I can be in expressing an opinion, — if the subject be within my range. I know that the work of such a person as — Mrs. Deland, for example — is beyond my limit; and I imagine that you would write of highly complex existences. . . .

Excuse my anxiety about my chicken. I want to feel sure that I can make him comfortable and warm if I do go to Cornell. I want to make all the money, too, that I honestly can earn, for his sake and the mother's. She will have some trying moments in the hour of parting with him. But there is no other future chance for him, and no educational place here to which I could trust him — least of all, the Jesuits. Very different it is with my second sturdy boy, who has no trace of European blood. His way is straight and smooth. I send his picture, that you may see the difference. And my third boy — sturdiest of all — will have other friends to help him, I fancy. . . .

LAFCADIO HEARN.

TO MRS. WETMORE

Tōkyō, January, 1903.

DEAR MRS. WETMORE, — It was a shock to receive your beautiful letter, because I had waited so long and anxiously, — fearing that the last gleam of hope in my Eastern horizon had been extinguished. It would be of no use whatever to tell you half my doubts and fears — they made the coming of your letter an almost terrible event.

Well, what *you* say about my work (always seizing upon the best in it, and showing such penetrant sympathy with its effort or aim) counts for more than a myriad printed criticisms.

My boy is accustomed to kissing — *from* his father only, who always so dismisses him at bedtime; and he understands very well the charm of Lady Elizabeth's sweet message, after hearing from me what the privilege signifies. But I have fairly given up the idea of taking him with me to America for the present. The risk is too great. I must try to make a nest for him first, and be sure of keeping alive myself.

In the mean time, I have been treated very cruelly by the Japanese Government, and forced out of the service by intrigues, — in spite of protests from the press, and from my students, who stood by me as long as they dared. To make matters worse, I fell sick; — I have been sick for months. About three weeks ago, I burst a blood-vessel, and I am not allowed to talk. So I fear that the lecture-business is out of the question; and I am not altogether sorry, because I do not know enough about the subject. I would wish never again to write a line about any Japanese subjects: all my work has only resulted in making for me implacable enemies.

The problem with me now is simply how I shall be able to live, and support my family. I must try to do something in America, — where the winter will not kill me off in a hurry. Literary work is over. When one has to meet the riddle of how to live there must be an end of revery and dreaming and all literary "labour-of-love." It pays not at all. A book brings me in about $300, — after two years' waiting. My last payment on four books (for six months) was $44. Also, in my case, good work is a matter of nervous condition. I can't find the conditions while having to think about home — with that fear for others which is "the most soul-satisfying" of fears, according to Rudyard Kipling. However, we are all right for the time being; and I can provide for the home before I go.

Thank you for telling me the name of your book. I had hard work to get your little volume of travel when it came out: ages pass here before an "ordered" book comes. But in America I can keep track of you. I want very much to see your book. It will either tell me very, very much about you — or it will tell me nothing of you, and therefore have the charm of the Unknowable. Oh! do read the divine Loti's "L'Inde sans les Anglais!" No mortal critic — not even Jules Lemaître or Anatole France — can explain that ineffable and superhuman charm. I hope you will have everything of Loti's.

Sometime ago, when I was afraid that I might die, one of my prospective regrets was that I might not be able to read "L'Inde sans les Anglais."

Much I should wish to see you in Japan — but human wishes! . . . Yet I think I could make you feel pleased for a little while — though our cooking be of the simplest. My little wife knows your face so well — your picture hangs now in her room. We have a garden, and a bamboo grove.

Now you must be tired reading me. As soon as I can feel well, I shall go to some fishing-village with my boy; and, if lucky, perhaps I shall leave for America in the fall. But nothing is yet certain. With all grateful thought from

LAFCADIO HEARN.

You cannot imagine how hungry and thirsty I have become to see you again, — or how much afraid I feel at times that I may not see you: though a season is short.

By waiting a few months more in Japan, I can, of course, make the lectures much better. But the time will seem long. Here the winter is very mild — but damp, as in New Orleans.

TO MRS. WETMORE

TŌKYŌ, 1903.

DEAR MRS. WETMORE, — You will probably have heard by this time that President Schurman cancelled the offer made me — by reason of the trouble at Cornell University. As I had taken several steps

in connection with that prospect, — the blow was
rather heavy; and this you will better understand
in view of the following facts: —

On the 31st March, as I anticipated, I was forced
out of the university — on the pretext that as a
Japanese citizen I was not entitled to a "foreign
salary." The students having made a strong protest
in my favour, I was offered a reëngagement at terms
so devised that it was impossible for me to reëngage.
I was also refused the money allowed to professors
for a nine-months' vacation after a service of six
years. Yet I had served seven years.

So the long and the short of the matter is that after
having worked during thirteen years for Japan, and
sacrificed everything for Japan, I have been only
driven out of the service, and practically banished
from the country. For while the politico-religious
combination that has engineered this matter remains
in unbroken power, I could not hold any position
in any educational establishment here for even six
months.

At my time of life, except in the case of strong men,
there is a great loss of energy — the breaking-up
begins. I do not think that I should be able to do
much that would require a sustained physical strain.
But if I could get some journalistic connection, assuring a regular salary, — for example, an engagement to furnish signed or unsigned articles, once or
twice a week, or even three times, — I believe that I
could weather the storm until such time as a political
reaction might help me to return to Japan. For my
boy's sake these events may prove fortunate, — if I

find an opportunity to take him abroad for two years.

At all events, O Fairy Queen, your gifts have "faded away" — even as in the Song, — and I am also fading away. I do not know whom else I should pray to, for the moment.

I have material evidence also that certain religious combinations want to prevent my chances in America; if you can help me to something journalistic, I imagine that it were better to let the matter remain unknown for the time being.

Perhaps I shall be able to leave Japan with McDonald (that would be nice!) — but only the gods know when *he* will return. Meantime, however, he gives me much comfort and promises me the fortunes of Aladdin. He seems to think I am quite safe and certain. But I am exercised about home — that is the chief trouble.

Please pardon this fresh appeal, — with all thanks for past kindness, and for those delightful letters.

Ever sincerely yours,
LAFCADIO HEARN.

TO MRS. WETMORE

TŌKYŌ, July, 1903.

DEAR MRS. WETMORE, — Your most kind letter is with me, — and I do not know what to say to thank you for the extraordinary interest and trouble that you have taken in my poor case. It is too bad that, having only one Fairy-Sister in the world, I should prove to her such a Torment. Perhaps I may be able to be at some future time a pleasure-giver — I shall pray to all the gods to help me thereunto.

Please do not worry about that Cornell matter: I suppose that President Schurman must have been in great anxiety and trouble when he wrote that letter.

You will be glad to hear that I am now much better than when I last wrote to you, and that I have finished most of the lectures — in rough draft. To polish them for publication will be at least a year's work, I fear; but I am now able, I think, to give a cultured audience a new idea of Japan, in large outline.

I have to be careful of my health for some time. Perhaps I shall get quite strong by the end of summer. But I am now only allowed to walk in the garden. . . .

I cannot write you a pretty letter: I have tried for two days, — but I feel so stupid.

What I want much is to get a little human sympathy and something quiet to do. Of course, I should like a university of all things, — but . . . is it possible? I have a new book in MS.; but as I was expecting to go to America, I did not send it to the publisher. It will chiefly consist of ghost-tales.

My dear Fairy-Sister, I now am writing only to reach you as soon as possible, — to thank you, and to reassure you about myself. So please excuse this poor effort, and believe me most gratefully worshipful.

LAFCADIO HEARN.

TO MRS. WETMORE

TŌKYŌ, 1903.

DEAR MRS. WETMORE, — Your letter from Virginia came, and made fires of hope burn up again, with changing vague colours, — like the tints of a fire of wreck-drift remembrance from the snowy winter of 1889. It has given me a great deal to think about — not merely as regards myself, but also as regards another and very dear person. . . .

I am delighted to read President Jordan's kind words. I shall write him a letter to-day, or to-morrow, enclosing it to you. From Johns Hopkins I have a reply, enclosed, — which does not promise much. I shall see what can be done there. But the Lowell Institute affair promises better. As for President Jordan, I should be glad to speak at Leland Stanford independently of salary, on the way going or coming — could no other arrangement be made. It strikes me, however, that there is danger of any and every arrangement being broken up. The power of certain religious bodies is colossal.

Spring would be the best time for me to go to America, if I can get through the spider-web now spun all around me. It would be the best time, because those lectures are taking handsome shape, towards a volume of 500 to 600 pp.; and it were a pity to leave anything unfinished before I go. Spring again would be the best time, because I am not yet so strong that I can face a down-East winter without some preparation. Spring would be the best time, because my fourth child is coming into the world.

Spring would be the best time, because I am getting
out a new book of ghost-stories, and would like to
read the proofs here, in Japan. I think it were im-
prudent to go before spring.

I have to think seriously about the money-question
— at 53, with a large family. To go to America
alone means $500 U.S., and as much to return —
that signifies 2000 yen; with which I can live in
Japan for two years. Then there are the necessary
expenses of living. To take my boy were a great
risk. Had the Japanese Government been willing
to pay me the vacation money they morally owed me
(about 5600 yen), I could have done it. (They told
me that I ought to be satisfied to live on rice, like
a Japanese.) Then I must be sure of being able to
send money home. At present there is no money
certainly in sight. But here I can live by my pen.
Since I was driven out of the university, I have not
been obliged to drop even one sen of my little hoard.
The danger is the risk to sight of incessant work;
but that danger would exist anywhere, except perhaps in a very hot country. And sooner or later the
Government must wake up to the fact that it was
wicked to me.

To go to America with some sense of security
would be mental medicine; and any success that I
could achieve there would make a good impression
here with friends. It would mean larger experience. It would mean also an opportunity to enter
some society that would protect liberal opinions.
I have not said much as to the pleasure I could look
forward to — that goes without saying. But I can-

not be rash on the money-question, or trust to my luck as in old days. To use a Japanese expression, "my body no longer belongs to me," — and I have had one physical warning.

Anxiety is a poison; and I do not know how much more of it I could stand. It was a friend's treachery that broke me up recently: I worked hard against the pain — only to find my mouth full of blood. With a boy on my hands, in a far-away city, and no certainties, I don't know that being brave would serve me much — the bodily machine has been so much strained here.

With a clear certainty ahead of being able to make some money, I could go, do good things, and return to Japan to write more books, — perhaps to receive justice also. In a few years more my boy will be strong enough to study abroad.

Very true what you say — no one can save him but himself, and unfortunately, though the oldest, he is my Benjamin. My second boy is at school, captain of his class, trusted to protect smaller boys. My eldest, taught only at home, between his father's knees, is everything that a girl might be, that a man should not be, — except as to bodily strength, — sensitive, loving pretty things, hurt by a word, always meditating about something — yet not showing any great capacity. I taught him to swim, and make him practise gymnastics every day; but the spirit of him is altogether too gentle. A being entirely innocent of evil — what chance for him in such a world as Japan? Do you know that terribly pathetic poem of Robert Bridges' — "Pater Filio"?

That reminds me to tell you of some obligations. You are never tired of telling me that I have been able to give you some literary pleasure. How many things did you not teach me during those evening chats in New York? It was you that first introduced me to the genius of Rudyard Kipling; and I have ever since remained a fervent worshipper. It was you who taught me to see the beauty of FitzGerald's translation, by quoting for me the stanza about the Moving Finger. And it was you who made me understand the extraordinary quaint charm of Ingelow's "High Tide" — since expounded to many a Japanese literary class. . . .

But this is too long a letter from

LAFCADIO HEARN.

TO MRS. WETMORE

TŌKYŌ, 1903.

DEAR MRS. WETMORE, — . . . I am getting quite strong, and hope soon to be strong, or nearly as strong, as before. The bleeding was from a bronchial tube, — so I have to be careful about getting cold. But my lungs are quite sound. For the sake of the lectures, it is better that I should wait a little longer in Japan. Most of them have been written twice; but I must write them all once more — to polish them. They will form a book, explaining Japan from the standpoint of ancestor-worship. They are suited only to a cultivated audience. If never delivered, they will still make a good book. The whole study is based upon the ancient religion.

I have also something to say about your proposed "Juvenilia."

I think this would be possible: —

To include in one volume under the title of "Juvenilia" — (1) the translations from Théophile Gautier, revised; (2) "Some Chinese Ghosts;" (3) miscellaneous essays and sketches upon Oriental subjects, formerly contributed to the *T.-D.*; (4) miscellaneous sketches on Southern subjects, two or three, and fantasies, — with a few verses thrown in.

For this I should need to have the French texts to revise, etc. Perhaps I shall be able to make the arrangement, and so please you. But I badly need help in the direction of good opinion among people of power. The prospect of "nothing" in America is frightening. I should be glad to try England; but scholars are there plentiful as little fleas in Florida; — and the power of convention has the force of an earthquake. When one's own adopted country goes back on one — there is small chance at the age of fifty-three.

Ever most gratefully,

L. H.

I tried to join the Masons here — but it appears that no Japanese citizen is allowed to become a Mason — at least not in Japan. The Japanese Minister in London could do it; but he could not have done it here.

TO MRS. HIRN

JULY, 1903.

DEAR MRS. HIRN, — Your very kind letter from Italy is with me. I am sorry to know that you have met with so painful a trial since I last wrote to you. Indeed, I hope you will believe that I am sincerely and sympathetically interested in the personal happiness or sorrow of any who wish me well, — and you need never suppose me indifferent to the affairs of which you speak so unselfishly and so touchingly.

By this time, no doubt, you will have seen much of the fairest land of Europe, and will scarcely know what to do with the multitude of new impressions crowding in memory for special recognition. Perhaps Italy will tempt you to do something more than translate: one who becomes soul-steeped in that golden air ought to feel sooner or later the impulse to create. I wish I could find my way to Italy: when a child I spoke only Italian, and Romaic. Both are now forgotten.

Thanks for the magazine so kindly sent me, and thanks for your explanation of that rendering of "ewigt" as signifying endlessness in space as well as time. That, indeed, settles the matter about which I was in doubt.

It is a pleasure to know that you received "Kotto," and liked some things in it. I thought your list of selections for translation very nice, — with one exception. "The Genius of Japanese Civilization" is a failure. I thought that it was true when I wrote it; but already Japan has become considerably changed, and a later study of ancient social conditions has proved to me that I made some very serious sociological errors in that paper. For example, in feudal times, up to the middle of the last century, there was really no possibility of travelling (for common people at least) in Japan. Iron law and custom fettered men to the soil, like the serfs of mediæval Europe. My paper, unfortunately, implied the reverse. And that part of the paper relating to the travelling of Japanese common people is hopelessly wrong as regards the past. As regards the present, it requires modification.

Your remark about the hard touch in Bellesort's book is very just. . . . He was accompanied by his wife, — born in Persia, and able to talk Persian. She was keener even than he, — a very clever silent woman, attractive rather than sympathetic. . . . Bellesort has been travelling a great deal; and "La Société Japonaise" is his best volume of travel. His book on South America is cruel.

I am not sure whether you would care for Nitôbé's book "Bushidō" — a very small volume, or rather treatise upon the *morale* of Samurai education. From a literary standpoint it would not tempt you: it is only a kind of "apology." But it is to some extent instructive. . . .

I suppose that Dr. Hirn will meet Domenico Comparetti, the author of "The Traditional Poetry of the Finns." I gave a lecture lately on the poetical values of the "Kalewala," and I found that book of great use to me.

Please excuse my loquacity, and let me wish you and the doctor every happiness and success. Perhaps I shall write you again — from America. Only the gods know.

Sincerely yours,
LAFCADIO HEARN.

TO MRS. WETMORE

TŌKYŌ, August, 1903.

DEAR MRS. WETMORE, — I am sorry for my dismal letter of the other day. I feel to-day much braver, and think that I can fight it out here in Japan. Anyhow, I have discovered that I have a fair chance of being able to live by my work — providing my health is good; and if I *must* live by my pen, there is no place in the world where I can do so more cheaply than here. When my boy is bigger, I may be able to send him abroad. Unless I could make money in America, it were little use to drop two thousand dollars (Japanese money) for going and coming. Besides, out of those lectures in book-form I shall make some money. . . .

For the present, I think that I shall simply sit down, and work as hard as Zola, — though that is to compare a gnat to an eagle. It only remains for me to express to you all possible devotion of gratitude. If I had dreamed of the real state of things, I should long ago have begged you to do nothing for me in high places. I have tried to break out of my chrysalis too soon, — but, with the help of the gods, my wings will grow. To have even one well-wisher like you in America, is much; — and I have a friend or two in England, some in France, some in Denmark, Sweden, and Russia. *Non omnis moriar* thus.

You will hear from me in print: — there I can give you pleasure, perhaps: I am not fit to write letters. But I am getting very strong again.

With reverential gratitude,

LAFCADIO HEARN.

TO MRS. WETMORE

TŌKYŌ, 1903.

DEAR MRS. WETMORE, — I have your kindest note of June 16th, and am returning, with unspeakable thanks, the letters forwarded. I have written also to President Remsen and to President Taylor, as you wished me to do, directly.

You will be glad to hear that I am almost strong again; but I fear that I shall never be strong enough to lecture before a general public. Before a university audience I could do something, I believe; but the strain of speaking in a theatre would be rather trying. The great and devouring anxiety is for some regular employ — something that will assure me the means to live. With that certainty, I can do much. Lecturing will, I fear, be at best a most hazardous means of living. But it may help me to something permanent. I have now nearly completed twenty-one lectures: they will form eventually a serious work upon Japan, entirely unlike anything yet written. The substantial idea of the lectures is that Japanese society represents the condition of ancient Greek society a thousand years before Christ. I am treating of religious Japan, — not of artistic or economical Japan, except by way of illustration. Lowell's "Soul of the Far East" is the only book of the kind in English; but I have taken a totally different view of the causes and the evolution of things.

I am worried about my boy — how to save him out of this strange world of cruelty and intrigue. And I dream of old ugly things — things that happened long ago. I am alone in an American city; and I have only ten cents in my pocket, — and to send off a letter that I must send will take three cents. That leaves me seven cents for the day's food. Now, I am not hard up, by any means: I can wait another six months in Japan without anxiety. But the horror of being without employ in an American city appalls me — because I remember. All of which is written in haste to catch the mail. How good you are! I ought not to tell you of any troubles of mine — but *if* I could not, what would have happened me?

LAFCADIO HEARN.

TO MRS. WETMORE

TŌKYŌ, October, 1903.

DEAR MRS. WETMORE, — I have had a charming letter from Vassar, — indicating that the president must be a charming person.

I have also — which surprised me — the most generous of letters from Sir William Van Horne,

President of the C. P. R. R., agreeing to furnish me with means of transportation, both ways, to Montreal and back to Japan. I shall have to do some writing, probably; but that is a great chance, and I am grateful.

French friends have taken up the cudgels for me against the Japanese Government — unknown friends. The *Aurore* had a 2-col. article entitled "*Ingratitude Nationale*," which somebody sent me from Italy. I am too much praised; but the reproach to Japan is likely to do me good. For I have really been badly treated, and the Government ought to be made ashamed.

I am *nearly* quite well, though not quite as strong as I should wish. My lectures, recast into chapters, will form a rather queer book — perhaps make a quite novel impression.

I have a little daughter; and all that anxiety is past. (If I could only get quite strong, I could make a good fight for myself later on.) Anyhow, I see no great difficulty about an American trip, once the sharp cold is over; and I think you will be glad of this note from your troublesome but always grateful

LAFCADIO HEARN.

TO MRS. WETMORE

TōKYō, December, 1903.

DEAR MRS. WETMORE, — . . . Of course your critics have been kind. Other things of yours seemed to have a distinct quality; but this is your Self, the clearest and dearest best of you. It is so much alive that I cannot believe I have been reading a story: I thought that I knew and remembered all the people and all that they said — surely none of the life in those pages could have been imagined! I am puzzled by the brightness of the memories and the freshness of the feeling: the real world of self-seeking has such power to dull and numb that I cannot understand how you could have conserved the whole delightfulness of child-experience in spite of New York. . . .

With me all the past is a blur — except the pain of it. It is not so much what one sees in your story, or what one hears folk say, that makes the thing so pleasing: it is rather the soft appeal made to one's moral understanding. I mean that I never imagined how good and brave and lovable those people were till you made me comprehend. And I felt about as "home-sick" as it is lawful for a Japanese citizen to feel. But I am afraid that your very own South is now of the past: — wherefore we can appreciate it incomparably more than when it was our every-day environment. . . .

LAFCADIO HEARN.

TO TANABE

TŌKYŌ, January, 1904.

DEAR MR. TANABE, — I received your kind New Year's greeting, and your good letter; and if I have delayed so long in replying, it has been only because, for some weeks past, I have not had five minutes to spare.

I was much touched by the sad news about your little girl, — and I can understand all that one does not write about such matters. Some nine years ago, I very nearly lost my little boy: we sat up with him night after night for weeks, always dreading that he was to be taken from us. Fortunately he was saved; but the pain of such an experience is not easily forgotten. As a general rule, the first child born to young parents is difficult to bring up. With the next, it is very different; — perhaps you will be more fortunate later on. One has to be brave about such matters. When Goethe was told of the death of his only son, he exclaimed: "Forward — over the dead!" and sat down to write, though the blow must have been terrible to him, — for he was a loving father.

I suppose that Mr. Ibaraki will soon be coming back to Japan. He deserves much success and praise; — for he had great obstacles to overcome as a student, and triumphed over them. I do not know who told him that I was going to England; but several persons were so — incorrectly — informed. Whether I shall go or not remains for the present undecided.

Of course the real philosophy of "Undine" is the development of what Germans call "the Mother-Soul" in a young girl. By marriage and maternity certain beautiful qualities of character are suddenly evolved, which had remained invisible before. The book is a parable — that is why it has become a world-classic.

What you tell me about your reading puzzles

me a little. One must read, I suppose, whatever one
can get in the way of English books at Kanazawa.
Still, if my advice be worth anything, I should
especially recommend you to avoid most of the
current novel literature — except as mere amusement. The lasting books are few; but one can read
them over so many times, with fresh pleasure every
time. I should think, however, that Stevenson
would both please and profit you, — the last of the
great nineteenth-century story-tellers.

May all happiness and success come to you is the
sincere wish of   Y. KOIZUMI.

TO ERNEST CROSBY

Tōkyō, August, 1904.

DEAR MR. CROSBY, — A namesake of yours, a
young lieutenant in the United States Army, first
taught me, about twenty years ago, how to study
Herbert Spencer. To that Crosby I shall always feel
a very reverence of gratitude; and I shall always
find myself inclined to seek the good opinion of any
man bearing the name of Crosby.

I received recently a copy of *The Whim* containing some strictures upon the use of the word
"regeneration," in one of my articles, as applied to
the invigorating and developing effects of militancy
in the history of human societies. I am inclined to
agree with you that the word was ill-chosen; but it
seems to me that your general attitude upon the
matter is not in accordance with evolutional truth.
Allow me to quote from Spencer: —

"The successive improvements of the organs of
sense and motion, and of the internal coördinating
apparatus, which uses them, have indirectly resulted
from the antagonisms and competitions of organisms
with one another. A parallel truth is disclosed on
watching how there evolves the regulating system
of a political aggregate, and how there are developed
those appliances for offence and defence put in action by it. Everywhere the wars between societies
originate governmental structures, and are causes
of all such improvements in these structures as
increase the efficiency of corporate action against
environing societies."

The history of social evolution, I think, amply
proves that the higher conditions of civilization have
been reached, and could have been reached, only
through the discipline of militancy. Until human
nature becomes much more developed than it is now,
and the sympathies incomparably more evolved,
wars will probably continue; and however much we
may detest and condemn war as moral crime, it will
be scarcely reasonable to declare that its results are
purely evil, — certainly not more reasonable than
to assert that to knock down a robber is equally
injurious to the moral feelings of the robber and
to the personal interest of the striker. As for "regeneration"— the Reformation, the development
of European Protestantism and of intellectual liberty, the French Revolution, the Independence of
the United States (to mention only a few instances
of progress), were rendered possible only by war.
As for Japan — immediately after her social organ-

ization had been dislocated by outside pressure, —
and at a time when serious disintegrations seemed
likely, — the results of the war with China were
certainly invigorating. National self-confidence
was strengthened, national discords extinguished,
social disintegrations checked, the sentiment of
patriotism immensely developed. To understand
these things, of course, it is necessary to understand
the Japanese social organization. What holds true
of one form of society, as regards the evil of war,
does not necessarily hold true of another.

Yours faithfully,
LAFCADIO HEARN.

I have reopened the envelope to acknowledge
your interesting sketch of Edward Carpenter. . . .
What an attractive personality.

But I fear that I must shock you by my declaration of non-sympathy with much of the work of
contemporary would-be reformers. They are toiling
for socialism; and socialism will come. It will come
very quietly and gently, and tighten about nations
as lightly as a spider's web; and then there will be
revolutions! Not sympathy and fraternity and justice — but a Terror in which no man will dare to
lift his voice.

No higher condition of human freedom ever
existed than what America enjoyed between — let
us say, 1870 and 1885. To effect higher conditions,
a higher development of human nature would have
been necessary. Where have American liberties
now gone? A free press has ceased to exist. Within

another generation publishers' syndicates will decide what the public shall be allowed to read. A man can still print his thoughts in a book, though not in any periodical of influence; within another twenty years he will write only what he is told to write. It is a pleasure to read the brave good things sometimes uttered in prints like the *Conservator* or *The Whim;* but those papers are but the candlesticks in which free thought now makes its last flickering. In the so-called land of freedom men and women are burnt at the stake in the presence of Christian churches — for the crime of belonging to another race. The stake reëstablished for the vengeance of race-hatred to-day, may to-morrow be maintained for the vengeance of religious hate — mocking itself, of course, under some guise of moral zeal. Competition will soon be a thing of the past; and the future will be to your stock-companies, trusts, and syndicates. The rule of the many will be about as merciful as a calculating-machine, and as moral as a lawn-mower. What socialism means really no one seems to know or care. It will mean the most insufferable oppression that ever weighed upon mankind.

Here are gloomy thoughts for you! You see that I cannot sympathize with the Whitmanesque ideal of democracy. That ideal was the heart-felt expression of a free state that has gone by. It was in itself a generous dream. But social tendencies, inevitable and irresistible, are now impelling the dreamers to self-destruction. The pleasure that in other times one could find in the literature of

humanity, of brotherhood, of pity, is numbed
to-day by perception of the irresistible drift of things.
Ever faithfully yours,

L. HEARN.

TO MRS. WETMORE

TŌKYŌ, September, 1904.

DEAR MRS. WETMORE, — To see your handwriting again upon the familiar blue envelope was
a great pleasure; and what the envelope contained,
in the same precious text, was equally delightful . . .
excepting some little words of praise which I do not
deserve, and which you ought not to have penned.
At least they might have been altered so as to better
suggest your real meaning — for you must be aware
that as to what is usually termed "life" I have less
than no knowledge, and have always been, and will
always remain, a dolt and a blunderer of the most
amazing kind. . . .

I left the dedication of the "Miscellany" un-
touched, — because the book is not a bad book in its
way, and perhaps you will later on find no reason to
be sorry for your good opinions of the writer. I
presume that you are far too clever to believe more
than truth, — and I stand tolerably well in the
opinion of a few estimable people, in spite of adverse
tongues and pens.

That little story of which you tell me the outline was admirable as an idea. I wish that you had
sent me a copy of it. But you never sent me any of
your writings, after I departed from New York —

except that admirable volume of memories and portraits. Of course, that paper about the morals of the insect-world was intended chiefly (so far as there was any intention whatever) to suggest to some pious people that the philosophy of Evolution does not teach that the future must belong to the strong and selfish "blond beast," as Nietzsche calls him — quite the contrary. Renan hinted the same fact long ago; but he did not, perhaps, know how English biologists had considered the ethical suggestion of insect-sociology.

In spite of all mishaps, I did tolerably well last year — chiefly through economy; — made money instead of losing any. I have a professorship in Count Okuma's university (small fees but ample leisure); and I was able to take my boys to live with the fishermen for a month — on fish, rice, and sea-water (with sake, of course, for their sire). I have got strong again; and can use the right arm as well as ever for swimming. . . .

The "rejected addresses" will shortly appear in book-form. The book is not what it ought to be — everything was against me — but it ought to suggest something to somebody. I don't like the work of writing a serious treatise on sociology. It requires training beyond my range; and I imagine that the real sociologist, on reading me, must smile —

"as a Master smiles at one
That is not of his school, nor any school,
Save that where blind and naked Ignorance
Delivers brawling judgement, unashamed,
On all things, all day long." . . .

I ought to keep to the study of birds and cats and insects and flowers, and queer small things — and leave the subject of the destiny of empires to men of brains. Unfortunately, the men of brains will not state the truth as they see it. If you find any good in the book, despite the conditions under which it was written, you will recognize your share in the necessarily ephemeral value thereof.

May all good things ever come to you, and abide.

Yours faithfully always,

LAFCADIO HEARN.

TO H. FUJISAKI

SEPTEMBER 26, 1904.[1]

DEAR CAPTAIN, — Your most welcome letter reached us to-day. It was a great pleasure to receive it, and to know that you are well and strong. You have often been in my thoughts and dreams. And, of course, we have been anxious about you. But the gods seem to be taking good care of you; and your position is, from our point of view, supremely fortunate. That a bright future is before you, I cannot doubt, — in spite of the chances of war.

As you see the papers here, it will not be worth while to send you any general news. As for local news, — things are very quiet, just as when you were here. But many men of Ōkubo-mura have been summoned to the front. Nearly all the young gardeners, fruit-sellers, kurumaya, etc., have been called. So the district is, perhaps, a little more

---

[1] The day of Hearn's death.

lonesome. We had regiments stationed here for a while. When the soldiers were going away, they gave toys to the children of the neighbourhood. To Kazuo they gave a little clay-model of a Russian soldier's head, and one said: "When we come back, we will bring you a real one." We prize that funny little gift, as a souvenir of the giver and the time.

Summer was dry, hot, and bright — we had very little rain after July. But during July, — the early part, — it used to rain irregularly, in a strange way; — and with the rain there was much lightning. Several persons in Tōkyō were killed by the lightning. I imagined that the war had something to do with the disturbed state of the atmosphere. After a heavy rain we generally had the news of a victory; so, when it began to rain hard, I used to say, "Ah! the Russians are in trouble again!"

We went to Yaidzu for about twenty days, and got strong and brown. Iwao was positively black when he returned. He learned to swim a little, and was able to cross the river on his back — where it was quite deep; — but the sea was rather too rough for him. We found that seventeen men of Yaidzu had been summoned to the war, — including several pleasant acquaintances.

Your good mother writes to us; and all your household seem to be as well and as happy as could be expected, — considering the natural anxieties of the war. Even for me, a stranger, the war has been trying; it was a long time before I could get used to the calling of the newspaper-lads, selling

LAFCADIO HEARN'S GRAVE

extras (*gogwai*). But the people of Tōkyō have
been very cheerful and brave. Nobody seems to
have any doubt as to the results of the campaign.

I am still hoping to see you next spring, or at
latest in summer. For this hope, however, I have
no foundation beyond the idea that Russia will
probably find, before long, that she must think of
something else besides fighting with Japan. The
commercial powers of the world are disturbed by
her aggression; and industrial power, after all, is
much more heavy than all the artillery of the Czar.
Whatever foreign sympathy really exists is with
Japan. In any event Russia must lose Manchuria,
I fancy.

What strange and unimagined experiences you
must have been passing through. Since the time
of the great war between France and Germany,
there were never such forces opposed to each other
as those that met at Liaoyang. It seems to me a
wonderful thing that I am able to send a letter to the
place of so vast a contest.

I shall try to send you something to read of the
kind you mention. My boys are writing to you —
Kazuo in English; Iwao in his native language.
May all good fortune be with you is the sincere
wish of your friend,

Y. KOIZUMI.

CONCLUSION

WITH Mrs. Hearn's quaint and tender record of Lafcadio Hearn's last days, his "Life and Letters" may fitly conclude.

About 3 P. M. Sept. 19th, 1904, as I went to his library I found him walking to and fro with his hands upon the breast. I asked him: "Are you indisposed?" Husband: "I got a new sickness." I: "What is your new sickness?" Husband: "The heart-sickness." I: "You are always over anxious." At once I sent for our doctor Kizawa with a jin-rikisha furnished with two riksha men. He would not let myself and children see his painful sight, and ordered to leave him. But I stayed by him. He began writing. I advised him to be quiet. "Let me do as I please," he said, and soon finished writing. "This is a letter addressed to Mr. Ume. Mr. Ume is a worthy man. He will give you a good counsel when any difficulty happen to you. If any greater pain of this kind comes upon me I shall perhaps die," he said; and then admonished me repeatedly and strongly that I ought to keep myself healthy and strong; then gave me several advices, hearty, earnest, and serious, with regard to the future of children, concluding with the words, "Could you understand?" Then again he said: "Never weep if I die. Buy for my coffin a little earthen pot of three or four cents worth; bury me in the yard of a little temple in some lonesome quarter. Never be sorry. You had better play cards with children. Do not inform to others of my departure. If any should happen to inquire of me, tell him: "Ha! he died sometime ago. That will do." I eagerly remonstrated: "Pray, do not speak such melancholy things. Such will never happen." He said: "This is a serious matter." Then saying "It cannot be held," he kept quiet.

A few minutes passed; the pain relaxed. "I would like to take bath," he said. He wanted cold bath; went to the bath-room and took a cold bath. "Strange!" he said, "I am quite well now." He recovered entirely, and asked me: "Mamma San! Sickness flew away from me. Shall I take some whiskey?" I told him: "I fear whiskey will not be good for heart. But if you are so fond of it I will offer it to you mixed with some water." Taking up the cup, he said: "I shall no more die." He then told me for the first time that a few days ago he had the same experience of pain. He lay down upon the bed then with a book. When the doctor arrived at our house, "What shall I do?" he said. Leaving the book, he went out to the parlour, and said "Pardon me, doctor. The sickness is gone." The doctor found no bad symptom, and jokes and chattering followed between them.

He was always averse to take medicine or to be attended by a doctor. He would never take medicine if I had not been careful; and if I happen to be late in offering him medicine he would say: "I was glad thinking you had forgot." If not engaged in writing, he used to walk in meditation to and fro in the room or through the corridor. So even in the time of sickness he would not like to remain quiet in confinement.

One day he told me in gladness: "Mamma San! I am very pleased about this." I asked him what it was. "I wrote this newspaper article: 'Lafcadio Hearn disappeared from the world.' How interesting! The world will see me no more — I go away in secret — I shall become a hermit — in some remote mountain, with you and with Kazuo."

It was a few days before his departure. Osaki, a maid, the daughter of Otokitsu of Yaidzu, found a blossom untimely blooming in one of the branches of cherry-tree in the garden. She told me about that. Whenever I saw or heard anything interesting I always told it to him; and this proved his greatest enjoyment. A very trifling matter was in our home very often highly valued. For instance, as the following things: —

To-day a young shoot appeared on a musa basjoo in the garden.

Look! an yellow butterfly is flying there.

In the bamboo bushes, a young bamboo-sprout raised its head from the earth.

Kazuo found a mound made by ants.

A frog is just staying on the top of the hedge.

From this morning the white, the purple, and the red blossoms of the morning-glory began to bloom, etc., etc.

Matters like those had great importance in our household. These things were all reported to him. They were great delight for my husband. He was pleased innocently. I tried to please him with such topics with all my heart. Perhaps if any one happened to witness, it would have seemed ridiculous. Frogs, ants, butterflies, bamboo-sprouts, morning-glory, — they were all the best friends to my husband.

Now, the blossom was beautiful to look. But I felt all at once my bosom tremble for some apprehension of evil, because the untimely bloom is considered in Japan as a bad omen. Anyhow I told him of the blossom. He was interested as usual. "Hello!" he said, and immediately approaching to the railing, he looked out at the blossom. "Now my world has come — it is warm, like spring," said he; then after a pause, "but soon it will become cold and that blossom will die away." This blossom was upon the branch till the 27th, when toward the evening its petals scattered themselves lonesomely. Methought the cherry-tree, which had Hearn's warmest affection for these years, responded to his kindness and bade good-bye to him.

Hearn was an early riser; but lest he should disturb the sleep of myself and children, he was always waiting for us and keeping quiet in the library, sitting regularly upon the cushion and smoking with a charcoal-brazier before him, till I got up and went to his library.

In the morning of Sept. 26th — the sad, last day — as I went to his library about 6.30 A. M., he was already quietly sitting as usual on the cushion. "Ohayō gozaimasu" (good-morning) I said. He seemed to be thinking over something, but upon my salutation he said his "good-morning," and told me that he had an interesting dream last night, for we were accustomed to tell each other when we had a pleasant dream. "What was it," I asked. He said: "I had a long, distant journey. Here I am smoking now, you see. Is it real that I travelled or is it real that I am smoking? The world of dream! . . . " Thus saying he was pleased with himself.

Before going to bed, our three boys used to go to his library and say in English: "Papa! Good-night! Pleasant dream!" Then he says in Japanese: "Dream a good dream," or in English: "The same to you."

On this morning when Kazuo, before leaving home for school, went to him, and said a "good-morning," he said: "Pleasant dream." Not knowing how to say, Kazuo answered: "The same to you."

About eleven o'clock in the morning, while walking to and fro along the corridor, he looked into my sitting-room and saw the picture hung upon the wall of alcove. The picture entitled "Morning Sun," represented a glorious, but a little mistic, scene of seashore in the early morning with birds thronging. "A beautiful scenery! I would like to go to such a land," he remarked.

He was fond of hearing the note of insects. We kept *matsu mushi* (a kind of cricket) this autumn.

Toward evening the plaintive notes which matsu mushi made at intervals made me feel unusually lonesome. I asked my husband how it sounded to him. He said: "That tiny creature has been singing nicely. It's getting cold, though. Is it conscious or unconscious that soon it must die? It's a pity, indeed." And, in a lonesome way, he added: "Ah, poor creature! On one of these warm days let us put him secretly among the grasses."

Nothing particularly different was not to be observable in all about him that day through. But the single blossom of untimely cherry, the dream of long journey he had, and the notes of matsu mushi, all these make me sad even now, as if there had existed some significance about them. At supper he felt sudden pain in the breast. He stopped eating; went away to his library; I followed him. For some minutes, with his hands upon his breast, he walked about the room. A sensation of vomiting occurred to him. I helped him, but no vomiting. He wanted to lie on bed. With his hands on breast, he kept very calm in bed. But, in a few minutes after, he was no more the man of this side of the world. As if feeling no pain at all, he had a little smile about his mouth.

APPENDIX

THE following was one of Hearn's general lectures at the University of Tōkyō as it was taken down at the time of its delivery by T. Ochiai, one of his students. It contains, together with some characteristic literary opinions, striking evidence of the curious felicity of Hearn's method of approach to the Japanese mind.

NAKED POETRY

Before beginning the regular course of literary lectures this year, I want to make a little discourse about what we may call Naked Poetry — that is, poetry without any dress, without any ornament, the very essence or body of poetry unveiled by artifice of any kind. I use the word artistically, of course — comparing poetry to an artistic object representing either a figure or a fact in itself, without any accessories.

Now for a few words about poetry in general. All the myriad forms of verse can be classed in three divisions without respect to subject or method. The highest class is the poetry in which both the words, or form, and the emotion expressed are equally admirable and super-excellent. The second divi-

sion in importance is that kind of poetry in which
the emotion or sentiment is the chief thing, and the
form is only a secondary consideration. The third
and least important class of poetry is that in which
the form is everything, and the emotion or sentiment is always subordinated to it. Now scarcely
any modern poem of great length entirely fulfils the
highest condition. We have to go back to the old
Greek poetry to find such fulfilment. But the second
class of poetry includes such wonderful work as the
poetry of Shakespeare. The third class of poetry
is very fairly represented in English literature by
the work of Pope and the dead classic school. To-day
— I mean at this moment in England — the tendency is bad: it is again setting in the direction of
form rather than of sentiment or thought.

This will be sufficient to explain to you what I
shall [mean] in future lectures by speaking of perfect
poetry, or second class poetry, or inferior poetry,
independently of qualifications. But I must also
ask you to accept my definition of the word poetry —
though it is somewhat arbitrary. By poetry, true
poetry, I mean, above all, that kind of composition
in verse which deeply stirs the mind and moves the
heart — in another word, the poetry of feeling.
This is the true *literary signification* of poetry; and
this is why you will hear some kinds of prose spoken
of as great poetry, — although it is not in any way
like verse; an important difference of the kind
above referred to has been recognized, I am told,
by Japanese poets.

They have, at all events, declared that a perfect

poem should leave something in the mind, — something not said, but suggested, — something that makes a thrill in you after reading the composition. You will therefore be very well able to see the beauty of any foreign verses which can fulfil this condition with very simple words. Of course when academic language, learned words, words known only to Greek or Latin scholars, are used, such poetry is almost out of the question. Popular language, in English at least, is the best medium for emotional poetry of certain kinds. But even without going to dialect, or descending to colloquialisms, great effects can be produced with very plain common English — provided that the poet sincerely feels. Here is a tiny but very famous little verse, which I would call an example of naked poetry — pure poetry without any kind of ornament at all. It has only rhymes of [one] syllable; but even if it had no rhymes at all it would still be great poetry. And what is more, I should call it something very much resembling in quality the spirit of Japanese poetry. However, you can judge for yourselves:—

> Four ducks on a pond,
> A grass-bank beyond,
> A blue sky of spring,
> White clouds on the wing:
> What a little thing
> To remember for years—
> To remember with tears!

It reads like nothing in particular until you get to the last line; — then the whole picture comes suddenly into your mind with a shock, and you understand. It is an exile's memory of home, one instant of childhood shining out in memory, after all the rest of memory has become dark. So it is very famous, and really wonderful — although there is no art in it at all. It is simple as a song.

Now English poetry contains very few inspirations like that — which, by the way, was the work of an Irishman, William Allingham. The remarkable thing about it is the effect made by so small a thing. But we have a few English poets who touched the art of divine simplicity—of pure emotion independent of form; and one of these was Kingsley. You know several of his songs which show this emotional power; but I am not sure whether you know "Airly Beacon."

"Airly Beacon" is a little song; but it is the story of the tragedy of life — you never can forget it after once reading it. And you have no idea what you are reading until you come to the last line. I must tell you that the place for "Airly Beacon" is a high place in Scotland, — from the top of which a beautiful view can be obtained, — and it is called Airly Beacon because in ancient time a signal-fire, or beacon-fire, used to be lighted upon it. Bearing this in mind you will be better able to judge the effect of the poem. I must also remind you that in England and America young girls are allowed a great deal of liberty in regard to what is called "courtesy" [courting?], that is to say, being wooed, or made love to under promise of marriage. The idea is that a girl should have sufficient force of will

to be able to take care of herself when alone with
a man. If she has not — then she might have [to]
sing the song of Airly Beacon. But *perhaps* the
girl in this case was not so importunate [un-
fortunate?]; we may imagine that she became a
wife and very early a widow. The song does not
say.

> Airly Beacon, Airly Beacon;
>> Oh, the pleasant sight to see
> Shires and towns from Airly Beacon
>> While my love climbed up to me.
>
> Airly Beacon, Airly Beacon;
>> Oh, the happy hours we lay
> Deep in fern on Airly Beacon,
>> Courting through the summer's day!
>
> Airly Beacon, Airly Beacon;
>> Oh, the weary haunt for me,
> All alone on Airly Beacon,
>> With his baby on my knee!

The great test as to whether verse contains real
poetry, emotional poetry, is this: Can it be translated into the prose of another language and still
make it appear emotional? If it can, then the true
poetry is there; if it cannot, then it is not true poetry,
but only verse. Now a great deal of famous Western
poetry will really bear this test. The little poem
that I have just quoted to you will bear it. So will
some of the best work of each of our greatest poets.
Those of you who study German know something
about the wonderful poems of Heine. You know
they are very simple in form and musical. Well,

the best foreign translation of them is a translation into French prose. Here, of course, the rhyme is gone, the muse is gone, but the real, essential poetry — the power to touch the heart — remains. Do you remember the little poem in which the poet describes the soldier, the sentry on guard at the city-gate? He sees the soldier standing in the light of the evening sun, performing the military exercises all by himself, just to pass the time. He shoulders his gun as if in receiving invisible orders, presents, takes aim. Then, the poet suddenly exclaims, — "I wish he would shoot me dead!"

The whole power of the little composition is in that exclamation; he tells us all that he means, and all that he feels. To a person unhappy, profoundly unhappy, even the most common sights and sounds of life give him thoughts and wishes in relation to death. Now, a little poem like that loses very little, loses scarcely anything by a littler [sic] translation; it is what I have called naked poetry; — it does not depend upon the ornaments of expression, all the decoration of rhyme, in order to produce its effect. Perhaps you will say that this essence of poetry may also be found occasionally in prose. That is true; — there is such a thing as poetry in prose, but it is also true that measure and rhyme greatly intensify the charm of emotional expression.

Suppose we now take something more elaborate for an example — this celebrated little poem written many years ago by an Oxford student, and now known everywhere. I call it more elaborate, only because the workmanship as to form is much more:

The night has a thousand eyes,
  And the day but one;
Yet the light of the whole world dies
  With the dying sun.

The mind has a thousand eyes,
  And the heart but one;
Yet the light of a whole life dies
  When love is done.

FRANCIS BOURDILLON.

An ancient Greek might have written something like that; it has the absolute perfection of some of those emotional little pieces of [the] Greek anthology — two thousand and even three thousand years old. The comparison of stars to eyes is very old. In every Western literature the stars have been called the eyes of the night; and still we call the sun the Eye of the Day, just as the Greeks did. Innumerable as are the stars of the night, they cannot be seen at all when the sun has well risen. They are not able to make light and joy in the world; and when the sun sets, everything becomes dark and colourless. Then the poet says that human love is to human life what the sun is to the world. It is not by reason, but by a feeling that we are made happy. The mind cannot make us happy as the heart can. Yet the mind, like the sky, "has a thousand eyes" — that is to say, a thousand different capacities of knowledge and perception. It does not matter. When the person that we really love is dead the happiness of life ceases for us; emotionally our world becomes dark as the physical world becomes when the sun has set.

Certainly the perfect verse and rhyme help the effect; but they are not at all necessary to the beauty of the thing. Translate that into your own language in prose; and you will see that very little is lost; for the first two lines of the first stanza exactly balance the first two lines of the second stanza; and the second two lines of the first stanza balance the second two lines of the second stanza; therefore even in prose the composition must assume a charming form, no matter what language it is rendered in.

But it does not follow at all that because a short composition in verse contains a great deal of meaning or happens to be very cleverly constructed, you can call it a real poem. Verses that only surprise by cleverness, by tricks of good words, have a very little value. They may be pretty; they give you a kind of pleasure, that is a small graceful object. But if they do not touch the heart as well as the head, I should never call them real poetry. For example, there is a French verse which has been translated into English more than a thousand times — always differently and yet never successfully. The English *Journal of Education* this year asked for translations of it, and more than five hundred were sent in. None of them were satisfactory, though some of them were very clever.

La vie est vaine:
Un peu d'amour,
Un peu de haine,
Et puis — bonjour !

La vie est brêve :
Un peu d'espoir,
Un peu de rêve,
Et puis — bonsoir !

Life is vain : a little love, a little hate, and then — good-bye !
Life is brief ; a little hope, a little dreaming, and then — good-night !

Of course, this requires no explanation, the French work is astonishingly clever, simple as it looks: the same thing cannot be done in the English language so well. As I have told you, at least a thousand English writers have tried to put it into English verse. So you will see that it is very famous. But is it poetry? I should certainly say that it is not. It is not poetry, because it consists only of a few commonplaces stated in a mocking way — in the tone of a clever man trifling with a serious subject. They do not really touch us. And they do not bear the test of translation. Put into English, what becomes of them? They simply dry up. The English reader might well exclaim, "We have heard of that before, in much better language." But let us take one verse of a Scotch song by Robert Burns which is known the whole world over, and which was written by a man who always wrote out of his own [heart].

"We two have paddled in the brook
From morning sun till noon,
But seas between us broad have roared
Since old lang syne."

When I put that into English, the music is gone, and the beauty of several dialect-words, such as "dine" (meaning the dinner hour, therefore the midday), and the melody have disappeared. Still the poetry remains. Two men in some foreign country, after years of separation, and one reminds the other of childhood days when both played in the village brook from the sunrise until dinner-time — so much delighted by the water! Only a little brook, one says; — but the breadth of oceans, the width of half the world, has been between us since that time. Now, anybody who, as a boy, loved to play or swim in the stream of his native village with other boys, can feel what the poet means; whether he be a Japanese or a Scotchman makes no difference at all. That is poetry.

And now, so much having been said on the subject of the emotional essence of poetry, I want to tell you that in the course of such lectures on poetry as we shall have in the course of academic year, I shall try always to keep these facts before you and to select for our reading only those things which contain the thought of poetry that will bear the test of translation. Much of our English poetry will not do this. I think, for example, that it is a great mistake to set before Japanese students such 18th century birth [work?] as the verse of Pope. As verse it is perhaps the most perfect of the English language, as poetry it is nothing at all. The essence of poetry is not in Pope, nor is it to be found in most of the 18th century school.

That was an age in which it was the fashion to keep all emotion suppressed. But Pope is a useful study for English classes in England, because of what English students can take from it through the mere study of form, of compact and powerful expression with very few words. Here, the situation is exactly converse. The value of foreign poetry to you cannot be in the direction of form. Foreign form cannot be reproduced in Japanese any more than French can be produced into English. The value of foreign poetry is in what makes the soul, the heart, the heart of all poetry: — feeling and imagination. Foreign feeling and foreign imagination may help to add something to the beauty and the best quality of future Japanese poetry. There I think the worth of study may be very great. But when foreign poetry means nothing but correct verse, you might as well waste no time upon it; as there is much great poetry which has good form as well as strong feeling.

INDEX

INDEX

Adulteration, in food and morals, II: 139–141.

Æsthetics, Y. Hirn's study of, II: 20, 21.

Africa, musical aptitudes of races of, I: 284, 353; transplantation of melodies of, to America, 356, 380, 411.

Ahriman, the Persian Spirit of Darkness, II: 118, 126.

Akizuki, teacher of Chinese at Kumamoto, I: 125; II: 66, 67, 73, 119, 177.

Albee, John, I: 83; letters from Hearn to, I: 276, 277; II: 358–361; his Prose Idyls, 360.

Albee, Mrs. John, I: 358, 359, 360.

Alden, Henry Mills, I: 286, 378, 405, 428.

Alexander the Great, I: 161.

Allen, Grant, Hearn's comment on, I: 394.

Allen, James Lane, II: 377.

Allingham, William, II: 522 ; a verse by, 521.

Amaron, lyrics of, I: 368.

Ama-terasu-Omi-Kami, II: 25.

Amenomori, Nobushige, I: 128, 139, 159; II: 217, 346, 353, 380, 390, 391, 392, 394; photograph of, 376.

Amicis, Edmondo de, his Cuore, I: 456; II: 102.

Amiel, Henri Frédéric, his Journal Intime, II: 400.

Ancestors, worship of, II: 28.

Andersen, Hans, Hearn's comment on, II: 251.

Angelinus, I: 256.

Anglo-American alliance, II: 384.

Anglo-Saxon race, future of, II: 137.

Antæus, II: 454.

Antilles. See West Indies.

Apes, treatment of, on board ship, I: 413, 414.

Apollo, Temple of, at Levkas, I: 3.

Apollonius of Tyana, I: 321, 322.

Arabia, hero-stories of, I: 234, 237.

Aristocracies, value of, II: 248.

Arnold, Edwin, I: 282, 335, 454; his Light of Asia, 291; Hearn's opinion of, 319; his translation of the story of Nala, 402.

Arnold, Matthew, Hearn's comments on, I: 318, 319.

Arnoux, ——, I: 465, 466; II: 347.

Arrows, used in Japanese rice-fields, II: 6.

Arrows of prayer, II: 6.

Art, nature of antique, I: 211; standards of, 216–218; sacrifices and rewards of, 237–239, 242, 243; return to antique, 254; money considerations should not enter into, 336; ghostliness of, II: 19, 20; use of the distorted in, 125–127; secret of literary, 345, 346.

Asai, Mr., II: 298, 299.

Assyria, ghost-stories of, II: 251.

Aston, William George, II: 484.

Atlantic City, N. J., I: 451.

Atlantic Monthly, I: 293, 317, 321, 397.

Aubryet, Xavier, I: 340.

Augustin, Jean, I: 70, 71, 363; II: 294.

Austin, Alfred, II: 302.

Azan, the muezzin's call, I: 280, 281, 283, 309, 317, 321.

Azukizawa, one of Hearn's pupils, II: 68.

Bacon, Francis, his idea of love, I: 316; Hearn's opinions of his Essays, 328.

Bagpipe, introduced by Romans into Scotland, I: 182.

Baker, Constance, II: 256, 259, 287, 288, 292.

Baker, Page M., I: 265, 267, 268, 280, 289, 321, 323, 334, 346, 361, 370; Hearn's description of, 70, 71; II: 203; letters from Hearn to, I:

87; II: 43–46, 90–95, 174–176, 253–256, 257–265, 285–289, 292–296.

Baker, Mrs. Page M., II: 265.

Ball, Rev. Wayland D., I: 83; letters from Hearn to, 250–267, 342–348; Hearn's advice to, regarding literary work, 265, 266, 267, 343, 346.

Ballads, a Japanese singer and seller of, II: 220; customs regarding, 221.

Balzac, Honoré de, II: 432; his Le Succube, I: 201.

Bamboula, music of, I: 325, 359.

Bangor, North Wales, a private museum in, I: 171, 172.

Banja, an African word, I: 339.

Banjo, I: 310, 311; use of, by Southern negroes, 337.

Baring-Gould, Sabine, his chapter on the Mountain of Venus, I: 279.

Barrera, Enrique, I: 228.

Barrie, James Matthew, II: 301; his Sentimental Tommy, 318.

Basutos, music of, I: 353.

Bath, the Japanese, II: 94.

Bathing, at Grande Isle, I: 90, 91, 92.

Batokas, multiple pipe of the, I: 297.

Bats, adventures with, I: 465–467.

Baudelaire, Pierre Charles, I: 197, 211; his phrase regarding Gautier, 82; Hearn's desire to translate his Petits Poëmes en Prose, 362.

Beaulieu, Anatole Henri de, I: 317.

Beauty, hatred of the many for, I: 27; nature of the first perception of, 28–30; Hearn's early love of, 29, 32, 48.

Bedloe, Edward, II: 408, 438, 439, 440, 443, 448, 454.

Beecher, Henry Ward, I: 52.

Beetles, Japanese, II: 143.

Behrens, Alice von, II: 411.

Belief, Hearn's philosophy of, I: 296; origin of religious, 347, 348.

Bellamy, Edward, II: 184.

Bellesort, André, II: 352, 353; his Société Japonaise, 471, 478, 479, 502.

Bellesort, Mme., II: 352, 353, 502.

Bennett, James Gordon, I: 54.

Béranger, Pierre Jean de, II: 412.

Bergerat, Auguste Emile, I: 222, 227.

Berlioz, Hector, I: 168.

Bernhardt, Sarah, II: 435.

Bhagavad-Gita, I: 316, 402.

Bible, revised version of the Old Testament, I: 350; grammatical usages in, II: 75, 76; Japanese hatred of some passages in, 320.

Bilâl, I: 280, 281, 282; Hearn's article on, 283, 284, 286, 295; biography of, 331.

Bisland, Elizabeth. See Wetmore, Elizabeth (Bisland).

Bizet, Georges, I: 385.

Björnson, Björnstjerne, I: 46.

Black, William, II: 301.

Blouet, Paul (Max O'Rell), I: 445.

Blue, significance of the colour, I: 394.

Boccaccio, Giovanni, his Decameron, I: 256.

Bodhisattvas, Japanese and Indian, II: 78.

Bon-odori, a Japanese dance, II: 37, 38, 46, 47, 52, 54.

Book of Golden Deeds, as a reading-book in a Japanese school, II: 102.

Books, Hearn's dislike of borrowing, II: 432.

Borrow, George, I: 205, 206, 459; his Gypsies of Spain, 201, 202.

Bourdillon, Francis, verses by, II: 525.

Bourgault-Ducoudray, Louis Albert, his Souvenirs d'une mission musicale en Grèce, I: 386.

Bourget, Paul, II: 84.

Bowditch, Thomas Edward, I: 354.

Brachet, Auguste, I: 374.

Brahma, I: 210.

Brahmins, example of magic given by, I: 322.

Brain, in civilized man and savages, II: 245.

Brantôme, Pierre de Bourdeilles, Seigneur de, I: 256.

Brenane, Mrs., Hearn adopted by, I: 8, 11, 12, 16; disposition of her property, 36, 37.

Bridges, Robert, his Pater Filio, II: 498.

Brittany, songs of, I: 189, 190.

Broca, Pierre Paul, I: 339; II: 245.

Brownell, William Crary, Hearn's comment on his French Traits, I: 457.

Browning, Robert, II: 190.

Brunetière, Ferdinand, II: 479.

Buddhas, Japanese and Indian, II: 78.

Buddhism, monistic idea in, strengthened by education, I: 112; introduction of knowledge of, into America, 265; the possible religion of the future, 291, 292; Christianity and, 347; in the light of modern science, 400; false teaching of, 401; Hearn's study of, II: 4; his love of, 26; suppression of, in hotels of Kizuki, 47; difficulty of study of, for foreigners, 82; effect of, on the foreigner, 85, 86; some tenets of, 135; theosophical and spiritualistic writers on, 431. See also Nichiren.

Buddhist catechism, projected by Hearn, II: 269, 270.

Bulwer-Lytton, Edward George Earle Lytton, first Baron Lytton, his The House and the Brain, II: 371.

Bulwer-Lytton, Edward Robert Lytton, first Earl of Lytton (Owen Meredith), his The Portrait, II: 294.

Bunchō, Japanese painter, II: 468.

Buonarroti, Michelangelo, I: 275.

Burke, Edmund, his Essays as a reading-book in a Japanese school, II: 102.

Burns, Mrs., II: 368.

Burns, Robert, a verse of, II: 527, 528.

Burthe, Honoré, I: 70, 71.

Business, hypocrisy of, II: 109; morality of modern men and methods of, 169–174, 177–179, 293; Hearn's hatred of, 294, 353, 354; extraordinary incidents of, 303.

Byron, George Gordon Noel, Baron Byron, French prose translations of, I: 245.

Byzantium, wind organs invented at, I: 166.

Cable, George Washington, I: 212; his study of Creole music, 175, 337, 359; his Grandissimes, 228, 229; character of his work, 289, 295, 296; negro Pan's pipe described by, 355.

Cæsar, Julius, I: 161.

Carlyle, Thomas and Jane, I: 139.

Carmen, the opera, I: 201, 202.

Carpenter, Edward, II: 511.

Castelar, Emilio, I: 275.

Castrén, Matthias Alexander, his work on Finnish mythology, I: 233, 235, 236.

Caterpillar, Hearn's story of a, II: 436.

Catholicism, Latin feeling surviving in, II: 312. See also Roman Catholic Church.

Cats, Japanese, II: 55, 56, 58, 59.

Cephalonia, Island of, I: 7.

Ceram, Island of, II: 211, 213.

Cerigo, Island of, I: 6.

Cerigote, Rosa. See Hearn, Rosa (Cerigote).

Chalumeau, or multiple pipe, I: 297.

Chamberlain, Basil Hall, I: 53; II: 63, 107, 306; his explanation of Hearn's inconstancy to his friends, I: 57–59; aid given to Hearn by, 110, 136; letters from Hearn to, 130, 131; II: 5–18, 23–43, 46–60, 198–251, 256, 257, 266–270, 273, 274, 276–278; his Kojiki, 6, 9; his Things Japanese, 60, 76–79, 90, 212; Hearn's suggestion for an illustrated edition of Kojiki, 58; his knowledge of the Japanese language, 117; project for a book on Japanese folk-lore by Hearn and, 129; Japanese appreciation of, 201; his version of the Kumamoto Rojō, 220, 221; his paper on the Loochoo Islands, 273, 274.

Charcot, Jean Martin, I: 441; story based on researches of, 399.

Châteaubriand, François René Auguste, Vicomte de, I: 191.

Châteauneuf, Agricole Hippolyte de Lapierre de, I: 256.

Chatto and Windus, I: 251, 253.

Chenières, Les, destruction of, I: 96.

Chinese gongs, I: 171, 172.

Choctaw Indians, I: 188; no longer a musical people, 166.

Chōzuba-no-Kami, II: 32, 33.

Christening ceremony, Shintō, II: 59.

Christern, F. W., I: 189.

Christian Band, The, II: 142.

Christianity, Buddhism and, I: 347; Oriental characteristics of, 400, 401; moral value of, II: 87; courtesy and, 132, 133; the higher, 146.

Cincinnati, Ohio, Hearn sets out for, I: 45; his first employment in, 49; his departure from, 63, 66; as an art centre, 182.

Cincinnati Enquirer, Hearn's work on, I: 50–52, 154.

Civilization, immoral side of Occidental, II: 111, 112; transmission of, from one race to another, 245; effect of American, on literature, 301.

Clapperton, Hugh, I: 354.

Clarke, James Freeman, sectarian purpose of his work on religions, I: 345.

Clifford, William Kingdon, II: 152, 190, 221.

Clive, Robert, Baron Clive of Plassey, I: 160.

Coatlicue, Mexican goddess of flowers, I: 436.

Cockerill, John, Hearn's sketch of, I: 53, 54.

Coleridge, Samuel Taylor, I: 377.

Colombat, Marc (Colombat de l'Isère), his work on diseases of the voice, I: 363.

Colour, æsthetic symbolism of, I: 394; sense of, 397.

Columbian Exposition, Chicago, II: 150, 152.

Comparative mythology, results of a study of, I: 345.

Comparetti, Domenico, author of The Traditional Poetry of the Finns, II: 502.

Concept, analysis of a mathematical, II: 241, 242.

Conder, Josiah, II: 117, 118.

Confession, Hearn's account of an experience at, I: 32, 33.

Confucianism, II: 27.

Congo, a Creole dance, I: 336.

Congo tribes, a superstition of, I: 313.

Coolies, West Indian, I: 415, 416, 433.

Corinthians, strait between Santa Maura and Greece cut by, I: 3.

Cornell University, lectures by Hearn proposed and abandoned by, II: 487–489, 490, 492, 495.

Cornilliac, Jean Jacques, I: 441.

Cosmopolitan, The (magazine), I: 452, 455.

Coulanges, Numa Denis Fustel de, I: 202.

Courtesy, Oriental and Occidental, II: 180; effect of industrialism on, 183.

Crawford, Francis Marion, II: 301, 377.

Creole sketches, Hearn's project for, I: 224.

Creoles, Hearn's collection of proverbs of, I: 83; patois of, 83, 189, 232, 417; music and songs of, 175, 188, 189, 337, 338, 356, 357, 359; of Louisiana, 188; Hearn's project for collecting legends of Louisiana, 193;

cruelty of French, 203; dances of, 297, 307, 336.

Crosby, Ernest, I: 85; letter from Hearn to, II: 509–513.

Crosby, Oscar, I: 85.

Cruise of the Marchesa, II: 218, 219.

Cuba, African influence on music of, I: 380.

Curiosités des Arts, extract translated from, I: 165, 166.

Curtis, George William, his Howadji in Syria, I: 196.

Cyrano de Bergerac, Rostand's, II: 435, 436.

Dai sen, mountain, II: 23.

Daikoku, Japanese deity, identified with Oho-Kuni-nushi-no-Kami, in Matsue, II: 13.

Daikon, II: 57.

Daily Item (New Orleans), Hearn's work on, I: 68.

Daimyōs, downfall of, in Japan, I: 116.

Dances, Creole, I: 297, 307, 336; Greek choral, 385, 386; Japanese, II: 21, 22, 31, 468. See also Bon-odori, Hōnen-odori, Mika-kagura.

Dancing-girls, Japanese. See Geisha.

Dardanas, I: 167.

Darfur, Africa, I: 277.

Darwin, Charles Robert, I: 292; II: 266; his hypothesis as to sexual æsthetic sensibilities in animals, II: 20; his contribution to the theory of evolution, 235.

Davitt, Michael, I: 361.

Death, Hearn's feeling about, II: 379.

Decadent school, II: 187, 188.

Deir-el-Tiu, monastery of, I: 328.

Deland, Margaret, II: 301, 489; her Philip and his Wife, 167, 222; her Story of a Child, 222.

Delpit, Albert, I: 361.

Demerara, gold-mines of, I: 413.

Dening, Walter, II: 77.

De Quincey, Thomas, his mastery of English, I: 132, 135; his Flight of a Tartar Tribe, 329.

Dictionaries, etymological, I: 374.

Dimitris, The, of Russia, I: 329.

Divinity, weight of the popular idea of a, II: 78.

Dobson, Austin, I: 253; II: 215.

Don Juan, not an Oriental type, II: 114.

Doré, Paul Gustave, Hearn's article on, I: 80, 268; his knowledge of gipsies, 201, 202; his illustrations for Poe's Raven, 317.

Dozy, Reinhart Pieter, I: 374.

Draper, John William, I: 326.

Drawing, Hearn's defence of Japanese methods of, II: 331.

Dreams, I: 442, 469.

Dublin, Ireland, Hearn family removes to, I: 7.

Du Maurier, George, II: 302; his Trilby, 187, 221.

Dumez, ——, I: 205.

Durham, Eng., Roman Catholic College at, I: 34.

Dutch East Indies, II: 218, 219.

Dutt, Toru, her translation of the story of Nala, I: 402.

Duveyrier, Henri, his Les Touâreg du Nord, I: 353.

Earthquakes, in Japan, II: 83, 84.

East, Shadows of the, II: 85, 87.

Ebers, Georg, I: 226.

Ebisu, Japanese deity, temple of, at Nishinomiya, II: 8; identified with Koto-shiro-nushi-no-Kami, in Matsue, 13; in Mionoseki, 37.

Education, of the emotions, I: 456; Hearn's attitude toward scientific, II: 163, 164, 275; decline of, in Japan, 216; ecclesiastical, 310.

Edwards, Bryan, his History of the West Indies, I: 297, 339.

Edwards, Osman, II: 402, 455; his Theatre in Japan, 222.

Eggs, eating of, in Japan, II: 96, 97.

Egypt, sistrum introduced into Italy by, I: 166; musical instruments of, 211, 212, 213, 311, 353; stories of the antique life of, 226; an ancient melody of, 286; ghost-stories of, II: 251.

Eitel, Ernest John, his identification of Japanese and Indian divinities, II: 78.

Electric light, G. M. Gould's paper on, I: 439.

Electricity, story based on evolution of, by the human body, I: 399.

Eliot, George, her Silas Marner used as a reading-book in Kumamoto, II: 79.

Emancipation, religious and political, II: 206.

Emerson, Ralph Waldo, I: 265; II: 174, 183, 441; his suggestiveness, I: 432; II: 190.

Emotions, education of, I: 456.

Endemann, Carl, music of the Basutos preserved by, I: 353, 354.

Enemies, value of, I: 153; II: 412, 414.

Engelmann, Willem Herman, I: 374.

England, distrust of American literary work in, I: 361; revision of treaty between Japan and, II: 185, 186; action of, after Chinese-Japanese War, 262; effect of religious conservatism on education in, 275; the reading public of, 446.

Environment, II: 239, 240; moral adaptation to, 136.

Erse tongue, I: 190.

Eskimo music, I: 330.

Estes and Lauriat, I: 250.

Etymological dictionaries, I: 374.

Euterpe, a periodical, II: 472.

Evolution, physical, Spencer's conservatism regarding further, I: 397; physical and moral, 432, 434–436; brain-growth a striking fact of, II: 245; psychological, 231–233, 238–243; popular effect of psychological, on fiction, 267.

Fairy-tales, Hearn's project for a set of philosophical, II: 339, 340.

Family, Oriental and Occidental ideas of the, II: 112, 113, 116, 117, 147.

Farny, H. F., I: 52, 53, 55, 280, 448.

Fashion, deformities of, I: 438.

Fauche, Hippolyte, his translation of the Ramayana, I: 402.

Feldwisch, ——, I: 221, 232, 292, 293.

Fenollosa, Ernest, letters from Hearn to, II: 381–384, 412–414.

Fenollosa, Mary McNeil, I: 153; II: 381, 383; letters from Hearn to, II: 401–403, 437, 440–442.

Feuillet, Octave, his M. de Camors, II: 84.

Fiction, Hearn's desire to write, I: 338, 339, 350, 352, 371, 372, 375, 430; II: 246, 341, 342, 348, 349, 378; Hearn's theory of that which lives, I: 454, 455; popular effect of evolutional psychology on, II: 267; Hearn's taste in, 276; requirements for the writing of, 341.

Figs, Louisiana, I: 170, 177, 178.

Finck, Henry Theophilus, his Romantic Love and Personal Beauty, II: 193.

Finland, music of, I: 191, 200; two epics of, 235; seen through the Kalewala, II: 469; social and political changes in, 469, 470; views in, sent to Hearn, 471, 472.

Fire-drill, for lighting the sacred fire, II: 10, 12, 13, 15, 23, 26, 29.

Fiske, John, II: 107, 190, 221.

FitzGerald, Edward, his translation of Omar Khayyám, II: 499.

Flameng, Léopold, I: 185.

Flammarion, Camille, his Astronomie populaire, I: 385.

Flaubert, Gustave, his Salammbô, I: 226, 248, 249; Hearn's translation of his Tentation de Saint Antoine, 247, 249, 251, 362; his literary generosity, 341.

Fleas, II: 448, 449, 450.

Flight into Egypt, a French painting of, I: 318.

Floods, in Japan, II: 307.

Florenz, Karl Adolf, II: 284, 311, 329.

Florida, Hearn's visit to, I: 341.

Flower, Sir William Henry, I: 438; his Hunterian Lectures, 314.

Flutes, antique, I: 185; double, 213.

Food, Japanese, II: 32, 91, 92; not suited to strain of higher education, 103, 104, 292. See Daikon; Sake.

Force, Oriental theory of the nature of, II: 339.

Forces, our knowledge limited to, II: 243, 244.

Fort-de-France, Martinique, I: 453.

Fox-superstition, II: 24, 29, 30.

Foxwell, E. E., II: 384; letters to, 455-457.

France, Anatole, I: 361; II: 491; Hearn's translation of his Crime de Sylvestre Bonnard, I: 102; quotation from, II: 345.

Freedom, love of Northern races for, II: 229.

Freemasons, Hearn's effort to join, II: 500.

Free will, I: 435.

Friends, the danger from, I: 153; II: 412-414.

Friendship, college, II: 197; basis of, 332, 333; nationality and, 432.

Fuji-san, climbing of, II: 375, 390, 391, 392; effect of a typhoon upon, 394; pilgrims to, 448.

Fujisaki, H., letter from Hearn to, II: 515-517.

Funeral rite, Shintō, II: 59.

Gaelic tongue, I: 190.

Galton, Francis, II: 229.

Gate of Everlasting Ceremony, II: 33, 317.

Gautier, Judith, II: 362.

Gautier, Théophile, I: 227, 231; Hearn's admiration for, 61, 82, 394, 430, 431; II: 44, 221, 222; translations of, I: 61, 62, 72, 73, 80–82, 213, 245, 248, 252, 253, 268, 269, 275, 276, 376, 396; Hearn's comment on his poetry, 253, 255, 269; pantheism of, 255, 256; his style, 269, 275, 324; his portrait, 318; posthumous poetry of, 327; his services ignored by Hugo, 340; his literary generosity, 341; his idea of art, 437; his Avatar, 252, 362, 442, 443; his Emaux et Camées, 82, 259, 260, 275; his Histoire du Romantisme, I: 317; II: 222; his Mademoiselle de Maupin, 248, 251, 254, 256, 257, 258, 259; his Roman de la Momie, 226, 253; his Spectre de la Rose, 244.

Geisha, II: 22, 73, 82, 94, 95, 114.

Gell, Sir William, his Pompeiana, I: 213.

Genghis Khan, I: 329.

Germans, in Japan, II: 199, 206, 207.

Germany, musical instruments furnished to the Romans by, I: 166; education in, II: 271.

Gessner, Salomon, I: 184.

Ghostology, Egyptian and Assyrian, II: 251.

Ghosts, Hearn's interest in, I: 15.

Gibb, George Duncan, I: 339.

Giglampz, Ye, Hearn's work on, I: 52, 53.

Gilder, Richard Watson, I: 342.

Gipsies, Hearn's interest in, I: 201, 205, 206; language of, 202.

Girls, liberty allowed to, in England and America, II: 522.

Gita-Govinda, I: 327.

Go-Daigo, Emperor of Japan, II: 186, 187.

Gods, pagan, teaching of the early church regarding, I: 26; Hearn's early interest in, 26, 27.

Goethe, II: 173, 266, 508.

Gongs, Chinese, I: 171, 172.

Gorresio, Gaspare, his translation of the Ramayana, I: 402.
Gōshō, one of Hearn's pupils, II: 465.
Goto, II: 119.
Gottschalk, Louis Moreau, I: 229, 356; his Bamboula, 325, 337; Creole musical themes used by, 359.
Gould, George Milbry, I: 97, 102; letters from Hearn to, 393–403, 421–443, 457–468; his pamphlet on the Colour-Sense, 394; Hearn's advice as to literary work, 426; his capacity for work, 457, 458.
Gould, H. F., wife of G. M., I: 468.
Gould, Jay, II: 173, 353; Hearn's defence of, 109, 110.
Government positions, exacting nature of, I: 383.
Gowey, John F., II: 369.
Grace, a savage quality, I: 438.
Grand Anse, Martinique, I: 422, 423, 465.
Grande Isle, I: 350, 414, 446; Hearn's description of, 87–95; destruction of, 96; II: 155.
Grant, Ulysses Simpson, I: 52.
Greece, musical instruments furnished to the Romans by, I: 166.
Greeks, Hearn's love of the mythology of, I: 26, 27, 28, 31; chastity of, 219, 220; sculpture of, 227; legends of, 227, 228; poetry of, II: 520.
Griffith, Ralph Thomas Hotchkin, his translation of the Ramayana, I: 402.
Griots, music of, I: 354, 355, 356, 377.
Grueling, ——, I: 282.
Guiana, British, Hearn's visit to, I: 97; a mocking-bird of, 357, 358.
Gulf of Mexico, Creole archipelagoes of, I: 333; bathing in, 341.
Gulistan, Saadi's, I: 280.

Hadramaut, I: 356.
Hadrian, Roman emperor, I: 328.
Hahaki, ancient name of modern Hōki, II: 58.
Halévy, Ludovic, II: 395.
Hall, Dr., II: 347, 348, 350, 374, 389, 405, 422, 428, 429.
Handwriting, Hearn's efforts to read character from, I: 340, 349.
Harper, Hearn's recollections of a Welsh, I: 13–15.
Harper and Brothers, their commissions to Hearn, I: 97, 102; Hearn

severs his contracts with, 109; his series of Southern sketches for, 268; their encouragement to Hearn, 338.
Harper's Magazine, Hearn's contributions to, I: 381.
Harps, of the Nyam-Nyams, I: 310.
Harris, Joel Chandler, I: 337.
Harris, Mrs. Lylie, I: 80.
Hart, Jerome A., his first acquaintance with Hearn, I: 80; letters from Hearn to, 244–250.
Harte, Francis Bret, II: 41.
Hartmann, Eduard, II: 235.
Hartmann, Robert, I: 297; his studies of African music, 353, 354.
Hastings, Warren, I: 160.
Hastings, battle of, I: 191.
Hat, highest evolution of, I: 94.
Hatakeyama, Yuko, story of, II: 142, 181, 268, 269; monument to, 277.
Hauck, Minnie, I: 201.
Havana, Cuba, music of, I: 202.
Health, influence of, on spiritual life, II: 34, 35.
Hearn, Surgeon-Major Charles Bush, father of Lafcadio, I: 5, 6, 9, 429; opposition to his marriage, 6; his elopement, 7; his return to Dublin, 7; his separation from his wife, 7, 8, 8 n.; his second marriage, 8.
Hearn, Elizabeth (Holmes), grandmother of Lafcadio, I: 6.
Hearn, James, brother of Lafcadio, I: 7; letter from Hearn to, 9–11.
Hearn, Lafcadio, a native of Santa Maura, I: 3, 7, 429; influence of the place upon, 4, 5; his ancestry, 5, 6; removes to Wales, 8, 12; effect of domestic conditions upon, 8, 9; his memory of his mother, 9, 10, 11; of his father, 11; his youthful characteristics, 15; autobiographical fragments left by, 15–32, 37–39, 41–45, 45–49, 100, 101, 159, 160; his interest in the weird, 15, 16, 17, 18; his experience with "Cousin Jane," 18–25; his love of beauty, 29, 32, 148; his early religious instruction, 16, 17, 19, 20, 32, 33; his interest in mythology, 26, 27, 28, 31; his education, 34, 34 n., 35, 36; becomes blind in one eye, 35, 36, 429; his poverty, 36, 37, 40, 100, 102; goes to New York, 39, 40; an incident of his early New York life, 42–45; goes to Cincinnati, 45, 49; an incident of

the journey, 46–49; becomes typesetter, proof-reader, private secretary, 50; his work on the Cincinnati Enquirer, 50–52, 53; on Ye Giglampz, 52, 53; character of his newspaper work, 55; his friendships, 55–59; his admiration for Spencer, 58, 85, 86, 365, 374, 375, 392, 394, 430, 431, 438, 459; ii: 20, 26, 44, 221, 222; for Gautier, i: 61, 82, 394, 430, 431; ii: 44, 221, 222; goes to New Orleans, i: 65, 66, 67; his letters to Krehbiel, 67; his work in New Orleans, 68, 72, 73, 167, 176, 197, 280, 363; his investments, 69, 198, 199, 230, 336; ii: 353; his library, i: 70, 278, 283, 290, 314, 336, 339, 350, 352, 364; ii: 305, 308; his associates on the Times-Democrat, i: 70, 71; his personal appearance and characteristics, 77–80, 428; ii: 466; his visit to Grande Isle, i: 87–95; his visits to and descriptions of the French West Indies, 97, 98, 100, 101, 409–419, 422–424; goes to Japan, 102; his early impressions of Japan, 103, 104, 107–109, 115; ii: 35; his love of the tropics, i: 105, 415, 420, 425, 449, 469; ii: 64, 211, 213, 217, 281; his work for Japan, i: 106; ii: 281; severs contracts with his publishers, i: 109; ii: 4; his friendship with M. McDonald, i: 109, 110, 153; ii: 107; his work at Matsue, i: 110–113; ii: 16, 30, 43, 46; his kindness of heart, i: 114, 118; his marriage, 116, 117; ii: 44, 60; his visits to Kizuki, i: 115, 122; ii: 7–11, 43; his Japanese name, i: 117; ii: 270, 292, 293, 299; his obligations as a Japanese citizen, i: 117, 136; ii: 44, 64, 81, 158, 191, 265, 270, 278, 279, 298; his household pets, i: 117, 118, 119; ii: 460; his popularity, i: 119, 120; his disregard of money, 122, 148, 336; his dislike of forms and restraints, 122, 123, 148; his study of Japanese with his wife, 123, 124; his appointment at Kumamoto, 124; ii: 63, 65; his life and work there, i: 125–128; ii: 93, 94, 100, 102, 103, 110; birth of his first child, i: 127; ii: 115, 116, 128, 149, 150, 156; enters the service of the Kōbe Chronicle, i: 128, 129; his growing indifference to externals, 129–131, 137; ii: 194, 195; his mastery of English, i: 132; facsimile of a first draft of his MS., 133, 134; goes to the University of Tōkyō, 136–138, 283; his methods of writing, 140, 141, 239, 373, 391; ii: 89, 272, 273, 396; his private life in Tōkyō, i: 141–152; ii: 295, 309; gives up his professorship, i: 154; ii: 368, 490, 493; lectures at Cornell proposed and abandoned, i: 154; ii: 487, 488, 490, 492, 495; accepts chair of English in Waseda University, i: 156; lectures in London and Oxford proposed, 156; his death, 156; buried according to Buddhist rites, 157–159; tributes to, 158, 159; his interest in primitive music, 165–167, 190, 231, 330, 339, 353, 354, 358–360, 380, 411; ii: 15; effect of Southern climate upon, i: 169, 170, 177, 195, 196, 288, 319, 421, 422, 423, 424, 425, 427, 440, 445; descriptions of his home in New Orleans, 172–174, 196, 222; his interest in gipsies, 201, 202, 205, 206; his fantastics, 220, 221, 226, 230, 231, 278; his proposed series of French translations, 252, 362, 363; of Oriental stories, 278, 295; of musical legends, 286; of strange facts, 298; of Arabesque studies, 321, 328, 331, 396, 403; of legends of strange faiths, 328; his ambition regarding his style, 276, 324, 364, 374, 379, 383, 393; ii: 359; his dread of cold, i: 279, 298, 379, 448; ii: 188, 211; his pursuit of the odd, i: 290, 291, 294; change in his literary inclinations, 293, 294; his desire to travel, 294, 295, 398, 424; ii: 351; his outline of an imaginary series of musical volumes, i: 299–304, 309; his use of classic English literature, 328; his ignorance of modern history, 329; his visits to the Gulf archipelagoes, 333; his study of Spanish, 334; thinks of studying medicine, 338; his desire to write fiction, 338, 339, 350, 352, 371, 372, 375, 430; ii: 246, 341, 342, 348, 349, 378; his visit to Florida, i: 341; his health, 344, 348, 366, 367, 371, 406, 407; ii: 14, 24, 25, 67, 73, 74, 129, 196, 197, 280, 292, 303, 304,

490, 493, 495, 506; result of his
study of comparative mythology, I:
345; his admiration for Viaud (P.
Loti), 377, 378, 396, 427, 452, 453;
his efforts to learn Chinese, 404; his
dread of New York, 405; II: 182,
476, 484; his desire to return to
America, II: 4, 175, 176, 202, 203,
473, 474, 475, 476, 477, 480–482,
484, 490, 493, 496, 497, 498, 499,
504, 505; translations of his books,
22, 466, 467, 468, 469, 472, 473, 485;
finds literary work in Japan difficult, 35, 60, 63, 89; his attitude
toward missionaries, 44, 45, 68, 109,
110, 311, 442; his legal seal, 46; difficulties of his position in Japan,
107–110, 175, 202, 252, 348, 490,
493, 497; his project for a book
with B. H. Chamberlain, 129; his
dislike of New Japan, 154, 161; his
method of teaching, 159, 160; his
literary success, 193, 277, 296, 297,
398; his dissatisfaction with his
work, 246, 277, 286, 333, 356, 375,
377, 380; criticisms of his work,
256, 257, 377, 466, 490; dislike of
women for, 265; his work at the
University of Tōkyō, 283, 298, 305,
306, 310, 311, 314, 327, 328, 357,
427, 429, 444, 481, 482, 486, 487;
his ignorance of every-day life, 340,
341, 399; a manuscript history of
his eccentricities, 350; his avoid-
ance of foreigners, 395, 397, 406,
456, 457; forces arrayed against,
404, 405, 493, 494, 496; his nose,
408; necessary conditions of work
for, 412–414, 424, 451, 452; his
method of teaching, 481, 486, 487;
protests against his treatment in
Tōkyō, 490, 493, 506; profits from
his books, 491; birth of a daughter
to, 506.

Writings:
Chita, I: 69, 86, 101, 371, 378,
393, 394, 396, 403, 404, 405, 411,
422, 430, 451; first form of, 96;
actual incidents related in, 96, 97,
426, 427; success of, 96, 97; criti-
cisms of, 98, 99, 445.
Dead Love, A, I: 74–76.
Dream of a Summer Day, quoted,
I: 4, 5.
Exotics and Retrospectives, I: 139;
II: 333, 401, 429; translations of, 467.

Gleanings in Buddha-Fields, I.
129, 131, 139; II: 466, 471.
Glimpses of Unfamiliar Japan,
II: 217, 270, 356, 359; quoted, I:
103, 111–113, 114, 115, 124, 125;
criticisms of, II: 187, 198, 209, 223;
translations of, 467, 468.
Gombo Zhêbes, a dictionary of
Creole Proverbs, I: 83, 278, 295,
335, 346.
Idolatry, quoted, I: 26–32.
Illusion, an autobiographical frag-
ment, I: 159, 160.
In Ghostly Japan, I: 139; II: 409,
411, 445.
In Vanished Light, an autobio-
graphical fragment, I: 100, 101.
Intuition, an autobiographical
fragment, I: 41–45.
Japan: an Interpretation, I: 115,
141, 155, 156; II: 499, 504, 505, 506,
514, 515.
A Japanese Miscellany, I: 140: II:
513.
Jiujutsu, I: 126.
Juvenilia (proposed), II: 500.
Kokoro, I: 129, 131; II: 193, 279,
289, 299, 300, 359, 471.
Kotto, I: 140, 146; II: 501.
Kwaidan, I: 141; quoted, 12, 156,
157.
Mountain of Skulls, II: 383.
My First Romance, an auto-
biographical fragment, I: 45–49.
My Guardian Angel, an auto-
biographical fragment, I: 16–25.
Naked Poetry, his lecture on, I:
137; text of, as taken down by T.
Ochiai, II: 519–529.
Notebook of an Impressionist
(proposed), I: 364, 383.
Out of the East, I: 127; II: 360;
quoted, I: 107, 108, 125, 126, 209;
impression made by, in England, II:
193; its title, 212.
Pipes of Hameline, I: 274.
Rabyah's Last Ride, I: 388, 389,
396.
Retrospectives. *See* Exotics and
Retrospectives.
Romance of the Milky Way, I:
159.
Shadowings, I: 140.
Some Chinese Ghosts, II: 43, 367,
469; dedication of, I: 60, 371;
characteristics of, 61, 73, 381, 388,

389, 405; difficulties regarding publication of, 83–85, 364, 370, 371, 375, 378; reception of, 407.
Stars, an autobiographical fragment, I: 37–39.
Stray Leaves from Strange Literature, I: 73, 83, 335, 340, 344, 346, 371, 376.
Torn Letters, afterward expanded into Chita, I: 96, 333.
Two Years in the French West Indies, I: 98, 102; criticisms of, 98, 99; his difficulties in writing it, II: 58.
With Kyūshū Students, I: 126.
Youma, II: 347, 466.
Translations:
Flaubert's Tentation de Saint Antoine, I: 247, 249, 278.
France's Crime de Sylvestre Bonnard, I: 102; II: 347, 348.
Gautier's Une nuit de Cléopâtre, etc., I: 61, 62, 73, 213, 245, 269, 275, 376, 396, 442, 443; estimates of, 80–82, 248, 268, 276.
Hearn, Richard, painter, I: 6.
Hearn, Rosa (Cerigote), mother of Lafcadio, I: 9; her meeting with Dr. Hearn, 6; her marriage, 7; her separation from her husband, 7, 8, 8 n.; her second marriage, 8, 429.
Hearn family, I: 5, 6; physical characteristics of, 11, 12.
Hearnian dialect, II: 62, 63, 81, 82.
Heck, Emile, a Jesuit priest, II: 284, 285, 310, 311, 312, 316, 320.
Hegel, Georg Wilhelm Friedrich, I: 438.
Heine, Heinrich, French prose translations of, I: 245; II: 524; Weill's reminiscences of, I: 341; poems of, II: 523.
Hell-shoon, superstition regarding, I: 313.
Hendrick, Ellwood, I: 102; letters from Hearn to, II: 60–65, 80–90, 98–101, 106–118, 120–129, 134–141, 149–152, 167–174, 177–180, 182–186, 187–191, 193–198, 251, 252, 270–273, 280–285, 299–303, 305–327, 332–340, 386–388, 398–401, 479–485; his marriage, 358.
Hendrick, Josephine, II: 332, 336.
Heracles, I: 316.
Heredity, Hearn's reflections on, I: 131, 399, 400; in the tropics, 429;

law of, II: 227–231, 232, 234, 237–243.
Heretic, fate of the modern, II: 107.
Herodias, I: 249.
Hershon, Paul Isaac, his Talmudic Miscellany, I: 287.
Hideyoshi, II: 77.
Hindola, I: 388.
Hindoos, legends of, I: 227, 228.
Hirata, I: 6.
Hirn, Yrjö, II: 502; letters to, 19–23, 466–472, 478, 479; his Origins of Art, 19–21, 468; his personal appearance, 467.
Hirn, Mrs., her translations of Hearn, II: 22, 466, 467, 468, 469, 501, 502; letters to, 472, 473, 501–503; Hearn's comments on one of her translations, 472, 473.
Hiruko, Japanese deity, II: 7, 8, 37.
Hobson, Richmond Pearson, II: 426, 427.
Hoffman, Ernst Theodor Wilhelm, I: 200.
Hōki, the modern name of ancient Hahaki, II: 58.
Hokusai, I: 103; II: 4.
Holmes, Edmund, I: 6.
Holmes, Elizabeth. See Hearn, Elizabeth (Holmes).
Holmes, Rice, I: 6.
Holmes, Sir Richard, I: 6.
Homer, I: 272.
Homing instinct, G. M. Gould's paper on, I: 439, 440.
Hommyōji, Nichiren temple of, II: 186.
Hōnen-odori, a Japanese dance, II: 38.
Hoppin, James Mason, his Old England, I: 234.
Houses, furnishings of Japanese, II: 93, 94.
Houssaye, Arsène, I: 361.
Howard, ——, and the Louisiana lottery, I: 205.
Howells, William Dean, I: 332.
Hueffer, Francis, his Troubadours, I: 361.
Hugo, Victor, his style, I: 269, 275; his selfishness, 340, 341; his Chant de Sophocle à Salamine, II: 215, 216.
Hugolâtres, I: 168.
Huxley, Thomas Henry, II: 190, 204, 221, 234, 235, 266, 404, 409; his Evolution and Ethics, II: 189.

Hyōgo, Kōbe, Japan, II: 192; Governor of, 191.
Hypocrisy, in religion, II: 87; in business and religion, 109.

Ibaraki, a Japanese student, II: 508.
Ibn Khallikan, I: 234, 331.
Iceland Spar, prediction concerning, II: 240, 241.
Ichibata, Japan, II: 15; Buddhist temple at, 17, 18.
Immorality, moral results of, II: 136, 137.
Immortality, Buddhist conception of, II: 473.
Improvisation, negro's talent for, I: 353.
Inada-Hime, Shintō deity, II: 8, 25; statue of, 105.
Inari, temple to, at Matsue, II: 24; no shrine of, at Yabase, 47; representations of, 77.
Inasa beach, II: 5, 6.
Individuality, Occidental theories of, II: 40.
Industrialism, its effect on good manners, II: 183; on liberty, 470, 511, 512.
Ingelow, Jean, her High Tide, II: 499.
Inomata, Teizaburō, I: 113; II: 291; letters from Hearn to, I: 64, 65; II: 131-133, 146-148, 160-162, 186, 187; his records of Hearn's Tōkyō lectures, I: 137, 138; his resolve to study medicine, II: 289, 290; text of one of Hearn's lectures as taken down by, 519-529.
Ionian Islands, I: 3; hatred toward England in, 6; ceded to Greece, 7.
Insects, caging of, in Japan, II: 335; ethical suggestions of the sociology of, 514.
Irish, similarities between faces of Mongolians and, I: 190; language of, 190.
Ise, Japan, II: 10, 29, 38; modernization of, 297.
Isle Dernière, L'. See Last Island.
Italian, Hearn's study of, II: 217, 218.
Italy, Spencer's theory of the education of the emotions in, I: 456; atmospheric influence of, II: 501.
Iwami, fox-superstition in, II: 29.
Izumo, Japan, II: 6, 10, 11, 13; Hearn's speech before the educational association of, 14; fox-super-

stition in, 29; Hearn plans a permanent home in, 270; an alternate name for Koizumi, 293.

James, Henry, II: 301, 396; literary criticisms of, I: 432, 434; obstacles to his popularity, II: 377.
Janet, Paul, II: 235.
January customs, Japanese, II: 80.
Japan, Hearn's commission to, I: 102; his early impressions of, 103, 104, 107-109, 115; II: 35; his work for, I: 106; II: 281; rigidities under the charm of, I: 107, 108; secret of the charm of, 108; absence of personal freedom in, 108, 109; position of foreign teachers in, 128; II: 68, 275, 283, 313, 316, 317; certain duties of subjects of, I: 136; Western influences in, 149, 150; II: 115, 154, 161, 177-179, 180, 199, 219, 291, 296, 485; art of, I: 405, 406, 407, 408; II: 3; nature in, 3; prices in, 4, 5, 43, 66, 67, 68, 69, 70; some bathing resorts of, 6; music of, 15; dances of, 21, 22, 31, 268, 297, 468; country people of, 31; prevalence of Shintō in interior of, 31, 32; food of, 32, 91, 92, 103, 104, 292; law of life in, 35; women of, 35, 36, 61, 87, 88, 90, 91; difficulties of literary work in, 35, 60, 63, 89; literature of, 40, 41, 114, 343, 344, 415; laws regarding marriage with a foreigner in, 44, 64; frankness of life in, 45; protracted labour uncommon in, 48, 49; cats in, 55, 56, 58, 59; English reading-books for students in, 79, 102, 105, 106, 283, 328; celebration of the New Year in, 80, 81, 82; drinking in, 82, 92, 93; earthquakes in, 83, 84; colourlessness of, 89; houses of, 93; children of, 99, 190, 191, 288, 306, 307; obstacles to higher education in, 103, 104, 291, 292, 307, 308; disintegration of, 144, 145, 323, 478; pay of native officials of, 158, 259, 265, 308; need of scientific men in, 163, 164, 275; politics in the public schools of, 166; war between China and, 175, 181, 182, 185, 186, 251, 258, 262, 281, 511; foreign treaties of, 185, 186, 262; naturalization of foreigners in, 191, 192; open ports of, 199, 298, 315, 341, 342; anti-

foreign feeling in, 201, 223, 252, 258, 262, 281; decline of education in, 216; girls' and boys' dress in, 253–255, 259, 260; songs of, 267, 268; floods in, 307; intrigue in, 321–323; Occidental indifference to stories of real life of, 362, 363; demands upon University professors in, 370; the educated woman in, 416–422; Occidental aggression in, 442; mania for organizations in, 461; Government service in, 470; rapidly changing conditions in, 471, 502; protests against Hearn's treatment by, 490, 493, 506; Hearn's proposed series of lectures on, 487, 495, 496, 499, 504, 505, 506, 514, 515; travelling of the common people in, 502; war between Russia and, 515, 516, 517.

Japan, Emperor of, II: 317. See also Go-Daigo.

Japanese, natural charm of, II: 4, 207; their genius for eclecticism, 28; unemotional nature of, 35, 60, 63, 85, 332; strange power of, 56; harder side of, 61; their fear of foreigners, 82 ; impossibility of friendship with, 99, 100, 159, 217; probable future characteristics of, 104; their reserve, 122, 123 ; their attitude toward nature, 125, 425, 426; their trickiness, 201, 202; deficiency of the sex instinct among, 209, 210; development of the mathematical faculty among, 210; psychology of, 214, 215; satire of, 217; their loyalty, 236, 237 ; an essentially military race, 258; their stature, 260; their chastity, 269; their affected religious indifference, 274; their hardihood, 292; their longevity, 324; management of, impossible to Occidentals, 386, 387, 388.

Jeannest, Charles, I: 313, 357; his Au Congo, 354.

Jerome, St., his letter to Dardanas, describing an organ, I: 166, 167.

Jesuits, animosity of, toward Hearn, II: 213.

Jesus y Preciado, José de, I: 334.

Jewett, Sarah Orne, II: 301.

Jews, ancient life of, I: 287; lost musical instruments of, 311.

Jizō, a festival in honour of, I: 126; legend of, II: 6.

Johns Hopkins University, II: 496.

Johnson, Charles, I: 307, 312, 314, 341.

Jordan, David Starr, president of Stanford University, II: 496.

Josephine, Empress of the French, anecdote of statue of, in Martinique, I: 417–419.

Journalism, rewards of, I: 169, 181; demands of, 242; restraints of, 271, 275; Hearn's desire to escape from, 274, 276, 363, 397; literary work and, 324; II: 222, 480; Hearn's abandonment of, I: 425; his proposal to return to, II: 493, 494.

Judæa, musical instruments furnished to the Romans by, I: 166.

Kabit, I: 388.

Kaka, Japan, II: 6.

Kalewala, II: 472, 502; its operatic possibilities, I: 233, 235–237, 239, 307, 308, 388; Hearn's translations from, 403.

Kalidasa. See Sakuntala.

Kamakura, II: 346.

Kano, II: 73, 104, 119, 279; his knowledge of English, 66; a teacher of ju-jutsu, 70.

Kanteletar, I: 235.

Katayama, Mr., II: 66, 68, 73, 291.

Kathā-sarit-sāgara, I: 237, 402.

Kazimirski, A. de Biberstein, his translation of the Koran, I: 327.

Keats, John, II: 215.

Keightley, Thomas, his Fairy Mythology, I: 279.

Kichijōji, temple of, II: 328.

Kihei, Masumoto, his charities, II: 309, 327.

Kikujirō, Wadamori, his exhibitions of memory, II: 279.

Kimi ga yo, II: 236.

Kingsley, Charles, his Greek Heroes, II: 102; Airly Beacon, 522, 523.

Kipling, Rudyard, II: 83, 190, 301, 336, 337, 348, 362, 363, 405, 485, 491; his morbidness, 84; his Jungle Book, 187, 189, 196; his story of Purim Bagat, 196; Hearn's admiration for, 319, 408, 499; his royalties, 377; his Day's Work, 408.

Kishibojin, worship of, II: 16, 17.

Kissing, different significance of, in Turanian and Aryan races, II: 263, 264.

Kiyomasa, Katō, legend regarding, II: 186.

Kiyomizu, Kwannon temple at, II: 28; scenery at, 30; Inari shrine at, 30.

Kizuki, Japan, II: 7, 11, 297; Hearn's visit to the temple at, I: 115, 122; II: 9, 10, 43; deity of, 8; society for preserving buildings at, 13; an entertainment given to Hearn at, 37, 38; custom regarding Shōryō-bune in, 38, 39; Buddhist temple (Rengaji) at, 42; revival of Shintō in, 47.

Kobe, Japan, Hearn's work in, I: 128, 129, 132, 139; disagreeable characteristics of, II: 197, 198, 199; flood in, 307.

Kobu-dera, Buddhist temple in Tōkyō, I: 142, 143.

Koeber, Raphael von, II: 284, 311, 315, 316.

Koizumi, Iwao, Hearn's son, II: 516, 517.

Koizumi, Kazuo, Hearn's eldest son, I: 127, 128, 150, 154; II: 165, 166, 175, 181, 190, 191, 196, 198, 231, 252, 255, 260, 275, 276, 280, 288, 291, 295, 305, 306, 307, 309, 351, 373, 374, 426, 434, 459, 460, 464, 474, 483, 485, 489, 490, 493, 497, 503, 505, 508, 516, 517; plans for his scientific education, 181, 270, 271; his sensitiveness, 300, 476, 498.

Koizumi, Setsu, II: 68, 74, 77, 81, 82, 90, 95, 96, 97, 110, 119, 128, 157, 159, 181, 190, 191, 192, 193, 276, 278, 279, 288, 295, 298, 317, 329, 336, 337, 386, 397, 489, 491; Hearn's marriage to, I: 116; her notes regarding their life, 117, 118, 119–124, 127, 138, 142–152, 155; her study of English, II: 106.

Koizumi, Yakumo, Hearn's Japanese name, I: 117; II: 270, 292, 293, 299.

Kompert, Leopold, his Studies of Jewish Life, I: 287.

Kompira, Japan, II: 153, 165.

Koran, various editions of, I: 327.

Koteda, Viscount Yasusada, Governor of Izumo, I: 119, 120; II: 14, 18, 104.

Koteda, Miss, II: 104; her gift to Hearn, I: 118; II: 19.

Koto-shiro-nushi-no-Kami, legend of, II: 7, 8, 97; identified with Ebisu, in Matsue, 13; in Mionoseki, 37.

Krehbiel, Henry Edward, I: 469; Hearn's friendship with, 55, 60; Hearn's letters to, 67, 73; text of the letters, 84, 85, 86, 165–244, 277–289, 292–314, 320–325, 330–339, 351–364, 367–380, 384–388, 405–408, 409–411; his Fantaisie Chinoise, 168, 171, 187; his musical essays, 187; his talks, 192; Hearn's comment on his style, 234, 240, 293, 372, 373; his work on the New York Tribune, 241; his musical criticisms, 386.

Krehbiel, Mrs. Henry Edward, I: 191, 223.

Krishna, I: 316.

Kūkedo, visit to cave of, I: 121, 122.

Kumamoto, Japan, Hearn's removal to, I: 124; his life at, 125–128; shrines of, II: 65; climate of, 66, 69, 73; Hearn's fellow teachers at, 66, 67, 70, 73; his household at, 67, 74, 81, 110; appearance of, 69, 70, 81; the Dai Go Kōtō-Chūgakkō at, 70, 71, 100; students at, 70, 79; religion in, 76; reading books used in, 79, 102.

Kwannon, temple of, at Kiyomizu, II: 28; representations of, 77, 78.

Kyōto, Japan, II: 130; middle school in, 142; Hearn's fondness for, 192; exhibition in, 257.

Kyūshū, Japan, II: 91; Europeanized, 99; students of, 129, 130.

La Beaume, Jules, his translation of the Koran, I: 327.

La Bédollière, Emile de, I: 200.

Labrunie, Gérard (Gérard de Nerval), I: 254, 255, 317; Hearn's desire to translate his Voyage en Orient, 362.

Lakmé, Delibes's opera of, I: 377.

Lamarck, Jean Baptiste de, II: 266.

Lang, Andrew, II: 215; his translation of Gautier's Contes, I: 62.

La Selve, Edgar, I: 353, 354.

Last Island, I: 95; destruction of, 96; the scene of Hearn's Chita, 96.

Latin races, cruelty of, I: 203; probable future absorption of, II: 300, 385.

Layard, Sir Austen Henry, I: 213.

Le Duc, Léouzon. See Léouzon Le Duc.

Lee, Charles, I: 168.

Le Fanu, Joseph Sheridan, his Bird of Passage, I: 201; II: 41.

Lefcada. *See* Santa Maura.

Le Gallienne, Richard, II: 299.

Legends, Greek and Hindoo, I: 227, 228; Talmudic, 287.

Leloir, Louis Auguste, I: 319, 320.

Lemaître, Jules Élie François, I: 434; II: 491.

Léouzon Le Duc, Louis Antoine, his edition of the Kalewala, I: 235, 236; II: 468, 469.

Lessing, Gotthold Ephraim, I: 211: his Laocoön, 269.

Letter-writing, different methods of, II: 247, 248.

Leucadia. *See* Santa Maura.

Levkas. *See* Santa Maura.

Lewes, George Henry, II: 190, 221; his recognition of Spencer, 235.

Liberty, effect of industrialism on, II: 470, 511, 512.

Life, law of modern, II: 134, 135; an intellectual battle, 135, 136; cost of, to the white races, 137; wastefulness of, 249.

L'Isère, Colombat de. *See* Colombat, Marc.

Lissajous, Jules Antoine, I: 385.

Literature, rewards of, I: 393, 430; Japanese, II: 40, 41, 344, 415; plan for a study of comparative, 271; teaching of English, 271; German, 290; American and English, 301, 302; Russian and French, 302; conditions of success in, 351; the personal equation in judgements of, 441; seriousness of, 463, 464; Hearn's theory of the study of English, in Japan, 464; no taste in America for good, 472; Hearn's equipment for, and method of teaching English, 480, 481–483, 486, 487; Hearn's advice about modern, 509.

Livingstone, David, I: 297.

Loennrot, Elias, his edition of the Kalewala, I: 235, 403.

Lombroso, Cesare, II: 276, 277.

London, University of, plan for Hearn to lecture at, I: 156.

Longfellow, Henry Wadsworth, I: 190; his Spanish Student, 205, 206.

Loochoo Islands, II: 91, 214; B. H. Chamberlain's monograph on, 273, 274.

Loti, Pierre, pseud. *See* Viaud.

Lotus, an article of diet, II: 45, 63.

Louisiana, some newspapers of, I: 204, 205.

Love, power of, I: 315, 316; decline of, 316; its effect upon literature, 326; varying attributes of, 438; a Buddhist view of, II: 138.

Lowell, Percival, II: 33, 117, 160, 200, 310, 317; his Soul of the Far East, I: 460, 461; II: 28, 30, 39, 150, 208, 479, 487, 505; his Chosön, I: 457, 461; II: 30; his papers on Mars, 202, 203, 204, 208, 479; his Occult Japan, 200, 204, 207, 208.

Lowell Institute, Boston, II: 496.

Loyalty, Japanese ideas of, II: 236, 237.

Lyall, Sir Alfred Comyns, I: 388.

Macassar, Celebes, II: 219.

Macaulay, Thomas Babington, Baron, his Lays of Ancient Rome as a reading-book in Japanese schools, II: 102.

McDonald, Mitchell, I: 153; II: 458, 459; Hearn's friendship with, I: 109, 110; letters from Hearn to, II: 340–342, 347–358, 361–381, 384, 385, 388–397, 403–412, 422–436, 437–440, 442–455; Hearn's proposal to, regarding a book of short stories, 341, 342, 348, 349, 350, 356; his Highbinder story, 348, 364; his belief in Hearn's work, 351, 375, 379, 494.

Mackintosh, Sir James, II: 136.

Magazine work, labour of, I: 283, 285; some effects of, 293; discouragements of, 317; Hearn's willingness to resume, II: 480.

Magic, musical, an example of, I: 322.

Mahabharata, I: 402.

Mahan, Alfred Thayer, II: 374.

Maiko. *See* Geisha.

Maine, battle-ship, destruction of, II: 358.

Malatesta, Giovanni, I: 271.

Mallock, William Hurrell, II: 196, 301; his opinion of Gautier, I: 254, 256; his translation of Gautier, 257; his morbidness, II: 84.

Malta, Island of, I: 7; II: 217; Hearn's recollections of, II: 213, 214.

Manila, P. I., II: 213; expedition against, 369.

Mantegazza, Paolo, II: 277.
Marche, Antoine Alfred, his Afrique
Occidentale, I: 354.
Marcus Aurelius, II: 446.
Margot, ——, I: 91, 94, 95.
Marie Galante, island, I: 413.
Marimba, musical instrument, I: 411.
Marion, ——, I: 88, 89, 90, 92.
Marriage, II: 98, 99; deity of, 8; Jap-
anese law regarding marriage with
a foreigner, 44, 64; Occidental views
of, 120; the educated woman and,
in Japan, 416–422.
Martinique, I: 97; costume colours of,
98; doll dressed as woman of, 410,
411; action in, after fall of Second
Empire, 418, 419; physicians of,
441.
Masayoshi, Kumagoe, II: 116, 130.
Massachusetts, application of Spencer's educational theories in, II: 275.
Matas, Rodolfo, I: 97, 263, 371, 380,
395, 445.
Mathematicians, indifference of, to
poetry, I: 461, 462.
Matsue, Japan, II: 154, 155, 330, 331;
Hearn's appointment at, I: 110–113,
137; situation and character of,
110, 111, 114, 115; Hearn's first residence in, 113; his departure from,
124, 125; ascendency of Shintō in, II:
13, 15; climate of, 23, 25; geisha at,
95; Hearn's desire to return to, 298.
Matsushima, Japanese flag-ship, II:
258.
Maupassant, Guy de, I: 72, 361; II:
348, 392.
Mazois, Charles François, I: 213.
Medical novels, I: 399, 437, 441.
Medicine, study of, II: 289, 290.
Medusa, legend of, I: 185.
Megara, choral dance of Greek wo-
men in, I; 385.
Meiji Maru, Japanese ship, II: 304.
Mélusine, periodical, I: 170, 284;
death of, 189.
Memory, transmutation of inherited,
II: 338.
Memphis, Tenn., I: 66.
Mephistopheles, Goethe's, II: 435.
Meredith, Owen. See Bulwer-Lytton.
Mérimée, Prosper, I: 205; his Carmen,
200, 201.
Métairie, the, New Orleans, I: 205.
Mexico, music of, I: 231; African in-
fluence on, 380.

Michelet, Jules, I: 227, 256; his
L'Amour, II: 277.
Middle Ages, musical instruments of,
I: 165–167; literary renascence in,
342.
Miko, Shintō priestesses, II: 21, 22, 31,
268, 297, 468.
Miko-kagura, Japanese dance, II: 38,
42.
Miller, Ed., I: 221.
Millet, Jean François, I: 6.
Milton, John, his Paradise Lost
used as a reading-book in Tōkyō,
II: 283, 328.
Mionoseki, Japan, II: 6; deity of, 7,
8, 37, 97.
Missionaries, Hearn's attitude to-
ward, II: 44, 45, 68, 109, 110, 311;
unmarried women as, in Japan, 441,
442.
Mississippi River, dangers to swim-
mers in, I: 176, 177.
Mocking-bird, of Guiana, I: 357, 358.
Mohammed, I: 280, 281.
Mombushō Readers, II: 105.
Money, power of, I: 348.
Mongolians, similarities between faces
of Irish and, I: 190.
Moon-of-Autumn. See Akizuki.
Moral development, immorality a
force in, II: 136, 137.
Moral sense, nature of, I: 434–436.
Morris, William, his Wood beyond
the World, II: 196.
Morrow, William C., II: 363, 364.
Mothers, II: 190, 191.
Motoori, II: 7.
Mountains, sadness produced by sight
of, II: 151.
Mud-dauber, I: 89.
Muir, John, I: 388.
Müller, Friedrich Max, his Sacred
Books of the East, I: 327.
Muezzin, call of the. See Azan.
Mukden, Manchuria, I: 106.
Mulock, Dinah, her John Halifax
used as a reading-book in Kuma-
moto, II: 79.
Murderer, Hearn's description of a,
I: 322, 323.
Murger, Henri, philosophy of his Bo-
hemianism, I: 242.
Murray, John, guide-book published
by, II: 37, 43.
Music, infinity of, I: 179; demands
of, 180; opportunities for studying,

182; antique, 211, 213; in the Talmud, 287; Spencer's essay on musical origination, 325; mathematics of, 385. *See also* Brittany, Creoles, Cuba, Eskimo, Finland, Griots, Havana, Japan, Mexico, Negro, Scandinavia, Timbuctoo, Wales, West Indies.

Musical instruments, I: 165-167, 211-213, 311, 353. *See also* Bagpipe, Chalumeau, Egypt, Flute, Greece, Harps, Judæa, Marimba, Negro, Sistrum, Syrinx.

Musset, Alfred de, I: 254, 255.

Mystic number, Japanese, II: 80.

Nakamura, Mr., II: 68.

Nala, story of, I: 402.

Names, of Japanese women, Hearn's article on, II: 445, 446, 447.

Nanji-umi, II: 30.

Naples, museum of, I: 213.

Napoleon I, II: 160, 173.

Natural selection, only one factor of evolution, II: 235.

Naturalism, in art and literature, I: 228.

Nature, in Japan, II: 3; attitudes toward, in East and West, 123-125, 131, 425, 426; immorality of, 189.

Negro, vocal chords of, I: 313, 339, 356; West Coast races and, 332; their talent for improvisation, 353; temperature of blood of, 356; music of the American, 358; musical instruments played by, in West Indies, 411.

Neith, Egyptian divinity, I: 315.

Neptune, festival of, I: 386.

Nerval, Gérard de, pseud. *See* Labrunie, Gérard.

Nervous system, weight of, II: 245.

New Orleans, La., Hearn removes to, I: 65, 66, 67; conditions in, after the war, 68, 69; yellow fever in, 69, 185, 186, 195; Hearn leaves, 97; description of an old Creole house in, 172-174; a Chinese restaurant in, 203, 204; maladministration in, 215; Hearn's disappointment in, 224, 225. *See also* Métairie.

New York City, Hearn goes to, I: 39, 40, 101, 102; his dislike of, 288, 405, 425, 443, 444; II: 182, 476, 484.

Newts, tradition regarding, at Sakusa, Japan, II: 26.

Nichiren, followers of, II: 27; prevalence of, at Yabase, 47; temple of, at Yabase, 55.

Nidānakathā, I: 287.

Nietzsche, Friedrich Wilhelm, II: 325, 514.

Nishida, Sentarō, I: 116, 122; II: 9, 23, 33; letters from Hearn to, II: 18, 19, 54, 55, 65-69, 72-76, 95-98, 101-106, 118, 119, 141-145, 153-160, 165-167, 180-182, 191-193, 274-276, 278-280, 291, 292, 296-299, 303-305, 327-332; his knowledge of English, 101; his ballad of Shuntoku-maru, 130.

Nishinomiya, Japan, II: 8.

Noguchi, Yone, I: 159.

Nordau, Max, false theories of, II: 277; his Degeneration, 456.

North, stimulus to literary production in, I: 194; conceptions of beauty in, 211; intellectual vigour of, 423; struggle for life in, 424.

Nude, the, in art, I: 30, 31.

Numi, a Japanese friend of Hearn, II: 465.

Occident, possible future domination of, by Orient, II: 29; indifference in, to stories of the real life of the Orient, 362, 363.

Ochiai, T. *See* Inomata, Teizaburō.

O'Connor, William D., Hearn's letters to, I: 73; his first acquaintance with, 80; text of the letters, 268-275, 290-292, 315-320, 326-329, 340, 341, 348-351, 364-367, 380-384; Hearn's advice regarding an illness, 365-367; his death, II: 432.

Odd, Hearn's pursuit of the, I: 290, 291, 294, 328, 329.

Odin, the Hávamál of, II: 428.

Œdipus, II: 168.

Offenbach, Jacques, I: 222.

Oho-kuni-nushi-no-Kami, Japanese deity identified with Daikoku, in Matsue, II: 13.

Ohokuni, legend of the son of, II: 6.

Ōiso, Japan, II: 6.

Oki, Japan, II: 96, 187.

Okuma, Count, university founded by, I: 156; II: 514.

Ō-Kuni, story of, II: 42, 43.

Olcott, Henry Steel, his Buddhist Catechism, I: 265.
Old Semicolon, nickname given to Hearn, I: 50.
Omar, Caliph, I: 281.
Omiki dokkuri no kuchi-sashi, form of, II: 80.
Onamuji-no-Mikoto, Japanese deity, II: 9.
Opposition, value of, II: 406.
O'Rell, Max, pseud. See Blouët.
Organization, tyranny of, II: 169, 170.
Organs, wind, adopted by Christians from Byzantium, I: 166; one described by St. Jerome, 167.
Orient, intellectual barriers between Occident and, I: 104, 105; possible future domination of the Occident by, II: 29.
Ormuzd, the Persian God of Light, II: 118, 126.
Ōsaka, Japan, II: 297, 298.
Osgood, James R., I: 320, 321.
Ōtani, Masanobu, I: 113, 118; II: 68; Hearn's aid to, I: 137, 138: his notes on Hearn, 137, 138; letters from Hearn to, II: 69-72, 79, 80, 162-165, 342-346, 414, 415, 461-464; advice to, regarding study of philology, 162, 164; Japanese poems collected by, 343, 415; a gift to Hearn from, 414, 415.
Ōtsu, flood in, II: 307.
Ōtsuka, Japan, Hearn's treatment in, II: 52, 53, 54, 55.
Ouadây, Africa, I: 277.
Overbeck, Johannes Adolf, his Pompeii, I: 213.
Overwork, penalties of, I: 241, 242; results of, 367, 383.
Oxford, University of, plan for Hearn to lecture at, I: 156.
Ōzawa, a teacher at Kumamoto, II: 66.

Pain, infliction of, II: 111; results of, 136; moral, 168; a factor in evolution, 243; results of, on Hearn's work, 272, 273, 393.
Paine, Thomas, I: 345.
Palmer, Edward Henry, his translation of the Koran, I: 351.
Parvati, Indian divinity, I: 210.
Patate-cry, I: 360.
Pater, Walter, II: 215.
Patti, Adelina, I: 240, 405.

Pearson, Charles Henry, his National Character, II: 137.
Pelée, Mt., I: 98.
Perron, Dr. A., his Femmes Arabes, I: 277, 315, 468.
Personality, invisible, I: 447; multiple, 474, 475.
Peterson Brothers, I: 250.
Petronius Arbiter, I: 256.
Phelps, Elizabeth Stuart. See Ward.
Philadelphia, Pa., Hearn's liking for, I: 449, 452, 469, 470.
Philistine, The, periodical, II: 369.
Philostratus, I: 321.
Photograph, scientific test of, II: 83.
Physicians, Hearn's regard for the career of, I: 436; women as, in France, 441; of Martinique, 441.
Physiology, effect of, upon the history of nations, I: 330.
Pickpockets, an adventure with, II: 391.
Pipes, ancient Samurai, II: 48; modern Japanese, 48-51.
Plato, II: 173.
Pleasure, changes in Hearn's ideas of, II: 194, 195.
Plympton, —, I: 360, 361.
Poetry, translations of, I: 245; value of form in, 271, 272, 294; indifference of mathematicians to, 461; vulgar, II: 343, 344; translation the test of, 344, 523, 526, 527, 528; three forms of, 519, 520; true literary signification of, 520; best medium of, 521.
Politeness. See Courtesy.
Politics, public schools and, II: 166.
Pompeii, musical instruments discovered in, I: 213.
Pontchartrain, Lake, I: 169, 176.
Poole, Captain, II: 304.
Pope, Alexander, II: 520, 528, 529.
Port of Spain, Trinidad, a silversmith at, I: 416.
Poseidon, festival of, I: 386.
Pott, Mrs. Henry, I: 364.
Prayer, the dilemma of the gods, II: 394.
Pre-Raphaelites, I: 211.
Professions, Hearn's estimate of, I: 398.
Proof, printer's, relation between copy and, II: 407.
Proof-reader, Hearn's terror of the, I: 387.

Prose, poetical, II: 524; Hearn's ambition regarding, I: 364, 374, 379, 383, 393.

Protestantism, II: 311, 312.

Provençal literature and song, Hueffer's treatment of, I: 361.

Public schools, politics in, II: 166.

Publishers, Hearn's opposition to the views of, II: 479, 480; their attitude toward authors, 484, 485.

Punctuation, Hearn's efforts to reform, I: 50.

Quacks, success of, I: 180, 181.

Quatrefages de Bréau, Jean Louis Armand de, I: 235, 236.

Rabyah, operatic possibilities of, I: 388.

Race expansion, intellectual, cost of, II: 98.

Ramayana, translations of, I: 402.

Raphael, I: 211.

Ravine-les-Cannes, I: 191.

Rawlinson, Sir Henry Creswicke, I: 213.

Regeneration, Hearn's use of the word, II: 509.

Rein, Johannes Justus, his work on Japan, II: 36.

Religion, the conservator of romanticism, II: 208, 209; Norse, 228; sects and, 131; characteristics common to all religions, 146, 147; science and, 148.

Rembrandt, I: 211.

Remsen, Ira, president of Johns Hopkins University, II: 504.

Renan, Ernest, II: 514.

Rengaji, Buddhist temple at Kizuki, II: 42.

Rhys-Davids, Thomas William, II: 380, 488.

Riess, Ludwig, professor at the University of Tōkyō, II: 312, 316.

Rights and duties, II: 115.

Rink, Henry John, I: 330.

Robert Clarke Company, Cincinnati, I: 50.

Robinson, ——, I: 187.

Roche, Louise, I: 357.

Roget, Peter Mark, his Thesaurus, I: 374.

Roland, Song of, I: 190, 246.

Rollins, Alice Wellington, I: 389; II: 299, 300.

Roman Catholic Church, Hearn's bitterness against, I: 33, 34.

Romanes, George John, I: 292, 439.

Romans, musical instruments adopted by, I: 165, 166.

Romanticism, religion the conservator of, I: 208, 209; Baudelaire on, 211.

Romanticists, pantheism of, I: 255.

Romany descent, mark of, I: 5.

Rossetti, Dante Gabriel, I: 211; II: 221.

Rouquette, Adrien, Indian missionary, I: 169, 188, 191, 206, 212.

Routine, merits of, I: 326.

Roy, Protap Chunder, I: 335.

Rufz de Lavison, Etienne, I: 442; II: 248, 347.

Ruskin, John, his comment on the Medicean Venus, I: 31.

Russia, feeling against, in Japan, II: 258, 262; war between Japan and, 515, 516, 517.

Rydberg, Viktor, I: 227.

Ryūkyū, II: 219.

Saadi. See Gulistan.

Sacher-Masoch, Leopold Ritter von, his Mother of God, I: 233.

Sadness, certain causes of, II: 150–152.

St. Augustine, Florida, I: 70.

St. Peter's Cathedral, Cincinnati, Hearn's description of a view from the spire of, I: 51.

St. Pierre, Martinque, I: 97; II: 347, 484; Hearn's record of, I: 98, 100, 101, 412, 413, 415.

Sainte-Beuve, Charles Augustin, I: 396; II: 222.

Saintsbury, George, II: 371.

Saionji, II: 279.

Sakai, Japan, II: 297, 304.

Sake, II: 57, 82, 92, 93.

Sakuma, his knowledge of literary English, II: 66.

Sakuntala, operatic possibilities of, I: 308.

Sakurai, headmaster at Kumamoto, II: 66.

Sakusa, Japan, Shintō shrine at, II: 15, 25, 26.

Sakusa-no-Mikoto, Shintō deity, II: 25.

Sale, George, his translation of the Koran, I: 327.

Samurai, I: 116.

San Francisco, Cal., Hearn's search for a publisher in, I: 246, 247.
Sanskrit, derivation of Greek and Latin from, I: 202.
Santa Maura, Island of, Hearn's birth-place, I: 3, 7, 429; situation and character of, 3, 4; its influence upon Hearn, 4, 5.
Sanza, Nagoya, II: 42.
Sanzo, Tsuda, II: 142, 143.
Sappho, I: 3, 238.
Sasa, a Japanese priest, II: 7, 8.
Satire, Japanese, II: 217.
Satni-Khamois, Egyptian romance, I: 238.
Sato, Mr., II: 68.
Sattee, a Hindoo, sent by Hearn to Krehbiel, I: 367–370, 393.
Scandinavia, music of, I: 190.
Schiefner, Franz Anton, his German translation of Kalewala, I: 235.
Schlemihl, Peter, II: 443.
Schopenhauer, Arthur, I: 447, 459, 460; II: 151, 235; basis of his phi-losophy, 266, 267.
Schurman, Jacob Gould, president of Cornell University, II: 488, 492, 495.
Schwab, Moïse, his translation of part of the Talmud, I: 287.
Schweinfurth, Georg August, I: 310, 354.
Science, influence of, upon literary style, I: 263, 264; unsatisfactori-ness of, II: 338, 339.
Scientific education, II: 163, 164, 275.
Scotland, bagpipe and kilt introduced by Romans into, I: 182, 183.
Secret Affinities, Hearn's translation of the pantheistic madrigal from Gautier's Emaux et Camées, I: 259–261.
Sects, religion and, II: 131.
Self-interest, the basis of most human relations, II: 188, 189.
Sensation, hereditary, II: 223, 225–227, 230, 233, 234, 235, 236, 237, 241, 250.
Senses, training of the, II: 86.
Sensibility, moral and physical, I: 434–436.
Serpent worship, II: 29.
Sex, influence of, on history, I: 256; a mystery of, 401; standards regard-ing the relations of, 438; Oriental and Occidental views regarding questions of, II: 112, 113, 114, 121,

122, 123; instincts of, deficient in Japanese, 209, 210.
Shakespeare, II: 520.
"Shall," and "will," Hearn's use of the words, II: 224, 225, 246.
Shelley, Percy Bysshe, II: 215.
Shimane, ken of, I: 115.
Shimbashi, II: 433; Hearn's adven-tures with pickpockets at, 391.
Shimo-ichi, II: 37, 41, 46.
Shinshū, a sect, II: 27.
Shintō, I: 112; ascendency of, in Mat-sue, II: 13, 15; nature of, 26, 27, 30; prevalence of, in interior of Japan, 31, 32; revival of, in Kizuki, 47; rituals, 59; Hearn's questions regarding Shintō home-worship in Izumo, 71, 79.
Ships of the Souls. See Shōryō-bune.
Shiva, the Hindoo god of destruction, I: 210, 211.
Shōryō-bune, II: 8, 38, 39, 41.
Simpson, Walter, his History of the Gipsies, I: 201, 202, 459.
Sinnett, Alfred Percy, I: 265.
Sistrum, introduced by Egypt into Italy, I: 166.
Siva. See Shiva.
Skeat, Walter William, I: 374.
Small-pox, in Martinique, I: 422.
Smoking, paraphernalia of, in Japan, II: 49–51.
Smyrna, I: 8.
Snake, sacred, II: 29.
Socialism, tyranny of, II: 184, 185, 205, 511, 512.
Societies, literary, Hearn's opinion of, II: 461–463.
Society, the nature of polite, II: 400; injury inflicted upon writers by, 451.
Society of Authors, London, II: 445, 446.
Society of Finnish Literature, I: 235.
Socrates, I: 41.
Solomon, Song of, I: 227.
Souls, sacrifice of, II: 410.
Souls, velvet, Hearn's definition of the phrase, II: 326.
Soulié, Melchior Frédéric, II: 231.
South, difficulty of literary production in, I: 194; conceptions of beauty in, 211.
Spanish-American War, II: 369, 373, 374, 376, 379, 380, 384, 385.
Specialization, necessity of, I: 263.
Spencer, Herbert, II: 108, 190, 207,

208, 221, 236, 247; Hearn's admiration for, I: 58; II: 44, 409, 509; his influence upon Hearn, I: 85, 86, 365, 374, 375, 392, 394, 430, 431, 438, 459; II: 20, 26, 221, 222; his Sociology, I: 312; his essay on musical origination, 325; his conservatism regarding further physical evolution, 397; his theory of education, 456; his criticism of the Mombusho Readers, II: 105; his theory of moral evolution, 137; history of good manners traced by, 183; socialism defined by, 184, 205; on heredity, 223, 226, 228, 234; on psychological evolution, 231; Darwin and, 235; his paper on the Method of Comparative Psychology, 249; application of his educational theories, 275; his views on eccentricity, 277; on war, 510.

Sphinx, riddle of the, II: 168.

Spinoza, Baruch, II: 173.

Stamboul, black population of, I: 355.

Stanford University, II: 476, 477; plans for Hearn to lecture at, 496.

Stauben, Daniel, his Scènes de la Vie Juive, I: 287.

Steamships, Hearn's account of the fatal effect of his presence upon, II: 433.

Stedman, Edmund Clarence, I: 332, 446.

Stevenson, Robert Louis, II: 190, 336, 383, 405, 509.

Strength, misuse of, II: 160, 161.

Sturdy, E. T., II: 380.

Style, literary, helps to formation of, I: 263, 264, 372, 373, 374; Hearn's ambition regarding his own, 276, 364, 374, 379, 383, 393; labour of acquiring an ornamental, 324.

Success, some requisites of, I: 431; II: 135.

Suicide, a Japanese, II: 273.

Susa-no-o, Japanese deity, II: 8.

Susa-no-o-no-Mikoto, Shintō deity, II: 16, 25.

Swimming, Hearn's fondness for, I: 176, 333, 334, 341; II: 47, 63, 303, 304, 448; of Japanese boys at Yabase, 48.

Swinburne, Algernon Charles, I: 432, 433; II: 427.

Sword-Dance, in Léon dialect, I: 305;

prose and metrical translations of, 305–307.

Swords, legends concerning, I: 185.

Symonds, John Addington, I: 220, 227; his praise of Whitman, 292; his Greek Poets, 329; his Wine, Women, and Song, 342.

Syrinx, musical instrument, I: 297.

Taillefer, I: 191.

Taine, Hippolyte Adolphe, his Art in Italy, II: 271.

Taka o gami-no-Mikoto, II: 25.

Takahashi, Dr., II : 304.

Takahashi, Sakué, II: 330, 331.

Takaki, Japanese boy, II: 278; head of, on title-page of Kokoro, 300.

Takamori, Senke, I: 115, 116 ; II: 7, 9, 10, 38, 145, 297; his gift to Hearn, 153; courtesy of, 180.

Takata, Dean, I: 150.

Talmud, I: 237, 311; legends of the, 287.

Tampa, Florida, I: 376.

Tam-tam, I: 411.

Tanabe, one of Hearn's pupils, II: 68; letter from Hearn to, 508, 509.

Tannery murder, Cincinnati, I: 51.

Taylor, Bayard, I: 266, 324; II: 215.

Taylor, James Monroe, president of Vassar College, II: 504, 505.

Tennessee, Hearn's account of an incident in, I: 67.

Tennōji, II: 297.

Tennyson, Alfred, Baron Tennyson, I: 221, 333; II: 190, 221, 302; his Princess used as a reading-book in Tōkyō, II: 283, 328.

Terminus, the god of boundaries, I: 184, 185.

Tetsujirō, Inoue, II: 284, 313.

Thomas, Theodore, I: 180, 182.

Thought, physiologically considered, II: 244.

Ticknor, William D., I: 332, 372.

Timbuctoo, music of desert nomads of, I: 353.

Time, value of, II: 194; no knowledge of the value of, in Japan, 461, 463.

Times-Democrat (New Orleans); Hearn's associates on, I: 70, 71; Hearn's work on, 72, 73, 176, 280, 363; letters to, afterward expanded into Chita, 96; purpose of its proprietors, 288.

Tison, Alexander, professor at the

University of Tōkyō, ii: 284, 312, 316.

Togo-ike, Japan, ii: 53.

Tōkyō, Hearn's private life in, i: 141–152; ii: 295, 309, 327, 329; his dislike of, ii: 192, 193; the foreign element in, 321, 456, 457; cheap living in, 329; appearance of, 333, 334; climate of, 366, 372, 385; lack of literary inspiration in, 378; work done by students in, 387; a silk-house at, 437, 438; Government service in, 470.

Tōkyō, University of, Hearn becomes Professor of English Literature at, i: 136–138; resigns this position, 154; ii: 368, 490, 493; students of, ii: 282, 283, 314, 315, 328, 388; the gate to public office, 282; Hearn's work at, 283, 298, 305, 306, 310, 314, 327, 328, 357, 427, 429, 444, 481, 482, 486, 487; professors at, 284, 285, 311, 312, 313, 315, 316; architecture of, 311; one reason for Hearn's appointment at, 313, 314.

Torio, Viscount, his theories of Western civilization, ii: 36, 40.

Toyokuni, ii: 77.

Toyoma, Masakazu, i: 122; ii: 298, 328, 329.

Tradesmen, enviable position of, i: 398, 399.

Translations, from the French, obstacles to publication of, i: 247, 248, 250, 251.

Trata, La, Greek choral dance, i: 385.

Trinidad, babies of, i: 416, 417.

Trinity, the Hindoo, i: 210.

Tropics, difficulty of reproducing the charms of, in literature, i: 99; Hearn's love for the, 105, 415, 420, 425, 449, 469; ii: 64, 211, 213, 217, 281; nature and human nature in the, i: 436; difficulty of literary work in, 422, 423, 424, 425, 449; heredity in, 429.

Trübner & Co., i: 325.

Trygvesson, Olaf, ii: 228.

Tunison, Joseph Salathiel, i: 288, 361, 405, 411; his comment on Hearn's work and characteristics, 54, 55, 62, 63, 64, 65, 66; Hearn's friendship with, 55; his comment on Hearn's friendships, 56; his book on the Virgilian Legend, 351; letter from Hearn to, 443, 444.

Turiault, J., his Etude sur la Langage Créole de la Martinique, i: 357.

Twins, Japanese, ii: 326, 327.

Tylor, Edward Burnett, ii: 8, 41, 57; an Australian chant quoted by, i: 312, 313; its construction similar to a Greek chorus, 312; his book on anthropology, ii: 14.

Tyndall, John, ii: 235.

Typography, Hearn's interest in, i: 50.

Uguisi, gift of, to Hearn, i: 118, 119; ii: 19.

Ukioye exhibition, ii: 382.

Undine, philosophy of, ii: 508.

United States, intellectual sterility in, ii: 478; liberty in, 511, 512; race-hatred in, 512.

Ushaw, Roman Catholic College, i: 34, 37.

Ushigome. See Tōkyō.

Value, close connection between ideas of weight and, ii: 74, 75, 76.

Van Horne, Sir William, his offer to Hearn, ii: 505.

Varigny, Dr., ii: 467.

Vedantic philosophy, ii: 236.

Venus, Medicean, Ruskin's comment on, i: 31.

Venus of Milo, i: 227.

Verlaine, Paul, ii: 187.

Very, Mary, ii: 441.

Viaud, Julien (Pierre Loti), i: 72, 334, 361, 431, 432; ii: 479; his L'Inde sans les Anglais, i: 72; ii: 491, 492; his Mariage de Loti, i: 249, 377; his Roman d'un Spahi, 249, 427; his Aziyadé, 250; Hearn's desire to translate some of his novels, 362; Hearn's admiration for, 377, 378, 396, 427, 452, 453; his Un Rêve, 434, 452, 453; his Madame Chrysanthemum, 434; his account of the French attack on the coast of Annam, ii: 373; offers his services to Spain, 385.

Vickers, Thomas, i: 50, 214.

Victoria, Queen of England, i: 164.

Vignoli, Tito, i: 292.

Villoteau, Guillaume André, i: 283; his Mémoire sur la Musique dans l'antique Egypte, 285.

Virchow, Rudolf, ii: 312, 316.

Vishnu, i: 210.

Voice, Colombat de l'Isère's work on diseases of the, I: 363.
Voudoo, the word, I: 360.
Voudoo songs, I: 192, 193.

Wagner, Richard, I: 236; II: 15.
Wales, Hearn removes to, I: 8, 12; music of, 190; language of, 190.
Wall Street, New York City, romance of, II: 182.
Wallace, Alfred Russel, I: 438; II: 211, 213, 221.
War, developing effects of, II: 509, 510, 511.
Ward, Elizabeth Stuart Phelps, II: 301.
Warner, Charles Dudley, I: 342, 392, 451.
Waseda University, professors of, I: 149, 150; Hearn accepts chair of English at, 156.
Watson, William, II: 215, 402.
Weight, close connection between ideas of value and, II: 74, 75, 76.
Weill, Alexander, his reminiscences of Heine, I: 341.
Weiss, John, I: 265, 432.
West Indies, dances of, I: 297, 307; transplantation of negro melodies to, 356, 360, 411; Hearn's plan to visit, 382; letters relating to, 409–419, 422–424; literary material in, 410, 414, 422, 426; formative influences of climate of, 441.
Wetmore, Elizabeth (Bisland), II: 65, 82, 83, 167, 333, 484; letters from Hearn to, I: 82, 388–392, 403, 404, 408, 409, 412–421, 445–457; II: 3–5, 457–460, 473–477, 486–500, 503–507, 513–515; Hearn's belief in her ability, I: 391, 414, 450; her marriage, II: 62.
White, Richard Grant, I: 350.
Whitman, Walt, II: 432; Hearn's opinion of, I: 271–274, 320, 432, 433; Symonds's praise of, 292; his ideal of democracy, II: 512.
Whitney, Charles, I: 70, 71.
Wilde, Oscar, his comment on the plagiarizations of life and nature, I: 96.
Wilkins, Peter, his Voyages, I: 212.
"Will" and "shall," Hearn's use of the words, II: 224, 225, 246.

Williams, Sir Monier, his translation of the story of Nala, I: 402.
Winckelmann, Johann Joachim, I: 211, 227.
Windward Islands, Hearn visits, I: 97.
Women, physical magnetism of, I: 401; as physicians, in France, 441; Japanese, II: 35, 61, 87, 88, 90, 91; compared with American, 36; intellectual, 98, 99; Occidental attitude toward, 112, 123; revelations made by men to, 189; marriage and the educated woman, in Japan, 416–422; emotional, 427.
Wordsworth, William, II: 215.
World, smallness of the, I: 472.
World, The (New York paper), J. Cockerill's work on, I: 54.
Worship, phallic, II: 32.
Worthington, Richard, I: 246, 248, 253, 276, 321, 376.
Wundt, Wilhelm Max, his colour-theory, II: 320.
Wüstenfeld, Heinrich Ferdinand, his edition of Al-Nawawi, I: 331.
Wycliffe, John, I: 350.

Yabase, Japan, II: 46, 47, 48, 54, 55.
Yaegaki san, deities worshipped at Sakusa, II: 25.
Yaidzu, Japan, II: 478, 516; Hearn's warning to M. McDonald regarding a visit to, 447, 448, 449, 450.
Yakushi Nyorai, Hearn's visits to the temple of, II: 17, 18.
Yasukochi, letter to, II: 464–466; his military experience, 465.
Yellow fever, in New Orleans, I: 185, 186, 195; in Martinique, 440.
Yokogi, death of, II: 72.
Yokohama, Japan, Hearn's visits to M. McDonald at, II: 346, 366, 367, 371, 388, 389, 390, 392, 393, 409, 422, 423, 438, 439, 442, 443.
Yriarte, Charles Emile, his life of Giovanni Malatesta, I: 271.
Yucatan, significance of darkness to ancient inhabitants of, I: 468.

Zilliacus, Konni, II: 467.
Zola, Emile, I: 228; II: 503; his L'Argent, II: 65; his Rome, 392.

THE END